ARBITRATION
AND THE
PUBLIC INTEREST

ARBITRATION
AND THE
PUBLIC INTEREST

PROCEEDINGS OF THE TWENTY-FOURTH
ANNUAL MEETING
NATIONAL ACADEMY OF ARBITRATORS

Los Angeles, California   ●   January 27-29, 1971

Edited by

Gerald G. Somers

Professor of Economics
The University of Wisconsin

and

Barbara D. Dennis

Editorial Associate
The University of Wisconsin

The Bureau of National Affairs, Inc.   Washington, D. C.

Printed in the United States of America

Library of Congress Catalog Card Number: 55-57413

International Standard Book Number: 0-87179-069-6

31

CONTENTS

CONTENTS

CHAPTER I

THE PRESIDENTIAL ADDRESS:
SEX AND THE SINGLE ARBITRATOR *

JEAN T. McKELVEY **

For a number of years members of the National Academy of
Arbitrators, in both their annual and their regional meetings,
have been engaged in a running appraisal of their role as administrators or guardians of public policy. While this examination has concentrated primarily on the respective roles of the
arbitrator, the National Labor Relations Board, and the courts, it
is but part of a larger issue which was posed by Bernard Meltzer
at the 20th Annual Meeting in San Francisco in 1967:

> ". . . what is the proper role of the arbitrator with respect to
> statutory or policy issues that are enmeshed with issues concerning
> the interpretation of the collective bargaining agreement?" [1]

Meltzer's own answer to this question was blunt and succinct:
Where there is an irrepressible conflict between the agreement
and the law, the arbitrator "should respect the agreement and
ignore the law." [2]

At the same annual meeting, Arnold Ordman and Robert
Howlett espoused a contrary position, urging arbitrators to accept the responsibility of considering and deciding questions
arising under the National Labor Relations Act where these
were intertwined with issues of contract interpretation. [3]

---

* Reprinted from the *Industrial and Labor Relations Review*, 24 (April 1971).
Copyright © 1971 by Cornell University. All rights reserved.

** President (1970-1971), National Academy of Arbitrators; Professor of Industrial Relations, New York State School of Industrial and Labor Relations, Cornell
University, Ithaca, N.Y.

[1] B. Meltzer, "Ruminations About Ideology, Law, and Labor Arbitration," in
The Arbitrator, the NLRB, and the Courts, Proceedings of the 20th Annual Meet-
ing, National Academy of Arbitrators, ed. Dallas L. Jones (Washington: BNA
Books, 1967), 1.

[2] *Id.* at 16.

[3] *Id.* at 47-110.

At the four workshop sessions which followed, the majority of those who spoke supported Meltzer's position that the arbitrator's job is to adjudicate the contract, allowing those with statutory responsibility to administer the Act.[4] One of the panelists, who essayed the role of mediator, offered this bit of sage advice to the combatants. He referred to a friend who recently had learned of the death of his mother-in-law. When asked by the undertaker, "Shall we embalm or cremate?" he replied, "Do both. Take no chances." [5]

Since no consensus emerged from these sessions, the Academy continued the debate at its next annual meeting in Cleveland. Seeking to occupy a middle ground between the polar positions advocated by Meltzer, on the one hand, and Howlett, on the other, Richard Mittenthal proposed that while the arbitrator might *"permit* conduct forbidden by law but sanctioned by contract," he should not *"require* conduct forbidden by law even though sanctioned by contract." [6] Neither Meltzer nor Howlett, however, yielded ground from their original positions, [7] while Theodore J. St. Antoine, who joined the fray, repudiated the mediatory efforts of Mittenthal, aligned himself with Meltzer, and delivered this final message:

> "Do the job for which you are best fitted—reading and applying contracts—and leave the statutes to the Board and the courts. If you find no value in my prescription, you can at least treat it as a health measure. Who, after all, has ever heard of an underworked member of this Academy?" [8]

Although the issue was laid to rest for a year, the matter was revived at the annual meeting in Montreal in 1970. In still another attempt to answer the question: When should arbitrators follow the federal law?, Michael Sovern joined the debate. After noting the range of positions explored at prior meetings, Sovern expressed his surprise at discovering that he "disagreed

---

[4] *Id.* at 111-228.

[5] *Id.* at 119. Another panelist commented: "I'm surprised to hear that the majority of you are opposed to arbitrators deciding legal questions or noncontract questions," *id.* at 193.

[6] "The Role of Law in Arbitration," in *Developments in American and Foreign Arbitration,* Proceedings of the 21st Annual Meeting, National Academy of Arbitrators, ed. Charles M. Rehmus (Washington: BNA Books, 1968), 50.

[7] B. Meltzer, "A Rejoinder," *id.* at 58; R. Howlett, "A Reprise," *id.* at 64.

[8] T. J. St. Antoine, "Discussion," *id.* at 75, 82.

in important ways with all of the positions advanced." [9] Sovern's formulation of his own position was as follows:

"I believe that an arbitrator may follow federal law rather than the contract when the following conditions are met:

"1. The arbitrator is qualified.

"2. The question of law is implicated in a dispute over the application or interpretation of a contract that is also before him.

"3. The question of law is raised by a contention that, if the conduct complained of does violate the contract, the law nevertheless immunizes or even requires it.

"4. The courts lack primary jurisdiction to adjudicate the question of law." [10]

With the advent of major new types of federal regulation of conditions of employment, in particular the ban on sex discrimination contained in Title VII of the Civil Rights Act of 1964, a similar dilemma confronts the arbitrator. Should he confine his judgment within the four corners of the collective bargaining agreement, or should he expand his jurisdiction to encompass the law as well? Are arbitrators applying the same standards as they do in NLRB situations—that is, do the majority of arbitrators espouse the conventional wisdom that their function is solely that of contract interpretation? Do a minority follow Howlett's injunction to consider the law as part of the contract? Do some follow Mittenthal's formulation? To what extent do Sovern's four criteria, or conditions, apply in Title VII cases? In other words: (1) How do arbitrators decide cases in which there may be a conflict between the contract and the law in the area of sex discrimination? (2) How do the administrative agencies and the courts regard arbitration decisions in this area? And (3), are we now on the threshold of developing a *Spielberg*-type doctrine for this area? [11] Finally, there is the whole question of election of remedies to be explored. Will resort to arbitration in a case alleging sex discrimination foreclose the charging party from resort to the courts?

---

[9] Sovern, "When Should Arbitrators Follow Federal Law?" in *Arbitration and the Expanding Role of Neutrals,* Proceedings of the 23rd Annual Meeting, National Academy of Arbitrators, ed. Gerald G. Somers and Barbara D. Dennis (Washington: BNA Books, 1970), 28.

[10] *Id.* at 38.

[11] The *Spielberg* doctrine emerged from a landmark decision of the NLRB defining the conditions under which the Board would honor an arbitration award rather than assert its own exclusive jurisdiction to decide an unfair labor practice charge. In the *Spielberg Mfg. Co.* case (112 NLRB 1080, 36 LRRM 1152

How Arbitrators Decide Cases Involving
Alleged Sex Discrimination

Although the decade of the 1960s witnessed the most dramatic changes in the evolution of legal sanctions against discrimination in employment, arbitrators were faced with numerous cases involving alleged sex discrimination in the reconversion period following World War II. These arose for the most part when employers sought to replace the female employees they had hired during the war with male employees who traditionally had performed certain jobs in the prewar period. One of the first arbitrators to deal with this problem was Charles C. Killingsworth, who decided 63 grievances between Bethlehem Steel Co. and the United Steelworkers of America involving a common charge that the company had improperly discharged female employees in violation of the agreement. The company's defense to these actions has a now-familiar ring: The women were temporary employees hired only for the duration of the war; they lacked the ability and physical fitness to perform the jobs as well as male employees could perform them; the Maryland laws regulating the employment of women made it uneconomical for a steel plant to employ them in most of its operations; a morals problem arises when a few women are employed on operations conducted almost exclusively by men; and the necessity of providing separate rest and welfare facilities for women creates an onerous and undue burden on the employer.

Arbitrator Killingsworth dealt with these contentions as follows: Although an employer was not required to continue to employ those who could not meet prewar standards of production, minor differences in efficiency did not warrant the

---

(1955)), an unfair labor practice charge had been filed with the Board, following an arbitration award upholding the discharge of certain striking union members. The Board declined to accept jurisdiction over the matter on the grounds that "the [arbitration] proceedings appear to have been fair and regular, all parties had agreed to be bound by the award, and the decision of the arbitration panel is not clearly repugnant to the purposes and policies of the Act." The Board later added the requirement that the arbitrator also should have considered the issue involved in the unfair labor practice in making his award. For further discussion of the implications of the *Spielberg* doctrine for arbitration, see Robert Howlett, "The Arbitrator, the NLRB, and the Courts," in *The Arbitrator, the NLRB, and the Courts* at 67-110; and Gerald A. Brown, "The National Labor Policy, the NLRB, and Arbitration," in *Developments in American and Foreign Arbitration* at 83-93.

replacement of females with males of lesser seniority. The statutory requirement that female workers be provided a 30-minute lunch and rest period did not justify the discharge of females where it could be shown that women matched male performance on an overall daily basis. As far as the alleged social and moral problem of permitting females to work in male company was concerned, the arbitrator noted that "industrial experience has generally been that men and women can work side by side without disrupting production." Inasmuch as separate facilities already had been provided for women, no weight could be given to this complaint of the company. Killingsworth then concluded that "the only important criterion to be applied in disposing of these grievances is whether or not the women were able to perform all of the regular and normal duties of their jobs." [12]

Most of the published decisions of this period indicate that arbitrators would not uphold a woman's right to a job if the consequence would entail a violation of state protective legislation by the employer. In fact, the dean of the arbitration profession, the late Harry Shulman, ruled that the existence of legal limitations on the work which women could do created a legal class disability which was not discriminatory because it was dependent "entirely on objective, indisputable tests of sex and weight, and is not subject to personal idiosyncrasy, differences of opinion as to physical capacity, or malingering for the purpose of securing a better job." [13]

---

[12] *Bethlehem Steel Co.,* 7 LA 163 (1947). Similar decisions rejecting the stereotyped concept of general female incapacity were issued by David A. Wolff in *Chrysler Corp.,* 7 LA 380 and 386 (1947). On the other hand, in a case involving the transfer of female quotation clerks from the floor of the New York Stock Exchange and their replacement by boys after the war, Israel Ben Scheiber upheld the employer's action as neither arbitrary nor capricious because he found that the atmosphere of noise, activity, nervous strain, and tension which prevailed on the floor was more distracting to female than to male employees. *New York Stock Exchange,* 7 LA 602 (1947).

[13] *Ford Motor Co.,* 1 LA 462 (1945); *Manion Steel Barrel Co.,* 6 LA 164 (1947), Robert J. Wagner; *Pittsburgh Corning Corp.,* 3 LA 364 (1946), C. W. Lillibridge; *U.S. Rubber Co.,* 3 LA 555 (1946), George Cheney. *See Republic Steel Corp.,* 1 LA 244 (1945), in which Harry Platt ruled that the company had no right to lay off employees with greater seniority than those who were retained merely because they were women so long as their ability and physical capacity were equal to that of junior males. In *Ohio Steel Foundry Co.,* 5 LA 12 (1946), Arbitrator Charles G. Hampton ruled that two women welders hired during the war were entitled to be recalled despite the company's reliance on the Ohio labor

In thus refusing to order employers to violate the mandates of state protective labor legislation, arbitrators were following the well-established legal doctrine that sex is a valid basis for classification.[14] They also were developing the principle which Mittenthal later formulated, namely, that the arbitrator should not require conduct forbidden by law even though sanctioned by contract.

If arbitrators experienced little trouble in dealing with cases of alleged sex discrimination where there was an apparent conflict between the contract and the mandates of constitutionally valid state protective labor legislation in the two decades following World War II (that is, where the law served as a defense against alleged breaches of the seniority provisions of the agreement, in particular), their real problems of accommodation began with the sweeping changes in federal public law affecting sex discrimination in the 1960s, especially Title VII of the Civil Rights Act of 1964.

The law itself was new, evolving, and unclear. The top administrative agency charged with its enforcement, the Equal Employment Opportunity Commission (EEOC), unlike the NLRB, had no enforcement powers, its role being limited to that of persuasion and conciliation. Enforcement as a matter of primary jurisdiction was entrusted to the federal judiciary. Finally, and most important for the arbitration profession, the validity of state protective legislation was now subject to challenge by state human rights commissions, by the EEOC, and, more significantly, by certain federal courts applying the doctrine of preemption.

What had been a relatively clear path for arbitral deference to the mandates of state legislation now became a thicket of state commission rulings, EEOC guidelines, and diverse and contradictory federal court decisions which arbitrators, for the most part, found impenetrable—a legal jungle to trap the unwary. Small wonder, then, that the dominant theme to be sounded

---

law, since no order to discharge female workers had yet been made by the state inspector.

[14] For an excellent treatment of this subject, see Leo Kanowitz, "Constitutional Aspects of Sex-Based Discrimination in American Law," 48 *Neb. L. Rev.* 131 (1968). See also Raymond Munts and David C. Rice, "Women Workers: Protection or Equality?" 24 *Ind. & Lab. Rels. Rev.* 3-13 (1970).

in arbitral decisions on sex discrimination was one of simple, harmonic contract construction, leaving any discordancies to the public authority virtuosos. No longer did arbitrators confront the simple dilemma of whether to apply the contract or the law. The real problem was discovering which law or laws to follow, should the arbitrator accept the view that the contract impliedly embodied the law.

Sex Discrimination in Employment

The inclusion of the prohibition against sex discrimination in employment in Title VII [15] was largely an historical accident resulting from a calculated effort by the opponents of Title VII to defeat its passage. As a result, there was scant legislative history to guide those entrusted with the enforcement of this provision of the statute.[16] In particular, the uncertainty as to how Title VII, state fair employment practice laws, and state laws protecting the employment of women were to interact or relate to each other created a situation which one commentator described as "colossally puzzling" to the employer, union, or employment agency,[17] and, one might add, to the arbitrator as well.

---

[15] 78 Stat. 253; 42 U.S.C. 2000 (e) (1964). This law (which covers employers in industries affecting commerce, employment agencies serving such employers, and labor organizations engaged in such industries) declares that it shall be "an unlawful employment practice" because of race, color, religion, sex, or national origin for those covered.

"(1) to fail or refuse to hire or to discharge any individual or otherwise to discriminate against any individual with respect to his compensation, terms, conditions or privileges of employment . . . or

" (2) to limit, segregate or classify his employees in any way which would deprive or tend to deprive any individual of employment opportunities or otherwise adversely affect his status as an employee. . . ."

[16] "The sex amendment can best be described as an orphan, since neither the proponents nor the opponents of Title VII seem to have felt any responsibility for its presence in the Bill." Richard K. Berg, "Equal Opportunity under the Civil Rights Act of 1964," 31 *Brooklyn L. Rev.* 79 (1964). For an account of the legislative history of Title VII, see Anthony R. Mansfield, "Sex Discrimination in Employment under Title VII of the Civil Rights Act of 1964," 21 *Vanderbilt L. Rev.* 484-501. This note also contains a good account of the interaction of the Equal Pay Act of 1963 (77 Stat. 56 (1963), 29 U.S.C. 206 (d) (1964)) and Title VII. See also Daniel Steiner, "Discrimination and Title VII of the Civil Rights Act," in *Collective Bargaining Today: Proceedings of the Collective Bargaining Forum—1969* (Washington: BNA, 1970) , 450-459. Because of limitations of space this article cannot deal either with the Equal Pay Act of 1963 or with Executive Order 11246 barring discrimination (including sex) by federal contractors.

[17] Mansfield, "Sex Discrimination in Employment . . .," at 501. Mansfield also

Central to the creation of the puzzle is, of course, the provision of the act which *permits* discrimination "in those certain instances where religion, sex, or national origin is a bona fide occupational qualification reasonably necessary to the normal operation of that particular business or enterprise. . . ."[18] Adding to its complexity in the matter of sex discrimination is the question whether state protective laws governing the employment of women constitute a bona fide occupational qualification (BFOQ) exception immunizing conduct which might otherwise constitute a violation of Title VII.[19]

The EEOC Guidelines

In approaching this problem of accommodating state protective labor legislation[20] and Title VII, the EEOC has issued a series of guidelines for compliance with Title VII.[21] At the outset, on December 2, 1965, the EEOC, in the belief that Congress had failed to overrule state protective laws, took the position that state laws constituted a legitimate BFOQ exception unless their clear effect was not to protect women but to discriminate against them.[22] A year later, on August 19, 1966, the Commission retreated, announcing that as a matter of policy it would pass no judgment on these laws but would advise complainants to litigate the matter in the courts.[23] Two years

---

notes that sex discrimination is "far more pervasive in our laws and customs than any form of racial discrimination. . . ." (p. 499). This same opinion is shared by M. O. Murray and P. Eastwood, "Jane Crow and the Law: Sex Discrimination and Title VII," 34 *Geo. Wash. L. Rev.* 232-256 (1965). See also Gunnar Myrdal, *An American Dilemma: The Negro Problem and Modern Democracy* (New York: Harper & Row, 1944), App. 5, "A Parallel to the Negro Problem," 1073-1078, for what has become the classic comparison between the social and economic status of Negroes and women.

[18] 42 U.S.C. § 2000 e-2 *(e)*. Note that this section omits mention of race or color.

[19] Here again the legislative history affords no clue. The debate in the House of Representatives was inconclusive on the point of whether state laws were to be preempted by Title VII. See 110 *Congressional Record* 2580 and ff. (1964).

[20] These laws in general prohibited the employment of women in certain occupations, established maximum hours and minimum wages for their employment, contained prohibitions against employment during certain night hours, set weight-lifting and carrying limitations, required special facilities for women such as rest rooms and seats, and specified lunch and rest periods. See Gola E. Waters, "Sex, State Protective Laws and the Civil Rights Act of 1964," 18 *Lab. L.J.* 344-352 (1967).

[21] See Robert J. Affeldt, "Title VII in the Federal Courts—Private or Public Law" (Pt. II), 15 *Villanova L. Rev.* 1-31 (1969).

[22] 30 *Fed. Reg.* 14926-28 (1965).

[23] *CCH Empl. Prac. Guide,* ¶ 16,900.001 n. 2 (1968).

later in 1968, the Commission rescinded its 1966 policy statement and reaffirmed its original 1965 guidelines.[24] In August
1969, however, the Commission announced that it would no
longer consider state laws regulating hours and weight lifting
as BFOQ exceptions:

> "The Commission has found that such laws and regulations do
> not take into account the capacities, preferences and abilities of
> individual females and tend to discriminate rather than protect."

Finding that these laws and regulations conflicted with Title
VII, the Commission announced that they would no longer be
considered "a defense to an otherwise established unlawful employment practice or as a basis for the application of the bona
fide occupational qualification exception." [25]

Because of these shifts in the EEOC guidelines, at least one
of the commentators suggested that the Commission look to
arbitration decisions as a compass in this uncharted wilderness:

> ". . . arbitrators have already met and fashioned solutions for
> many of the programs [sic] which arise under Title VII. . . .
> It would seem that the large number of these arbitration decisions
> might well provide guidelines for the EEOC to consider in the
> solution of its problems." [26]

Not surprisingly, these guidelines furnished by the sample arbitration awards reviewed by the commentator upheld the denial
of recall, promotion, or bumping rights to women as not discriminatory when state laws set statutory limits on the weights
that could be lifted by female employees.[27] In almost all the

---

[24] 33 *Fed. Reg.* § 3344 (1968). The guidelines also had provided that "an
employer may not refuse to hire women because state law requires that certain
conditions of employment such as minimum wages, overtime pay, rest periods, or
physical facilities be provided." Where state laws provided for administrative ex-
emptions, the Commission stated its expectation that the employer would make a
good-faith effort to obtain such exceptions.

[25] 1969 EEOC Guidelines on Discrimination Because of Sex, 34 *Fed. Reg.* 13367,
§1604.1 b(2). See also Decision No. 70382, Dec. 16, 1969, dealing with a District of
Columbia law limiting the hours which females might work. The EEOC, finding
probable cause of violation of Title VII by an employer, stated that the later
statute had impliedly repealed the District of Columbia law which clearly was repugnant to and inconsistent with Title VII, 2 FEP Cases 338. An excellent recent
compilation of the statutes, guidelines, and executive orders dealing with sex
discrimination has been published by the Women's Bureau of the U.S. Department of Labor, *Laws on Sex Discrimination in Employment* (1970.).

[26] Mansfield, "Sex Discrimination in Employment . . .," at 491.

[27] *Id.* Among the cases cited were *Lockheed Georgia Co.*, 46 LA 931 (1966), H.
Ellsworth Steele; and *Apex Machine and Tool Co.*, 45 LA 417 (1965), Arthur E.
Layman.

cases cited, the contract also contained a clause barring discrimination for reasons of sex, but this clause generally was interpreted as modified by state protective labor legislation where such existed.

This writer's research into the published arbitration awards in the period following the enactment of Title VII supports the conclusion that arbitrators in general have held that state laws act as a defense not only against a charge of violating contract bars on sex discrimination but also against the allegation that Title VII has been violated likewise.

Thus, Joseph Shister held that a female employee was properly denied a leadman's job because of safety and health considerations related to the requirement that an average weight of 40 to 45 pounds be lifted for 10 to 20 percent of each day. Here the parties had abandoned a separate listing of male and female jobs in conformance with Title VII. Moreover, the state in question, Pennsylvania, had no weight-lifting restrictions, but the arbitrator accepted the company's argument that such restrictions could be implied from International Labour Organisation and U.S. Department of Labor standards. The arbitrator also was impressed with the testimony of the company physician that females as a class should not be assigned to jobs involving heavy lifting because

"(a) females are more prone to low back pain due to their anatomy; (b) intra-abdominal pressure can lead to the displacement of the pelvic organs; (c) weakness and fatigue during the menstrual period can be aggravated by lifting; (d) there is the danger of miscarriage during pregnancy."[28]

Prevailing Opinion

Perhaps the clearest (and certainly the best researched) statement of the prevailing view of the arbitration profession was that of Edwin Teple in a 1967 case.[29] Here, under a contract

---

[28] *Robertshaw Controls Co.*, 48 LA 101 (1967). See a pre-Title VII award by Joseph Klamon stating that despite the fact that Mississippi had no statute limiting weights for females, it was the duty of the company to protect the health and safety of its employees even though they were willing to perform the jobs. *Mengel Co.*, 18 LA 392 (1952).

[29] *General Fireproofing Co.*, 48 LA 819 (1967). See also *Capital Mfg. Co.*, 50 LA 669 (1968), Harry Dworkin.

barring sex discrimination and providing for recall from layoff on the basis of seniority and physical fitness to perform the work, the arbitrator held that the employer's determination that females were not physically fit to perform many of the jobs was reasonable under the Ohio law which barred women from jobs requiring the regular or frequent lifting of weights in excess of 25 pounds. The arbitrator also expressed the view—then shared by the EEOC—that Title VII's reference to sex was not intended to wipe out state protective labor laws. He felt that medical opinion favors lighter work for females "because of the physical nature and function of their bodies."[30]

These candid arbitral views that females as a class are to be regarded as "the weaker sex" were given most eloquent and definitive expression by Arbitrator Peter Seitz:

"Anti-discrimination provisions do not, however, abolish or eliminate biological differences between people. The recognition of differences between the sexes, I am confident, will survive anti-discrimination provisions, not only in labor contracts, but in Federal and State laws. There is no basis on which it would seem sound to deny to the Company the right to indulge the assumption made in most of the States in this nation that females, *as a class,* and because of their biological structure and function, require more protective regulation as a part of the labor force than males."[31]

A few arbitrators, however, have rejected the assumption that women workers should be protected as a class. One of these is Ralph Roger Williams who held, under a contract barring sex discrimination, that a company could not lay off five senior females as a class, instead of five junior males, despite the company's contention that the jobs required undue muscle power and physical strength not normally possessed by women. Observing that "some women are stronger than some men," the arbitrator held that the company must make its determination "on the basis of the individual employee's qualifications, skill

---

[30] Edwin Teple cited a long list of other published awards holding similarly. In addition to *Robertshaw Controls Co., supra* note 28, he gave *Marathon Electric Mfg. Corp.,* 31 LA 656 (1958), Fidelis O'Rourke; *Rheem Mfg. Co.,* 32 LA 147 (1959), Paul Prasow; *National Gypsum Co.,* 34 LA 41 (1959), Paul M. Hebert; *Electrical Engineering and Mfg. Co.,* 35 LA 657 (1960), Thomas T. Roberts; *Three Boys Food Mart,* 38 LA 817 (1962), Paul L. Kleinsorge; *Advanced Structures,* 39 LA 1094 (1963), Thomas T. Roberts et al.; *Minute Maid Co.,* 40 LA 920 (1963), Alfred J. Goodman; and *Sperry-Rand Corp.,* 46 LA 961 (1966), Peter Seitz.
[31] *Sperry Rand Corp.,* 46 LA 961 (1966) (emphasis added).

and ability, including *his* or *her* physical ability to do the work." [32]

Another is E. J. Forsythe who, in a 1966 case, rejected the company's contention that the merger of male and female seniority lists "could not of itself eliminate the differences in the physical capacity between male and female employees," and ruled that the female employee who was denied a job as material handler should be given the work because of her demonstrated ability to perform it.[33]

Between the purveyors of the conventional wisdom and the minority who regard women as individuals rather than as a class, there are some who express their views in the form of dicta. One of these is Walter Seinsheimer. Although he upheld management's right to determine that female employees did not possess the physical ability necessary to perform jobs to which their seniority would otherwise have entitled them in the face of a layoff, he expressed some reservations about the "weaker sex" presumption:

> "I am well aware that there are some women who are as physically able as most men to do what is considered men's work. All one has to do is travel to the rural areas of this country to see women doing heavy farm work, lifting loads far beyond what was usually required in the work in question. And all of us have seen pictures of women in foreign countries doing heavy physical labor—from digging ditches to hod carrying to operating heavy equipment." [34]

Another, David C. Altrock, sought to solve the conflict between the no-discrimination clause of the agreement and the Ohio laws regulating the employment of women by ordering the company to request the state to evaluate all the jobs that had been filled by junior males instead of senior females during a layoff in order to determine their suitability for women. Although the arbitrator did not feel free to ignore state law or regula-

---

[32] *International Paper Co.*, 47 LA 896 (1966) (emphasis added). The arbitrator also stated that the BFOQ exemption of Title VII had no application to the case and that the mandate of the Title was as clear in barring sex discrimination as was the similar contract clause. See also *Paterson Parchment Co.*, 47 LA 260 (1966), W. Roy Buckwalter.

[33] *Buco Products, Inc.*, 48 LA 17 (1966).

[34] *Pitman-Moore Division*, 49 LA 709 (1967). The arbitrator went on to say, however, that his decision was influenced strongly by the fact that the women and their union had accepted and agreed to their "weaker sex" role in the plant!

tions, he could not resist the temptation to express his opinion that they were outmoded or archaic. Referring to the state's administrative opinion that lifting 25 pounds once an hour or longer could be termed frequent and repeated, Altrock snapped:

> "So be it, although I cannot avoid saying that that seems to me to be ridiculous on its face. Women daily lift grocery bags, laundry bundles, and children that weigh more than twenty-five pounds. It is a part of the way of life of any healthy woman during normal working years." [35]

Other Interpretations

Still another arbitrator who sought an accommodation between contract and law was A. Dale Allen, Jr., who ruled on the general question whether the company could select only males for credit trainee jobs because certain features of the job such as extensive travel, geographic relocations, long hours, and occasional abusive language made it in the company's view unsuitable for females. Allen held that he could not view the contract in a legal vacuum. Although recognizing limits on his jurisdiction since he was not the Missouri Commission on Human Rights, Allen directed the company to request that commission to evaluate its selection practices and determine whether they were in fact discriminatory.[36]

In *Weirton Steel Co.*, a 1968 case, Samuel Kates also referred to both Title VII and state weight restrictions in interpreting a contract provision barring sex discrimination. Holding that the law need not be applied literally, but in the "light of reason and practicality," Kates upheld the company's refusal to assign women to jobs outside the assorting room because to do so would require the company to provide seats and separate rest-room facilities. Although the arbitrator conceded that there might be a few women "of rare strength and endurance" capable of performing the jobs in question, it was not reasonable

---

[35] *Alsco, Inc.*, 48 LA 1244 (1967).

[36] *Phillips Petroleum Co.*, 50 LA 522 (1968). Since the contract contained a no-discrimination clause, it is not clear why the arbitrator could not have made this determination. For comment on this case and on the subsequent noneffectuation of the remedy, see William G. Gould, "Labor Arbitration of Grievances Involving Racial Discrimination," 24 *Arb. J.* 226 (1969).

in his judgment to require the company to provide separate facilities for "these especially endowed women." [37]

In one case where three female employees sought to be removed from a particular job because they were "nervous wrecks" and suffered pain in their arms, necks, chests, and backs, the arbitrator, John A. Hogan, citing the contract clause against sex discrimination and Title VII, refused their plea, holding that it would be discriminatory to reserve the job for men alone.[38] And in a case where men sought to bump into a shade department, hitherto the private preserve of women workers, the arbitrator, Walter J. Gershenfeld, upheld their right to a trial period despite the company's contention that the work in question required skills of dexterity in handling delicate fabrics "not possessed by men in general." [39] One could, perhaps, classify this particular arbitrator as a "male liberationist"!

On the whole, however, most of the arbitrators generally interpreted contract provisions in cases involving alleged sex discrimination in the light of the restrictions imposed by state protective labor laws governing the employment of women.[40] On this point, arbitrators were in accord with the EEOC, at least until 1969.

At this time, however, a new problem arose. As the EEOC, state commissions, and, most significantly, some of the federal courts began to interpret Title VII as repealing state protective legislation, arbitrators were faced with the argument that a new accommodation should be made in harmonizing contractual provisions with the more sophisticated doctrine that the capacities of female workers should be judged individually, not as a class. For the most part, arbitrators in general now retreated to familiar ground, holding that their assignment was only to interpret the contract, *not* the law.

---

[37] *Weirton Steel Co.,* 50 LA 795 (1968).

[38] *Allen Mfg. Co.,* 49 LA 199 (1967). See also *Owens-Illinois Inc.,* 50 LA 871 (1968), Joseph Klamon.

[39] *Creative Industries, Inc.,* 49 LA 140 (1967).

[40] A similar conclusion, based on a somewhat different sample of cases, has been reached by A. Dale Allen, Jr., in his article "What To Do About Sex Discrimination," 21 *Lab. L. J.* 563-576 (1970).

Before "Women's Lib"

Even before the new "doctrine" of women's liberation began to be enunciated by administrative agencies and the courts, a sizable number of arbitrators rejected contentions that Title VII was being violated as outside the scope of their authority or jurisdiction.[41]

In the airline marriage-rule cases, however, the arbitration fraternity split apart, exhibiting no consensus on the propriety of using legal rules as an aid to contract construction. In *Braniff Airways,* Walter Gray, as chairman of the System Board, held that the airline was not justified in discharging married stewardesses despite the fact that the airline had individual agreements with each stewardess that she would resign upon marriage and that the company had for 25 years maintained a policy of using only unmarried stewardesses. In its decision the board stated that it was "impressed with the language of the Civil Rights Act which also expressed, on a wider basis, the modern trend of thought concerning discrimination based upon sex." [42] Just a year later, in a memorable and often-quoted decision, Saul Wallen similarly denied the right of Southern Airways to "ditch" its married stewardesses, stating:

> "In our opinion, while management may indubitably establish initial employment standards for stewardesses and thus hire anyone it chooses, once such a person is hired and acquires seniority pursuant to the contract's terms, that seniority may be terminated only in accordance with the contract's terms. And this, in turn is permitted only if the original or altered rule is a reasonable one.
> "That the rule in question is not a reasonable one has already been shown. Its justification as a safety measure is minimal. . . . Its value as a sales promotion device is doubtful. While it has been upheld in arbitration as reasonable in several prior cases, all these decisions were made in the context of a universal application of such a rule in the industry. *Now times have changed and views have been altered by experience.*" [43]

---

[41] In *Pitman Moore Division, supra* note 34, Seinsheimer disposed of a Title VII contention by saying the company action "may well have been, or may be in violation of the Civil Rights Act, but it is my opinion that it is not up to an Arbitrator to interpret the Federal Law." See also *Great Atlantic and Pacific Tea Co.,* 49 LA 1186 (1967), Clair Duff; and *Studebaker Corp.,* 49 LA 105 (1967), Harold W. Davey. Davey commented that he wished "to make clear in unmistakable terms that he is not commissioned to interpret Title VII of the Civil Rights Act of 1964."
[42] *Braniff Airways, Inc.,* 48 LA 769 (1965).
[43] *Southern Airways, Inc.,* 47 LA 1135, 1141 (1967) (emphasis added).

The fact that some of the stewardesses might be married and therefore unalluring to the passengers was answered by Wallen in an oft-quoted riposte that this would merely add "zest to the hunt." [44]

This same line of thinking was followed in the *Allegheny Airlines* case by Peter M. Kelliher in 1967, when, although saying that he was following only the contract and not Title VII, he commented that "unreasonable restrictions upon marriage are against public policy." [45]

The day after Wallen's award was handed down, Peter Seitz, in an equally memorable opinion in the *American Airlines* case, reached the opposite conclusion as to the reasonableness of the no-marriage rule and the responsibility of the arbitrator to consider questions of public policy.

"I do not think that an arbitrator should second-guess the employer on such a matter as the kind, quality, and character of stewardess performance it requires on its planes. This is as much a matter of managerial and entrepreneurial prerogative as the determination of the kind of equipment that should be run and the kinds of services to be made available to customers by the stewardesses and others. . . .

"I am not called upon to agree or disagree with the Company's belief that marriage disqualifies stewardesses from performing efficiently. In fact, I entertain very serious doubts that the generalization is entirely valid to the extent claimed. The question, however, is, rather, whether on the record of this case the Company has presented sufficient facts to justify its decision as a rational one. I believe that it has done so. . . .

"This Board has no franchise to administer the penal laws or governmental statutes such as the Civil Rights Act. . . . Only

---

[44] Wallen's more extended comments on the airline's argument that it sold "atmosphere" in addition to transportation are worth repeating: "The logic on which this proposition is based is dubious. An attractive girl loses none of her charm when she marries; in fact, it may be enhanced. While something might be said for the argument that a small segment of the traveling public may be influenced in its choice of a carrier (where it has a choice) by the fact that its stewardesses are attractive, it is highly doubtful that any but the most predatory of males bother to consider whether they are 'encumbered.' Moreover the predatory ones are not likely to be deterred if they are 'encumbered.' . . . For the passenger lured on board by the prospect of the chase, the presence of a few 'encumbered' ones among the quarry is likely to be an obstacle which merely adds zest to the hunt." *Id.* at 1140.

[45] *Allegheny Airlines, Inc.,* 48 LA 734 (1967). This comment provoked a strong dissent from the company members of the board who held that alleged violations of public policy were beyond the scope of the arbitrator's authority. *Id.* at 742.

mischief can result from this Board acting as though it were an agency of government with the power and authority to fulfill public policy." [46]

Arbitrators Are Not Legal Administrators

In the *United Air Lines* case in 1967, Mark Kahn, after making an agonizing appraisal of these various marriage decisions, lined himself up on the side of Seitz. Finding that in the *United* case the rule against marriage had been a long-established and consistently administered past practice, surviving 10 or more collective agreements since its initiation, Kahn upheld the policy. Stating that the merits or wisdom of the policy were not matters for the arbitrator to decide, Kahn commented, "The jurisdiction of this System Board does not extend to interpreting and applying the Civil Rights Act." [47]

Almost three years later the U.S. District Court, Northern District of Illinois, found United's policy unlawful and held that discharges of married stewardesses violated Title VII of the Civil Rights Act of 1964.[48]

One final statement of the prevailing arbitral view of the need for separation of powers should suffice. In a 1966 case Lou Yagoda, as chairman of a board of arbitration, confronted the issue of determining whether separate seniority lists based on sex and negotiated before Title VII became law were still valid. Dismissing the union's claim that the seniority clauses

---

[46] *American Airlines, Inc.* (Sept. 15, 1966) grievance of Shirley Weiss, Case No. SS-465, unpublished decision. The following year, after the parties had negotiated a new clause stating that the company at its option may "release from employment a married stewardess at any time following the expiration of six (6) months after marriage or on pregnancy," Seitz was called upon to determine whether this gave the company a blanket option to terminate *all* married stewardesses six months after marriage. Reflecting the impact of what might be called "creeping liberation," Seitz held that the company was obligated to exercise its option *only* on an individual case-by-case base. *American Airlines, Inc.*, 48 LA 705 (1967).

[47] *United Air Lines, Inc.* 48 LA 727 (1967).

[48] *Sprogis* v. *United Air Lines*, 308 F.Supp. 959, 2 FEP Cases 385 (D.C. Ill. 1970). The court held that sex or single status did not constitute a BFOQ exception. United hired both male and female flight attendants but did not apply its ban on marriage to the males. On the other hand, in *Cooper* v. *Delta Air Lines, Inc.*, 274 F.Supp. 781, 1 FEP Cases 241 (E.D. La. 1967) where the airline hired only female flight attendants, the court found the nonmarriage rule was not sex-based discrimination but only discrimination based on marital status and therefore not unlawful.

were now illegal, the board stated that it must act on the presumption that the agreement is valid:

> "It is true that the arbitrators may and should, if contract provisos are patently and unambiguously in violation of the law, take cognizance of clear public policy and resist the upholding of illegal contract provisions. But whenever they do so, they should take great care that (a) the violation is unmistakably apparent; (b) they are not substituting themselves for the authority, expertise and procedures which have been established by and are responsive to the statute in implementing the law.

> "We are not the Equal Employment Opportunity Commission and should not put ourselves in its place in terms of our rights and ability to enforce the law which they administer."

Arbitrators, the board concluded, should not engage in the futile act of trying to preempt the authority of a legal body.[49]

An exception to the general arbitral reluctance to resolve questions of law which are intermingled with questions of contract interpretation is to be found in a recent decision by Arnold Zack. Pursuant to a Pennsylvania rule requiring that female employees were entitled to a 30-minute rest period after five continuous hours of work as well as two rest periods of at least 10 minutes "to eat and rest at such intervals as shall preserve their physical well-being," the Weyerhaeuser Company had for eight years granted an unpaid 30-minute lunch period and a paid 15-minute relief break to its female employees, who thus were paid for 7½ hours instead of for the 7¼ hours actually worked. Male employees who worked and were paid on the basis of an eight-hour day had no scheduled breaks.

After the Pennsylvania Human Relations Act was amended in 1969 to bar discrimination on the basis of sex, the attorney general advised the commonwealth's secretary of labor that any preferential laws according disparate treatment on the basis of sex were impliedly repealed. Accordingly, the company by notice eliminated the scheduled breaks for its female employees. When the matter came to arbitration, the company defended its action on the ground that the contract contained a clause stating that hours of work and premium pay were subject to change by federal or state laws and directives and additionally

---

[49] *The Ingraham Co.*, 48 LA 884 (1966).

that for it to perpetuate different hours of work for its female employees would be violative of Title VII.

Although conceding that law enforcement and interpretation are the primary responsibilities of government agencies and the courts, Zack stated that the arbitrator "must certainly be mindful of the law, particularly when the parties' Agreement stipulates compliance with it." In upholding the company's action, he stated:

> ". . . we are mindful of the public policy of equality of treatment in employment for females as expressed in both Federal and Pennsylvania statutes. This policy is continually and even more vocally being reinforced by the protests of the woman's 'lib' movement." [50]

In the recent *Simoniz Company* case, Robert Howlett ruled against a company that refused to consider the bid of a senior woman worker for promotion to a job which required overtime. The company defended its refusal on the basis of an Illinois statute forbidding women to work over 48 hours a week. After reviewing the various attitudes which arbitrators have held on their role, Howlett, as might be expected, reiterated his own view that the arbitrator should apply the law to each collective bargaining agreement. He therefore stated:

> "The Illinois statute is in conflict with the Civil Rights Act of 1964. . . . Management's refusal, relying on the Illinois statute, to recognize grievant's bid deprives grievant of an employment opportunity in direct contravention of the Civil Rights Act of 1964." [51]

Not only may an employer find himself on the horns of a legal dilemma after receiving such an award, but also the arbitrator may risk a reversal at the hands of a court. In one case involving state restrictions on weight lifting by female employees, the arbitrator's decision ordering the company to give senior women a trial period was denied enforcement by the

---

[50] *Weyerhaeuser Co.*, 54 LA 857 (1970). To the best of my knowledge this marks the first appearance of the woman's "lib" movement in an arbitration award! Ironically, of course, the women lost 15 minutes' pay—but this is the price of equality!

[51] 70-1 ARB ¶ 8024. See *Dayton Tire and Rubber Co.*, 55 LA 357 (1970), in which Samuel Kates held that the new EEOC guidelines did not automatically invalidate state hours' laws.

federal district court on the ground that the award was contrary to public policy.[52]

Court Decisions

Like the arbitrators and the EEOC, the courts also have found themselves in a quandary in determining the impact of Title VII on state protective labor legislation, although there now seems to be a clear trend toward preemption.

In *Rosenfeld* v. *Southern Pacific Co.* a California district court held in 1968 that a plaintiff who had been denied a promotion because this would violate California's hours and weight-lifting legislation governing the employment of women had been discriminated against. The court decided that the California laws did not create a BFOQ exception and that they were void and of no effect because of the supremacy clause (Article XI, Clause 2) of the U.S. Constitution. This decision was somewhat blunted, however, by the court's finding that the laws were discriminatory because the standards they established were "unreasonably low." [53]

A stronger stand was taken by the district court in Oregon in 1969.[54] A female employee had been denied promotion to the job of press operator because the collective agreement required that all females receive rest periods, and the Wage and Hour Commission of Oregon, under its Order No. 8, prohibited women from lifting over 30 pounds. The court granted relief to the plaintiff, holding that

> "Individuals must be judged as individuals and not on the basis of characteristics generally attributed to . . . sexual groups. The particular classification in Order No. 8 may be reasonable under the Equal Protection Clause, but it is no longer permitted under the Supremacy Clause and the Equal Employment Opportunity Act. . . ." [55]

In two cases district courts which have upheld state protective labor laws as constituting a BFOQ exception to Title VII have

[52] *W. M. Chace Co.*, 48 LA 231 (1966), Erwin Ellman. Reversed in *UAW Local 985* v. *W. M. Chace Co.*, 262 F.Supp. 114, 64 LRRM 2098 (D.C. Mich. 1966).
[53] 293 F.Supp. 1219, 69 LRRM 2826 (C.D. Cal. 1968).
[54] *Richards* v. *Griffith Rubber Mills*, 300 F.Supp. 338, 1 FEP Cases 837 (D. Ore. 1969).
[55] *Id.* at 340.

been overruled by their circuits. In *Weeks* v. *Southern Bell Telephone and Telegraph Co.*,[56] the plaintiff, Mrs. Lorena Weeks, who had 19 years of seniority, applied for the open position of switchman and was denied it on the ground that Georgia had a regulation restricting weights which women could lift to 30 pounds. The Fifth Circuit, showing deference to the EEOC's now-narrow construction of the BFOQ exemption, found that the Georgia regulation had since been withdrawn and replaced by one prohibiting any employee, male or female, from lifting weights that caused undue strain or fatigue. In any event, the court rejected the use of class stereotypes as applied to women, such as the notion that few women are able to lift over 30 pounds or that a job requiring late-hour calls was too dangerous for women, stating that

> ". . . Title VII rejects . . . romantic paternalism as unduly Victorian and instead vests individual women with the power to decide whether or not to take on unromantic tasks. Men have always had the right to determine whether the incremental increase in remuneration for strenuous, dangerous, obnoxious, boring, or unromantic tasks is worth the candle. The promise of Title VII is that women are now to be on equal footing. We cannot conclude that by including the bona fide occupational qualification exception Congress intended to renege on that promise." [57]

The second case, *Bowe* v. *Colgate-Palmolive Company*, involved a Title VII action brought by a group of female employees against both the company and the union. Their complaint was directed against a rather unusual seniority system in which employees each week completed a job preference sheet for the following week because available jobs fluctuated from week to week. Separate seniority lists restricted women from bidding for jobs which required lifting over 35 pounds. The lower court found this restriction a reasonable BFOQ exemption (based on an analysis of state weight-restriction laws in general)

---

[56] 408 F.2d 228, 1 FEP 656 (5th Cir. 1969).

[57] It should be noted that this is the same court which shortly thereafter itself appeared to renege on that promise in the *Phillips* v. *Martin Marietta Corp.* case (411 F.2d 1, 1 FEP Cases 746 (5th Cir. 1969)) by upholding an employer's rule that it would not hire women with preschool children. This decision was vacated by the Supreme Court on Jan. 25, 1971, and remanded to the lower courts for further evidentiary findings on whether the existence of conflicting family obligations is "demonstrably more relevant to job performance for a woman than for a man."

since Indiana, where the Colgate plant in question was located, had no such restriction. The Seventh Circuit, however, disagreed, commenting:

> "If anything is certain in this controversial area, it is that there is no general agreement as to what is a maximum permissible weight which can be safely lifted by women in the course of their employment. . . . Most of the state limits were enacted many years ago and most, if not all, would be considered clearly unreasonable in light of the average physical development, strength and stamina of most modern American women who participate in the industrial work force." [58]

The court went on to advocate the consideration of individual physiological qualifications as well as technological conditions. Although it ruled that Colgate might retain its 35-pound limit "as a general guideline for all its employees, male and female," it directed the company to permit any employee who desired to demonstrate *his* or *her* ability to perform strenuous jobs and to permit those who so demonstrated to bid on jobs according to their seniority.[59]

Although one cannot predict with certainty what the ultimate resolution of this question will be, it seems safe to conclude that Title VII will be interpreted as superseding state protective laws unless they apply to males and females alike.[60] It also seems clear that the elimination of sex discrimination in employment will be achieved by judicial decision rather than by arbitration. There remains the question whether aggrieved employees may pursue their claims both in arbitration and in law or whether they must choose between one forum or the other. Here the courts have spoken in a multitude of tongues.

---

[58] 416 F.2d 711, 2 FEP Cases 121 (7th Cir. 1969), reversing 272 F.Supp. 332, 1 FEP Cases 201 (S.D. Ind. 1967). See *Cheatwood* v. *South Central Bell Telephone*, 303 F.Supp. 754, 1 FEP Cases 644 (M.D. Ala. 1969).

[59] The suit against the union was dismissed by the court for failure of the plaintiffs to comply with the jurisdictional requisites for filing a suit against the union.

[60] See Donald A. Garcia, "Sex Discrimination in Employment or Can Nettie Play Professional Football?" 4 *U. San Francisco L. Rev.* 323-352 (1970). A federal district court has recently held that the Illinois Female Employment Act is unenforceable insofar as it restricts the hours which female employees may work, because the state law conflicts with Title VII and in addition sets unreasonably low standards for the employment of women. *Caterpillar Tractor Co.* v. *Grabiec*, 317 F.Supp. 1304, 2 FEP Cases 945 (D.C. Ill. 1970). Administrative or judicial officers of the District of Columbia, Ohio, Oklahoma, Michigan, and Pennsylvania also have held that their statutes are preempted by Title VII.

The Problem of Election of Remedies [61]

In the *Bowe* case, discussed earlier, the trial court had ruled that the plaintiffs had to choose whether they would pursue their action in court or in arbitration, since they could not elect both. The court of appeals, however, found it was "error not to permit the plaintiffs to utilize dual or parallel prosecution both in court and through arbitration," with an election of remedy proper only after adjudication to prevent duplicate relief which might result in unjust enrichment or a windfall to the plaintiffs. According to the appellate court, "the analogy to labor disputes involving concurrent jurisdiction of the N.L.R.B. and the arbitration process is not merely compelling, we hold it conclusive." [62]

The Fifth Circuit agrees with the Seventh. In a recent Title VII case, *Hutchings* v. *U.S. Industries*,[63] the plaintiff, a Negro, alleged that he had twice been denied a leadman's job solely because of his race. He already had taken his grievance to arbitration under an antidiscrimination clause in the contract and had lost. The court held that he had not thereby forfeited his right to relitigate the matter in court:

> "An arbitration award, whether adverse or favorable to the employee, is not per se conclusive of the determination of Title VII rights by the federal courts, nor is an internal grievance determination deemed 'settled' under the bargaining [*sic*] contract to be given this effect."

Judge Ainsworth noted that Title VII was entirely silent on the role that private grievance arbitration was to play in the resolution of disputes involving discrimination in employment. Moreover, picking up a cue from Harry Platt,[64] he stressed the point that grievance arbitration involves rights and remedies

---

[61] Since this problem is not confined to sex discrimination alone, as was true in the case of the BFOQ exemption, we shall be dealing here with decisions involving race, religion, and sex discrimination.

[62] Case cited *supra* note 58.

[63] 428 F.Supp. 303, 2 FEP Cases 725 (5th Cir. 1970), *rev'g and reman'g* 309 F.Supp. 691, 2 FEP Cases 599 (D.C. Tex. 1969). On the threshold question of the statute of limitations, the circuit court held, in accordance with its decision in *Culpepper* v. *Reynolds Metals Co.*, 421 F.2d 888, 2 FEP Cases 506 (5th Cir. 1970), that the statute is tolled once an employee invokes the grievance procedure to seek a private resolution of his complaint.

[64] Harry H. Platt, "The Relationship Between Arbitration and Title VII of the Civil Rights Act of 1964," 3 *Georgia L. Rev.* 398-410 (1969).

different from those involved in judicial proceedings under
Title VII.

> "The trial judge in a Title VII case bears a special responsibility
> in the public interest to resolve the employment dispute, for once
> the judicial machinery has been set in train, the proceedings
> takes on a public character in which remedies are devised to
> vindicate the policies of the Act, not merely to afford private
> relief to the employee." [65]

But having thus confined the arbitrator and the judge each
to his separate sphere, Judge Ainsworth, essaying the peace-
maker's role, dropped hints for bringing them together in a
kind of mutual-assistance pact. Thus, on the one hand, he suggested that the arbitrator, consistent with the scope of his
authority, might (like the EEOC) encourage and effect voluntary compliance with Title VII. On the other hand, he suggested (in a footnote, to be sure) that arbitration awards and
grievance settlements properly might be considered as evidence
and evaluated by the courts in deciding issues of violation and
relief in Title VII cases.

Finally, he suggested the possibility of evolving a *Spielberg* [66]
approach to the question:

> ". . . we leave for the future the question whether a procedure
> similar to that applied by the Labor Board in deferring to arbi-
> tration awards when certain standards are met might properly be
> adopted in Title VII cases."

Two weeks before the Fifth Circuit's decision in *Hutchings*
was handed down, the Sixth Circuit reached a contrary conclusion in *Dewey* v. *Reynolds Metals Co.* concerning the elec-
tion-of-remedies problem. The *Dewey* case involved a complaint
of religious discrimination. The plaintiff, who was a member
of Faith Reformed Church, had refused to work Sundays as
scheduled overtime because of his religious beliefs. Dewey
processed his complaint through his union to arbitration and
simultaneously began proceedings before the Michigan Civil
Rights Commission. In June 1967 the arbitrator denied the
grievance. Ultimately, Dewey prevailed before the EEOC and

---

[65] Here he cited the *Enterprise* decision (363 U.S. 593, 46 LRRM 2423 (1969))
that an award based "solely upon the arbitrator's view of the requirements of
enacted legislation exceeds the scope of the submission" (at 597).
[66] *Supra* note 11.

the Federal District Court for the Western District of Michigan, which found that the employer had violated Title VII. This judgment was reversed by the Sixth Circuit on the ground, among others, that Dewey had made a binding election of arbitration and once an award had been made he was thereby foreclosed from a lawsuit.

Any other construction would be unfair, the court held, since the employer but not the employee would be bound by the arbitration. "This result could sound the death knell to arbitration of labor disputes which has been so usefully employed in their settlement." The court went on to point out that the great increase in civil rights litigation probably would increase resort to the act in labor disputes. "Such use," said the court, "ought not to destroy the efficacy of arbitration." [67]

A similar view of the finality of arbitration awards in the area of civil rights was expressed by the Connecticut superior court in *Corey* v. *Avco Corp.*, another case involving alleged discrimination for religious beliefs. Here, too, the matter had been submitted both to arbitration and to the Connecticut Commission on Human Rights and Opportunities. The arbitration award which upheld the company also was confirmed in court. After losing in arbitration, the complainant prevailed before the Connecticut commission. The superior court, however, found that the commission had erred by reason of failure to give effect to the findings and award of the arbitration tribunal and by permitting the relitigation of the same facts and issues. Such an approach, the court held, "would serve to render

---

[67] *Dewey* v. *Reynolds Metals Co.*, 429 F.2d 324, 2 FEP Cases 687 (6th Cir. 1970). It is interesting to note the court's reference to this bit of legislative history (citing 1964 *U.S. Code Cong. and A News*, at 2516) : ". . . management prerogatives and union freedoms are to be left undisturbed to the greatest extent possible. Internal affairs of employers and labor organizations must not be interfered with except to the limited extent that correction is required in discrimination practices." Some two months later the court denied a petition for rehearing based on the *Hutchings* decision. In the Sixth Circuit's opinion, *Hutchings* was not correctly decided in the light of *Boys Markets, Inc.*, 398 U.S. 235, 74 LRRM 2257 (1970). Moreover, "our case [Dewey] is even stronger than *Boys Markets* because the grievance here was submitted to arbitration and the arbitrator made an award which was final, binding and conclusive on the parties. It is as binding as a judgment." *Dewey* v. *Reynolds Metals Co.*, 429 F.2d 324, 2 FEP Cases 869 (612 Cir. 1970). In January 1971 the Supreme Court granted *certiorari* in the *Dewey* case.

nugatory the policy of this State and the United States which clearly favors such agreements for arbitration." [68]

Commentaries

So much, then, for arbitration opinions, EEOC guidelines, and court decisions in this area. What do the commentators say as to the respective roles of arbitrators and the courts with respect to the problem of jurisdiction?

Three members of the National Academy of Arbitrators— Harry Platt, Alfred W. Blumrosen, and William B. Gould— have contributed to the literature in this field.[69]

Platt believes that arbitrators should move cautiously in this area, especially where questions of public policy are concerned. Sensitive to the possibility that arbitral upholding of discriminatory contractual provisions may "engender minority group allegations of conspiracies between the arbitrators and the parties," he suggests that in this type of case the arbitrator "bow out" and refuse to make a decision.[70]

Blumrosen, who has had experience both as an arbitrator and as a staff member and consultant to the EEOC, likewise has expressed skepticism as to the ability or inclination of arbitrators to decide questions of public policy in the area of employment discrimination.

> "The instinct, self-interest and the training of the arbitrator as well as the body of law surrounding his work, all call out for him to accept that position which will secure the assent of both of [sic] union and management. Union and management want him to operate within the framework of contractual principles which *they* have established, rather than range over their relationship with a roving commission to implement federal legislative policy." [71]

---

[68] *Corey* v. *Avco Corp.*, No. 137-318, May 28, 1970, Conn. Super. Court, Fairfield County, 2 FEP Cases 738.

[69] Platt, "The Relationship Between Arbitration and Title VII . . . ," at 398; Alfred W. Blumrosen, "Labor Arbitration, EEOC Conciliation, and Discrimination in Employment," 24 *Arb. J.* 88 (1969); and Gould, "Labor Arbitration of Grievances . . . ," at 197.

[70] Platt cites *Hotel Employers Ass'n of San Francisco*, 47 LA 873 (1966) as an egregious example of arbitral mischief and meddling in the civil rights area.

[71] Blumrosen, "Labor Arbitration, EEOC Conciliation . . . ," at 94. Blumrosen's criticism is based on the *Local 12, Rubber Workers* case (45 LA 240 (1965)), especially on the action of the NLRB in referring the issue of racially segregated

Arbitrators in situations involving third-party interests cannot be neutral, according to Blumrosen, because in fact and in law they are the agents of the parties who are alleged to have discriminated.

The EEOC, in Blumrosen's view at the time he was writing, likewise lacked experience in handling such issues, although he noted that unlike arbitration it provided a multilateral forum for the resolution of controversies involving discrimination in employment. Therefore, only the courts can provide the answers.

> "Administrative abdication and narrow arbitration interpretations seem the order of the day. At the root of this phenomenon lies the fact that there is only one institution in our society capable of the difficult tasks of articulating the meaning of modern antidiscriminatory statutes in the complex setting of labor relations. The courts must speak before the less formal processes can operate effectively." [72]

Once the courts decide the questions of substantive law, then arbitrators and administrators might move back into the arena of shared decision-making.

The institutional deficiencies of arbitration as a forum for the just resolution of grievances alleging racial discrimination (and one infers sex discrimination as well) also have been explored by William Gould, who has made a number of suggestions for procedural and other remedial reforms of arbitration. Many of these, as Gould concludes, would modify "the voluntary and private nature of labor arbitration." Whether "the leaky ship" of arbitration is worth patching, or whether it would be "better to build a new ship constructed in the form of government labor courts more responsive to public law" is a question that Gould raises but does not answer. [73]

Conclusions

Certain generalizations can be made at this point in time on

---

jobs to an arbitrator who was not in a position to handle it as a contractual issue. See 150 NLRB 312, 57 LRRM 1535 (1964); confirmed 368 F.2d 12, 63 LRRM 2395 (5th Cir. 1966), *cert. denied.* 389 U.S. 837, 66 LRRM 2306 (1967). Like Platt, he also is critical of the *San Francisco Hotel Association* award.

[72] Blumrosen, *id.* at 105.

[73] Gould, "Labor Arbitration of Grievances . . . ," at 227.

the basis of the foregoing review of arbitral and judicial decisions in the area of employment discrimination.

1. Arbitrators in general, in this field perhaps more than in others, are reluctant to administer public policy. They adhere to the Meltzer doctrine of the separation between contract and law, and they likewise follow in practice the Sovern command to stay out of an area where the courts have primary jurisdiction.

2. The courts for the most part adhere to the same principle, refusing to cede jurisdiction to arbitrators, although some have expressed a preference for arbitration rather than the courts as the forum for resolving these disputes.

3. There are signs of the emergence of a new *Spielberg* doctrine of deference to arbitral awards which meet criteria still to be established.

Should this latter development occur, what response may be expected from the profession? If past discussions of arbitration, the NLRB, and the courts are any guide, this writer anticipates that most arbitrators will continue to refuse the responsibility of deciding issues of public policy.

This negative attitude is alarming. It seems outmoded and irresponsible. As more and more contract issues—once regarded purely as matters of consensual law—become subject to overriding public regulation and control, the once-tight little ship of private adjudication is indeed becoming a leaky vessel. More and more we are witnessing challenges to vested institutional arrangements. Not only the civil rights movement but also the youth movement and the women's "lib" organizations are "pressing the industrial relations system to accommodate to [their] demands." [74] If the institution of arbitration is to survive and to be "relevant" to the emerging needs of a new social and economic order, it cannot afford simply to remain as a part of "the Establishment."

As court decisions in the area of civil rights evolve and the law of employment discrimination becomes more settled, there should be no irreconcilable or irrepressible conflict between the

---

[74] Blumrosen, "Labor Arbitration, EEOC Conciliation . . . ," at 88.

law and collective bargaining agreements, most of which contain little Title VII antidiscrimination provisions of their own. Once the question of federal preemption of state protective laws is answered in the affirmative (as this writer thinks it will be), there will be less reason for arbitrators to use the contract as a shield against public policy.

There remains the question of expertise or competence. Here the profession has either been unduly modest—or to put it more starkly—too specialized. Many who are experts in the law of the shop shy away from the notion of learning more about the law of the land. But this merely means that like every profession, arbitrators are in need of continuing education. In addition to worrying about the training of new arbitrators, perhaps arbitrators should be concerned about retraining themselves to face the challenge of accommodating an old and valuable institution to the new movements of social change. In other words they would mind their BFOQ's!

Chapter II

ARBITRATION IS A VERB

W. Willard Wirtz *

Madame President, Father McIntosh, Ladies and Gentlemen:

Father McIntosh, as one with my own future behind me, I can only express total admiration for the confidence with which you contemplate a reckoning that lies ahead of you. You must feel your credit rating is pretty high in the bank you draw on. If I recall your Invocation accurately, you asked divine assistance in assuring that the food be good, the waiters polite, the conversation pleasant, and the speeches short. Even recognizing your Sponsor in His tripartite capacity, which some here have some question about, it remains that never have so few been asked for so much by so many.

Father, I'd appreciate your importuning your Client for forgiveness, too, if I were to say to Him that if I had the Bible to write over again, after listening to this noon's Presidential Address, I would make one little change in it . . . right at the beginning, in the first book, in that Garden of Eden bit. On reflection, it wasn't an apple that Eve gave Adam; it was a big, round, red raspberry!

Every man here has spent this afternoon thinking back to that idyllic period in arbitration before we made God's second mistake. There were snakes around then, but we males weren't taking any serpentine testimony. We stuck to interpreting agreements, and the thought of nibbling at the forbidden fruits of that tree of knowledge of good and evil never crossed our minds. Our clients here tonight would testify that we didn't know right from wrong. We were doing all right; we were naked but unashamed.

It's plain after this noon, though, that someplace along the

---

* Member, National Academy of Arbitrators, Washington, D.C.

line, Madame President, you let that viper whisper sweet nothings in your ear. We don't know why; but lady, that's your problem. You said something this noon about two bites at the apple. One is enough. Don't try to eat your apple and have us eat it, too. We're not going to bite on this good-and-evil business. We make a decent living not bothering about the facts or about who's right . . . just splitting the difference. If you want to be equal, find something better to be equal to than men. Tell your EEOC-BFOQ troops that if they want to raise their skirts and lower their necklines, even if the twain meet, that's all right with us. But none of this fig-leaf stuff. We're getting along just fine.

One other thing, though, Jean. The truth is that we know you're dead right. Our problem is trying to figure out how to admit it without sounding condescending. All this banter is just the last hurrah of a bunch of stags at bay. We love you, and whatever it is we're still entitled to do, now and forevermore, Amen. Or even Ah-women.

I am an enemy of after-dinner speeches and never give them except for pay or under the influence of strong spirits. It has been a lifetime rule not to open my mouth when sober except at somebody else's expense. Now I find myself paying $30 just to listen to what's going to drop from me. So I have taken, with the rest of you, the trinity of liquid measures necessary to lessen the pain.

There remains, though, the sobering recollection of Cy Ching's comment that no man has more than one speech in him; and, as you have already been reminded, I have made mine here twice before. There is the compensating corollary to Ching's Law, though, that no audience ever remembers anything a speaker says anyway.

This corollary was confirmed Wednesday afternoon, when I came into the executive session of the Academy to find the brethren wrestling again with the problem of the "agreed," or "fixed," arbitration award. It is appropriate to explain to the ladies that this is the situation in which representatives of the parties come to the arbitrator to tell him that they have in fact worked out their problem, that they have agreed on what the award ought to be, but that one of them lacks what it takes to admit it so they want to go ahead with a sham proceeding. The arbitrator goes through a Kabuki dance with his conscience, trying to figure out how to maintain his self-esteem without diminishing his fee. He finds some way of doing this and then comes to the annual meeting of the National Academy of Arbitrators where he engages in a mass confession before Father Brown. Then Leo gets up, as he did Wednesday afternoon, and provides mass absolution with some comment to the effect that arbitration is "nothing but a matter of smell" anyway.

What was particularly bothersome about that 45-minute mass catharsis Wednesday, though, was that Bob Fleming and Ben Aaron and I conducted a complete, exhaustive questionnaire among the whole Academy in 1958. We got all the answers to the rigged-award question, and then I went to the St. Louis meeting and delivered a learned text on the subject. Abe Stockman rose in confirmatory comment in the panel session, and we all agreed upon exactly what the answer was. Yet there wasn't one single reference to that Wednesday afternoon!

What's worse, I can't for the life of me remember what it was we agreed upon in St. Louis. As Ralph Seward might have said last year in Montreal, "Plus ça change, plus sic transit gloria!"

On another occasion, addressing this august body in Chicago, I made the mistake of prefacing a message of undiluted wisdom with some mixed metaphors. Only the metaphors survived.

So there will be no jokes this year. This is also out of deference to the Administration, the media, and the younger degeneration. Each of these forces is obviously hell-bent on exterminating the other two. I wish all three of them total success. But you wonder why they all have to be so sour about it. This country needs a Will Davis to remind us again that whom the gods would preserve they first make laugh, or at least smile just a little bit.

Jokes, though, are only plays on the truth, and the amateur who has to wait until after dinner hasn't a chance these days with the whoppers that come out of Washington during working hours. Some of you may have missed this story in the morning edition of the *Los Angeles Times*. I quote—a little loosely: Dateline Washington: "The combined rise last month in prices, unemployment, and the number of civilian advisors in Cambodia represented a smaller increase, conveniently adjusted, than during any comparable period in the nineteenth century, thus constituting a great ideological victory." With an instinct for the jocular, they live in a constant state of euphemism; but how they can lay one lemon after another and come up cackling like a rose is an enema to me.

But it's time, and past, to get down to business. And time for brevity even at the risk of seeming offense to contemplative reason.

Jean McKelvey, in her Presidential Address this noon, returned to the issue of the extent to which "third party" participation in disputes settlement extends properly beyond the function of "neutral" interpretation of what the contracting parties have agreed upon, to include a recognition and effectuation of broader "public policy." Her discussion was primarily of this issue as it arises in connection with the arbitration of grievances under collective bargaining agreements, particularly those involving the question of whether the myth of men's having been created equal is to be extended to women.

Sharing fully Jean's view about the particular point, I'd like to say a little about some broader aspects of it. For the extension of the third-party function—not in the collective bargaining area alone, and perhaps least of all in the settlement of grievances—seems to me a matter of increasingly critical importance in a period of escalating confrontation in the society as a whole. And I venture, perhaps presume, to suggest that the relative reticence of the arbitration profession's advocacy of this extension is in part the product of our having entered it under inhibiting circumstances.

We came in, many of us in the 1940s, as part of the single most significant development of arbitration in American history. Organized labor and large corporate management had decided, almost suddenly and as the product of the Washington Conference of 1946, to establish a terminal point for disputes which developed under the agreements which companies and unions had entered into. It was important for a variety of reasons that the "private" nature of the arbitration procedure they adopted, and its total commitment to acceptance of the will of the contracting parties, be emphasized and respected. We, as arbitrators, accepted those terms. Even a determination as to whether an employee had been discharged for "just cause" was cast in terms of being only a matter of divining the parties' cryptically expressed consensus. If the issue of a possible conflict between something in the agreement and some public law came up, which it rarely did, it was part of the conventional technique to devise some approach or circumlocution which respected the law without offending clients closer at hand. The emergent institution of free, private collective bargaining needed, at that point, an arbitration function sternly disciplined to the dictates of a self-abnegating "neutralism." We performed that function.

There were accompanying attitudes about some related matters. Arbitration of new contract disputes, obviously requiring something more than "neutral interpretation," was considered a kind of aberration; and there was unanimous agreement that "compulsory arbitration" was a plague to which we couldn't risk exposing ourselves under any conceivable circumstances. (The fact that arbitration of contract grievances had been required by law in the Railway Labor Act was not mentioned in serious company.) And the companion gospel developed in the neighboring province of "mediation" was that what was good for General Motors *and* the UAW was good for the country. Which is not to fault the mediators of that period. Collective bargaining was considered a *private* process. The country, furthermore, was concerned about disputes being settled and totally unconcerned about settlement terms.

I urge it a little that relevant and significant circumstances have changed; that it is possible, indeed accurate, to believe that the third-party function served collective bargaining and the public interest well by being kept essentially and narrowly "neutral" during that formative period; but that concepts which became virtually part of the definition of "arbitration" and "mediation" at that stage have an inhibiting effect on the extension of this third-party function to meet the demands of contemporary and prospective circumstance. It is unfortunate that words don't grow the way ideas do—and significant that in the hard sciences, unlike such soft disciplines as politics and public affairs, new vocabularies are developed to better accommodate the growth of reason.

This is not the hour for historical analysis, even as much as there has already been here. Yet it seems clear beyond the need for supporting detail that one thing which is happening in the society is a breaking down of the once sharp distinction between public and private interests. It is part of this that there is general recognition that the obligation of all "private" institutions includes taking account of the "public interest." The issue, so sharply debated 30 or 40 years ago, of whether a corporate board of directors was even *entitled* to take the public interest into account is now totally anachronistic. George Meany would not consider Samuel Gompers's answer—"More. More. More."—to the question of what organized labor's purpose is. Private representatives are on literally hundreds of public committees and commissions. And new forms of broader "public" participation in the working of the "private" sector are the subject of widespread interest and varied proposals.

Perhaps there are good reasons for not extending this changing logic of pluralism to the role of third parties in labor-management relations. I don't know them. Having grown up, or old, professionally, on the idea that "the right to strike and to lock out are the essential motive forces of collective bargaining," I know that this no longer seems to me the absolute we made it into. A perquisite of retiring from the field is the privilege of not feeling the compulsion to cower like one of Pavlov's dogs whenever anybody mentions "compulsory arbitration." Now I can dislike it, but feel that the fair reaction is along the lines of the housewife's answer when she is asked, "How's your husband?" and replies, "Compared with what?"

Perhaps it will appear a matter of having run up openly at my masthead the skull and crossbones of corporate piracy; but recognizing the Academy's rule against bringing here any case a member has under advisement at the moment, let me put a hypothetical:

Suppose there were an industry which had gotten into such deplorable shape that part of its service was being taken over in desperation by the government, most of the industry was in deep financial trouble, and the largest unit in it had gotten to the point where it was losing over $300 million a year and was therefore put into bankruptcy.

What the trustees in bankruptcy would find would be that the interests of that corporation's shareholders—its creditors, those with judgments against it, the local taxing districts dependent on that property to support schools and the like—were all subject to what is in effect third-party disposition. But not the interests of the employees.

Suppose the trustees found that over 65 percent of that corporation's operating costs were for labor, that wage levels were about to be raised some 35 percent in the next three years, that the whole system of work rules was a travesty on good sense, and that the business could probably be run equally well with 10 to 20,000 fewer employees on the rolls. But they would also find that with respect to the employment relationship, unlike that with creditors, shareholders, claimants, and taxing authorities, there is no provision at all for effective recourse to reason; that the bankruptcy laws specifically leave this to collective bargaining.

And suppose it were the situation that in this particular industry there hadn't been any real collective bargaining for at least 20 years; that there was still talk about the right to strike and to lock out, but that whenever there was a serious resort to these measures, a court or the Congress intervened to deny the alleged right; and that things were so bad that it had been necessary three times recently for the Congress to decide—what it had not had to with respect to any other industry—how particular disputes should be settled.

Sorry to have violated the rule so grossly. The point should have been made more directly. It is that one big reason for the condition the railroad industry is in today—although by no means the only one—is the stubborn insistence that its labor disputes be settled without resort to some kind of effective third-party determination. I think it is also a fact that the Penn

Central could be made a viable and effective operation again—without asking the Congress to supply $100-million lines of credit, indeed without *any* further cost to the public—by changing the bankruptcy laws to provide for third-party determination of questions involving (even aside from wages) disputes about labor terms and conditions.

We are paying a high price for trying to preserve as an absolute the principle of leaving labor disputes to the exercise of the disputants' economic strength regardless of the effect of their unreconciled disagreement.

It is not only the problem of disagreements. No fair-minded assessment of the present crisis of inflation in the country blames it all on rising wages, leaving out the other forces which contribute to rising costs. Neither does any reasonable assessment leave out the fact that the imbalance of bargaining power in the construction industry has resulted in agreements that include unconscionable and epidemic wage settlements.

Nor is it only in the labor field that the need for a broader concept of arbitration is increasingly imperative. I suspect there is an operative principle that as a society and its economy become more complex and more highly organized, and more sophisticated and powerful, and that as the pace of change is accelerated, confrontation increases and expands and becomes more dangerous. It is a corollary that under these circumstances the necessity for the arbitrament of reason—as against any other form of dispute settlement—increases.

With the splitting of the atom and the reducing of the miles and hours that used to separate nations to inches and seconds, the arbitrament of war—anywhere in the world—changed from fallacy to insanity. There *has* to be a way to put the disputes between governments to some kind of arbitrament of reason.

The past 10 years have seen the development of at least two new areas of organized confrontation: between people whose distinction is the color of their skins, and between those who are younger and those who are older. And now there is the emergence of organized consumer groups, where before we were organized almost exclusively in our capacity as producers.

The new conflicts these developments are producing are unquestionably painful, but by no means all regrettable. They are
probably an inevitable part of coming out of a trance of
hypocrisy and bigotry in which we committed outrageous mis-
demeanors of one kind or another.

In an address by Mr. Justice Holmes to the Bar Association
of New York in 1913, he spoke about the timing of the role
of law. Paraphrasing from memory, he said about this: That
as long as conflicting notions and opposite convictions still
keep a battlefront against each other, and the idea destined to
prevail has not gained the field, the time for law has not yet
come. Perhaps that's true of the law, although Holmes would
probably say it a little differently today. But if this is true of
the law, it is not true of the whole broader need for the arbitrament of reason.

In each of these areas of confrontation and in others, it
seems increasingly plain that new forums, perhaps even more
than new laws, are called for—new procedures which permit
bringing to bear on a dispute, sometimes with terminal authority, the views and influence of someone other than the
disputants. Or perhaps just "public interest" arbitration.

There will be the objection that the "public interest" is too
vague and indefinable to permit or warrant its use as a guide
to the exercise of the authority of either a mediator or an
arbitrator. A little about this, and then I am done.

There is no point in pressing the question of whether iden-
tifying the "public interest" is actually any harder than finding
the "neutral" answer to a good many issues which parties to a
contract never thought about when they wrote it. Few arbitrators would say, as Mr. Justice Roberts almost did, that grievance
arbitration is only a matter of laying the facts beside the contract and measuring them as with a ruler. It could be won-
dered, too, how many of the cases Jean referred to this noon
were cases in which the arbitrator managed in his *award* to
serve the "public interest" more fully than might be suggested by
his deference in his *opinion* to the gospel of "neutralism"
and the gods of the parties. You can question the whole dichot-
omy between "neutralism" and the "public interest."

Better, though, to question the assumption that the public interest is the mystique it is sometime considered.

I can't define the "public interest" any more clearly than I could one night, probably in 1945, when President-elect Gill and I were sitting as public members on a War Labor Board case that had to be settled before morning. We took a recess about 11 o'clock so that the labor members could get on the phone and find out what the labor interest was and the industry members could call their clients and find out about the industry interest. Public Member Gill and I went over to the window in that board room at the back of the fifth floor in the Labor Building and looked up at the stars, and he said— "Iewconically"—"Too bad we don't have a phone to up there."

A year or so ago now, when we were deciding where to dig a well for a piece of heaven we've found in West Virginia, I discovered that I am possessed of the powers of the water witch. The forked willow branch bent sharply down in my hands at just the spot it had for the professional well digger, and we hit water at 37 feet. My fellow dowser was surprised at this sharing of his powers. He was an untutored type—who wouldn't even understand the difference between "compulsory arbitration" and "mediation to finality"—so I didn't tell him I had been in a similar line of occult divination ever since the War Labor Board days.

Which is all nonsense. The "public interest"? No, I can't define it. But in every case I can think of there has been a common sense of the right answer which most of the people close to it shared in substantial part.

Most of the mystery about the public interest comes from thinking of it as a noun. As a noun it's a big, fat, prostitute phrase continually compromised by rakes, not for their passions but for their pleasures. It was Buckminster Fuller's comment, in one of his earlier articles, that "God is a verb, not a noun." The stature of Fuller's thought has been diminished a little by his entitling his most recent book, *I Seem To Be a Verb*. But the point survives the sacrilege. The public interest is a verb, not a noun.

Part of it is doing those things rational people know by quite general consent need to be done, but which for some constraining reason—a tired habit or a rusty precedent or a retreating majority—can't be done easily.

The public interest has to be served in substantial part by an "adhocracy." When things are changing at the rate they are now, it demands that there be forums freed of the tyranny of precedents, in which every hard and fast rule is suspect and the seed-grain of experience is separated out from the chaff of custom and habit.

But if the service of the public interest is in administering change, it doesn't permit misconceiving change as being good in itself or as having any sense of conscience of its own—which change isn't and hasn't. That service is sternly disciplined according to one central principle: that only the individual counts.

It takes its procedures from that principle. Some of us were talking at breakfast this morning about a case, utterly insignificant in itself, at the U.S. Rubber plant at Passaic 20 years or so ago. Two men were discharged for fighting in the plant. We all knew the rule: Both had to go. It didn't matter that Joe, the big fellow, had thrown cold water on pint-sized Steve in the shower room, then taunted him about being a runt, and thrown in some reflections on his ancestry—until Steve finally tried to climb up Joe's frame. Lacking stone or sling, Steve's efforts were futile. But he mixed it up long enough to bring the inexorable rule into effect. Then, at the arbitration hearing, Steve got up and said just one thing: "Mr. Arbitrator, what would you have did?" I hope Steve is still there.

But a good deal more than procedures comes from the uncommon law of arbitration that only the individual matters. Nothing else. Not the individual as a remote and uncertain beneficiary of something called progress or the gross national product. Not the individual as a sparrow to be fed by gorging the horses. No. The individual as the owner of rights and interests—job rights, personal rights, human rights—at least as much entitled to protection as a piece of real estate or machinery. The individual as somebody the system is designed for instead of the other way around.

There is a strongly emergent sense today of the need to re-
new the idea of the supremacy of the individual. A book as
third rate as *The Greening of America* becomes a best seller
because it makes, even absurdly, a point that catches this sense.
We're listening to "the kids," even in their sometimes out-
rageousness, because they're saying the truth about our having
put the system ahead of the individual. They talk about "feeling" instead of "understanding." We only half get it—because
we don't understand. But we know they are right that the
"public interest" has to be served with the realization that
"the public" is a myth. The reality is people.

Well, we seem to be a long way from where these remarks
started, and yet at the same time tiresomely close. Listening to
what you've just heard, I think of Holmes's apostrophe to the
woodpecker: "Thou sayest such undisputed things in such a
solemn way."

It is simply that I think of arbitration as an instrument with
a potential for meeting infinitely greater needs than those we
have spent most of our professional lives putting it to. What
we do in using it to decide grievances under collective bargaining agreements—and regardless of what we conclude about restricting it there to the "neutral" interpretation of agreements—
is not enough reason for defining it in those terms or confining
it to those uses.

Feeling deeply, almost desperately, that the society is becoming
mortally dependent on the arbitrament of reason—that the
future may depend, even whether there will be a future, on
the development of a jurisprudence built around people instead
of the system of things—I speak for arbitration, too, as a verb.

CHAPTER III

THE ROLE OF ARBITRATION
IN STATE AND NATIONAL LABOR POLICY

EDGAR A. JONES, JR. *

I.

There is an immediate and insurmountable difficulty in trying to think about *the* role of arbitration in the formulation and
administration of labor policy in the United States. In one
word, the difficulty is diversity. There is marked diversity of
education and viewpoint among those who serve as arbitrators
in the various regions and among the many industries of this
vast country. There is considerable diversity of expectation
among the participants as well as among those who are concerned about the quality of life among our citizens and of
justice among disputants. There is diversity of responsibility
among the forums and jurisdictions from whose labors emerge
the dynamic crosscurrents of purpose and action that we choose
to call "national labor policy."

Arbitration has become Argus, the watchful giant of Greek
mythology, enshrouded in contemporary mythology, Argus of
the 100 eyes and, today in America, several times over as many
tongues.[1]

Consider the state of labor arbitration as we move into the
decade of the 1970s. We are participating in what Professor
Harry Wellington has aptly called "this quiet revolution." [2]
Professor Bernard Meltzer remarked its "substantial invisibil-

---

* Vice President, National Academy of Arbitrators; Professor of Law, University
of California, Los Angeles.
[1] We need not here speak of the circumstances of the creature's demise.
[2] Wellington, *Labor and the Legal Process* (New Haven: Yale University Press,
1968), 98.

42

ity." [3] But, none doubt its impact on the quality of justice in the United States. Professor Wellington accurately described arbitral decision-making in labor disputes as "one of the most rapidly developing segments of American jurisprudence." [4] But it would abort the significance of that observation were "jurisprudence" in that sense to be narrowly conceived as limited to what courts are deciding.

Dean Leon Green, one of the first and surely the most durable of the legal realists of the 1920s, conceived of "law" as "the power of passing judgment." [5] His view was and is sociologically sound. A modern legal sociologist, concerned to identify "law" in terms of legally sanctioned and enforceable decisions resolving disputes in contention between citizens, would not hesitate to encompass in that definition arbitral awards resolving labor disputes.

Numbers indicate the dimensions. For the six years 1964-1969 there was a purposeful research effort by the Academy's Law and Legislation Committee to identify and comment upon all the federal and state court decisions that dealt with pre-award and post-award labor arbitration.[6] Over the six years the total judicial output uncovered cumulated 765 court decisions rang-

---

[3] Meltzer, "Ruminations About Ideology, Law, and Labor Arbitration," in *The Arbitrator, the NLRB, and the Courts,* Proceedings of the 20th Annual Meeting, National Academy of Arbitrators, ed. Dallas L. Jones (Washington: BNA Books, 1967), 1 at 19.

[4] *Supra* note 2, at 98.

[5] L. Green, *Judge and Jury* (1930), 41.

[6] The annual reports, covering the years 1964-1969, appear in the BNA volumes reporting the Academy's annual proceedings of the following years: 1965, at 219-240 (Jones and Gould) ; 1966, at 366-398 (Jones and Kranwinkle) ; 1967, at 381-404 (Jones and Anderson) ; 1968 at 201-266 (Jones and Anderson); 1969, at 187-212 (Jones and Finkel) ; 1970, at 213-252 (Jones and Peratis). In 1964 the Law and Legislation Committee report identified about 175 reported cases dealing with labor arbitration in which state and federal courts had been called upon to intervene either before or after an arbitral award had issued; 74 percent of those cases were federal and, interestingly, the New York Supreme Court, actually a trial court in these matters, held a monopoly of two thirds of all state decisions. In 1965 there were about 150 decisions in the courts, 64 percent being federal and the New York Supreme Court accounting for half the state decisions. In 1966 there were 120 court cases, 83 percent being federal and the New York Supreme Court again accounting for half the state decisions. In 1967, 130 court cases were counted, 83 percent federal, but the New York Supreme Court output dropped off to a quarter of the state decisions. In 1968 only 81 court cases were found, 86 percent being federal and only two decisions (surely there must have been more unreported) coming out of the New York Supreme Court. Finally, in 1969 there were 109 court cases, 78 percent being federal and, once again, the justices of the New York Supreme Court were back up at the plate swinging at 50 percent of the state decisions.

ing from the Supreme Court down to local trial courts, of which
75 percent were federal and 25 percent state in origin. The
annual totals ranged from 81 (in 1968) to 175 (in 1964),
averaging 120 court decisions a year.

In each of those six years only a handful of cases—almost
literally—involved refusals by courts to order arbitration when
requested. And in each year the overwhelming majority of suits
to review arbitral awards resulted in confirmation. A consistent
pattern of judicial self-restraint, preservative of the discretion
of the arbitrator, was manifest throughout the six years.

In the fiscal year 1968 the National Labor Relations Board
closed 1,414 unfair labor practice cases at various stages in the
pipeline of decision,[7] from after a hearing had opened before
a trial examiner to after the Supreme Court had taken some
action. Of them, 1,111 were closed after a Board order had
issued. That same year in the circuit courts of appeals, the
federal appellate judges decided 301 proceedings on petitions
for enforcement or review of Labor Board orders. The 11 circuit courts modified, set aside, or remanded in 41 percent of
those cases. A reading of a number of those court decisions will
support the conclusion that the federal judges have no hesitancy
in making substantial changes in Board orders when they proceed to "modify" them, and that the differences reflect policy
conflicts over which interests among employers, unions, and
individual employees shall receive preferential protection.

Thinking only in terms of quantity, then, we have state and
federal courts deciding about 120 Section 301 cases a year on
average and about 300 or so cases reviewing decisions of the
Labor Board. The Board itself contributes upward of 1,000 of
its own decisions, no more than a couple of dozen of which are
concerned with arbitrators' awards or the prospect of arbitration
as an alternative to Board procedures. (Of course I have not
referred to the office practice of the Board's regional offices
which must cope with a torrent of cases heading for the 50,000
mark, of which the vast bulk are handled in the regional offices
with finality. My reference in these remarks is to litigated
matters, since they afford a meaningful comparison to the activities of arbitrators.)

---

[7] *33rd NLRB Annual Report* (1968), Tables 8, 19, and 19A.

Look now to the activity of arbitrators, still thinking only of numbers. First of all, my correspondence with practitioners in the 50 states indicates to me that there are fewer than 500 men and women in the United States categorizable as active labor arbitrators, even making two or three decisions a year. My discussions with Federal Mediation and Conciliation Service and American Arbitration Association people over the years, added to my informal survey of the various states, has convinced me that there are probably fewer than 300 truly active arbitrators in the country, handling at least a dozen cases a year resulting in awards. By contrast, the U.S. district courts number about 365 district judges, and the Labor Board uses the services of about 75 trial examiners who apparently conduct an average of about a dozen hearings a year.

Bearing in mind the informed guess that there are about 300 or so active arbitrators in the country, recall the 1962 study of the Academy in which 158 members responded to a survey, disclosing the issuance of 6,279 decisions for the year.[8] Extrapolating those figures, it seems a conservative estimate to me that upward of 10,000 final and binding awards are being issued each year by labor arbitrators. That is a very awesome figure! Just in sheer numbers it is impressive enough. But it derives its awesomeness for me from the speculation it compels about the effect of this outpouring of awards upon the quality of justice in our country, for these arbitral awards are multiplied almost exponentially in their effects upon the conduct of workers, supervisors, and managers who consciously try to be guided by these awards or the anticipation of them.

It is a fact today that no one can realistically purport to describe the quality of American justice unless he can relate the substance of what labor arbitrators are actually doing in their conduct of hearings and in the issuance of decisions on the variety of issues that are brought before them by grievances during the terms of collective bargaining agreements. Unfortunately in that regard, the 1962 survey of Academy members also disclosed that less than 10 percent of the arbitral decisions

---

[8] In *Labor Arbitration: Perspective and Problems*, Proceedings of the 17th Annual Meeting, National Academy of Arbitrators, ed. Mark L. Kahn (Washington: BNA Books, 1964), at 295.

become available for study through publication. As of now, it must be said, awareness of what arbitrators are actually doing in their dispositions of grievances is only knowable, if at all, by observing the few decisions that do make their censored appearance in print and through conversation by and with arbitrators and those whose business it is to keep track of what's going on in labor-management affairs. (Every now and then, of course, as we have witnessed annually, one of them can also be lured out of his insulated anonymity of judgment to make ill-considered disclosures, the only result of which is active note-taking on the programs—"Strike him!"—as he lives to regret that fleeting temptation to vanity unsuppressed. If I were Peter Seitz, at this point I would utter a striking poetic image; but Seitz incites insights that only Seitz insights sight.)

How then shall we look for what is "national labor policy"? It becomes necessary to think of labor arbitrators engaged in their highly individual and personal acts of judgment—almost, but not quite, immune to post-award review albeit *jointly* selected by the disputants in the first place—and to relate their activities, not just to one another and to their cumulative impress on American labor policy, but also in terms of their interaction, conscious or unconscious, with other governmentally sanctioned tribunals engaged in fashioning labor and other public policy. There must be reckoned the administrative apparatus of the National Labor Relations Board—its regional officials, the General Counsel and his staff, the 75 or so trial examiners, and the five members of the Labor Board. But we must also view arbitrators and their decisional activities relative to the 50 state court systems. And then as kind of a capper we have to be mindful of the federal judiciary, the 365 or so federal district judges sitting throughout the states and the 11 federal circuits sitting in three-judge panels or *en banc* to review the decisions of the Labor Board, or of lower federal courts reacting to the prospect or actuality of arbitral decisions. If that were not enough to bedazzle the would-be synthesizer, there is the further necessity to reckon the federal Equal Employment Opportunities Commission and its state facsimile agencies. And now over the horizon stirs the Goliath of public sector employment with its own infinite variety of public service functions and agencies—federal, state, and local—and millions of employees whose grievances are as numerous in the contemplation as are the grains of sand on the Santa Monica beach.

How in the name of God can all of this frenetic decisional activity be harnessed to any common purpose? Forty mules could be harnessed to bring water to Death Valley, despite the conventional wisdom about mules. What about 40 times 40 forums? The mules drew one element—water. No one in this room is so naive as to think that 40 forums draw one element—justice! We are all too knowing about the frailties of human reason and its susceptibility to the setting of judgment —time, circumstance, and personalities—to be deluded by the single-minded myth of single-minded justice.

II.

At the outset of their classical study of the history of English law, Pollock and Maitland at the turn of this century defined the conditions of acceptance in the community of a national mode of disputes resolution. "Different and more or less con- flicting systems of law," they wrote, "different and more or less competing systems of jurisdiction, in one and the same region, are compatible with a high state of civilization, with a strong government, and with an administration of justice well enough liked and sufficiently understood by those who are concerned." [9]

For its time and locale that was a remarkably sophisticated view. It could well have been written today and for us, not as theory but as descriptive of our experience with labor arbitra- tion and its interactive state and federal tribunals in America. But it does also constitute a sound theoretical premise for that tribunal interaction. It accepts a diversity of viewpoint about what justice might be in particular circumstances. But impliedly it also posits the existence of some kind of commonality loosely holding it all together.

This is what another English scholar, Professor Percy Winfield of Cambridge, identified a few years later as "the common stock of legal ideas without which no civilized community can exist." He was reflecting on the implications of public policy in the evolution of English law. His thought was turned back to the formative era from which we in America as well as our English

---

[9] Pollock and Maitland, *History of English Law* (1911), xxv.

cousins draw many of our currently compelling legal ideas. "The whole of that era," he wrote, "was one of rapid building in our law, and it had to be developed more by analogies, by logic, and by a broad perception of what was wanted than by precedents of which there were few compared to the mass that exists in more modern law." Nonetheless, there was some kind of reservoir from which each would be apt to draw some "common stock of legal ideas" radiating notions of fairness whereby human affairs in that community might reasonably be expected to be ordered. This reservoir of conviction and commitment has come to be referred to as "public policy." "In tracing the history of public policy," Professor Winfield wrote, "two things must be clearly distinguished. One is the unconscious or half-conscious use of it which probably pervaded the whole legal system when law had to be made in some way or other, and when there was not much statute law and practically no case law at all to summon to the judges' assistance. The other," he added, "is the conscious application of public policy to the solution of legal problems. . . ." [10]

Mark the parallel between the contemporary labor arbitrator and the common law judge of that formative era of our heritage described by Winfield and bearing in mind Leon Green's identification of law as "the power of passing judgment." Observe, if you will, how labor arbitration fits into the Pollock and Maitland scheme of systems of jurisdiction and law in a state of continuing but understood and accepted tension one with another. Those early judges had little or no legal precedent to command them. Nor do contemporary labor arbitrators. Review of those early court decisions was rare, sporadic, and unstructured, as it is today of arbitral awards. Statutory law seldom if ever laid its legislative arm on their discretion, nor does it today on arbitrators. The early judges may have thought to pay some attention to each other's patterns of decision, but they had no structured means—other than the King's Own Good Pub—whereby to share concern about the rightness of decisions in recurrent mutual problems, and so it is with us. But they did share that "common stock of legal ideas" and it was evident

---

[10] P. Winfield, "Public Policy in the English Common Law," 42 *Harv. L. Rev.* 76, 79-81 (1928).

in the evolution of their decisions that their thinking did have a common gene pool. I would suggest that we are similarly situated today as labor arbitrators.

My colleague Melville Nimmer recently undertook a study for the Israeli Ministry of Justice of the uses of judicial review in Israel's present quest for a constitution. His effort led him to seek to identify the sources of a "higher law" (short of the Deity, I should add, as this was not a rabbinical work) which might afford a stability for the fundamental societal values inherent in the commitment to freedom of expression and of worship and to the equal protection of the laws. He concluded that such a higher law was necessary to which all could subscribe despite their differences and from which, as a consequence, there could be derived "meaningful assurance that the societal values of freedom and equality will endure." [11] This is a modern affirmation observable in the circumstances of a nation newly forging constitutional ideas that reflects the same kind of reliance upon Winfield's "common stock of legal ideas" that makes possible Pollock's and Maitland's coexistent diversity of systems of law and jurisdiction. There is a vital lesson to be drawn from our legal history in this connection. In Professor Nimmer's words, "if the delicate balance between majority rule and the preservation of minority rights, both of which are essential to a democratic state, are to be preserved, it is essential that all segments of the population play by the rules and that the rules themselves not be susceptible to easy change by transient or intolerant majorities." Nor, we might add, by final and binding decision-makers who simply ignore them.

Several years ago in his thoughtful remarks to this Academy Professor Bernard Meltzer advised arbitrators to construe collective agreements where possible so as to avoid invalidating confrontations with countermanding law. Although he evidently credited arbitrators with competence to engage in that kind of subtle interpretive maneuver, positing as it does a knowledge of the contours of the obstacle around which it would be necessary to maneuver, he nevertheless disqualified them as a group, and the arbitral process as a system, to resolve "irrepressible

---

[11] M. Nimmer, "The Uses of Judicial Review in Israel's Quest for a Constitution," 70 *Colum. L. Rev.* 1217, 1257 (1970).

conflict" when the mandates of the collective agreement and those of some "higher law" external to it come unavoidably into conflict. In that posture, he declared, the arbitrator "should respect the agreement and ignore the law." [12] And there is little doubt that his counsel reflected the conviction of most of the arbitrators present, and I suspect that that balance would probably still exist among us today.

In dissent, I sense an unperceived and mischievous potential for the continued good health and utility of labor arbitration in the assumption that ignorance is not only bliss, but virtue as well. If I have been successful in prodding your thinking up to this point in my remarks, you should be prepared to join me in what I would now press upon you to be an important distinction. It is that between "law" in a narrow sense and "public policy" in the broader sense of that "common stock of legal ideas" that we all share.

Mr. Justice Holmes once defined "law" in a famous phrase. It was for him "the prophecies of what the courts will do in fact," [13] and no more. I have no hesitancy whatsoever in joining Professor Meltzer in abjuring law as the pursuit of arbitrators if by "law" we may accept the Holmes definition. If an arbitrator is indeed fearful today of what courts will do in fact in response to a decision he is contemplating, he is needlessly so if the pattern of adjudication and arbitration interaction teaches us anything at all these past six years. Such an arbitrator would have to believe that judges fly on brooms in search of wayward arbitrators. (I should drop a caveat here, and that is that I am referring to the pattern of interaction of courts and arbitrators in the private sector, not as to public employment problems where, as we shall see, it is as yet uncertain what the pattern of interaction may shape up to be.)

We may surely stipulate together that arbitrators should not, and need not, fret about law in the Holmesian sense of "prophecies of what courts will do in fact." Having done so, I would then like to propose to you that *all* labor arbitrators should feel in conscience bound to be concerned about how their deci-

---

[12] Meltzer, *supra* note 3, at 16.
[13] Holmes, *Collected Legal Papers* (1920), at 173.

sional conduct accords with "the common stock of legal ideas without which no civilized community can exist," as Professor Winfield saw it. Then, to the hindmost with the courts! The critical query is whether in these thousands of arbitral decisions we as labor arbitrators are leaving this country with a higher or a lower quality of justice. I believe, with Professor Nimmer, that it *is* essential that all segments of the population play by the elemental rules or, more precisely, *try* to play by them. It seems to me that it would be most destructive if our societal values of freedom and equality were being warped and diminished across the land because arbitrators felt themselves to be above the law, or felt that they should not be concerned to be the spokesmen of those values rather than ignorant or heedless of them. Thousands of grievants are bringing before supervisors asserted rights which are being measured against what arbitrators have been deciding and saying in like circumstances. These values radiating from our commitments to freedom and equality have historically always been embattled. They have always required strong and courageous guardians to insure that the weak and easily overwhelmed shall enjoy them. After all, they are the least able to lay assured claim to their benefits and the most needful of them.

If the guardians will not guard, who shall guard the guardians? I have a deep sense of presentiment that were it to become evident that labor arbitrators were issuing awards in significant numbers contrary to the spirit of the "common stock of legal ideas" protective of our freedom, arbitration would then have dealt a mortal wound to collective bargaining. Juvenal asked, "Who guards the guardians?" [14] For our purposes here I have little doubt in my own mind that the answer will run in the alternative: The conscience of the guardian, informed and sensitive, must guard the guardian; or the guardian will be dismissed and his house dismantled.

III.

The circuitry along which we thread our thoughts on this subject of the roles of public policy in labor arbitration has a number of breakers strung out along it which seem to short-

---

[14] Juvenal, *Satires VI.* Professor Nimmer refers to this conundrum as "the perennial problem of jurisprudence." Nimmer, *supra* note 11, at 1217.

circuit communication rather frequently. Since I have experienced this short-circuit phenomenon a number of times, let me take heed of at least some of the obvious circuit breakers with the following affirmations. First, I have never heard any participant in the labor arbitral processes seriously advance the notion that collective bargainers, using the usual general language of a broad arbitration clause, intend to or do create an arbitral ombudsman who may properly roam at will among the equities of a dispute in response to the distressed summons of either of the parties or of affected employees.

Second, I share the view expressed a dozen years ago by Willard Wirtz, and I take it to be expressive of the minds of practically all, if not all, arbitrators with whom I have ever discussed the subject. He observed then that " 'due process' is a symbol borrowed from the lexicon of law, and therefore suspect in this shirtsleeves . . . business of arbitration." [15] The sense of his caution was that uncritical adoption of ideas grown in another milieu is a dangerous business and, secondly, that any application of ideas adapted from the "lexicon of the law" had to have their utility demonstrated, and this *before* being engrafted on arbitral function. He went on to wonder if "protection of certain individual interests" might be more effectively accomplished by holding elected representatives to standards of fair representation, perhaps by penalizing them through the ballot box, or by a forum like a court or the Labor Board, rather than by "endowing the umpires of controversy with the obligation and authority." [16] I have extrapolated some of Bill Wirtz's thoughts and, having done so, I should add that the actions of the courts in the intervening 12 years have, in my judgment, so enhanced the power of arbitrators by further insulating their judgment against judicial review as to create more rather than less reason for arbitrators to seek to preserve public policy rights protective of individual freedom and equality and, I should add, dignity.

Third, I would ally myself without hesitancy with Abe Stock-

---

[15] Wirtz, "Due Process of Arbitration," in *The Arbitrator and the Parties*, Proceedings of the 16th Annual Meeting, National Academy of Arbitrators, ed. Jean T. McKelvey (Washington: BNA Books, 1958), at 1.

[16] *Id.* at 5.

man's observation, [17] at the same meeting at which Bill Wirtz spoke in 1958, that there is no automatic analogy linking the rights of a person accused of a crime, and involved in law enforcement procedures, with the rights of an employer, an employee, and a union, all of whom are concerned about the investigation of a problem, for example, of warehouse thefts. And, finally, I know of no arbitrator who would be willing, let alone merely be reluctant, "to blanket the arbitration process with due process considerations." [18]

There are, nonetheless, recurrent situations in plants in the course of which the necessity for an arbitrator to assess "the common stock of legal ideas" about what is tolerable in our society is well nigh inescapable. A decade ago Professor Alfred Blumrosen studied the disposition of various public issues by arbitrators and by the courts as disclosed in published awards. Interestingly, he found, "Arbitrators consider it their duty to take account of public policy considerations involved in labor-management relations. In not a single case has it been suggested that the employer-union relationship is a private affair, and that the public interests should not affect a decision by a person privately selected by the parties to resolve some of their private disputes." [19] His survey convinced him that arbitrators, lawyer or no, tended to "handle public policy considerations with understanding and intelligence," and were not "blinded by the

---

[17] *Id.* at 39-40.

[18] H. Edwards, "Due Process Considerations in Labor Arbitration," 25 *Arb. J.* 141, 143 (1970). Unfortunately Professor Edwards has misread a decision of mine, deducing from it a position contrary to the views to which I subscribe and which are stated above in the text. See *Thrifty Drug Stores Co.,* 50 LA 1253 (1968), Edgar A. Jones, Jr. The thrust of the reasoning in that opinion was expressed thus: "Of course, we are not here concerned with 'the forces of the law.' . . . But our concern is not unlike that of the courts when they are coping with the testimonial privilege or with custodial interrogations by police. We must determine whether there was truth-telling despite these custodial interrogations as they were conducted in the Company's security cubicles in the absence of union representatives. It is sometimes overlooked and certainly underemphasized that those procedures which impose pressures on interrogated persons to disclose incriminating facts are unreliable as eliciters of truth and that their unreliability mounts in direct proportion to the increase in the pressures." 50 LA 1260-1261. "The question here is whether the statements are so tainted by compulsions created by the manner of their taking as to make it too speculative for a trier of fact—the Arbitrator—to give them credence as evidence against those whom they would implicate." *Id.* at 1262.

[19] Blumrosen, "Public Policy Considerations in Labor Arbitration Cases," 14 *Rutg. L. Rev.* 217, 235 (1960).

importance of policy considerations into an ill-considered weighing of evidentiary factors." [20] I *think* that remains valid as a
description, although I feel disturbingly ignorant of what all
those thousands of unpublished awards are accomplishing in
this regard.

In discussing the relevances of public policy to arbitral decision-making, it is essential to be fact-oriented. Public policy is
not a disembodied voice speaking commandingly from a cloud.
It is a concern which arises from a perceived set of facts, and in
our context the set of facts will always involve contractual differences. It is a contract we are expounding (with proper
deference to Chief Justice Marshall); it is not a constitution.
But Mr. Justice Black, no ingenuous acceptor of the untram-
meled virtues of arbitration in all settings, expressed the Court's
basic view when he wrote that a collective agreement "is not
an ordinary contract for the purchase of goods and services, nor
is it governed by the same old common-law concepts, which control such private contracts." [21] The Court has been firm in its
acceptance of Dean Harry Shulman's definition of arbitration
as "an integral part of the system of self-government. And the
system is designed to aid management in its quest for efficiency,
to assist union leadership in its participation in the enterprise,
and to secure justice for the employees." [22] Professor Wellington
has well described the agreement as "one episode in a continuing, joint history of a firm and a union. It is a temporary
calm in a restless, shifting relationship." [23] But in my judgment it is vital for us to realize that it is also the instrument
for the ordering of aspirations, achievements, and frustrations of
individual employees for whose freedom and equality our society
has the most pressing concern, men and women who move
impersonally in and out of our enterprises in this incredibly
mobile society of ours in which it is not at all uncommon for
a work force to be almost wholly renewed in five years.

---

[20] *Id.* at 236.
[21] *Transportation-Communication Employees Union* v. *Union Pacific Railroad Co.*, 385 U.S. 157, 161, 63 LRRM 2481 (1966); see discussion of this case in Jones, "A Sequel in the Evolution of the Trilateral Arbitration of Jurisdictional Labor Disputes—The Supreme Court's Gift to Embattled Employers," 15 *UCLA L. Rev.* 877 (1968).
[22] Shulman, "Reason, Contract and Law in Labor Relations," 68 *Harv. L. Rev.* 999, 1024, (1955).
[23] Wellington, *supra* note 2, at 120.

Arbitrators do indeed interpret the collective agreement. They do not, and I do not suggest that they should, dissociate themselves from the agreement in order to undertake to expand upon the Constitution, the Civil Rights Act, the National Labor Relations Act, the Railway Labor Act, the Norris-LaGuardia Act, the Sherman Anti-Trust Act, or any other resource of national policy. But many important public policies are latent in the terms of collective agreements. To ignore them, wittingly or unwittingly, is to frustrate them.

I recently participated in the filming of a movie for use in secondary schools in a series designed to illumine the Bill of Rights.[24] My role was to sit as "arbitrator" to hear a grievance by a white senior employee who had bid on a leadman job that was awarded to a bidding black junior employee. It was dramatized in the film that these men were relatively equal in ability as well as in economic and educational status. The worthy aim of this employer was to move black workers in the plant into leadership roles in order to remedy one aspect of the historic pattern of racial discrimination. Ultimately the viewers were left to answer the question whether that aim could be held to justify deviation from the plain meaning of the seniority provision. The latter dictated setting aside the black worker's promotion to leadman and awarding the job to the white senior employee. This film had a "Lady and the Tiger" ending, with the arbitrator summing up the considerations on either side of the issue and then concluding with the statement that he would be in touch with them when he had reached his decision. (I have to confess I have run into time-bind problems from time to time in getting awards out, but I shudder as I contemplate viewers of that movie for years asking me, "You mean you haven't gotten that decision out *yet*?")

That situation of the black junior, in my judgment, exemplifies the kind of public policy preemptive reasoning that should not be regarded as proper for the arbitrator to justify deviation from the plain meaning of the seniority provision. I have never been able to figure out any convincing way to answer the white senior's question, "Why *me*?" While I realize that some think

---

[24] "The Bill of Rights in Action—Equal Opportunity," Film 716, Bailey-Film Associates, Los Angeles, Calif. (1969).

that seniority is an antiquated mechanism for making choices among employees, I do not so regard it. I have yet to hear anyone set forth a system that can evenhandedly and uniformly, without discrimination, enable an employer to decide who shall go out on layoff and who shall stay—the obnoxious lout who is supporting a crippled mother and 11 fine children (who all take after their mother) or the great guy who has no children and works only because he doesn't think he should live on his inheritance lest he lose the common touch. I do not think that coloring them black or white makes the decision any the more readily just.

Employers who wish to pursue that worthy goal of true integration ought to seek an agreement with the union, with or without EEOC involvement, to set aside some percentage, realistic for the particular plant, of occasions when the employer may promote minority employees without regard to seniority. If the whole work force bears the responsibility of that kind of accommodation at a time when it has not yet become personalized into a choice between this fellow right here and that fellow right there, I think such a policy would be viable and fair. But I repeat what the arbitrator said in the film: "What can I say to this particular white worker that reasonably ought to cause him to believe that it is rational and right for him to give up his own welfare and that of his family in favor of achieving a worthy social goal, *not* at the expense of society, but at his own right-here-and-now personal expense?" From whence may I be said to derive the supervening power as an arbitrator to veto the express terms of a collective agreement when one of the bargainers refuses to waive its right? Is is not a rational distinction to interpret ambiguity, or silence, or malleability of application, to comport with public policy while declining to reverse explicit contractual mandates?

In contrast to the seniority problem of racial preference, it thus seems perfectly proper in a case in which relative seniority is not a problem for an arbitrator to take into consideration the public policy favoring integration of our races. Thus where there is doubt whether a black employee may be said to have the qualification to perform a job as to require a trial period, fairly administered, he should be preferred if he has made any kind of a decent showing of aptitude or experience. Similarly, in discipline cases I have observed that arbitrators are inclined to lean over backwards a bit, not to penalize employers with unfair back-pay awards, but with give-him-another-chance awards without back pay. This is in circumstances when, to be quite blunt about it, the discipline of a white employee would not be mitigated.

On the other hand, there are obviously instances—I have had a couple and heard of others—when a minority employee is so wound up tight about his racial realization that he is incapable of conducting himself in a manner that will enable him to work with the particular people who are his supervisors. If I am satisfied that there is neither objective nor subjective discrimination—which is to say, supervision is clean, free both of unintended but nonetheless discriminatory conduct and of plain, old-fashioned, you-better-believe-it racial discrimination [25]—I am not prepared, and I do not see how any arbitrator can be prepared, to condone conduct that is incompatible with the necessities of the supervision of the work force.

The Supreme Court is currently busy with Title VII cases that will be of great interest to arbitrators. Thus an arbitrator upheld the discharge of an employee of Reynolds Metals Co. when he joined a religious sect that forbade working on Sunday, so that he refused to work contractually mandatory overtime and counselled a possible replacement not to do overtime work either. Mr. Dewey, the employee, then sued in the federal district court for the alleged violation of the Civil Rights Act of 1964.[26]

Parenthetically, had he sued before arbitrating, it is likely that

---

[25] See the discussion in *Allison Steel Mfg. Co.*, 53 LA 101 (1969), Edgar A. Jones, Jr., discussed in Jones and Peratis, "Arbitration and Federal Rights Under Collective Agreements in 1969," in *Arbitration and the Expanding Role of Neutrals*, Proceedings of the 23rd Annual Meeting, National Academy of Arbitrators, eds. Gerald G. Somers and Barbara D. Dennis (Washington: BNA Books, 1970), 219-220. The *Allison Steel* case is perhaps a classic instance of the pressures that warp the lives of those who suffer racial indignities. While a federal district court's refusal to enforce the remedy fashioned by the arbitrator was pending on appeal before the Ninth Circuit—with good reason to anticipate reversal of the lower court—the unemployed grievant and his wife split up (according to the union's counsel) and in the personal turmoil that followed, he shot and killed her and then committed suicide. The appeal was dismissed as moot.
[26] *Dewey v. Reynolds Metals Co.*, 291 F.Supp. 786, 1 FEP Cases 440, 69 LRRM 2601 (W.D. Mich. 1968).

he would have been told to exhaust his contractual remedies first. The district court held, however, that the arbitral award did not preclude the later action by Mr. Dewey under the Civil Rights Act. The Sixth Circuit reversed, directing dismissal of the action. It felt that it would "sound the death knell to arbitration of labor disputes" to hold otherwise, since the employer would admittedly have been bound by the arbitral award and the employee not, under the district court's reasoning. "The tremendous increase in civil rights litigation leads one to the belief that the Act will be used more frequently in labor disputes," said the court. "Such use ought not to destroy the efficacy of arbitration." [27]

The Supreme Court will have to decide whether the employee, disappointed in the arbitration, is entitled to another chance to overturn the employer's discharge action under Title VII. What shall the role of an arbitrator be in these statutory discrimination cases? Should the arbitrator uphold the right of a religious believer to tithe his employer to support his religion? I cannot believe it. We shall see shortly how the Court views it.

In another case,[28] the Court reportedly came to grips with Women's Lib last week. In a *per curiam* opinion the Court remanded to the Fifth Circuit for further development of the record. If there is to be sexual discrimination in hiring practices, it indicated, there would have to be a showing of such "conflicting family obligations" as to warrant preferring male to female employees. Mr. Justice Thurgood Marshall, concurring, expressed his concern lest his brethren had "fallen into the trap of assuming that the act permits ancient canards about the proper role of women to be a basis for discrimination." The Court's conclusion was apparently that a woman with a young child might pose such "conflicting family obligations" in a particular industrial setting as, for example, to warrant an employer's not promoting her to a leadlady position requiring availability for unexpected overtime assignments.

Martin-Marietta may suggest a decision adverse to Mr. Dewey. But the difficult dimensions of these discrimination cases are

---

[27] *Id.* at 429 F.2d 324, 2 FEP Cases 687, 691 (6th Cir. 1970).
[28] *Phillips* v. *Martin-Marietta Co.*, 400 U.S. 542, 3 FEP Cases 40 (1971). The remarks in the text were made on Jan. 28, 1971.

suggested by the argument reportedly made by the Department of Justice in this *Martin-Marietta* case just decided: to sustain this employer's policy of not hiring mothers of small children "will cause unwarranted hardship to families in which the mother is the only available breadwinner." [29] The harsh facts of life are that this kind of worker-mother situation may also quite possibly have a double discriminatory aspect if the mother is also black.

When an arbitrator is confronted with a grievance in this kind of case, I believe he will be found trying to assess the claim in conscience, balancing the realistic needs of the particular employer involved, setting the public policy pull on his judgment in tension with the industrial realities evidenced before him. One helpful way to look at this kind of situation, if you happen to be a representative of an employer or a union, is to regard it as largely a problem of proof. To do so is at least to make a focused effort to get in tune with the felt dilemma of the labor arbitrator in 1971 who tries to balance his role as a contract interpreter with that of final and binding decision-maker, creature of the contract, indeed, but also guardian of the received genetic complex of public policy concepts applicable to *this* specific configuration of facts now presented to him in the context of the necessity of decision in *this* case.

IV.

The growing body of arbitral awards and opinions dealing with grievance arbitration in the public sector points up an interesting and significant element distinguishing the public from the private sector arbitration of grievances. Arbitrators making decisions in the private sector have often been hesitant to rationalize (or acknowledge their rationalization) in terms of public policies whose sources are external to the collective agreement. Still, there is a certain amount of disingenuousness in this posture. It is quite evident in the published reports of private sector awards that a large number of decisions, regardless of express rationalization, have been prompted by notions of propriety and fairness surely not to be found other than by wholly creative deduction from a silent agreement.

---

[29] *Los Angeles Times*, Jan. 25, 1971, p. 7, col. 1.

And it could hardly be otherwise when the dispute at hand is covered by that amoebic phrase "just cause." Its fluid mandate inevitably and strongly has to be influenced by shared convictions that have accumulated in the community concerning how institutions and individuals ought to interact in our society. I confess to a certain amount of pish-tosh as I listen to the knee-jerk complaints of those who willingly execute a "just cause" provision in a contract and then later excoriate an arbitrator for "going outside the agreement" to draw on constitutional, statutory, common-law, or, for that matter, umbilical ideas to give content to that phrase. Typically, the complaining party didn't have the nerve to define it in the terms that it now urgently argues should have been inferred by an arbitrator.

In the public sector, however, arbitrators in grievance cases involving the rights of employees will quite foreseeably constantly be pressed to reckon public policy. State, county, and city legislative bodies, commissions, special purpose districts, boards of education, boards of trustees, and so on, are all intricately hedgerowed by specific grants of constitutional and statutory powers. These will frequently require interpretation by an arbitrator concerning the public employer's discretionary powers and his own authority. Furthermore, although private sector employers are rarely disposed to litigate disappointing awards, public sector managers appear on occasion to be compulsively litigious. It appears to reflect a yearning to be assured, before venturing out on a policy limb for any distance at all, that the limb will be judicially declared safe to climb at any speed without fear of being shaken off by gusts of second-guessing by politicians or local editorial writers.

At least until the court of last resort of the particular jurisdiction promulgates a universal rule of deference in grievance cases to public sector arbitral awards, it is foreseeable that an arbitral award in a grievance case that appears to compel anything remedial other than the most innocuous and routine of managerial action may well have to be judicially enforced before the public administrator will feel free to implement it.

This is in marked contrast to the private sector. And experience over the years with judicial reluctance to let go of the merits in private sector arbitration also suggests that the courts to which resort will have to be had in these cases may well exhibit the same compulsive difficulty with judicial forbearance. This judicial instinct to intervene—ostensibly to "accomplish justice"—is likely to be heightened considerably in the public sector by the sovereignty syndrome that is already hampering the needed acceptance of public sector grievance arbitration. That syndrome senses a certain sanctity of sovereign prerogative even in the shoveling of garbage, and it is not going to be easily curbed, except perhaps in cases of unshoveled garbage.

It is really going to be up to the judges of first instance, hopefully encouraged by early and acerbic appellate counselling, to demonstrate the kind of withholding of hands that the Supreme Court has required in the private sector. For it will still be true that in a suit to compel public sector grievance arbitration, a court ought not to weigh the merits but should order arbitration even of what it may consider to be a frivolous claim. When a judge thinks a particular grievance, or an arbitral award responsive to it, is foolish, even outrageous, it may well be that he simply does not understand the problem involved.[30] Thus, for example, misguided concern for unnecessary costs for the overburdened taxpayer may well create far greater economic costs for him in bad labor relations and in consequent deteriorated or interrupted public services. Undoubtedly it came as a rude and wholly unexpected shock to the New York judges a couple of weeks ago when the explosive wildcat "job action" (as unlawful public strikes are now euphemistically called) of the New York policemen erupted after an appellate decision

---

[30] By no means do I mean to belittle the judicial function in this area. It does not lie easy on the conscience of a judge to abstain from righting what he is convinced is a wrong-headed decision. But the Supreme Court has made it a mark of professional competence to exercise judicial self-restraint in these matters, and the rationale is a sound one: "The labor arbitrator performs functions which are not normal to the courts; the considerations which help him fashion judgments may indeed be foreign to the competency of courts. . . . The ablest judge cannot be expected to bring the same experience and competence to bear upon the determination of a grievance, because he cannot be similarly informed." *United Steelworkers* v. *Warrior & Gulf Navigation Co.*, 36 U.S. 574, 581-582, 46 LRRM 2416 (1960). For an example of the judicial forbearance needed in these cases, see *Local 1011 IBEW* v. *Bell Telephone Co. of Nevada*, 254 F.Supp. 462, 63 LRRM 2167 (D. Nev. 1966), discussed in Jones, "The Name of the Game Is Decision—Some Reflections on 'Arbitrability' and 'Authority' in Labor Arbitration," 46 *Texas L. Rev.* 865, 868-869 (1968).

forestalled a wage increase seemingly assured by a lower court. It was a classic illustration of the blowup potential inherent in a court decision that unwittingly frustrates expectations reasonably created by earlier favorable negotiations or rulings by other public functionaries.

The standard established by the Supreme Court in *Warrior & Gulf* [31] is going to have to be transplanted to the public sector by an understanding judiciary. The grist for the forum, after all, is substantially the same—issues of discipline and discharge, applications of provisions for seniority, vacations, holidays, wages, hours, conditions of employment, work assignments, transfers, overtime, jury duty, and even time off to vote out of office the elected officials who are still sitting on the last fact-finding wage recommendation. [32] Past practices will be apt to be a more fruitful source of dispute in the public than in the private sector as thousands of little bureaucratic empires crumble under the stress of negotiation followed by impartial scrutiny of the eroded remains.

Courts undoubtedly will be confronted with nonarbitrability arguments by public administrators and their supportive lawyers in government service, reflecting the familiar sovereignty syndrome and graphically raising the specter of the suffering taxpayer to avoid being compelled to submit particular issues to arbitration. The courts, if grievance arbitration is to work in the public sector—*which it had better*—will have to echo the Supreme Court in *Warrior & Gulf* that arbitration will not be denied "unless it may be said with positive assurance that the arbitration clause"—whether it be a negotiated agreement or a legislative enactment—"is not susceptible of an interpretation that covers the asserted dispute. Doubts should be resolved in favor of coverage." [33] Similarly, public sector arbitral awards, where brought before the courts in grievance cases, will have to receive a circumspect judicial review that does not manipulate the merits but seeks instead to enforce an award as long as, in the words of the Ninth Circuit Court of Appeals in a

---

[31] *United Steelworkers* v. *Warrior & Gulf Navigation Co.*, 363 U.S. 574, 46 LRRM 2416 (1960).

[32] See Robert Howlett, "Arbitration in the Public Sector," in *Labor Law Developments* (Albany: Matthew Bender, 1969), 268.

[33] *United Steelworkers, supra* note 31, at 582.

recent private sector case, "it is possible for an honest intellect to interpret the words of the contract [or, we may add, the statute or ordinance] and reach the result which the arbitrator reached." [34] Although it may be that knowledge of "industrial common law—the practices of the industry and the shop" as part of the arbitrator's "source of law" may at first appear inapposite in the public sector grievance arbitration, further reflection suggests that this is not so. Arbitrators typically have become experienced in dealing with a great variety of industries and working conditions, each with unique and differing worker problems and managerial necessities, and they will hardly be astonished to find that work assignments in a municipal zoo [35] will differ substantially from those encountered by helicopter-flown firefighters.

Indeed, it is this marked variety of past experience that should prompt the courts to reason in the public as in the private sector that this successful method of dispute resolution is deserving of judicial forbearance as the rule rather than the exception. The Supreme Court observed in *Warrior & Gulf* of the private sector arbitrators who are now also serving in the public sector, "The labor arbitrator performs functions which are not normal to the Courts; the considerations which help him fashion judgments may indeed be foreign to the competence of Courts. . . . The ablest judge cannot be expected to bring the same experience and competence to bear upon the determination of a grievance, because he cannot be similarly informed." [36]

As arbitrators move increasingly into the public sector in grievance disputes, they will find themselves being confronted with the necessity to make arbitrability rulings as to which top governmental employees—or more accurately, the managerial administrators—will make essentially the same argument against arbitrability that was made against governmental participation in binding grievance arbitration in the first place. That is,

---

[34] *Newspaper Guild* v. *Tribune Publishing Co.*, 407 F.2d 1327, 70 LRRM 3184 (9th Cir. 1969).

[35] See, for example, *Zoological Society of San Diego*, 50 LA 1 (1967), Edgar A. Jones, Jr. This arbitration and the transcript of testimony quoted in the opinion may not afford a reliable test whereby questions about sexual identity may be self-resolved, but it does afford a like opportunity for those who may feel insecure about their identification with mammals as against birds, or vice versa.

[36] *United Steelworkers, supra* note 31, at 581-582.

that state or local legislation, or a constitution or a charter, has vested the employer with "plenary" power over the terms and conditions of employment which cannot lawfully be delegated to a "third party," a "private person," or assumed by that person. Although the parties wouldn't even be before an arbitrator if that reasoning hadn't been rejected by responsible governmental authority, it is evident that many an arbitrator will hear it repeated lower down the governmental scale of advocacy on specific issues sought to be arbitrated by unions representing governmental employees. As in the private sector, however, the primary legal source of the arbitrator's authority is the agreement containing provision for it in terms negotiated between the union and the governmental employer.

An arbitrator has to be wary of crediting arguments against arbitrability—in contrast to those for or against a certain result on the merits of the grievance—that are rooted in sources external to that agreement. There is a very real danger already visible in the reports of awards that the adaptation of arbitration to the public sector—initiated to meet demonstrated and often pressing needs to assure stability of public services— may be seriously hampered by uncritical or unduly timorous deference by arbitrators to foreclosing public policy arguments unwisely pressed upon them by public administrators in order to avoid arbitration.

If the administrator has a serious concern about the legality of arbitrating a particular dispute, let him refuse and by court order either be vindicated in his refusal or be compelled to proceed. In the private sector, top management normally will not long tolerate the expense of futile resort to the courts in place of good-faith participation in the jointly adopted dispute resolution procedure of arbitration. We may anticipate that the instinct to dig in heels and resist the intrusion of "that outsider" reviewing the propriety of managerial decisions—as psychologically expectable and explicable in the public as in the private sector and certainly visible in either on occasion today—will pass in time, in part because of economically motivated negative reactions by those who supervise supervision.

In the meantime, the burden of demonstrating lack of arbitrability of a particular grievance from sources extraneous to the operative agreement should be a considerable one before court or arbitrator. Public policies external to the agreement may very well influence, even dictate, a particular disposition on the merits. But the presumption of arbitrability should be, if anything, heightened in the public sector, far more than in the private. This is so precisely because the alternative right of public employees to strike will remain for some time quite limited, if not wholly outlawed.

Public administrators and arbitrators—not to mention courts —will do well to reflect long and hard on the significance of those angry, frustrated New York cops surging out the doors of their precincts in unplanned outrage.

Once again, that ancient truism comes to mind: "He who builds a pressure cooker had better vent the steam or blow the scene!"

Comment—

CHARLES J. MORRIS *

Ted Jones has taken a complex question—What is the role of arbitration in state and national labor policy?—and he has given a thoughtful and descriptive answer, synthesizing the diversity which characterizes arbitration and providing an overview of what arbitrators actually do. I find myself in agreement with much, but not all, of what he has said about private sector arbitration; and I whole-heartedly second his motion about public sector arbitration: that if grievance arbitration is to work in the public sector, it will have to echo the *Warrior & Gulf* [1] presumption of arbitrability, and further, that public sector arbitral awards, where brought before the courts in grievance cases, should receive circumspect judicial review that does not manipulate the merits of the dispute. I shall say no more on this occasion about public sector arbitration, for Ted has done an exceedingly good job in his treatment of this sensitive subject.

It is with regard to the role of arbitration in the private sector that I find myself in some disagreement with his position.

---

* Member, National Academy of Arbitrators; Professor of Law, Southern Methodist University, Dallas, Tex.
[1] *United Steelworkers* v. *Warrior & Gulf Navigation Co.*, 363 U.S. 574, 46 **LRRM** 2416 (1960).

To the extent that he is describing what most arbitrators do, I have no quarrel with his characterization of the arbitrator's role. But to the extent that he is postulating what the role ought to be, I cannot agree. At the risk of applying another beating to what by now should be a dead horse, I must dissent from his dissent. Professor Jones purports to dissent from Professor Meltzer's thesis regarding the interrelation of the arbitration award with law applicable to the dispute but external to the collective bargaining agreement. Professor Meltzer's much-quoted advice, given from this platform four years ago and repeated three years ago in a rejoinder to Dick Mittenthal, was to the effect that "where there appears to be an irrepressible conflict between a labor agreement and the law, an arbitrator whose authority is typically limited to applying or interpreting the agreement should follow the agreement and ignore the law." [2] Professor Jones says that he agrees with Professor Meltzer if by law he means what Mr. Justice Holmes defined as "the prophecies of what the courts will do in fact." The illustrations which Meltzer provided in his paper and also in his rejoinder would seem to indicate that he was referring to law in the Holmesian sense. But whether he was or not, Ted Jones has now submitted his own definition of the role of arbitration vis-à-vis the law. In so doing, Ted might also be accused of beating the same old horse, for this horse has been beaten previously by at least seven other distinguished members of the Academy. In addition to Bernie Meltzer, the list of horse beaters includes Bob Howlett, Dick Mittenthal, Harry Platt, Mike Sovern, Bill Gould, and Ted St. Antoine—to name only a partial list of the participants in this exercise. The fact that eight such eminent scholars and arbitrators have given at least six different answers to the same question is persuasive proof that the horse they have been beating is indeed very much alive. It is so much alive that the Supreme Court has just granted certiorari in a case which involves at least part of this same

---

[2] Meltzer, "Ruminations About Ideology, Law, and Labor Arbitration," in *The Arbitrator, the NLRB, and the Courts,* Proceedings of the 20th Annual Meeting, National Academy of Arbitrators, ed. Dallas L. Jones (Washington: BNA Books, 1967) , 16; Meltzer, "The Role of Law in Arbitration: A Rejoinder," in *Developments in American and Foreign Arbitration,* Proceedings of the 21st Annual Meeting, National Academy of Arbitrators, ed. Charles M. Rehmus (Washington: BNA Books, 1968), 58.

subject, *Dewey* v. *Reynolds Metals*,[3] which Ted noted in his paper. I shall later comment briefly about that case, but first I think it would be useful to line up the spectrum of the foregoing positions and then discuss in greater detail the new position which Ted has advanced.

At one end of the spectrum, not surprisingly, is Professor Meltzer's statement that the arbitrator "should respect the agreement and ignore the law." [4] Ted St. Antoine has expressed general agreement with that position.[5] At the other extreme is Bob Howlett's view that "arbitrators *should* render decisions on the issues before them *based on both* contract language and law. Indeed, [according to Howlett] a separation of contract interpretation and statutory and/or common law is impossible in many arbitrations." [6] He notes a single exception: where the employer and the union advise the arbitrator that they have chosen him to decide the contractual issue only and that actual or potential statutory questions are to be presented to the NLRB. In such a situation, Howlett recognizes that the arbitrator must comply or withdraw from the case; and he suggests withdrawal as the wiser course, allowing the parties to pursue their remedy before the Board and thus avoid two hearings and two decisions.

Harry Platt has taken a position between the two extremes, at least with regard to cases involving civil rights and the Title VII area.[7] His position seems to be located in both the Meltzer and the Howlett camps. First, he questions whether the Meltzer approach will suffice in the civil rights area, noting that:

> "Many earnestly believe that if arbitration is not to become a contradiction of public policy and a forum in which racial tensions are exacerbated, third party impartials should think twice about legitimatizing discriminatory provisions which thwart the proper advance of Negro workers. To do otherwise, it is urged, would be to demean the arbitral process and to engender minority group allegations of conspiracies between the arbitrator and the parties."

---

[3] *Dewey* v. *Reynolds Metals Co.*, 429 F.2d 324, *rehearing denied*, 429 F.2d 324, 2 FEP Cases 687 (CA 6, 1970), *aff'd* by equally divided Court, 402 U.S. 689, 3 FEP Cases 508 (1971).

[4] Meltzer, "Ruminations . . . ," *supra* note 2, at 16.

[5] St. Antoine, in *Developments in American and Foreign Arbitration, supra* note 2, at 75.

[6] Howlett, in *The Arbitrator, the NLRB, and the Courts, supra* note 2, 67 at 83.

[7] Platt, "The Relations Between Arbitration and Title VII of the Civil Rights Act of 1964," 3 *Ga. L. Rev.* 398 (1969).

Notwithstanding that admonition, Platt cites *Hotel Employers Ass'n* [8] to demonstrate "the potential mischief in the arbitral fashioning of legal opinions about civil rights law," [9] and he concludes on a cautionary note which brings him perhaps closer to the Meltzer position than he may have intended. He states:

> "Whatever might be said in favor of harmonizing law and the contract, when possible, arbitrators should move cautiously and should be loathe to make statutory and legal interpretations, certainly in the absence of clear legal precedent. Where there are substantial doubts about the contract's legal viability—and I am talking particularly about racial discrimination grievances—deferral to the courts and the EEOC would appear to be the wisest course. Where the parties' intent can move in concert with statutory objectives, affirmative relief can issue. But, arbitral meddling in the law as well as 'contingent awards' which are based upon illegalities seem to be unavailing. Otherwise, the utility of arbitration in discrimination disputes may be seriously impaired." [10]

Dick Mittenthal and Mike Sovern also occupy the middle ground—but not the same ground. Mittenthal suggests that:

> "The arbitrator should 'look to see whether sustaining the grievance would require conduct the law forbids or would enforce an illegal contract; if so, the arbitrator should not sustain the grievance.' This principle, however, should be carefully limited. It does not suggest that 'an arbitrator should pass upon all the parties' legal rights and obligations.' . . . Thus, although the arbitrator's award may *permit* conduct forbidden by law but sanctioned by contract, it should not *require* conduct forbidden by law even though sanctioned by contract." [11]

Sovern buys some of Mittenthal and some of Meltzer, but injects different reasons and additional conclusions. According to the Sovern formula, an arbitrator may follow federal law rather than the contract when the following conditions are met:

> "1. The arbitrator is qualified.
> "2. The question of law is implicated in a dispute over the application or interpretation of a contract that is also before him.
> "3. The question of law is raised by a contention that, if the conduct complained of does violate the contract, the law nevertheless immunizes or even requires it.

---

[8] 47 LA 873 (1966), Robert E. Burns et al.

[9] Platt, *supra* note 7, at 409.

[10] *Id.* at 409-410.

[11] Mittenthal, "The Role of Law in Arbitration," in *Developments in American and Foreign Arbitration, supra* note 2, 42 at 50.

"4. The courts lack primary jurisdiction to adjudicate the question of law." [12]

Dean Sovern illustrates his fourth condition by noting that the courts are entrusted with primary jurisdiction to decide Title VII questions, contrasted with the absence of such court jurisdiction for NLRB questions; therefore, when Title VII questions arise the arbitrator should decide the issue on the basis of the contract only, making it absolutely clear that he is not deciding the Title VII issue. Sovern suggests that in the ensuing action to enforce or set aside the award the court can apply Title VII to the award and, if appropriate, invalidate it.

Bill Gould, writing close to the Howlett end of the spectrum, rejects the view that there is a sharp demarcation between public and private law in the arbitral process.[13] With particular emphasis on Title VII questions he argues that:

"New approaches to the use of arbitration in grievances involving racial discrimination are needed. For if racial discrimination cases cannot be heard by arbitrators, the uniformity to which *Vaca* [14] has given honor and consideration will be undermined by a dual system composed of public and private routes—the first for racial cases and the second for nonracial." [15]

Citing Mr. Justice Douglas's flattering dictum in *Warrior* [16] (flattering, that is, to arbitrators), Gould says that "arbitrators are infinitely more capable than government officials and judges in interpreting labor contracts and fashioning remedies," [17] and "[i]f arbitration can be adapted to cope with racial discrimination, a relatively expeditious forum for the redress of grievances would then be available." [18]

So much for the pre-Jones spectrum. Time does not permit direct discussion of these various positions on the Meltzer-Howlett scale; but I should try to answer the question of where

---

[12] Sovern, "When Should Arbitrators Follow Federal Law?" in *Arbitration and the Expanding Role of Neutrals,* Proceedings of the 23rd Annual Meeting, National Academy of Arbitrators, eds. Gerald G. Somers and Barbara D. Dennis (Washington: BNA Books, 1970), 29, 38.
[13] Gould, "Labor Arbitration of Grievances Involving Racial Discrimination," 118 *Pa. L. Rev.* 40 (1969).
[14] *Vaca* v. *Sipes,* 386 U.S. 171, 64 LRRM 2369 (1967).
[15] Gould, *supra* note 13, at 50.
[16] *United Steelworkers* v. *Warrior & Gulf Navigation Co.,* 363 U.S. 574, 582, 46 LRRM 2416 (1960).
[17] Gould, *supra* note 13, at 51.
[18] *Id.*

the Jones position fits into the spectrum. I am not at all sure—
but this may be because I am not sure that I fully understand
Ted's position.

Ted rejects the view that an arbitrator should apply law in
the Holmesian sense; and I assume that to mean, for example,
that an arbitrator should not apply the law of Title VII as it
might relate to the construction of a seniority provision in a
collective bargaining agreement. However, Ted makes a distinction between "law" in the narrow sense and " 'public policy'
in the broader sense of [a] 'common stock of legal ideas' that
we all share." He proposes "that all labor arbitrators should feel
. . . conscience bound to be concerned about how their decisional
conduct accords with 'the common stock of legal ideas' without
which no civilized community can exist." He says: "To the
hindmost with the courts! The critical query is whether . . . we
as arbitrators are leaving this country with a higher or a lower
quality of justice." These are indeed lofty ideals. But I am
uncertain as to whether Ted would include statutory law, such
as the Age Discrimination in Employment Act of 1967,[19] or
Title VII of the 1964 Civil Rights Act,[20] or Section 8(e) of
the Taft-Hartley Act [21] among the "common stock of legal ideas"
upon which an arbitrator might draw. Apparently he would not,
at least not in a direct way. Nevertheless, in some vague way
he would rely on the conscience of the arbitrator to guarantee
that arbitrators would not issue awards in significant numbers
that are contrary to the "spirit of our common stock of legal
ideas."

His approach is reminiscent of the Supreme Court debates
over the "absorption" doctrine whereby so-called "fundamental
rights" in the Bill of Rights were deemed applicable to the
states through the concept of Fourteenth Amendment due process.[22] The question was frequently asked: What are those
fundamental rights? And how does one distinguish them from
the subjective views of the individual Justices? Emphasizing the

---

[19] 29 U.S.C. § 621.
[20] 42 U.S.C. § 1971.
[21] 29 U.S.C. § 158(e) .
[22] *E.g., Palco* v. *Connecticut,* 302 U.S. 319 (1937); *Adamson* v. *California,* 332 U.S.
46 (1947) ; *Rochin* v. *California,* 342 U.S. 165 (1952); *Pointer* v. *Texas,* 380 U.S.
400 (1965).

subjective element in the doctrine, Mr. Justice Douglas dubbed the concept, especially as it was articulated by Justices Frankfurter and Harlan, as a recurrence of a theory of natural law. Is Professor Jones suggesting a like theory of natural law which should guide labor arbitrators? I would agree that an arbitrator must often look to his conscience to aid him in reaching a decision, but his mandate is to interpret the contract. We have been reminded that a labor arbitrator "does not sit to dispense his own brand of industrial justice." [23] I would be suspicious of a system which says to the arbitrator: Let your conscience be your guide. I am quite certain that Professor Jones is not suggesting that one's conscience or one's subjective view of common legal ideas should ever be more than an aid to construction, not a substitute for construction. And he is on sound footing when he insists that public policy in arbitration be fact-oriented, and that for the arbitrator facts will involve contractual differences. However, I am unsure of his meaning when he declines to include specific labor statutes and basic constitutional guarantees among the common stock of legal ideas on which an arbitrator should rely.

I fail to see why one would reject statutory law as a direct source of fundamental rights and at the same time allow the arbitrator to apply a subjective standard based on public policy in a broad sense. Surely statutory laws specifically enacted to cover the employment relationship (I am not referring to nonspecific laws, such as general criminal laws) embody the most reliable standard to tell us what public policy is. But Ted Jones emphasizes that "[i]t is a contract we are expounding." And by that he means *only* a contract, one that is independent of the law around it, for he says that:

> "Arbitrators do indeed interpret the collective agreement. They do not, and I do not suggest that they should . . . undertake to expand upon the Constitution, the Civil Rights Act, the National Labor Relations Act, the Railway Labor Act, the Norris-LaGuardia Act, the Sherman Anti-Trust Act, or any other resource of national policy."

I suggest that if such advice is taken literally, labor arbitration will stand to lose much of its relevance. It is too late to turn

---

[23] *United Steelworkers* v. *Enterprise Wheel & Car Corp.*, 363 U.S. 593, 46 LRRM 2423 (1960).

the clock back to the collective agreement of an earlier day, though we might long for that day, and some of us might wish that we could return to it. It is an inescapable fact that the agreement is no longer the exclusive province of the immediate parties. The Supreme Court, in numerous familiar decisions,[24] and Congress, in a series of statutes, have dictated the allowable contours of both the collective agreement and, to a large extent, the role which arbitration plays in the implementation of national labor policy. Collective bargaining agreements can and do embody the Constitution, the Civil Rights Act, the National Labor Relations Act, the Norris-LaGuardia Act, and even the Sherman Anti-Trust Act.[25] The contract and the arbitration process are thus the product of more than an agreement between the union and the employer. To illustrate: Congress, through the National Labor Relations Act, has sharply circumscribed the types of collective bargaining provisions on which the parties may agree. Shall an arbitrator ignore the law relating to subcontractor clauses, picket line clauses, union standards clauses, union security clauses, and numerous other areas where the NLRA establishes patterns of lawful bargaining and standards of lawful conduct affecting employee rights? Shall an arbitrator, in construing seniority provisions, ignore still other congressional mandates regarding discrimination based on race, sex, religion, national origin, and age?

It is undoubtedly true that many arbitrators will choose to ignore these laws; but to the extent that arbitration awards conflict with these laws, or perhaps even to the extent that such awards ignore the legal issues which federal—and sometimes state—laws impose upon the interpretation of the collective bargaining agreement, arbitration will surely lose its relevance. And minority groups in particular will have reason to object to a labor relations system where arbitrators conceive of their roles so narrowly. Any grievance system which fails to resolve a sig-

---

[24] *E.g., United Steelworkers v. Warrior & Gulf Navigation Co.*, 363 U.S. 574, 46 LRRM 2416 (1960); *Teamsters Local 174 v. Lucas Flour Co.*, 369 U.S. 95, 49 LRRM 2717 (1962); *National Woodwork Mfrs. Ass'n v. NLRB*, 386 U.S. 612, 64 LRRM 2801 (1967).

[25] See *United Mine Workers v. Pennington*, 381 U.S. 657, 59 LRRM 2369 (1965); *Amalgamated Meat Cutters Local 189 v. Jewel Tea Co.*, 381 U.S. 676, 59 LRRM 2376 (1965).

nificant number of important employee disputes, or resolves them contrary to public law, invites alienation from the system.

Let us, as arbitrators, not make the mistake of refusing to change where the need for change is dictated by inherent changes that have already occurred, and are still occurring, in the institution to which we devote our services.

Time limitations will not permit a detailed discussion of the familiar legal doctrine whereby applicable law is deemed incorporated automatically into contracts. The U.S. Supreme Court over 100 years ago provided the classical statement of that rule:

> "It is . . . settled that the laws which subsist at the time and place of the making of a contract, and where it is to be performed, enter into and form a part of it, as if they were expressly referred to or incorporated in its terms. This principle embraces alike those which affect its validity, construction, discharge, and enforcement." [26]

Whether that rule may be literally applied in all situations is irrelevant to the present discussion.[27] What is important is that in the field of collective bargaining, federal labor laws have generally provided the framework and the limits within which contracts are construed and enforced. Stating the proposition in its broadest form, Bob Howlett reminded us that:

> "Arbitrators, as well as judges, are subject to and bound by law, whether it be the Fourteenth Amendment to the Constitution of the United States or a city ordinance. All contracts are subject to a statute and common law; and each contract includes all applicable law. The law is part of the 'essence [of the] collective bargaining agreement' to which Mr. Justice Douglas has referred." [28]

The extent to which the collective bargaining agreement incorporates external law depends ultimately on the question and answer which Mr. Justice Douglas posed in his *Lincoln Mills* [29] opinion. His question was: "What is the substantive law to be applied in suits under §301 (a) ?" His now familiar answer was: "[F]ederal law, which the courts must fashion from the policy of our national labor laws." The debate thus boils down to a point of policy: whether arbitrators can and should

---

[26] *Von Hoffman* v. *City of Quincy*, 4 Wall (U.S.) 535, 550, 18 L.Ed. 403 (1967).
[27] *Williston on Contracts*, 3rd ed., 615 (W. Jaeger, ed., 1961).
[28] Howlett, *supra* note 6, at 83.
[29] *Textile Workers Union* v. *Lincoln Mills*, 353 U.S. 448, 40 LRRM 2113 (1957).

make legal determinations which embrace the effect that various labor statutes might exert on the interpretation and application of collective agreements. Put simply, is the national labor policy better served by arbitrators assuming this additional role? Or is it preferable for them to decide their cases within the comfortable symmetry of the collective agreement, as if shielded by blinders shutting out all other legal principles, even principles which might ultimately be dispositive of the issue? There are some who would argue that an arbitrator, having been chosen by and being paid by the union and the employer, is thereby unqualified to apply laws designed to regulate union and employer conduct. Such critics may ultimately be right; but if so, arbitration in a great variety of cases will have ceased to be a reasonably fair and reasonably successful dispute-settling institution. I am not prepared to admit such premature failure of the arbitration process to adjust to the expanded role which new laws and changing conditions have thrust upon it. I prefer to believe that arbitration is sufficiently resilient to adapt satisfactorily to most of these new demands affecting employee disputes.

I am also impatient with the view that arbitrators are not qualified to apply law considered external to the collective bargaining agreement. In the first place, the law with which we are concerned will never be—or should never be—entirely *external* to the agreement. It is only in cases involving the interpretation of an agreement, or conduct pursuant to or in violation of an agreement, or conduct which is contrary to an agreement because it is alleged that the law prohibits literal compliance with the agreement, that the arbitrator will be called upon to interpret and apply the law. But in so interpreting and applying the law, he is first and foremost interpreting and applying the contract, which after all is his ordinary and traditional obligation. There will of course be situations in which the statutory issue is unclear; in such cases the arbitrator might be well advised to heed Harry Platt's admonition to avoid making statutory interpretations in the absence of clear legal precedent. But in cases where the statutory issue is squarely presented and the ultimate disposition of the dispute is likely to hinge on the application of the statute, the arbitrator should give full consideration to the legal effect which the statute has upon the grievance.

As to the matter of the arbitrator's legal competence, it is not likely that an arbitrator who is incompetent to handle a complex legal issue will necessarily accept such a case, just as arbitrators who are incompetent to handle highly technical wage-incentive cases generally do not accept them. However, I am confident that most professional arbitrators will rise to the occasion if necessary, particularly when they have the assistance of legal briefs which they have the right to expect the parties to furnish whenever a case contains difficult statutory issues.

As to the arbitrator's objectivity, we must rely primarily upon the maintenance of the highest professional and ethical standards to guarantee that arbitrators will have the moral courage to decide cases solely on their merits. If arbitrators cannot do this with reliability, then they should not accept the responsibility of deciding unpopular cases—indeed, they should not be arbitrating at all. But if high professional standards do not suffice, the corrective response will likely come from the courts in the form of expanded judicial review of the arbitrator's award. Properly limited, such review should not be unwelcome.

Admittedly, many hard problems will be encountered when and if arbitrators generally apply the law as well as the contract in deciding grievance cases. In particular, one can foresee problems relating to the reception which other tribunals will accord the award. It is in this regard that I would not be surprised if the Supreme Court, pursuant to its own *Lincoln Mills*[30] mandate, ultimately clarifies the *Enterprise*[31] rule to provide for limited judicial review of the arbitrator's application of statutory law, at least in those areas, such as Title VII cases, where the courts have primary jurisdiction. Indeed, it seems consistent with the broad rule of *Enterprise* to reason—assuming that the contract does incorporate the law—that if an arbitrator ignores the law and limits his award solely to construing the bare bones of the contract, then the words of the arbitrator, in the language of *Enterprise,* will "manifest an infidelity to the agreement."[32] If the *Enterprise* rule is thus

[30] *Id.*
[31] *Supra* note 23.
[32] *Id.* at 597.

expanded, arbitrators should not fear such limited judicial review—provided of course that this review is confined to the
arbitrator's application and interpretation of the relevant statute
but otherwise goes no further than the present review. (I
daresay that most of us would not want to return to the days
of *Cutler-Hammer*.[33]) The prospect of judicial review of an arbitrator's construction of a statute that directly concerns the employment relationship could prove beneficial to the arbitral
process. Such review, or the availability of such review, would
serve the dual purpose of providing both a strong incentive for
the arbitrator to arrive at a correct legal decision and also a
judicial check against his arriving at a wrong decision.

When an arbitrator consciously determines a contract dispute
with reference to applicable statutory law, for example, Title
VII, it does not follow that in an independent Title VII
action the U.S. district court would or should be deprived of
jurisdiction. In *Hutchings* v. *U.S. Industries, Inc.*,[34] where the
matter in dispute was subject to the concurrent jurisdiction of
an arbitrator under the collective bargaining agreement and a
federal court under Title VII, the Fifth Circuit stressed that

> "[t]he trial judge in a Title VII case bears a special responsibility
> in the public interest to resolve the employment dispute, for once
> the judicial machinery has been set in train, the proceeding takes
> on a public character in which the remedies are devised to vindi-
> cate the policies of the Act, not merely to afford private relief to
> the employee." [35]

Supremacy of court jurisdiction over arbitral jurisdiction in
such cases is not sufficient reason, however, for an arbitrator to
ignore the statute. Should he ignore the statute and thereby render
the wrong decision, he would accordingly weaken collective bargaining and contribute to the irrelevancy of its grievance procedure. But should he conscientiously apply the statute, his
award might settle the dispute. Even where it does not, however, the arbitrator will have added the weight of his fact-
finding and his reasoning to the ultimate judicial disposition of

---

[33] *Int'l Ass'n of Machinists* v. *Cutler-Hammer, Inc.*, 271 App. Div. 917, 67 N.Y.S.
2d 317, 19 LRRM 2232, *aff'd.* 297 N.Y. 519, 74 N.E.2d 464, 20 LRRM 2445 (1947).
[34] *Hutchings* v. *U.S. Industries, Inc.*, 428 F.2d 303, 2 FEP Cases 725 (5th Cir.
1970).
[35] *Id.* at 311.

the case. The effect to be given his award in a subsequent judicial proceeding—whether in an independent action or in an action to enforce or review an arbitration award under Section 301 [36]—should depend on a variety of factors: for example, the importance of the statutory question to the contractual issue, the extent to which the parties have litigated the statutory issue in the arbitration proceeding, the adequacy of the grievant's representation, and the degree of his participation in the selection of the arbitrator. The presence or absence of such factors may prove to be significant in the future development of a modified doctrine of judicial review and in the ultimate demarcation of lines defining the concurrent jurisdiction of arbitrators and courts.

My allotted time does not permit further speculation or theorizing about the problems which might be posed by such areas of concurrent jurisdiction. It may be noted, however, with reference to an issue in *Dewey v. Reynolds Metals*,[37] pending in the Supreme Court, that the doctrine of election of remedies, to which Professor Jones referred in his description of that case, makes common and legal sense only where the first tribunal—in that instance an arbitration board—either has decided the external legal issue, or could have decided it, and the grievant was aware or should have been aware that he was electing a remedy and thereby waiving his right to file a court action. It is my understanding that those conditions did not prevail in *Reynolds Metals*. *Reynolds* will be an interesting decision to watch, for the Court might use that case to provide some guidelines relating to the arbitrator's role when the grievant's statutory rights are enmeshed with rights under the collective bargaining agreement.[38]

Let me close on this note. Ted Jones has given us a thoughtful and provocative paper. I suspect that the real differences in our views are miniscule, and that the various positions on the Meltzer-Howlett spectrum are but evidence of our collective groping for a conceptual theory to define the role of labor arbitration in a rapidly changing collective bargaining structure. I

---

[36] 29 U.S.C. § 185.
[37] *Supra* note 3.
[38] *Id.*

also suspect that we shall be beating the same live horse for a long time to come.

Comment—

DAVID E. FELLER *

Earlier today I heard about garbage collectors, and now, at this session, I am described as the clean-up man coming after a live horse. My role has, I suppose, been adequately described.

I want to say, first of all, that I am like Charley, only more so, in my state of unpreparedness. I had done some preliminary thinking about "The Role of Arbitration in State and National Labor Policy," but I had done no thinking about the role of state and national labor policy in arbitration until I read Ted's very provocative piece at about 10 o'clock this morning. And, of course, I never had the slightest idea as to what Charley Morris was going to say. So, rather than clean up after him, I guess I had better just get on the horse and place myself in the spectrum he has described.

Let me say flatly: I am with Meltzer. I am not sure that I quite understand Ted's view that arbitrators must be concerned that their decisional conduct accords with "the common stock of legal ideas without which no civilized community can exist." If he means that arbitrators must adjudicate the disputes which come before them in the light of the "public policy rights" applicable to the dispute, then I quite agree with Charley Morris that the arbitrator must take into account not only vague notions of social policy but also the statutory law which, today, most often reflects social policy.

Ted recoils from that ultimate conclusion to his view because it necessarily implies, as he says, that the arbitrator must then undertake to expound the Constitution, the Civil Rights Act, the National Labor Relations Act, and the other sources of national policy. And he explicitly rejects any suggestion that they should do so. The reason is that this would make clear the essential contradiction in his position.

He begins by reviewing the course of decision of the past several years in the Supreme Court. He sees that the courts

---

* Member, National Academy of Arbitrators; Professor of Law, University of California, Berkeley.

have given arbitrators an extraordinary freedom from judicial review. This freedom, he then finds, requires the introduction into the arbitral process of what I will call extraneous considerations of public policy because the arbitrator is now the final and binding, nonreviewable, decision-maker. But the very premise of this reasoning, the freedom of arbitration from judicial review, was built upon the notion that arbitrators were expounding the agreement and not the law.

I am not the author of the words that are so frequently quoted from the *Warrior & Gulf* case as to the special expertise of arbitrators. I think the words in my brief in that case were a little more modest, but a little more accurate. They were, however, to the same effect: The nature of the decision which the arbitrator makes is one which he is peculiarly competent to make and which the courts are not competent to make. That is the essential premise upon which the freedom from review which the courts have granted to arbitrators rests.

Ted's argument implicitly, and Charley's extrapolation of it explicitly, involves a different premise: that the arbitrator determines not only what the agreement means but what the law is. Alternatively phrased, the premise is that the arbitrator decides what the agreement means on the assumption that all applicable common and statutory laws are engrafted into it. The problem is that on that premise there is no reason at all to assume that the arbitrator is more competent than the judge. There is certainly no reason to assume that his judgment should be unreviewable, while the district judge who is deciding Title VII questions, and the Labor Board which is deciding NLRA questions, are subject to being reviewed by a whole hierarchy of courts.

I therefore think that the role which Charley and Ted project for the arbitrator is essentially a bootstrapping one. You simply cannot start from the premise that the arbitrator is working within a particular sphere in which he is uniquely competent and therefore should be free from judicial control and then conclude that, since he is free from judicial control, he is obliged to work outside that sphere.

Of course, there are some notions of what you may want to

call public policy which an arbitrator must take into account. There are considerations of fairness and justice that arbitrators obviously utilize, and must utilize. I can even agree that arbitrators utilize those concepts because they are part of "the common stock of legal ideas without which no civilized community can exist." But the civilized community to which reference is properly made is the industrial relations community, not the society at large.

Obviously, in interpreting and applying an agreement, an arbitrator must discover and explicate many things which are not expressly set forth—indeed, many things which are not dealt with at all. At the Santa Monica meeting of the Academy I urged that arbitrators had been given a charter by the Supreme Court to act like judges and urged that they go forth and act like judges. But that does not mean for a moment that they should act like judges in saying that the agreement, fairly read, means X, that Title VII fairly read requires Y, and that the result in the case to be decided should therefore be Y and not X. To the contrary. What I said there, and what I would like to repeat here, is that an arbitrator's function in interpreting and applying an agreement is very much like a judge's function in interpreting and applying a statute.

To paraphrase what Learned Hand once said, it is the surest mark of an immature jurisprudence to rely on the plain meaning of words to determine what a statute means. Indeed, Judge Hand, in a famous case, once interpreted the numbers 1916 to mean 1941, a rather astonishing result which he justified by saying that a court should not make a fortress out of a dictionary. The case is, concededly, an extreme one, but he was doing what the courts do all the time in interpreting statutes. He looked at what the purpose of the statute was in order to interpret its words. The term "purpose" is used in an entirely fictional sense. What the courts seek, and properly so, is the objective which the Congress was intending to accomplish by a statute. With a sympathetic understanding of that objective, they must make that determination of the particular dispute before them (to which Congress may not have adverted at all) which is most consistent with the entire scheme of the congressional enactment.

Now what an arbitrator should do—and all he should do—is to deal with a collective bargaining agreement in precisely the same way. Of course, in doing that he must make certain assumptions as to what the parties thought about concepts of fairness, justice, and equality. To the extent that it is consistent with the entire scheme of the agreement to do so, it is entirely proper for him to take such concepts into account. But his competence ends when he has finished that kind of interpretation of the agreement.

It seems to me that as soon as an arbitrator goes further and relies upon external sources of authority, he not only subjects his judgment to review by others equally or more competent to apply that external authority and destroys any claim of the uniqueness, but he also disappoints the expectations of the parties. Without glorifying the expectations of the parties, I think it may be fairly said that a system of justice under law is one which, by and large, produces results in controversies most in accordance with the expectations of the community within which that system of law operates. The community within which the arbitrators' system of law operates is the community to which the collective bargaining agreement applies—the industrial community. The result in a controversy as to the meaning of the law governing that community should accord with the expectations of the parties who establish that law, not the expectations or the scheme envisaged by those who enacted the external law except as it may fairly be said that the parties intended to incorporate that law into their agreement.

To use a simple example: The notion of "just cause" as expressed in a collective agreement is a reference to an undefined standard. Yet it is not a charter for arbitrary decision. There is some reference point. That reference is not to "just cause" as it is understood under some statute, or in some other situation, or in the halls of Congress, but "just cause" as it is understood in the industrial community to which the agreement applies. It is that standard, and no other, which the arbitrator is charged to apply.

My adjurations concerning the appropriate reference source for arbitrators apply equally in the other direction. Every time I read an NLRB decision in which the Board unfortunately

gets into the business of interpreting a collective bargaining
agreement, I am shocked by the ineptness of the performance
(although perhaps I am not as shocked by that as I am at the
quality of the performance in the few instances I've seen where
arbitrators have tried to interpret the National Labor Relations Act).

The Board is enforcing a statute. Insofar as it enforces that
statute, it has some expertise. When a dispute arises as to the
proper application of the Act to particular facts, the Board has
to resolve that question. That's its job and, as well, the job
of the courts in reviewing what the Board does. The fact that
the dispute which the Board resolves as to the proper application of the statute arises between parties who have agreed to
arbitrate disputes as to the proper application of their agreement has little or no relevance, except as disputes relating to
the facts or to the meaning of the agreement may bear on the
Board's resolution of the controversy as to whether there has
been a violation of the National Labor Relations Act.

One of the classic blunders of the Labor Board in failing to
recognize that principle was the much-discussed *International
Harvester* case, in which the question was whether an employer could be required to discharge a man for failing to pay
his dues. The dispute arose under a union-shop contract which
had been executed in a right-to-work state before the passage
of the right-to-work law. By the time the case came to arbitration, however, the right-to-work law had become effective
and a new contract had been executed which did not contain
the union-shop provision. The question was whether the employer had violated the agreement by not discharging the employee initially, and if he had, what remedy should now be applied in view of the existence of the right-to-work law and the
new agreement.

David Cole, in deciding that case, confined himself pretty
clearly to interpreting the agreements which the parties had
made and applying the law which the parties had acknowledged,
by their agreements, to be applicable. He said that the company
should have fired the man before the old contract expired.
Since it did not do so, and since he could not now be fired
under the terms of the new agreement which had been exe-

cuted in the light of the right-to-work law, he concluded that the employee should be treated as having been fired but subsequently rehired as a new employee on the effective date of the new agreement.

The employee then filed a charge with the Board that this action violated the National Labor Relations Act on the theory that it violated the state right-to-work law and any violation of a state right-to-work statute also violated the NLRA. The Board decided that it did not have to decide whether the action violated the Act because the dispute had been resolved by an arbitrator!

Of course, David Cole didn't purport to decide whether the relief which he found was called for under the agreement would violate the Act. The result is that there was never a decision by anybody on that particular question. The case came out right anyway, but just by good luck, not because the adjudication of the proper application of the National Labor Relations Act fell between tribunals.

So I would conclude these brief remarks by affirming that, yes, arbitrators must be sympathetic and understanding of the public policy issues which are involved in the disputes which they hear. But they should be sympathetic and understanding only insofar as it may be fairly said—not arbitrarily and by virtue of a legal presumption—that the parties themselves are conscious of those considerations and, it can be assumed, would have dealt with the particular question before the arbitrator in the indicated way because of those considerations.

Beyond that, I think that the arbitrator, if he moves, moves not only at his peril but also at the peril of the relative immunity of all arbitrators from judicial review which has developed primarily because they have not taken the broader view here urged.

Chapter IV

DISCRETION IN ARBITRATION

Gabriel N. Alexander*

I.

I recall, somewhat ruefully, the conversation between Dick Mittenthal and myself during which he asked if I would work up for delivery at this meeting a discourse about arbitrators and the exercise of discretion. We were seated in the lobby at the Chateau Champlain near the end of last year's annual meeting in April. I demurred a bit, as I remember it, and pointed out to Dick that, unlike himself and others, I have no bent for scholarly research. He continued to press me, of course, as any good Program Chairman should. I think he tried to be reassuring and made some reference to my tendency to philosophize about the arbitrator's function, which I foolishly took as a compliment, and I began to respond to his invitation with increasing enthusiasm. After 15 minutes or so of what at the time seemed like a lively exchange of ideas, I took the hook. But I asked Dick to do two things for me: first, to write me a letter sketching out what he had in mind, and second, to keep after me by phone about once a month. He promised to do so, and did. In his letter he said in part: "You asked me to write in more detail as to what I had in mind. That's not easy to express. For this is an elusive subject, one which concerns the many unstated assumptions and judgments which enter into our awards. . . ."

Over the months intervening since last April 1, I have from time to time grappled with the subject. It is indeed an elusive one. Eel-like, no matter at which point I sought to take hold of it, it slipped from my grasp and slithered on the desk before me. Eventually I managed to creel my prey, and with your

---

* Member and Past President, National Academy of Arbitrators, Oak Park, Mich.

indulgence for the next half hour or so I shall display it. Whether my catch is a delicacy to be savored or trash to be thrown on the garbage pile rests in the palate of you, my audience.

Insofar as any ultimate conclusions are concerned, I am probably no further ahead nor much behind where I was in 1962 when I addressed the Academy under the title "Reflections on Decision-Making." At that time I ventured into a brief analysis of what goes on in the mind of an arbitrator between the time the evidence and arguments are fully submitted to him and the time he affixes his signature to an opinion and award and sends it out for the parties, and perhaps others, to see.

My thesis then was that decision-making by arbitrators is a dynamic mental and emotional process which includes nonrational, as well as rational, elements, and that awareness of such dynamics is essential to a proper understanding of it. But the area of interest encompassed by this paper is intended to be narrower than that with which I previously dealt. Today I propose to explore those aspects of decision-making by arbitrators which may be encompassed by the word "discretion."

Roughly divided, what I have to say comprises three parts: an inquiry into the meaning and usage of the word "discretion"; a look at some of the pros and cons as to the exercise of discretionary authority by arbitrators; and an argument that arbitrators are affected by normative forces which constrain them toward objectivity and accepted notions of justice and fairness, when, occasionally, they exercise "discretion."

Much of the elusiveness which characterizes today's subject emanates from the variety and generality of the meanings suggested by the word "discretion." Webster's *New International Dictionary* lists about six definitions, some of which are clearly foreign to present interest. The definition from which I proceed toward closer analysis reads as follows: "Power of free decision; individual judgment; undirected choice."

In the administration of justice, "discretion" as thus defined is generally regarded as evil. For persons in authority to exercise "free decision; individual judgment; [or] undirected choice" smacks of tyranny and an authoritarianism which is incompatible with fundamental conceptions of liberty and justice.

As I shall attempt to make more clear hereinafter, however, it is impossible to avoid all indulgence in "discretion" in the administration of justice, and there have grown up two modified concepts which (with some misgivings) are generally regarded as beneficial. I have in mind the terms "judicial discretion" and "administrative discretion." The following observation by Professor Frank Cooper in his book *Living the Law* illuminates the point:

> "Exercise of discretionary powers (in the classical meaning of the term defined as 'unrestrained exercise of will') is alien to judicial tradition. True, judges are free to exercise a degree of discretion in ancillary matters (such as determining trial dates, or the order of proofs or whether to grant extraordinary equitable remedies). But even here, it is said that the Courts exercise a 'judicial discretion' meaning that the trial judge's freedom of choice will be limited by established norms and standards." [1]

Accordingly, in the literature of the law we find definitions of, and discourses upon, "judicial discretion," a term that implies something narrower than wholly unrestrained exercise of will, but something broader than close adherence to rules of law. Attempts to define the more benign meaning of discretion connoted by "judicial discretion" are fraught with semantic uncertainties. The following definition of "judicial discretion" taken from a respected dictionary of legal terms may draw some wry amusement from those of you who, as I try to do, look closely at words to discern exactly what they mean. "Judicial discretion" is there defined as:

> "A liberty or privilege allowed to a judge, within the confines of right and justice, but independent of narrow and unbending rules of positive law, to decide and act in accordance with what is fair, equitable and wholesome, as determined upon the peculiar circumstances of the case, and as discerned by his personal wisdom and experience, guided by the spirit, principles, and analogies of the law." [2]

What to me is a more realistic definition is to be found in the following extract from a monograph by B. X. Meyer appearing in the *New York State Bar Journal* for April 1966. "Judicial discretion" was there defined as describing

> ". . . the area in which an appellate court will accord deference, but not finality to the determination of the lower court judge

---

[1] Cooper, *Living the Law* (Indianapolis: Bobbs-Merrill, 1958), 99.
[2] *Black's Law Dictionary*, 375 (2d ed. 1910).

. . . [resulting] from the difficulty of establishing hard and fast rules . . . typically . . . reversal will be accompanied by the statement that the lower court 'abused' or 'improvidently exercised' its discretion." [3]

This definition affords greater recognition to the interrelationship between a lower court and a reviewing court. It takes into account the dynamics of such relation and points up the inescapable fact that a discretionary ruling by a lower court will be reversed when the reviewing court disagrees with the ruling so strongly that it will use the words "abuse" or "improvident" to describe that ruling.

Consider now the concept of "administrative discretion," so important in modern law that it is doubtful if our complex society could be regulated without resort to it. As Professor Cooper put it, "Administrative agencies, on the other hand, thrive on the grant of broad discretionary powers. It has been said that discretion is the very life blood of the administrative process." [4] Nevertheless, experience reveals an appellate court will, when sufficiently aroused, also reverse a discretionary choice made by an administrative agency. The following words by Mr. Justice Douglas, dissenting in *New York* v. *United States,* verbalize the traditional concern of courts for the "unrestrained exercise of will" by administrative authority:

"Unless we make the requirements for administrative action strict and demanding expertise, the strength of modern government can become a monster which rules with no practical limits on its discretion. *Absolute discretion like corruption marks the beginning of the end of liberty.*" [5] (Emphasis added.)

The point I would stress to you before leaving my analysis of the meaning of "discretion" is that exercises of both "judicial discretion" and "administrative discretion" are subject to review by appellate courts. Such review, of course, is only on the question, as commonly put, whether such discretion was "abused," but even as thus limited it places direct restraints on the freedom of choice which may be exercised by any court or tribunal vested with "discretionary" powers. It is to the appellate courts that one must look for practical application of

[3] Meyer, "Judicial Discretion in Matrimonial Actions," 38 *N.Y.S. Bar J.* 119 (1966).

[4] Cooper, *supra* note 1, at 99.

[5] Dissenting opinion in *New York* v. *United States,* 342 U.S. 882, 884; 72 Sup. Ct. 152 (1951).

the restraints upon "discretion" which modifies the concept from its classical definition, "unrestrained exercise of will," to its accepted meaning in the administration of justice.

The question then may be asked, how, if at all, may the notion of "arbitral discretion" be defined and utilized? Assuming for discussion that an arbitrator is empowered specifically or by reasonable implication to exercise his "discretion," what if anything in theory or practice narrows such discretion to the limits to which exercises of "judicial discretion" or "administrative discretion" are subjected? There are, of course, limits beyond which an arbitrator may not exercise his will without being subject to reversal by a reviewing court, but I am unaware of any legal principle which asserts that an award will be upset on the ground that a *discretionary power* clearly vested in an arbitrator was exercised improvidently. Does it follow that as to matters lying within an arbitrator's discretion, there are, or should be, no limits on his exercise of will? In other words, is or should the concept of "arbitral discretion" be equated with "discretion" in its classical sense? I do not relish such a consequence.

So much for the difficulties that emanate from the meaning and connotations of the word "discretion." I turn now to passing comment on three matters relevant to the necessity or advisability of authorizing or permitting an arbitrator to exercise "discretion" as to any matter.

II.

First: There exists a perceivable parallel between the complexities of society at large and the complexities of the industrial relations society in which arbitrators function as decision-makers. While a major thrust by organized labor and a major concession by the managers of enterprises have been in the direction of objectifying the rules and standards governing life in industrial establishments (to create a society "governed by laws, not men"), experience demonstrates the impossibility of putting into words specific rules and standards to cover all circumstances. Our late respected colleague, Harry Shulman, described the problem in his 1955 Holmes lecture. After expressing the view that it is wholly impractical for unions and employers to deal with labor relations problems on a purely case-by-case basis, he said:

"So the parties seek to negotiate an *agreement to provide the standards* to govern their future action.

"In this endeavor they face problems not unlike those encountered wherever attempt is made to legislate for the future in highly complex affairs. The parties seek to foresee the multitude of variant situations that might arise, the possible types of action that might then be available, the practicalities of each and their anticipated advantages and disadvantages . . . ." [6] (Emphasis added.)

And as to an agreement resulting from negotiations, Dean Shulman said that it

". . . becomes a compilation of diverse provisions: Some provide objective criteria almost *automatically applicable;* some provide more or less specific standards which require *reason and judgment* in their application; and some do little more than *leave problems to future consideration* with an expression of hope and good faith." [7] (Emphasis added.)

Second: Although, as Dean Shulman observed, parties engaged in collective bargaining face problems similar to those encountered in legislating complex affairs, experience reveals that by and large they did not resort to a device similar to the administrative agency: that is, they did not create offices, sole or *en banc,* with power to make and enforce *general rules* within *broadly defined policies.* Rather, employers and unions reserved to *themselves* the right and duty of applying their collective bargaining agreement directly to the incidents of day-to-day life in the factory and provided for third-party intervention only on the limited scale encompassed by the system of grievance arbitration as it generally exists. I assume that all would agree that, on the whole, with certain exceptions aside to which I will advert hereinafter, arbitrators are *not expressly* empowered to exercise "discretion" as to any matter.

From my own experience I had thought this was so. In my early deliberations on this discourse I could recall seeing only three collective agreements in which there are provisions expressly authorizing an arbitrator or umpire to exercise "discretion," as such, with respect to any matter. Being chary of

---

[6] "Reason, Contract and Law in Labor Relations," 55 *Harv. L. Rev.* 999, 1003 (1955).
[7] *Id.* at 1005.

generalizations based on one man's experience, however, I inquired by mail of 20 members of the Academy whether they could cite to me out of their experience any labor agreement usages of the word "discretion" to describe either by way of expansion or limitation the authority of an arbitrator. The replies received by me confirm my impression based on my own experience. I now regard it as a safe generalization to say that, ordinarily, express affirmative grants of authority to arbitrators to exercise "discretion" are found only in provisions relating to the modification of disciplinary action imposed on employees by management. Otherwise, in the grievance arbitration system as we know it, the authority of an arbitrator to exercise "discretion" emanates from the inherent nature of his role, or by implication from other contract provisions which do not contain the word.

Third: An explanation for the absence, by and large, of express delegation of "discretion" to grievance arbitrators probably lies in two factors. One is the voluntarism by which, particularly in the years prior to 1960, our grievance arbitration institution has been characterized. While government (at the level of the War Labor Board, the President's Labor Management Conference of 1945, and the Congress in the Labor Management Relations Act, 1947) has lent *impetus* to the acceptance of grievance arbitration, all important expressions of that impetus emphasize the notion that employers and unions would create and shape their own proceedings. For example, Section 206 (d) of the Act states only that

"Final adjustment by a *method agreed upon by the parties* is hereby declared to be the desirable method for settlement of grievance disputes arising over the application or interpretation of an existing collective-bargaining agreement." (Emphasis added.)

The other factor was *apprehension*, most marked in management circles but not unknown in labor circles, lest arbitrators issue awards which seriously diminished the rights or freedoms of the parties, or created impracticable results.

The most common manifestation of this apprehension is seen in the provision, found in almost all arbitration clauses, to the effect that the arbitrator shall have no power to add to, detract from, or modify any of the provisions of the agreement. More forceful expressions in the same vein appear in some labor agreements, one example of which reads in part as follows:

> "He [the arbitrator] shall have no power to substitute his discretion for the Company's discretion in cases where the Company is given discretion by this Agreement or by any supplementary agreement,
> . . .
>
> ". . . In rendering decisions, an arbitrator shall have due regard to the responsibility of Management and shall so construe the Agreement that there will be no interference with such responsibilities except as they may be specifically conditioned by this Agreement."

III.

To recapitulate to this point, I have sought to explain that "discretion" in its classical sense is abhorrent to our fundamental conceptions of justice, but that as the complexities of life prohibit the formulation of specific rules to cover every contingency there have arisen a concept of "judicial discretion" within which the courts of first impression may act, and a concept of "administrative discretion" within which regulatory boards and commissions may act. Application of those limited concepts of discretion involve recourse to appellate courts, and the concepts are better understood by those who recognize the dynamics inherent in the process of judicial review. By contrast, labor arbitration agreements seldom specifically authorize arbitrators to exercise "discretion" although, as Harry Shulman and others have pointed out, companies and unions face problems not unlike those encountered in complex legislative matters.

Nevertheless, I submit, closer examination of the subject reveals that, as to a variety of matters, arbitrators are expected to, do, and indeed must act in a manner which, although not styled "discretionary," is identical with, or closely similar to, the exercise of discretionary power.

Let us put aside for the moment the word "discretion" and substitute for it its classical definition, "unrestrained exercise of will." Let us then look to the sources, if any, of restraint upon the exercise of will by arbitrators. The primary source, it is clear, is the text of the labor agreement or submission from which the arbitrator derives his authority. The arbitrator, faithful to his trust, like the judge, applies the rule which is clearly prescribed by his source of law or principle. Judge Cardozo put it in these words: "The rule that fits the case may be supplied by the constitution or by statute. If that is so the judge looks no farther. *The correspondence ascertained, his duty is to obey.*" [8] (Emphasis added.)

But in the grist of the business coming before labor arbitrators, the terms of an agreement are seldom clear enough to supply the rule, and *pro tanto* the arbitrator is less than explicitly restrained in the exercise of his will. A contract may be devoid of any affirmative invitation to the arbitrator to exercise "discretion," as such, but it may be replete with words which are so general in their meaning as to compel him to exercise his will with little or no specific contractual restraint. I cite the following clauses as illustrative:

> 1. "An employee seniority shall be broken and all employment rights terminated if an employee is absent for three working days, unless he has a *satisfactory reason* for such absence."
> 2. "The arbitrator shall decide the question of *equitable incentive compensation.*"
> 3. "The Company shall not exercise its right to discipline . . . any employee except for *good and just cause.*"

None of these clauses, which are representative of many clauses which arbitrators are regularly called upon to interpret and apply, affirmatively grants arbitrators authority to exercise "discretion," but none of them provides much guidance or restraint upon the arbitrators' exercise of will with respect to the outcome of a dispute over the application of the clause to a situation.

In terms of the underlying consideration, "restraint upon the exercise of will," how much, if any, real difference can be found between a clause which grants an arbitrator authority to exercise "discretion" with respect to how much incentive employees should earn and a contract clause which empowers the arbitrator to decide whether incentive compensation available under a plan is "equitable"?

Illustrative of how arbitrators actually behave in this uncertain area are two lines of holdings, one by the United States

---

[8] Cardozo, *The Nature of the Judicial Process* (New Haven: Yale University Press, 1921), 14.

Steel-Steelworkers Board of Arbitration and the other by the General Motors-United Automobile Workers umpires. In the former, the Board of Arbitration has made it clear that it will decide whether a plan provides "equitable incentive compensation" by reference to what is fair, just, and reasonable on a case-by-case basis, and will not establish any intermediate principle or precedent for such a determination.[9] In one opinion in this series, the Board said:

> "Since it [the Board] proceeds on a case by case basis . . . in applying the 'fair just and reasonable' test, it seems essential that the Board *refrain from theorizing or rationalizing the decision here announced.*"[10] (Emphasis added.)

In effect, as I see it, the Board has asserted that it will exercise its will to reach decision in these cases unrestrained by principles or concepts which are more specific than the terms, "fair, just, and reasonable." I find it hard to distinguish between such an assertion and one which says that these kinds of cases will be decided by exercise of "arbitral discretion." Indeed, in a recent incentive case heard by me involving another steel company, counsel for the Steelworkers used the word "discretion" to describe to me the latitude of consideration which permeates decisions on the question of equitable incentive compensation made by the Board of Arbitration.

The line of decisions to be found in the General Motors-United Automobile Workers umpire rulings arises under one of the few agreement clauses which does affirmatively grant "discretion" to an arbitrator. Since 1941 the GM-UAW national agreement has contained a clause which states in part, "The Corporation delegates to the Umpire full discretion in cases of violation of shop rules. . . ."

However, and for present purposes by way of contrast with the refusal of the United States Steel Board to lay down more specific guideposts, the umpires have said that they would generally adhere to the unifying concept of corrective discipline in exercising that delegated "discretion." In one opinion, it was put in these words:

> "*Full discretion* is an extremely broad term and connotes a

---

[9] *U.S. Steel,* 5 Basic Steel Arbitrations [hereinafter cited as BSA] 3177 (1955); *U.S. Steel,* 6 BSA 3939 (1957); U.S. Steel, 6 BSA 4317 (1958).
[10] 4 BSA 2343 (1954).

freedom of choice not hampered by formal rules or precedents. Nevertheless, in order that the parties might have some guide to indicate the probable outcome of disputes over the reasonableness of penalties, the Umpire has announced that, with certain exceptions not now material, he will exercise his contractual full discretion within the doctrine of 'corrective discipline'. . . ." [11]

The contrast between these two lines of decision is best understood as a manifestation of the importance which the respective arbitrators attached to considerations beyond those affecting the particular disputes ruled upon. In the line of decisions dealing with disciplinary penalties, the GM-UAW umpires were apparently most concerned lest lack of guideposts for the probable outcome of appeals would obstruct the settlement of discipline cases at the lower steps of the grievance procedure. In the line of decisions pertaining to equitable incentive wages, the Board of Arbitration was apparently most concerned lest the broad standard ("equitable incentive compensation") set forth in the contract become subservient to specific industrial engineering principles or incentive wage theories.

The results achieved by both arbitration tribunals are viable, having withstood tests of subsequent experience, and in my opinion were wise. The holdings illustrate not only that "discretion," or something closely akin to it, is a factor which affects decisions upon diverse matters, but also indicate that the extent to which "discretion" will be exercised by arbitrators is itself a question which at times may and properly should lie in the arbitrator's discretion. Nothing in either the General Motors agreement or the United States Steel agreement, as far as I can find, instructs the arbitrator as to the importance which he must attach to conflicting relevant considerations which are brought to bear on a dispute. In most arbitration cases where the outcome turns upon value judgments, the arbitrator has no alternative to making his choices on the broad basis of experience and wisdom.

Does it follow that as to any matter upon which the labor agreement does not specifically supply the rule to be applied, the arbitrator's will is wholly unrestrained? Not in the overall grievance arbitration system in which we practice. One important constraint which influences most arbitrators is the quasi-

---

[11] Decision G-15 (1951).

DISCRETION IN ARBITRATION

professional status of our calling, a status for which the National Academy has diligently exerted its efforts for almost 25 years. Rare indeed on today's labor arbitration scene is the well-meaning but uninformed prominent citizen called upon to act the role of Solomon. Grievance arbitrators are selected for qualities of expertise as well as their personal dedication to justice.

Another influential constraint upon the exercise of will by grievance arbitrators comes from the practice of explaining awards in written opinions. The necessity of recording a reasoned conclusion includes the necessity of calling forth reason to explain the decision. A reasoned exercise of will is not an unrestrained exercise of will. And Judge Paul Hays to the contrary notwithstanding, what to me are the legitimate and beneficial aspirations of arbitrators to maintain the respect of their fellows and of their clientele constitute a third source of constraint against the "unrestrained exercise of will," or arbitrary or tyrannical behavior.

IV.

What I have thus far discussed concerns the exercise of discretion, or something like it, by arbitrators as to the *substantive outcome* of a dispute. There are other aspects of arbitration as to which arbitrators are called upon to make rulings (exercise their will) entirely and frankly as a matter of "discretion." I have reference to the multitude of matters that arise with respect to the conduct of a hearing. Usually one does not find in a collective bargaining agreement a complete set of rules for the fixing of time and place of hearing, or the manner and sequence of the presentation of evidence and argument, or the winding-up of the case. Within the limits of "due process and fair hearing" to which the parties are entitled as of right, there are many details the resolution of which reposes in the "discretion" of the arbitrator by force of necessity from his role as president of the tribunal, and by force of customary expectations of the disputants. In this area the arbitrator exercises discretion identical with that exercised by a trial judge.

In another area, both substantive and procedural, arbitrators may be called upon to exercise discretionary authority. I refer to the formulation of a specific remedy for a proved violation of the agreement. This is a complex area, and time limitations preclude me from delving deeply into it. I call your attention to the following:

> 1. On occasion parties will stipulate the issues to be decided in substantially the following terms: "Did the Company violate the Agreement when it did not promote Grievant to Electrician Leader? If so what shall the remedy be?"[12]
>
> 2. In *United Steelworkers* v. *Enterprise Wheel & Car Corp.* Mr. Justice Douglas said: "When an arbitrator is commissioned to interpret and apply the . . . agreement he is to bring his informed judgment to bear. . . . This is especially true when it comes to formulating remedies. There the need is for flexibility. . . ."[13]
>
> 3. The J&L Steel-Steelworkers Agreement states: "The decision of the Board will be restricted as to whether a violation of the Agreement as alleged in the written grievance . . . exists and if a violation is found, to specify the remedy provided in this Agreement."

So much for the arbitrator's discretion as to remedies. Let me call attention to another aspect of the grievance arbitration system as it exists today—the writing of opinions explaining decisions.

I think most experienced arbitrators would agree that the writing of opinions is an arduous task which does not become easier with the passage of years. The arbitrator is never more on his own with little or no restraint or guidance than when he is putting words to paper. Entirely within his "discretion" are the questions of what to say and how to say it. To whom is he addressing himself? His clients alone, or a wider audience? Shall he write broadly for the purpose not only of recording disposition of the subject case but also of giving guidance to the parties for the future? Or shall he write narrowly so as to avoid the pitfalls of affecting matters not known to him? Shall he call a spade a spade and characterize one or the other of the parties in strong or blunt terms? Or shall he let his words fall gently, either completely masking his feelings or only hinting at them? Or shall he say something nice about one or the other or both sides? It is almost entirely a matter within his discretion, or "style," or personality. Yet the arbitrator's writings are what most people rely on to form judgments about his skill and ability, and decision-writing forms a most important element of the system.

---

[12] See *Allied Chemical*, 47 LA 554 (1966), Carroll R. Daugherty; *General Slicing Machine Co.*, 49 LA 823 (1967), Louis Yagoda.
[13] 363 U.S. 593, 46 LRRM 2423 (1960).

And, finally, I call your attention to the one area, closely interwoven with both procedure and substance, as to which restraint or guidance to the exercise of the arbitrator's will is not only lacking, but is also unavailable from any reliable or authoritative source. I have reference to the jury function—the acceptance, qualification, or rejection of belief in conflicting versions of fact as related by witnesses. The real and underlying truth of this matter, as experienced practitioners recognize, is that the outcome of a case which turns upon which of conflicting versions is believed is a matter which lies wholly within the "discretion" of the arbitrator. It is at this point that the whole of the arbitrator's personality, experience, outlook on life, sympathies known to him or buried in his subconscious, etc., all come into play.

I have heard some men say they could always know who was telling the truth and who was lying. I have seen arbitrator's opinions which assert as a principle that a grievant is less credible than a contradicting foreman because the grievant has an interest in the outcome of the case but a supervisor does not. I would be more at ease with myself and the world if I shared those views, and in a way I envy others who do. But experience has not led me to do so, and I have searched in vain for authoritative principles of law, psychology, or any science or art upon which I could confidently rely for guidance or restraint upon my exercise of will as to matters of belief. I need not remind this audience that the "facts" upon which an arbitrator bases his conclusion are not the "facts" as they occurred at the time the dispute arose, but are rather the "facts" as understood by the arbitrator from the presentation made to him by the parties during the course of the hearing. No one who understands the psychological processes of observation, recall, and narration by witnesses can fail to perceive that difference and the dynamics that affect the understanding and decision-making by arbitrators, by administrative tribunals, by judges, and by juries.

As I said at the outset, I find myself not much ahead or behind the position I took in my 1962 discourse. We profess belief in a society governed by laws, not by men. We reject tyranny and absolutism. We find truth in the saying, "Power tends to corrupt; absolute power corrupts absolutely," and we share the

feelings of Mr. Justice Douglas when he said, "Absolute discretion, like corruption, marks the beginning of the end of liberty." But in 1971, as in 1962, I see no way of escaping the
realities which affect our institutions for the administration of
justice. One cannot ignore the necessity of resolving disputes
on the basis of judgment, or the elements of personality that
affect human judgment. Although seldom invested with specific
authority to exercise "discretion," arbitrators could not reach
or express their judgments without exercising their will. Justice demands that such exercise should not be wholly unrestrained, but it is simply not possible to restrain it to a degree
that eliminates "discretion" in a sense comparable to "judicial
discretion" or "administrative discretion."

Comment—

PHILIP G. MARSHALL *

Perhaps the soundest approach I could make in commenting
on Gabe's dissertation would be to say "Amen" and be seated.
But the program calls for something more than that, so for the
next 10 minutes or so I shall try my analytical best to explore
further the subject of "Discretion in Arbitration."

Gabe has said that he has "no bent for scholarly research,"
and indeed the very title of his paper gives evidence of that.
The simple and descriptive title, "Discretion in Arbitration,"
has no scholarly clout. Anyone who pretends to be a scholar
would have picked a title that has some real sock. Evidently
Gabe doesn't know that at least 90 percent of all doctoral dis-
sertations, papers, monographs, or just plain everyday academic
speeches bear such titles as "The Impact of Something on
Something Else" or "The Influence of Something Upon a Whole
Flock of Other Things." Even though Gabe's original paper
bore that simple title, "Discretion in Arbitration," the acade-
micians on the Program Committee could not sit still for so
simple and forthright a title. Hence, in the printed program,
it was changed to "The Role of Discretion in Arbitral Decision-
Making." Thus, we see that the key words to demonstrating
erudition are "impact," "influence," and "role."

Quite properly, Gabe begins with a number of definitions of

---

* Member, National Academy of Arbitrators, Milwaukee, Wis.

"discretion," each of which quarrels with the others. Recognizing this, he proceeds to differentiate between certain categories of discretion, that is, judicial discretion, administrative discretion, arbitral discretion, and also what he refers to as discretion in its "classical" sense. It was Cardozo who observed that there is an ancient maxim of the law which runs, "Peril lurks in definitions," [1] as, indeed, it does. If one consults *Words and Phrases*,[2] that legal reference work which preserves for posterity almost every judicial definition of every word or phrase which has been reduced to print in the entire West Publishing Company Reporter Series, you will find a curious but quite understandable variation in definitions, particularly by appellate judges, depending on whether they affirm or overrule a lower court or administrative body. A typical opinion overruling the exercise of discretion by an inferior judge reads as follows:

> "The discretion of a judge is said to be the law of tyrants. It is always unknown; it is different in different men; it is casual, and dependent upon constitution, temper, and passion. In the best, it is oftentimes caprice; in the worst, it is every vice, folly, and passion to which human nature is liable."—Judgment reversed.

On the other hand, when appellate judges affirm the exercise of discretion by an inferior court, the opinion most frequently cryptically states: "Discretion is the freedom to act according to one's judgment."—Judgment affirmed. Thus, it appears that "discretion" can be defined or categorized in many different ways, depending on whether there is approval or disapproval of the manner in which it has been exercised and the resultant judgment.

I find it difficult to determine any real difference between the proper exercise of judicial discretion, administrative discretion, or arbitral discretion. All must be judicial and all must be based on sound reasoning. It is likewise true that in every case there should be no abuse of discretion, nor should discretion be improvidently exercised.

In the early 1940s there was a great hue and cry about the unbridled, improvident, and uncontrolled exercise of discretion by federal administrative bodies and the executive branch of the Federal Government. To correct these alleged abuses, Senator

---

[1] Cardozo, Address before the New York State Bar Association Meeting, Jan. 22, 1932, *New York State Bar Association Report* (1932), 274.

[2] *Words and Phrases* (St. Paul: West Publishing Co.), Vol. 12A, 327 *et. seq.*

Pat McCarran in 1944 introduced a bill into the Congress which subsequently was enacted as the Administrative Procedure Act. Section 10 of that Act provided for judicial review of any administrative action "except so far as (1) statutes preclude judicial review or (2) agency action is by law committed to agency discretion." [3] When Senator McCarran was asked whether this provision would preclude judicial review of "an abuse of discretion," he denied that such would be the case and explained: "It must not be an arbitrary discretion. It must be a judicial discretion; it must be a discretion based on sound reasoning." [4] Thus, we see that Senator McCarran was equating "administrative discretion" with "judicial discretion."

Of course, it is true that administrative bodies are generally ceded the right to exercise discretion in many areas where a judge in an ordinary suit at law is bound by the rigor of statutes or the common law, as fortified by the doctrine of *stare decisis*. However, though the area of discretion is admittedly broad in the field of administrative law, the manner in which it is exercised should nevertheless be subject to the same limitations that apply in courts of law or in arbitration proceedings.

Arbitrators, as well as judges or administrative bodies, are bound by the written word of the statute, regulation, or contract under which the dispute is being resolved; each is bound in equal measure. The area within which each is empowered to exercise his discretion, however, may vary markedly. In many cases the arbitrator's area of discretion is the broadest of all. Very often the parties in effect say to the arbitrator, "We got a problem. Here it is. Give us your solution." Very often neither side even alludes to the contract, and frequently the contract consists of a recognition clause, a termination clause, and little or nothing in between that bears any relationship to the issue presented. It isn't even a question of resolving an ambiguity; it is purely a question of judgment unconfined. A colleague of ours, Mike Ryder, in a paper delivered at our 21st Annual Meeting, put it another way: "After all, an arbi-

---

[3] Administrative Procedure Act, Public Law 404, 79th Cong., 2d Sess., Sec. 10.

[4] Administrative Procedure Act, Legislative History, 1944-46, 79th Cong., 2d Sess., Senate Document No. 248, 310 ff.

trator is engaged in a legislative function when he is asked to interpret and decide a negotiated ambiguity." [5]

Perhaps the closest approach to the exercise of this kind of unbridled discretion is to be found in the old English Court of Requests, which first appeared in 1493: "Under Henry VII it was, in effect, a committee of the Council for the hearing of poor men's causes and matters relating to the King's servants." [6] The sole curb on its discretion was that its decisions were required to square with the King's conscience, which was notoriously flexible. And let the institution of labor arbitration beware, as Professor Plucknett in his *History of the Common Law* observed, "Toward the end of its career it lost its reputation owing to the growing complexity, slowness and expense of its proceedings." [7]

Gabe quotes our Program Chairman as being principally concerned with "the many unstated assumptions and judgments which enter into our awards." I suspect that if the full truth be known, hunch or intuition is frequently the principal ingredient. Cardozo, to whom I must credit this observation, in an address before the New York State Bar Association in 1932 stated:

"In the business of choosing between . . . competitive offerings in the legal mart, we hear a great deal now-a-days of the intuitive judgment, more picturesquely styled the hunch, as the real arbiter of values (Hutcheson, The Judgment Intuitive; The Function of the Hunch in Judicial Decisions, 14 Cornell L.I. 274)." [8]

Cardozo points out, however, that pure hunch or intuition, or what might more properly be called the "intuitive flash or inspiration," seldom comes to those who are untutored and inexperienced in the field which gives rise to the intuitive flash. As he explains:

"Accidental discoveries of which popular histories of science make mention never happen except to those who have previously devoted a great deal of thought to the matter. Observations

---

[5] Meyer S. Ryder, "The Impact of Acceptability on the Arbitrator," in *Developments in American and Foreign Arbitration,* Proceedings of the 21st Annual Meeting, National Academy of Arbitrators, ed. Charles M. Rehmus (Washington: BNA Books, 1968) , 107.

[6] Theodore F. T. Plucknett, *A Concise History of the Common Law* (Rochester, N.Y.: Lawyers Co-operative Publishing Co., 1929) , 142.

[7] *Id.* at 142.

[8] Cardozo, *supra* note 1, at 285.

unillumined by theoretic reason is sterile. . . . Wisdom does not come to those who gape at nature with an empty head." [9]

In other words, pure and unadulterated hunch without the "value of conceptions, rules and principles" is tantamount to being a denial of "the value of all logic" and to proclaim that "Whirl is King." [10]

As arbitrators we have been frequently accused of being inconsistent, as indeed we are—and so indeed are all who serve as judges. As Oliver Wendell Holmes observed:

> "The truth is, that law hitherto has been, and it would seem by the necessity of its being is always approaching and never reaching consistency. It is forever adopting new principles from life at one end, and it always retains old ones from history at the other which have not yet been absorbed or sloughed off. It will become entirely consistent only when it ceases to grow." [11]

I think that there are really only two characteristics which distinguish arbitral discretion from judicial discretion. The first is that the judgment of an arbitrator, once given, is rarely subject to review. Every trial judge faces the prospect of having his judgment scrutinized by an appellate court, while an arbitrator can walk away from his mistakes with only the curse of the immediate parties in his wake.

The second characteristic of arbitral discretion which is different from the manner in which judicial discretion is normally exercised is the absence of a jury to decide the issues of fact.

These two characteristics—the absence of review and the absence of a jury—place upon the arbitrator a responsibility which is grave indeed, and transcends that of the average trial judge.

The area which Gabe and Abe and I are attempting to explore today has been better and more thoroughly done by Cardozo in his *The Nature of the Judicial Process,* by Karl Llewellen in his *Bramble Bush,* and by Morris Cohen and Jerome Frank in their numerous books and articles. As the three great jurisprudential scholars have observed, anyone who hears con-

---

[9] *Id.* at 286.
[10] *Id.* at 287.
[11] *Justice Oliver Wendell Holmes, His Book Notices and Uncollected Letters and Papers* (Brooklyn, N.Y.: Central Book Co., 1936), 12.

flicting sides of an issue, exercises discretion, and renders a judgment, is more influenced by subconscious forces than conscious ones. Indeed, if we could rule out the subconscious decision-making forces, we wouldn't need judges, commissioners, or arbitrators at all; we could resort to a computer.

As Cardozo observed, ". . . it is through these subconscious forces that judges are kept consistent with themselves and inconsistent with one another." [12]

Comment—

ABRAM H. STOCKMAN [*]

Gabe Alexander has told us, in essence: first, that under our system of grievance arbitration, arbitrators in their role as decision-makers do exercise discretion; second, that notwithstanding they are seldom granted such authority, they inescapably must do so in resolving disputes; and finally, that the professional nature of the arbitrator's calling, the need to substantiate decisions by written opinion, and the desire to maintain respect among colleagues and clients all serve as restraints upon the possibility of an unrestrained exercise of discretion.

There is little to quarrel with what Gabe has said. The fact of the matter is that, somewhat uncharacteristic of Gabe—at least insofar as Academy meetings are concerned—he has not adopted a polemical position. On the contrary, as I construe his paper, he has merely sought to explore and explain certain aspects of the decision-making process as seen through the eyes of a professional arbitrator. And need I add that, as a professional arbitrator, Gabe is among the most experienced as well as among the most esteemed in the profession.

There have been other occasions at these meetings which have been devoted to discussions of the decision-making process. Who can forget that tour de force in 1962 by none other than Peter Seitz on the subject, "How Arbitrators Decide Cases: A Study in Black Magic"? [1] You may recall that it was Peter's conclusion

[12] Benjamin Nathan Cardozo, *The Nature of the Judicial Process* (New Haven: Yale University Press, 1921), 12.

[*] Member, National Academy of Arbitrators, New York, N.Y.

[1] *Collective Bargaining and the Arbitrator's Role,* Proceedings of the 15th Annual Meeting, National Academy of Arbitrators, ed. Mark L. Kahn (Washington: BNA Books, 1962), 159.

that arbitrators decide cases much in the manner in which his grandmother—and he made it quite clear that it was his maternal grandmother who was involved—chose and bought a melon at the fruit store. Digging deep into the bottom of the pile, she would pick one out for color, heft it for weight and volume, pressure the ends for ripeness and maturity, sniff it for fragrance, and then, turning her back on the evidence of her senses, choose another, relying upon "the ineffable and completely subjective criteria for judgment that are acquired only with having and coping with a problem for a long time. . . ." In that same year Gabe delivered his Presidential Address entitled "Reflections on Decision Making," [2] and it was his thesis that decision-making by arbitrators is a dynamic process which includes not only rational elements but nonrational elements as well. One cannot but be struck by the extraordinary coincidence of a meeting of the minds between Alexander and Seitz. We know of no other instance where that has occurred, and we strongly doubt that it will ever occur again. And so, if only because of that coincidence, if not for more cogent reasons, I am prepared to accept, and indeed endorse, the proposition that every decision represents a combination of both rational and nonrational elements.

In his talk today, Gabe concentrates on what he conceives to be a narrower aspect of the decision-making process—namely, an exploration into the discretionary aspect of the arbitrator's function. And he concludes, "Although seldom invested with specific authority to exercise 'discretion,' arbitrators could not reach or express their judgments without exercising their will."

I have no difficulty in accepting that conclusion, but I confess to some perplexity because I am never quite certain in what sense he is using the word "discretion" in the various ways he deals with this subject throughout the paper. Thus, I can never be sure whether he is speaking of discretion as "undirected choice" or "unrestrained exercise of will," or in some narrower sense, as "freedom of choice . . . limited by established norms and standards." And furthermore, in whatever sense he is using the term, I find myself equally uncertain in determining whether he is addressing himself to a specific grant of authority to exercise discretion, or to a reasonable implication to do so from the language, or to the inherent necessity to interpret and apply

---

[2] *Id.* at 1.

language as such. But I cannot and would not fault him for these uncertainties or my perplexities because I realize that we are here dealing with a subject that is at best quite elusive. In its broader context, it inescapably concerns the very nature of the decision-making process itself—a subject that has challenged the thinking of philosophers and jurists over the ages and, in our own time, of figures no less eminent than a Holmes or a Cardozo. Since none of us speaking this afternoon purports to be a professor of jurisprudence, I think we are entitled to a degree of fuzziness which may or may not be characteristic of jurisprudence professors.

Let us return, for a moment, to the statement, "Although seldom invested with specific authority to exercise 'discretion,' arbitrators could not reach or express their judgments without exercising their will." Of course, this is true. And it is a truism which extends throughout the arbitration proceeding from the moment the arbitrator accepts an appointment until he has discharged his responsibilities and issued his decision and award. Why is this so? Because in the very nature of the grant of authority to a third party to decide a dispute, the contesting parties have necessarily conferred upon the third party the power to exercise his discretion in freely choosing as between the facts and arguments presented by each and the decision which each seeks to have him render. Whatever his reasons, whether or not they conceal his motivations, and to whatever extent they may be dictated by nonrational elements, his decision in that case imposes on the parties his judgment, indeed his will, and represents to that extent an act of fiat. In short, by virtue of the authority invested in him by the parties, he decrees that the act be done.

Lon L. Fuller, professor of jurisprudence at the Harvard Law School, in his perceptive analysis of Cardozo's legal philosophy entitled *Reason and Fiat in Case Law*,[3] has pointed out that Cardozo was singularly aware that every decision in case law embraces the antinomies of reason and fiat. In epitomizing Cardozo's philosophical approach to that inherent contradiction, Fuller said: "For him law was by its limitations fiat, by its

---

[3] *Reason and Fiat in Case Law* (New York: American Book-Stratford Press, 1943) .

aspirations reason, and the whole view of it involved a recognition of both its limitations and aspirations." [4]

In like manner must we recognize the limitations and aspirations of the decision process in arbitration. Its aspirations are to persuade by reason that justice has been accomplished, but its limitations as an institutional device no less abound in the exercise of discretion that represents a measure of personal fiat. And in the context of the arbitration of industrial disputes, concerned as it generally is with the interpretation and application of a written agreement, neither the absence of express authority to exercise discretion nor the presence of a restraining clause proscribing additions, detractions, or modification of the terms of the agreement can divest the arbitrator of the need to exercise his personal judgment. Hence, on that proposition, Gabe and I are in complete agreement. If there is any sense of difference between us, it is only as to a matter of emphasis in his attempt to treat the discretionary aspects of decision-making as something distinguishable from the decision-making process itself.

Believing, as I do, that the exercise of discretion permeates every aspect of the arbitrator's role, I am led to these conclusions. First, I do not think that one can meaningfully discuss the part that discretion plays in decision-making on any overall basis without reference to the particular substantive problem involved. Let me explain. In Dick Mittenthal's letter to Gabe detailing what he had in mind in suggesting the subject—the nature and exercise of arbitral discretion—he speaks of the many unstated assumptions and judgments which enter into our awards, and he cites, among others, the example of the selection of the rationale or theory on which a case is decided. Thus, he says: "Frequently we have a wide choice. Sometimes we choose the most forceful theory (i.e. the one which is most persuasive); other times we choose the safest theory (i.e. the one which is most likely to be acceptable); still other times we choose the most reasonable theory (i.e. the one which produces the 'correct' result notwithstanding contract-fact complexities); and so on." And he concludes: "Do we tend to exercise this kind of discretion in the parties' interests or in our own interests?"

Leaving aside, for the moment, the latter question about

---

[4] *Id.* at 3.

which I will have some comment later, any discussion concerning the choice of the most forceful, safest, or reasonable theory upon which to rest a decision can only be meaningful in the context of a consideration of the particular substantive problem involved. Is it to be doubted that the choice may be influenced by whether we are discussing wages and compensation, or vacations and holidays, or promotions, layoffs, premium pay, discipline, or any one of the great variety of provisions customarily included in the collective bargaining agreement? For example, Gabe has addressed himself to two substantive areas: one dealing with the question of equitable incentive compensation; the other dealing with just cause in disciplinary matters. In the situation dealing with the matter of equitable incentive compensation, he points out that the Board of Arbitration, in the cases he cited,[5] determined that it would proceed on a case-by-case basis in applying a "fair, just and reasonable" [6] test and would refrain from theorizing or rationalizing the decision, apparently because of a concern that the broad contractual standard might become subservient to specific industrial engineering principles or theories. In the situation dealing with discipline, the umpire, in the exercise of the "full discretion" [7] delegated to him by the contract, determined that he would exercise that discretion on the basis of the doctrine of "corrective discipline," [8] having in mind the need to provide guideposts so as to encourage the settlement of discipline cases at the lower steps of the procedure. Gabe concludes that in any arbitration case where the outcome turns upon value judgments, the arbitrator is compelled to make his choice broadly as a matter of "discretion." But where does that leave us? Informative as the cited examples may be about the considerations which entered into the exercise of discretion in choosing the particular theory upon which to rest the decision, in the final analysis we are really not much further advanced about this matter of discretion except as it relates to the specific substantive matter involved. In short, I suggest that the nature and exercise of discretion cannot all be wrapped up in one ball of wax, and my own personal opinion

---

[5] *U.S. Steel,* 5 BSA 3177 (1955); *U.S. Steel,* 6 BSA 3939 (1957); *U.S. Steel,* 6 BSA 4317 (1958).
[6] 4 BSA 2343 (1954).
[7] Decision G-15 (1951).
[8] *Id.*

is that any attempt to do so would not represent much of a contribution to the jurisprudence of industrial relations.

The second conclusion that I derive from my view that the entirety of the arbitration process encompasses the exercise of discretion concerns the matter of constraint. Gabe has indicated that, in contrast to the restraints imposed by appellate review in the exercise of judicial and administrative discretion, the likelihood of a reversal of an arbitrator's award for the improvident exercise of an *express* grant of discretionary power is, in the main, rather remote. This may well be true, and I am content to rely upon his research for that conclusion. But from my point of view, I find it significant that our own Academy Committee on Law and Legislation has found in its analysis of reported judicial decisions that, consistently over the years, the majority of arbitration awards, challenged for *whatever reason* in judicial proceedings, were enforced or confirmed by the courts.[9]

Hence, I think it fair to conclude that, in general, the only restraint upon the arbitrator not to abuse his power of discretion is not judicial restraint but self-discipline. Self-discipline, according to Gabe, will necessarily result from the impact of such factors as the professional nature of the arbitrator's calling, the need to substantiate the decision by a written opinion, and the desire to maintain respect among colleagues and clients.

As I earlier indicated, there can be no quarrel with those conclusions. But since I do not regard the arbitrator's power to exercise discretion as something tangential to the process, but regard it rather as something inherent and inescapable by virtue of the very nature of the process, I would urge that the only safeguard which the parties have against the possibility of an improvident exercise of that discretion is the professionalism and integrity of the person they select as arbitrator.

When I speak of professionalism, I have in mind one who, by training and experience in the adjudication of industrial re-

---

[9] Edgar A. Jones, Jr., and David G. Finkle, "Arbitration and Federal Rights Under Collective Agreements in 1968," in *Arbitration and Social Change*, Proceedings of the 22nd Annual Meeting, National Academy of Arbitrators, ed. Gerald G. Somers (Washington: BNA Books, 1969), 200; Jones and Kathleen Peratis, "Arbitration and Federal Rights Under Collective Agreements in 1969", in *Arbitration and the Expanding Role of Neutrals*, Proceedings of the 23rd Annual Meeting, National Academy of Arbitrators, ed. Gerald G. Somers and Barbara D. Dennis (Washington: BNA Books, 1970), 229.

lations disputes, has demonstrated the attributes of competency
in its various facets, ranging from a thorough and intimate knowledge of labor relations to an ability to write a clear and persuasive opinion of the reasons which form the bases for his
decision.[10] And when I speak of integrity, I have in mind a
demonstrated awareness of the proprieties so necessary to the
proper functioning of the office of arbitrator and so vital to
preserving the integrity of the process of arbitration. In the
final analysis, professionalism and integrity are most apt to provide the parties with the assurance that the arbitrator they
have chosen to decide their dispute will exercise his discretion
in a manner least calculated to result in unwarranted damage
to them and, I might add, in a manner that would serve their
interests and not his own. The concept of a government of
laws, so characteristic of our society, is not without its antinomy
in being dependent for the implementation and interpretation
of those laws upon man. Hence, we are constantly faced with
the challenge of seeking to insure that only persons of competence and integrity are selected or elected as judges. That challenge is, I submit, not without its relevance to the quasi-judicial
process with which we have been concerned here this afternoon.

---

[10] For a fuller discussion of professional competence, see Stockman, "Now, Who
Shall Arbitrate?" 19 *Stanford L. Rev.* 707 (1967).

CHAPTER V

IMPLEMENTATION OF ARBITRATION AWARDS

LAURENCE E. SEIBEL, CHAIRMAN *
RAYMOND E. SHETTERLY **
ALEXANDER C. MEKULA ***
BEN FISCHER ****
GEORGE A. MOORE, JR.*****

CHAIRMAN LAURENCE E. SEIBEL: It seems to me rather curious that the problem of this morning's meeting has never been the subject of a program or workshop of the Academy. Some years ago there was a discussion of seniority and promotion cases, but that dealt primarily with the correctness of the arbitrator's reversal and his decision to promote younger men.

Today's program is not primarily concerned with the correctness of the arbitrator's decision in altering or overturning the action taken by one of the parties, generally the company. Rather, it is concerned with what flows from that decision. Unfortunately, neither in law nor in arbitration is an affirmative decision generally self-enforcing. The affirmative decision that one of the parties shall do so-and-so must be implemented. Theoretically, in a perfectly presented case, correctly decided, there should be no doubt as to what should be done. But is this true?

Even under such a theoretical model rather significant problems may arise when the award is implemented. But the millennium has not yet arrived, and we know that cases are not always perfectly presented nor are the conclusions of the arbitrator al-

---

* Member, National Academy of Arbitrators, Washington, D.C.
** Director, Arbitration Services Department, United Auto Workers, Detroit, Mich.
*** Manager, Arbitration Proceedings Department, Labor Relations Staff, Ford Motor Co., Dearborn, Mich.
**** Director, Contract Administration Department, United Steelworkers of America, Pittsburgh, Pa.
***** Manager of Labor Relations, Bethlehem Steel Corp., Bethlehem, Pa.

ways clearly set forth, with due regard as to how that conclusion should be implemented.

I have made no survey, nor do I know of a grievance with respect to the implementation of awards. We can look forward today to having these matters developed and commented upon by our speakers.

The UAW View

MR. RAYMOND E. SHETTERLY: Voluntary grievance arbitration is an escape by the contesting parties from the consequences of their own failure to settle their differences. Common law courts have been found to be a costly and dilatory proceeding. Likewise, the resort to strike action over failure to settle such differences has not met with universal appeal. The parties have chosen the route of the "power of logic" over the route of the "logic of power" as the most sensible final step to grievance determination in the majority of our labor contracts. The process, being entirely voluntary in nature, is still on trial, and the major factor which will dictate its continued use is the confidence which the parties place in it. This implies not only an obligation on the parties to carefully investigate, evaluate, and prepare their cases, but it also implies a willingness of the parties to give dignity and meaning to the process by accepting the award in good faith, whether they agree with the award or not. The future, then, of labor arbitration depends on the competence and integrity of the advocates of the two parties as well as on the methods and techniques used by the arbitrator in his opinion to "sell" his award to the "losing" party and, of course, to insure that he has a "salable product."

Unquestionably, the arbitrators cannot be held responsible for most shortcomings in the practices of the various arbitration advocates, but they can be held accountable for the acceptability of their own awards. We are not unmindful of the fact that the advocate who loses an arbitration case is inclined to feel that the arbitrator has, under the guise of interpretation, engaged in "judicial legislation," but this is not the real problem when deciding acceptability. Most experienced arbitrators are as insulated against such excoriation as the football referee is to the criticisms he receives from the fans in attendance at the game. But where objective and significant censure now is appearing, it seems that this reproof must be taken into account if the institution is to retain its usefulness and/or acceptability.

What, then, needs examination? What are the areas of legitimate censure?

1. *Awards are too costly.* In this day of accelerated inflation, who can say what is too costly? I think the criticism goes not to the daily per diem, but rather to the number of days for which the arbitrator charges. Sometimes it defies credulity to accept as justifiable the number of days the arbitrator studies and prepares.

2. *Grievance arbitration is too time-consuming.* Here the complaint is justified, but the parties themselves in most instances are the major culprits.

3. *Availability of acceptable arbitrators.* Something should be worked out to permit so-called apprentice arbitrators to break in on cases that would, by agreement, be non-precedent-setting.

4. In writing an award, if the arbitrator sets forth in any degree of detail the position of one party, it would seem to us that he should be bound to set forth the position of the other party to the proceeding. Otherwise, it would surely appear to be an ex parte hearing.

5. Finally, to the subject of our particular problem, *the implementation of the award once it is received.* First, of course, the parties should both read the award with understanding and then accept its directive. The adverse influence on the general relationship of the parties which results from any attempt to circumvent or tamper with that award should, of course, lead to the obvious conclusion that the parties must take the award to be inviolate.

But what are the actual facts?

Item. In one case, an illustrious member of this Academy reinstated a discharged employee without back pay. The company contended that the arbitrator misstated one fact and it refused to comply with the award. For some unexplained reason, that employee is still discharged. I might add that the misstated fact alluded to by the company dealt with the question of whether a letter of suspension pending a decision was in fact a letter of discharge since the writer of that letter admitted under cross-examination that when he wrote the letter of suspension, he had already decided to convert the suspension to discharge after the "five day cooling-off period" imposed by the contract.

In discussing this item, it is almost unbelievable that the company would refuse to reinstate the grievant on the flimsy technicality raised by its legal department, but nevertheless it did. Apparently, if the arbitrator had placed quotation marks around the word "discharge" in referring to the disputed letter, or if he had referred to the letter as a suspension, the company would have viewed the matter differently. It is our judgment that the company's legal department established the "straw man" to justify the company's real position: that is, a blatant refusal to comply with the clear language of the reinstatement award. Our conclusion, then, must be that awards should be written with extreme care by the arbitrators to make sure that no technical flaw can be developed by either side to the arbitration proceedings.

Item. In another case, after an award on a subcontracting dispute upholding the union had been received, the company contended that a particular statement by the arbitrator, in his discussion but not in his award, about notification had somehow granted unusual rights for the future. It required another hearing with the arbitrator to straighten out that problem.

In discussing this item, it is our judgment that again the company placed a severe strain on credibility in order to make a case of an objective contention that the arbitrator somehow intended to change for them their negotiated obligations concerning notification to the union of anticipated subcontracting arrangements. They seized upon some observation in the body of the opinion, but not repeated in the award, and contended that this remark somehow made a meaningful distinction between a letter of notification and a letter of intent. Again we point out the necessity of examining opinions critically prior to their being mailed to the parties in order to eliminate any possibility of confusion and/or giving comfort to the losing party in the arbitration proceeding by some inadvertent reference that seemed logical at the time of writing but which could be seized upon by that losing party to try to make some "bricks" for the future out of the "straws of his losing efforts" in that particular proceeding.

Item. In still another case the arbitrator told the company that the failure to pay a Christmas bonus after years of past practice was in fact a bargainable issue and that the bonus could not be discontinued unilaterally. He remanded the matter to the parties with instructions to both sides to bargain the amount since in the past it had depended on a formula developed by the company according to its profit picture. The company then took the position that the award only obligated it to bargain—not to reach an agreement. A subsequent award by the same arbitrator ordered the company to use the last formula, since it refused even to discuss the profit picture with the union. The company completely ignored this last award.

In discussing this item, we can only suggest that the award in the first instance should have made clear that a failure to reach a negotiated agreement after the issue was clarified and remanded back to the parties would result in a second award upon the request of either party. The arbitrator did make it clear that the matter was bargainable and arbitrable in the first award, but he did not make it clear that the failure of the parties to negotiate a settlement would result in a final and binding arbitration award on the amount of the Christmas bonus. The arbitrator also made it clear in his second award that the failure of the company to provide the necessary data with which to negotiate the Christmas bonus formula used previously by the company was the cause of the breakdown in negotiations ordered by his first award, and in fact left him in the position of having no objective criteria upon which to establish a proper bonus in the dispute before him. Therefore he was forced, through necessity, to order the company to figure the disputed bonus based upon the same formula used in the most recent bonus prior to the Christmas period then in dispute. In spite of all this logic, however, the company based its refusal to carry out the second award on the specious claim that the arbitrator lost his authority simultaneously with the signing and mailing of the first award.

Item. In yet another case, an employee who was discharged for suspected but not proven theft was reinstated with full back pay, less, of course, the usual offset of earnings since the date of discharge. However, because of his lack of seniority standing in the company which paid these earnings, he was forced to work a night shift and all overtime that the senior employees declined. As a result, his total pay over the eight-week period, when measured against 14 weeks of lost wages as a result of his improper discharge, left him only $90.00 short. For the six weeks that he was without a job, the company was required to pay him only the $90.00, according to its interpretation of the award.

In discussing this item, we get into an area of not only mixed emotions but, we feel sure, mixed opinions as far as the arbitrators themselves are concerned. We are speaking now of the problem of lost earnings opportunity as a result of the imposition of an improper penalty. It is our judgment that in considering this area of the award, the arbitrators ought to address themselves only to the question of whether the discipline imposed by the company was proper, and not whether some form of discipline was called for. We understand the well-reasoned criteria on the one side of the coin that suggests caution as far as the correction of an improper penalty resulting in a so-called windfall to the employee; but we also call attention to the inequity created by the arbitrator when he goes overboard in his desire to prevent such so-called windfalls. The whole purpose, as we understand it, behind the process of voluntary arbitration is to search for the solution to a problem. In doing so, it seems to us that the award ought to nudge the parties themselves toward searching for their own solution in future cases of like nature. In the case of discipline, since management is the moving party, it would seem that it ought to be encouraged to make the proper disciplinary decision in the first place. If managements were thus faced a few times with awards containing this doctrine, it is our judgment that they would use more objective criteria, or practice a great deal more restraint, when imposing the original penalties. In many instances, if the company had imposed a more reasonable penalty or at least something less than discharge, the union might have accepted that penalty as being for just cause, thus saving the wear and tear on both the process of arbitration and the union treasury. When the company imposes discharge and it is determined by the arbitrator not to have been for just cause, it seems to us perfectly reasonable to question any offset in earnings during the period of the unreasonable discharge. We recognize immediately that this might create a problem with some arbitrators in those areas where the grievant's case is close to that line of demarcation between a discharge for just cause and one that is not for just cause and swing the scales against the grievant; but if we examine what is really at issue, we feel certain that this should create no particular problem. In other words, in discipline cases, one of the primary objectives as far as the future is concerned is to instill in management a desire to issue discipline fairly. That desire can best be instilled in managements, in our opinion, by giving them the necessary incentive to issue the proper discipline in the first place. If the members of this organization find our suggestions in this area unacceptable, then please consider the alternative: When writing your awards dealing with an offset in wages, make the offset on an hour-for-hour basis. Surely you must agree that if an employee loses a month's work as a result of an improper discharge, he should be paid for that month regardless of how much he earns after he acquires subsequent employment. We agree that the make-whole principle would apply to all fringe benefits, but as far as lost earnings are concerned, we believe that the usual damage principle does not apply. Rather, the contractual-relationship principle should apply in dealing with the matter of lost earnings.

Item. Finally, in a case involving the return of a number of foremen to the bargaining unit, the company permitted these ex-foremen to exercise bumping rights and displace unit employees from the higher priced unit jobs. When an award was handed down to the effect that the company violated the rights of the grievant employees, the company chose this time to raise numerous questions regarding the future before it would place the clear language of the award into effect.

In discussing this item, the arbitrator cannot be faulted in any manner. Our only point in raising it in this paper is to show that the companies, too, are mindful of the position in which the union is placed when a company flatly refuses to implement an award. It is our judgment that only because of this knowledge did the company in our item contend that it would not apply the award as the union stated it should be applied unless it received certain concessions for the future in return.

I hope our comments have not sounded too much like technical fault-finding with the arbitration process. They are not so intended. But you must be aware, we feel sure, that arbitration is the *quid pro quo* for the right to strike and, as such, in many instances was arrived at reluctantly as far as the union is concerned—reluctance mostly because of fears of inadequacy on our part and of management's so-called sovereignty. When these fears are sharpened and magnified by company refusal to properly implement an award, then the "venture of faith and hope" embarked upon by the union will eventually be regarded as a failure, and therefore it will request a return to direct confrontations including only the two parties.

We believe this would be a tragic error, but the fact remains that the process of arbitration will "self-destruct" unless an answer can be found to insure the proper implementation of the award, once it is issued. The reasons are manifest. The employees have voluntarily given up the right to settle grievances against the employer in a manner that they understood and where they had complete control of the end result. They have accepted, in return, a different way—one which they have been assured will be more beneficial as far as logic and cost in terms of man-hours lost are concerned. When they see management blithely accepting the results of grievances lost by the union and then arrogantly refusing to abide by the results of grievances won by the union, the conclusion is reached that they are the victims of the "Heads I win, tails you lose" attitude. We believe, then, that an arrangement should be insisted upon by all arbitrators that would commit both parties of an arbitration proceeding to be bound by the award unless they are able to have the award set aside through proper court action. When the union dislikes an award, it must either accept it or sue to vacate it; when the company dislikes an award, it simply fails and/or refuses to implement it. We hasten to make clear that this does not include the majority of companies, but it does include enough to make the problem burdensome. Generally speaking, the permanent umpireships, such as General Motors, accept the results of the awards in good faith, but far too many ad hoc relationships seek to avoid such good-faith acceptance. We hope that this body, with its vast capacity to evaluate and provide the answers to problems, can find an answer to this problem: that is, this abortion of justice taking place in certain areas in the name of impartial arbitration.

The Ford Experience

MR. ALEXANDER C. MEKULA: When Program Chairman Dick Mittenthal extended his gracious invitation to appear here today, we briefly discussed the subject of my paper. He was somewhat surprised to learn that the implementation of arbitration awards has been a relatively minor problem at Ford for a good number of years. And this is so despite the fact that the company has over 27 years of arbitration experience dealing with some 16 unions and involving thousands of decisions.

I should emphasize that there is a marked difference between the problems resulting from technical implementation and the problems sometimes resulting from the psychological trauma that an arbitration advocate, a labor relations administrator, or a plant manager experiences in first swallowing, then digesting, then implementing the "essential justice" provided by the arbitrator. While we have relatively little trouble with the former, the latter phenomenon is something else again. I should like to suggest that the disordered psychic state which accompanies the implementation of certain arbitration awards presents a tantalizing subject for a future Academy meeting. As a matter of fact, several of my colleagues have already expressed their willingness to undertake such a paper, provided that the meeting will be held in Hawaii, Pago Pago, or Puerto Rico revisited.

Not only has Ford Motor Co. implemented thousands of arbitration decisions dealing with some 16 unions, but I should also point out that these decisions were the product of 30 or so arbitrators. These numbers are cited here for two reasons:

First, I am well aware of the perils associated with generalizing from specific situations in the labor relations field. The great differences between the various industries and between employees and employers in a given industry with respect to such matters as nature of the service or product, operating conditions, union organizational background, and even personalities of the arbitrators, tend to make an industry's problems unique. While I will deal essentially with the Ford experience, I believe that the figures I have cited give me greater license to slip in a few generalizations.

Second—and this may come as a bit of a shock to some of our arbitrator hosts today—many arbitration advocates (especially management advocates) are by nature kind, sensitive, warm people who also view as an important part of their job the dispensing of "essential justice." Of course, advocates are also known to be pragmatic. Therefore, by referring to some 30-odd arbitrators, I can protect the guilty from unnecessary embarrassment which might—through some subliminal process—make the implementation of some future award more or less of a problem.

The first part of my paper, which can be subtitled "Incongruous Decisions Made by Some of the 30 Arbitrators That I Have Known," will deal with some specific instances where the implementation of the award caused management extracurricular problems. The second part of my paper deals with that naughty five-letter word which has caused many a management advocate to emote for periods ranging from ad nauseum to ad infinitum—*dicta*. That part of my paper received a ready-made subtitle from the Program Chairman when he suggested that I might address myself to "What Difficulties Are Presented by Dicta in the Arbitrator's Opinion."

One of the worst implementation problems that Ford has faced over the years is one which placed it in an operational dilemma. The company was confronted with two arbitration awards ordering that certain work be assigned to two different skilled trades, each represented by a different union. As a matter of convenience, I'll refer to the unions as A and B and the arbitrators responsible for the awards as 1 and 2. I should point out that these designations are purely symbolic and are not intended as an indication of my opinion as to the relative merit of those involved.

Union A protested work being assigned to members of Union B. The company continued to assign the work to members of Union B pursuant to the award given by Arbitrator 1. Union A proceeded to arbitration and then to the federal district court, seeking enforcement of the award it received from Arbitrator 2. Union B moved to intervene and its motion was granted. Later, it was stipulated by the parties that the court should take no action until a decision was rendered under the AFL-CIO internal disputes plan. Since the decision under the union's internal procedures resulted in an award against it, Union A finally stipulated to the dismissal of its action in federal court.

In this particular case the company had no objection to the resolution of the conflict under the union's internal procedures system. However, this should be viewed as the exception rather than the rule. In this case it did not make very much difference which trade was assigned to the work; in many other cases it does.

While the case represents a single instance at Ford, the generalization which I seek to draw from it is also applicable to a number of arbitration awards in industries other than auto. Too often there is a tendency among arbitrators to view jurisdictional disputes confronting industrial employers as solely interunion or intra-union problems, with management having no interest in the final result other than to see that the job is covered. To be sure, there are instances where this may be true, but more often than not, management's interest is totally separate from and paramount to .that of the disputing unions.

Arbitrators should give far more serious consideration to the third possibility—that neither contending trade has an exclusive right to the work. Most of us here would undoubtedly agree that unjustifiable or artificial lines of demarcation between classifications of employees can lead to gross inefficiency and featherbedding. Absent any clear language in the parties' agreement to the contrary, the arbitrator should recognize that it is probably in everybody's best interest to resist any encroachment on management's right to assign work in the most efficient manner with full utilization of available skills.

Ford has experienced a far more common problem with respect to the implementation of arbitration decisions. It occurs when arbitrators decide to dispose of cases before them by laying down certain ground rules presumably calculated to resolve a particular grievance or grievances, and then remanding the cases back to the parties to develop their factual determinations in line with the general conclusion of the award.

Remanded cases are sometimes accompanied by a thought-provoking phrase such as, "The parties should reexamine their earlier positions and attempt to adjust the grievances." Still another favorite interim disposition is: "The parties agree in principle, but strongly dispute the facts. The case must be remanded to the parties for investigation and determination of facts and settlement of the matter in accordance with undisputed principle." Then the arbitrator probably breathes a sigh of relief as he advises the parties, with a tone of solemn paternalism, "I will retain jurisdiction of these cases until I am notified as to the outcome of the parties' negotiations." As you may recall, in his address to this distinguished Academy several years ago, Peter Seitz strongly supported the use of the interim decision by arbitrators.[1]

I, for one, am opposed generally to the partial or temporary resolutions of arbitration cases. My feelings in this regard are more akin to those expressed by the late Jesse Frieden in his appearance before the Academy in 1964 when he said:

> ". . . what the parties expect and what they ask an arbitrator to provide is a final resolution of their grievance, of their difference; not a temporary one, not a partial one, not an interim one, but a final one; and I submit to you that this finality is itself a quality of worth, for it accomplishes a most useful purpose—it brings a difference to an end—the very purpose that the parties intended the arbitration procedure to   provide." [2]

It has been our experience at Ford that interim decisions, in nearly every instance, prove unsatisfactory to the parties and foster discord between them. The very things in issue, most often factual disputes, remain unresolved, and the parties merely find themselves where they started—haggling over the facts. The consequence is usually a prolongation of the dispute and further friction between the parties. There is a great temptation for the parties, in desperation, to engage in mere horse-trading

---

[1] Seitz, "Problems of the Finality of Awards, or Functus Officio and All That," in *Labor Arbitration—Perspectives and Problems,* Proceedings of the 17th Annual Meeting, National Academy of Arbitrators, ed. Mark L. Kahn (Washington: BNA Books, 1964) , 165.

[2] Frieden, "Remedies in Arbitration: Discussion," in *Labor Arbitration—Perspectives and Problems* at 203.

with the hope that the same problem will not arise in the foreseeable future.

From management's point of view these interim arbitration decisions are particularly disconcerting because in all but discipline cases, the burden of proof rests with the union. If the grievance has not been proved, it should be denied; it's as simple as that. All too often the interim award encourages trial grievances and provides the other party with an opportunity to rehabilitate a weak position or a losing case. In short, such decisions frustrate the state of finality which arbitration was designed to provide the parties.

As a backdrop for my discussion *re dictar,* I should like to point out to you that it is known by other names as well. In fact, one of my union friends, and I won't quote him exactly, likens it to a common barnyard commodity. His colorful reference to dicta also provides us with some insight into what he and others in the union may think of dicta in an arbitration award.

At Ford we employ a fast rule in the implementation of arbitration decisions with respect to dicta. We simply instruct personnel who are responsible for the administration of our labor agreement to ignore it. However, although this measure is generally adhered to, the problems which do emanate from dicta are not so easily dismissed.

The one type of problem which the parties in general have experienced with respect to dicta involves the generation of grievances by the dicta that frequently appear in arbitration decisions. It is frustrating, to say the least, to find yourself grappling with grievances arising out of decisions which were assumed to have laid to rest a particular issue. This problem is relatively common in labor relations; almost any time an arbitrator flavors his decision with dicta, he's sowing the seeds for new grievances. However, with my allotted time growing short, I will not dwell on the point, important as it may be.

The aspect of dicta I would like to discuss with you in a little more detail is the impact dicta can and do have on the parties' contract negotiations.

Consider this simple fact situation involving a provision that

Ford has in its agreements with several unions. Under our agreements, an employee who absents himself from work for five scheduled working days may be terminated after another five days upon being sent a registered letter to report—unless, of course, it is not possible for him to respond. In one particular case an employee who was absent from work for the aforementioned number of days was sent a registered letter. Upon his failure to report, he was terminated. Subsequently, he filed a grievance in which he invoked a defense that is most commonly used by the union or an employee. He contended that he did, in fact, respond to the company's letter by telephone within the required five-day period. At arbitration, the company substantiated the fact that a registered letter was sent to the aggrieved's last known address. Also, the company produced its logs of incoming hourly employee telephone calls covering the period in question. These were accepted as proof that no telephone call was received from the aggrieved. The aggrieved employee volunteered that he may have placed a call beyond the time allowed by the contractual provision and that it was made to the wrong company representative. On the basis of all the evidence, the arbitrator issued a decision denying the employee's grievance. It would appear that no company should encounter the slightest difficulty in implementing such a favorable decision or have any other problem with it. Right? Wrong! Unfortunately, the arbitrator who decided that case felt compelled to offer what we may refer to as a few "pearls of wisdom." Pearl No. 1: "It seems most unfortunate that this relatively slight degree of negligence should place in peril the job equity the aggrieved has established over 16 years." Pearl No. 2: "Alternatively it is for the parties to devise some improvement in the administrative procedure that will eliminate the contention that a call was or was not made. For example, a tape of phone calls such as this."

Of course, the company did not introduce the fact that the employee in question had a deplorable disciplinary record and was a habitual absentee who had a short time earlier placed himself in the position of being the recipient of similar termination notices on three different occasions. In these instances, however, he had conveniently responded on the very last day permissible.

Actually, the import of that decision went far beyond the mere implementation of the arbitrator's award. The aforementioned dicta gave birth to a cause célèbre and became the basis for a serious demand by the union at the national negotiating table concerning the long-established quit provision. The company was charged with invoking technicalities to rid itself of high-seniority employees. In addition, the union demanded that a system of taping phone calls suggested by the arbitrator should be instituted for the protection of the employees.

After a countless number of valuable hours at the negotiating table, the union was finally convinced that the provision (already one of the most liberal in the industry) was not employed in a harsh fashion. An example cited by the union of a high-seniority employee's being terminated was found to be the exception. The record was replete with instances of high-seniority employees' being reinstated following their terminations under the contractual provision in question. Moreover, the union was advised of the fact that the taping of telephone calls was not only an expensive proposition, but was also unduly burdensome. When one considers that an employee had five days within which to place such a call, it is not unlikely that a labor relations representative could spend some 100 hours listening to tapes in order to determine whether an alleged call was, in fact, made by a particular employee. I'm sure most of you know that the labor relations field is not so barren that it is unable to provide the parties with a surfeit of difficult problems. Additional problems induced by an arbitrator's advice are wholly unappreciated.

I have come to the conclusion that the parties and the arbitrator should strongly resist any tendency that would give the arbitrator pivotal importance in their relationship. In my judgment, the examples I have submitted for your consideration indicate that some arbitrators—deliberately or otherwise—place themselves in such a position. All too often this leads to the arbitrator's effecting some significant changes in the parties' relationship either by suggesting or telling the parties what their agreement *should* provide or by laying down extremely broad dicta heavily laden with his own notions of the parties' commitments.

Personally, I am convinced that no third party can construct good agreements for a company and a union. No arbitrator, regardless of how familiar he might be with the parties and their problems, is really close enough to make their agreements for them. No arrogance is intended by this statement, but I might add that I do subscribe to the concept that arbitration is vital in labor relations.

Of course, for my part, I admire the arbitrator who has either the humility or wisdom, or a touch of both, to respect the positions of the parties and refrain from supplying unwanted observations. It is, unfortunately, naive to expect that in every instance the arbitrator will listen to the evidence and arguments of both parties and base his award only on these items. All too often the arbitrator fashions his own theories for the basis of his award, and these theories frequently collide with principles long established between the parties, or they generate new issues for future arbitrations. Probably the best defense in the long run against an arbitrator's intrusion and inventiveness is an alert, perceptive, and thoroughly knowledgeable advocate who is prepared to meet all possible theories in a case.

It is essential, of course, that the answer the parties seek can be arrived at from the facts and on the theories presented at the hearing. And the arbitrator must understand that the parties are seeking an answer in a specific fact situation, and any dicta or advice beyond the scope of that situation would be best received over a martini after the decision is rendered.

On reflection, one of the reasons I think the implementation of awards has remained a relatively minor problem at Ford is because Ford and the unions with which it deals have met the test stated by Harry Shulman when he wrote:

> "The important question is not whether the parties agree with the award but rather whether they accept it, not resentfully, but cordially and willingly. Again, it is not to be expected that each decision will be accepted with the same degree of cordiality. But general acceptance and satisfaction is an attainable ideal." [3]

This test certainly assumes that the arbitrator's final judgment is the product of reason applied on the basis of the standards and the authority the parties entrusted to him. To the extent

---

[3] Shulman, "Reason, Contract, and Law in Labor Relations," 68 *Harv. L. Rev.* 1019 (1955).

that we at Ford have been able to have the arbitrators understand this view, we have been able to minimize the problems discussed today. The Ford arbitrators generally have responded positively to the views expressed by both company and union spokesmen concerning the parties' desire for finality in arbitration. They have used their remand authority sparingly and they have, for the most part, refrained from fattening their opinions with that starchiest of all food for thought—*obiter dicta*.

The Steelworker's View

MR. BEN FISCHER: The subject which we have been asked to discuss is a little complicated and so elusive that the best I can do is to make some interim remarks and remand it back for some future resolution.

I am really tempted, faced with this distinguished group of arbitrators as well as leaders of management and labor, to talk about what's wrong with arbitrators, how inexpert they are, and how often they goof. But I hesitate to do this because for many years I have dreaded the day when the Academy would be so rude as to schedule a session on how inexpert labor and management are in their negotiations, and how extensively they goof in developing their collective bargaining agreements which we then impose upon arbitrators to interpret very strictly. So I'm going to try to be kind today, even though many of you may think it's out of character.

The arbitration process is a part of the labor-management relationship. It will rise or fall on the basis of the performance of labor and management, both in collective bargaining and in contract administration. Arbitrators can help; arbitrators should help; arbitrators can sometimes make things more difficult. But the essential responsibility, I am afraid, rests with the representatives of labor and with the members of management, and this we cannot evade.

The arbitration process as it has grown up, and as we know it, has run into some difficulty. Some people call it trouble; some people call it distress. Whatever it is, there is reason to be concerned.

Arbitration is costly, as is everything else, including this hotel.

I hope Alcoa takes some of the results of these enormous prices and puts them on the bargaining table a few months from now.

There is difficulty—very real difficulty—because of delay, and delay is not uncommon. There is delay within management in the decision-making process; there is delay within the union and its decision-making process. There is delay in the court system; there's delay in the legislative system in our country, in our states, and in our communities. Perhaps because of the tremendous complexity of modern organization and modern relationships, delay is being built into almost all portions of our life. There's even delay in getting from one place to another because of traffic and scheduling difficulties. But delay in the arbitration process is placing very great strains on that process, and delay in implementation of arbitration awards is increasing that strain.

To some extent the arbitration process is in trouble because it tends to become removed from the everyday shop problems. We're getting arbitrators who are experts; we're getting labor people who are experts and management people who are experts —and as they gain more expertise, they become more removed from the real problem as it is understood by the worker and as it is understood by foremen.

There is an alienation, not only between the average union member and the arbitration process, but between the average supervisor, who has to run a plant or some portion thereof, and the arbitration process.

Many people take it for granted that the labor-management contract establishes justice—what is right and what is wrong. I submit that it doesn't do so at all. There's nothing right about paying time and a half for overtime; it's just the rate that's provided in the contracts. There's nothing right in saying that if you're absent for five days or three days or two hours, you'll be penalized. That's just a rule, established one way or another, and everybody has his own essentially self-serving concept of what he would like justice to be.

Thus, since it is the arbitration process that dramatically portrays what the contract really does provide, the arbitration process bears much of the burden for the inevitable shortcomings of the labor-management collective bargaining process and what the resultant contract inevitably creates.

So the parties have a very real problem.

I don't know how much we're going to solve the problem of cost. A local union that brings 18 representatives to an arbitration case where two would do well or better should hardly complain about the fee of the arbitrator. And there are other phases of cost.

Some arbitrators charge too much money. But that depends on how one defines too much money—a difficult concept for us as we are in the first of a series of collective bargaining negotiations with major industries. I suppose that too much money is the amount of money you pay, and too little money is the amount of money you receive.

The parties and the arbitrators, and the arbitration community, can do a great deal about delay. They must do a great deal about delay, and they're not going to do it just by making speeches about it or by doing things the way we've always done them. I think we have to be innovative, imaginative, and bolder, but that's not the subject of this morning's discussion.

We can do something about moving the arbitration process closer to the people, and it is something we should bear in mind. But again, that's not quite the subject of this morning's discussion.

The fact that people, faced with a problem that affects them, be they management people or union people, invariably seek some kind of justice as they see it, is something that is just going to continue. In no instance can man possibly establish standards of justice to govern arbitration that will be acceptable to everybody at all times. It is with this in mind that it seems to me that you ought to do what you can to mitigate the strain and distress inherent in the arbitration process.

Insofar as the implementation of arbitration awards is concerned, it should not contribute to delay; it should not contribute to the real cost to the parties and to the grievant and to their distress. To the extent that implementation problems help to create confusion and a lack of understanding of what the process is all about, and to the extent that implementation contributes still further to the frustration of the whole process of grievance handling, we have a problem, and we ought to try to improve our performance.

I don't know whether I'm right or not (I'm kind of like an arbitrator; they never know whether they're right or not, but I assume they do the best they can), but I have the feeling that despite many remarks made here, the present permanent umpire system works pretty well. That's not where we run into our problem. More problems arise in the ad hoc field, which creates the essential climate in the labor-management community.

I suspect it is of very great importance that if one thinks in terms of how to improve the thousands of individual ad hoc contract situations, in industry after industry, involving many, many unions and many, many companies, it is well to start with what kind of tone and leadership is provided by the major situations where there are usually permanent umpire setups. It is in that context that I speak, and that's one reason I'm not doing much castigating of arbitrators.

Arbitrators can help to fashion the process of implementation by the nature of the award that they issue—by the way in which they compose and organize it. It should not be necessary to have second awards. But we do have interim awards and awards that remand back to the parties. We also have second arbitrations where the award may be clear, but one party or the other doesn't understand it the way the arbitrator does, or the way the other one thinks it ought to be understood.

It seems to me that arbitrators can make a contribution. They can do so by being fairly emphatic; they can do so in the conduct of their hearings by trying to make sure that they have before them the kind of facts and the kind of information, the kind of guidance from the parties, that will enable them to finally dispose of the issue at hand.

But I recognize that the extent to which an arbitrator can do that is limited. I know that in one major corporation, an arbitrator sitting here in the audience today started asking the attorney for the corporation too many questions. There was a recess because this attorney didn't know anything about the case; he was just reading from notes that had been furnished to him, and he was most embarrassed by any effort of the arbitrator to probe his mind—because his mind was not probeable. He had come well prepared, not to answer the arbitrator's questions, but to say only what he had been told to say.

That's an extreme case, but in many situations an arbitrator can get only limited help, and he has to decide at some point that there's no point in going much further in his probing because he isn't going to get anywhere anyway. Nevertheless, somehow he must figure out this case or do a job not quite as precise and expert as he should like to do.

The essential responsibility, in my judgment, for proper implementation of arbitration awards rests with the companies and the unions. It rests in the first place with the collective bargaining process, and it rests in the second place with their attitude toward the process and toward what you do with it once you do get the award.

In the collective bargaining process, it seems to me, it is the obligation of the company and the union to set the kinds of standards and the kinds of guidance that are going to minimize the perplexities and the difficulties of implementation. This is not always easy, and it's getting to be pretty rough. Union leadership in collective bargaining, and even management leadership, is not very easy, and is not going to get any easier. This does lead to some temptation to slough things off, and this is something we're going to have to resist increasingly.

I don't know whether I should say this here, but I think most of the arbitrators know some of our secrets. We not only have the situation to which we always refer where arbitrators slough things off and say, "I'm not going to solve this problem because I don't know how"; labor and management have this problem, too. We kind of slough things off, and we remand to the arbitrators. We do it on a wholesale basis. We don't describe, in most of our agreements, what is just cause for discharge. We could, but for lots of reasons we don't generally do it. And when we don't do it, what we're really saying is that through our administrative procedures we will try to develop the skin and the sinews around this bare bone of just cause or proper cause—but if worse comes to worst we've got some arbitrators, and gradually, over a period of 5, 10, or 15 years and a few hundred thousand dollars' worth of fees, they'll let us know what this means.

That's just a dramatic example. I can take you through any steel, can, or aluminum agreement, on issue after issue, and show the precise degree to which the parties—these expert negotiators who know all the answers because they're close to the picture; they're on top of everything—will say, "The hell with it; it's getting late. Let's put some gobbledygook words in there and somehow something will happen some day, but meanwhile we'll have an agreement and we'll be able to go to sleep."

So it's not only arbitrators who engage in remanding. The parties do, too, but we do it in a much more refined and sophisticated and expert fashion. I think we have to resist this. We're not going to avoid it entirely because there does come a time when you've got to make an agreement. There's one advantage arbitrators have; they never have to make decisions. They can put them off day after day and week after week.

That's one luxury we don't enjoy. There comes a time when we've got to make a decision or else those plants are going to shut down or they're not going to reopen, whichever the case may be. It's a costly kind of delay. So in many respects we're even more tempted than the arbitrator to resort to this remanding device.

I think that arbitrators, on the other hand, can do a good deal more to ease this process of implementation. They can do so by the nature of their awards, or the way in which they address the parties and deal with them, perhaps by anticipating and trying to avoid trouble. I'm not sure how much of that can be done in any meaningful, useful way. The arbitrator has the tools that are given him. He has the contract; he didn't write it. And with all due respect, I don't know of any arbitration dicta that have influenced us or the fellows we deal with in collective bargaining, but unbeknownst to me they may have. We have our share of dicta from arbitrators—and if you pick Peter Seitz as your arbitrator, you not only get dicta, you're going to get poetry along with it!

I want to deal very briefly with a few areas in which implementation has developed into a very real problem, as I see it. One is the notion that a company can violate a contract and get slapped on the wrist, and if it violates the contract a second time, it will be slapped, presumably, on the other wrist. I don't know what the arbitrator does with the third violation; he runs out of wrists, so he can, perhaps, slap them elsewhere.

I don't know to what extent this is the fault of the arbitrator. I suspect it is more specifically the fault of the collective bargaining process, and this peculiar device whereby management agrees to something but agrees in such a way that if they don't do what they agree to, nothing is likely to happen. There are several outstanding contract areas in which this kind of thing happens.

Management says: "Foremen won't work." And when they do work, management says: "That's wrong. We're going to look into this and do something about it." They do, and the foreman is told not to work—and this keeps going on and on until you go to arbitration, and then you've got a new kind of remedy. Now the arbitrator says that the foreman shouldn't work.

And the way you implement this is by giving the foreman a copy of the award, and if he can read he knows he violated the contract. Perhaps management takes him aside, if he can't read, and explains it to him. But nothing happens. If you think it's a great deal of satisfaction to a union member to say, "We won!" when it costs us $1,200 to get this little lecture to the foreman, you are quite wrong. People are not that concerned with this sort of elusive victory.

I don't know that this is the arbitrator's problem; I think it is the parties' problem. It seems to me that in responsible collective bargaining at this late date, if you're going to say that there is a rule, then you ought to say that there should be some penalty for its violation. When a member of the union violates a rule, there's a penalty; there's not much of a problem involved in that. When management violates a rule, there ought to be a penalty, and it is not primarily—in my judgment—the responsibility of the arbitrator to fashion such a remedy. If he can do so, God bless him—and I'll help him if I can—but I'm not going to lose sight of the fact that it is the contract itself that really fashions the remedy.

This is not just a moral problem. It is a very practical problem because this sort of thing will alienate the worker from the arbitration process—and even to some extent from the collective bargaining process itself.

If you want to develop that kind of alienation, this is one good way to help do it. Set up the rule and provide no remedy that is meaningful. And this is the source, in my experience, of very great concern. As the work force becomes more sophisticated, more knowledgeable, and where more and more of our members get to be lawyers without portfolio—and we surely have a lot of them and I'm one—this becomes more and more the problem. So in terms of the validity of the process we're talking about—its acceptability and its durability—it seems to me very important that management understands that rules that are violated must lead to some kind of penalty.

Then we have this growing monstrosity: You make whole the employee who was fired improperly or was suspended for a long period of time. And how do you do that? You pay him what he would have received from the company less what he did get from other unrelated employment. This is a humdinger. How it all came about I don't know; all I know is that it's here, and I don't want, at this late date, to waste your time by attributing blame.

This has become an intolerable circumstance. Let me give you just some of the reasons. One is that it puts a premium on the guy who can find some way to make money in a manner that is not recorded. Then you have the question: "What are the outside earnings?" And what do you do about the moonlighter? We've had such problems. One distinguished arbitrator here had precisely this problem—"I always had two jobs." As a matter of fact, the man got fired because he had two jobs, and the arbitrator put him back to work. Now what do you deduct?

Then what about the fellow who doesn't have two jobs; he has only one and a quarter jobs. What do you deduct? What about the fellow who runs a gas station or owns a little grocery store or has other means of earning money? Just what is it that you're deducting? So you have very practical problems.

And then you have another very real problem. You don't make him whole. You never make a discharged employee whole by putting him back to work. In this day and age, when workers are developing dignity and status in the community and in their family, and you operate almost in an industrial goldfish bowl, you can't make him whole. He was offended; he was embarrassed; his family was embarrassed. "I saw your husband the other day. Isn't he working? What's the matter?" Do you reply, "He was fired"? Or, "He's ill"? Or, what do you do to avoid the stigma? How do you make that whole? What do you do about the guy who loses his car, whose TV is picked up, who has to borrow money and pay interest, who loses his home? We've had those cases. How do you make him whole?

I don't think you can tolerate this kind of thing any longer. You're not dealing with the working man of 30 years ago, who lived in a little hut or hovel and perhaps had one Sunday suit. You're dealing with a different breed of people. You're dealing, if you will, with a relatively affluent society, and a society in which the worker today treasures his dignity and his peace of mind. And why not?

The time has come to correct this horrible inequity contractually, through collective bargaining—and I don't plead here with the arbitrators to save our necks. I hope we don't need you for this, and if we needed you, you wouldn't be available anyway. Labor has to face up to the fact that it must extract from management a termination of this "less deductions" baloney. You can't really make the wrongfully penalized employee whole, no matter what you do, so at least give him the few pennies or the few dollars that are involved instead of adding insult to injury.

And then, I think parties must have the proper respect for arbitration awards. I'll tell you what I mean by that. We're all pretty smart; the fellows we deal with are pretty smart. We know how to chisel; we know how to evade; we know how to create all kinds of gimmicks. If this whole process is to be wholesome and healthy in its development and strengthening, and consistent with our whole democratic system, parties have to accept an arbitration award in fact and in full. They ought to put their minds to work, now that the arbitrator (that nut!) did this ridiculous thing, as to how to abide by his award by really restoring the situation to what it was before, instead of devising some new gimmicks to add oil to this fire. And it's being done.

Every time you hire a nice, young, well-educated fellow who wants to become vice president in four years instead of 40, he's going to put his mind to work on that. These men are well trained; I have respect for our educational process. It surely teaches young people how to be chiselers! And it surely teaches young people how to be "wise guys." It's up to responsible management, and in some cases responsible labor leadership—it's not all one-sided— to see to it that arbitration awards are accepted in good faith and in good grace, without putting to work a whole chain of: "How are we going to get around this one?"

That doesn't mean—and I don't want to be misunderstood— that management or labor doesn't have the right to say, "Well, that's the award, but we may try this same case again." I don't advocate trying cases over and over again, but sometimes you *do* try a case again. Of course, when it gets to be again, and again, and again, and again, it gets to be kind of irritating. But under reasonable circumstances a second crack, when you perhaps put a little more steam behind it and a little more expertise, may be in order.

The "sore loser" kind of thing is not doing any of us any good. It's having a very unfortunate effect, and it is one of the reasons for disenchantment with the arbitration process. I daresay if you could somehow dig deeply enough, it's one reason why we hear that the workers are rebellious and don't accept contracts, and so on. I think these things mesh together. It is a total situation of no faith in what is going on. The good-faith efforts of all of us are urgently needed.

Finally, I want to talk about the computer. If there is one thing that's screwing up the arbitration process, it's the computer. I don't know of any computers that can implement arbitration awards, and more and more companies have fired everybody except the computer. As a consequence, when they have to make some manual calculations, there's just nobody around any more to make them. We therefore find that months and months go by and the workers don't get what the arbitrators said they should get. Nobody is arguing about the facts, but somebody has got to make the damned calculation and there's nobody working at it any more, except the few who run computers.

Somehow we have to resolve this; I don't know how. I don't think you're going to abandon the computers and you're not going to make them that much smarter. So we have to find some simplified methods of paying off promptly—maybe not with the same precision that ordinarily we have been accustomed to call for—or some other device. Maybe every company will have to have someone in charge of doing what the computer can't do, so that he's available with these ancient instruments like pencils, pens, paper, and things of that sort, to carry out arbitration awards.

This is a matter of very great distress to us, and I don't know what an arbitrator can do. You can go back to him and say, "They didn't pay us," and the company will say, "That's right, we haven't." The arbitrator says, "Pay!" but that's what he said in the first place, so he isn't really adding anything to it. He can say, "Pay immediately!" But, still, who is around to make the calculations?

Finally, may I close on this note. This whole arbitration process, its implementation, and various things I've been referring to, are the responsibility in part of the arbitration community. I think you have to take them seriously. You must address yourselves to them as individuals and as groups.

I think these things are the responsibility of the management community. But I have no illusions. The essential responsibility is the responsibility of labor leadership.

There is a new myth that's grown up in this country among a lot of people that somehow arbitration was created either by arbitrators or by management which wanted to take away the workers' right to strike. That has not been my experience.

Arbitration is something that was developed as a result of the struggles, the strikes, and the insistence of great and powerful unions. It was imposed upon management, and then, one way or another, some people created this profession of arbitration which, in turn, produced this Academy.

The revitalization of the arbitration process is essentially going to have to come from labor. I say this not only because this is where the necessity arises, but also because I'd rather have it that way. I don't trust management, not because they're not nice fellows, but because they're not in the business of making labor-management relationshps work in the interests of the workers. That just isn't their business. That's the business of unions and union leadership. If this revitalization and a program to remove much of the source of current alienation are to be successful, in a manner which is compatible with the interests of the workers and the progress of unionism and of labor in this country, then that leadership is going to have to come from labor, including the top leadership of American labor.

It's time that the leadership of American labor understands that this is a matter of very high priority and not just some off-shoot, technical problem that does not require all of the imaginativeness and all of the initiative and all of the militancy and power of the labor movement. Some of the things I'm talking about, and many things I haven't talked about, aren't going to be solved merely by intellectual persuasion. They're going to be solved mostly in the same way problems have been solved over the years—with the strength and ingenuity, the intelligence and determination of organized labor.

Personal Observations on Implementation Problems

MR. GEORGE A. MOORE, JR.: Last May, when I learned of this opportunity to speak on the implementation of arbitration awards before this body consisting of the nation's renowned arbitrators, I undertook the assignment with relish. I did so because after nearly two decades of representing the managements of companies as diverse as the Bethlehem Steel Corp. and the Pennsylvania Railroad, I was, I thought, the possessor of not just a few wounds inflicted by various Academy members in the form of adverse awards with subsequent implementation problems. As a consequence, this occasion appeared to provide an excellent opportunity for me to turn the tables and experience the pleasure derived from that old Biblical exhortation best stated as, "It's better to give than to receive." I was also sure, with respect to this subject at least, of the inapplicability of the universal excuse of arbitrators; that is, the fault of the decision does not lie with the arbitrator but with the parties, all represented by able counsel, who were responsible for the poorly drafted and highly ambiguous contract provision in dispute.

In initially sorting my thoughts on past arbitration awards, I must admit that I somewhat hastily concluded that difficulties in implementing arbitration awards occurred frequently and, furthermore, that these difficulties were generally attributable to less than judicious work by the arbitrator involved. Further investigation revealed that this initial judgment was less than circumspect and resulted from certain rather vividly remembered experiences requiring extremely imaginative efforts on my part to comply with what, at the time, appeared to be exceedingly abstract or obtuse decisions. As a result of that initial thinking, I was quite unprepared to discover, after a review of the more than 4,700 grievances which have been arbitrated by Bethlehem Steel Corp. and its union associates since 1942, how infrequently situations have arisen where the company has had actual difficulty in implementing a particular arbitration award. Of course, this newly formed opinion may have been unduly influenced by the fact that at least 75 percent of the awards rendered were, without question, clear, concise, and unambiguous—that is, they all concluded with the phrase, "This grievance is denied."

As an aside, I might note that even with respect to at least a few of those denied grievances, our victory has been somewhat bittersweet. This irony has occurred because of an occasional penchant by the arbitrator to burden his decision with unnecessary grievance-generating dicta. A good illustration of this point was a recent Bethlehem arbitration award involving a claim by an employee that he should have been assigned to work on a particular day when his job had been left vacant. The issue, as presented at the hearing to the arbitrator, was a rather narrow one, namely, whether the seniority provisions in the agreement supported the employee's claim that the job had to be filled. The arbitrator, in denying the grievance, found that there had not been any violation of the seniority provisions by management's refusal to fill the job. This, of course, was a very acceptable conclusion from the company's standpoint. Unfortunately, the umpire, in his conclusion, continued on in a rather gratuitous vein and noted that if the grievant had raised a past-practice claim under another provision in the agreement, the outcome of the arbitration decision might have been different. Without belaboring the point, this sort of unasked-for dicta is, of course, quite disturbing to the management in the light of the already proven ability of our union associates and employees to generate substantial grievance litigation without assistance. In fact, such speculation on the part of the arbitrator is quite harmful to the successful disposition of a problem.

An examination of those remaining cases which had resulted in decisions adverse to the company's announced position at hearing also quickly revealed that, with but few exceptions, implementation problems were minimal. This latter discovery has prompted me to conclude and suggest here that Bethlehem has indeed been fortunate because it has been graced by an honor roll of arbitrators who have, with but rare lapses, done a magnificent job in examining those controversies presented to them for consideration and then issued decisions which, although calling in some instances for remedial or affirmative actions, have taken into consideration the practical aspects of the day-to-day working relationship of the parties. I also believe that some credit for this record must also go to enlightened union and management leadership with a mutual goal of solving problems and not creating more.

This is not to say, however, that we have had a total absence of problems when implementing arbitration awards. Thus, I am able, in spite of our fine past record, to touch briefly upon several of the implementation difficulties that Bethlehem has experienced over the years, even with decisions rendered by men of such stature and capability as Ralph Seward, Irving Bernstein, Ben Aaron, Lewis Gill, Bill Simkin, Rolf Valtin, and the late Scotty Crawford.

Before reviewing those award-implementation problems, I think it would be helpful initially to note for background purposes that Bethlehem has, for years, utilized a permanent umpire arbitration system as provided for in our principal collective bargaining agreements covering shipbuilding and steelmaking operations. Under these agreements, the authority of our various arbitrators has generally been expressed in rather broad terms; that is, they have been given wide latitude to apply and interpret the provisions of our agreements as long as these provisions are not altered. Furthermore, the scope of our arbitrators' authority runs the entire range of the agreement with respect to subject matter and, as a consequence, covers such varied topics as crew sizes, contracting, incentives, safety, and vacation scheduling. Thus, the subjects susceptible to arbitration in the Bethlehem agreements are far more numerous than, for example, those arbitral subjects found in the electrical industry agreements of General Electric or Westinghouse.

Having given you this brief background résumé with respect to Bethlehem's arbitration history and experience, I will now review several problems which we have had in award implementation.

The first of our award-implementation trouble spots—and probably the most universally faced from an employer's standpoint—occurs when the suspension or discharge of an employee is overturned and the company is directed to reinstate the suspended employee and to make him whole. Representative of questions that can arise where the arbitrator's award and the contract are silent as to what constitutes making a grievant whole are the following:

1. Should earnings from other sources of employment during the suspension period be used to reduce back-pay liability?

2. Should unemployment compensation be used as an offset?

3. Should a poor past history of absenteeism be projected forward into the suspension period to mitigate the employer's liability? If so, how?

4. Should "make whole pay" include missed overtime earnings, loss of incentive performance payments, and other similar somewhat speculative earnings opportunities?

At least one of these questions recently proved to be very troublesome at Bethlehem even though we have developed extensive arbitral *stare decisis* in this area. Illustrative of this is a discharge case which was arbitrated at one of our West Coast plants. The grievant had been discharged for excessive absenteeism. Subsequently the arbitrator set the discharge aside—not on the merits of the case but on the basis of a procedural misadventure by the plant management. The award, when rendered 15 months after the discharge, directed plant management to reinstate the grievant and make him whole for any loss of earnings.

As might be expected, the union demanded that back pay for the grievant should be calculated on the basis of a full 40-hour week for each week during the 15-month period, subtracting from that amount only earnings from other employers. On that basis, the management's liability would have amounted to several thousand dollars.

In formulating its position with respect to the implementation of the award, however, the management believed that it was entitled to take into account not only the grievant's earnings from other employment, but also his perfectly horrible attendance record which had been the basis for this discharge. Projecting that attendance record forward to the 15-month period in question to establish the number of days it could reasonably be estimated that he would have worked resulted in a situation whereby the grievant would not be entitled to any back pay. On balance, he earned more money from his other employment than he would have earned from us, based on his past attendance track record. Countering that position, the union retorted that if we were to project the grievant's attendance forward to determine what he would have earned had he continued to work for us, then we must, in fairness, project the record against his actual outside employment during that period, thereby reducing our offsetting figure attributable to outside earnings during that period with the result that we would owe the grievant money. In spite of the fact that this decision was rendered on March 30, 1970, the parties are still discussing the monies due the grievant.

A second and more significant problem area for Bethlehem in the award-implementation area arises from those occasional decisions which are vague in their requirements as to what action should be taken by the management to resolve a violation of the agreement as determined by the arbitrator. A recent illustration of this problem from Bethlehem's standpoint is a contracting-out issue which was decided at one of our eastern plants in September 1969. In his holding the umpire concluded that three out of four phases of a continuing multifaceted job involving disposal of slag debris from a newly opened basic oxygen furnace facility had been assigned to an outside contractor improperly when, in fact, the members of the plant work force should have been given the work. The umpire, after reviewing the case and arriving at this conclusion, merely summarized his decision by noting that the grievance was "in part sustained and in part denied." Thereafter, in subsequent discussions with the union during an eight-month period, arrangements were made to train plant employees to perform the work in question and then to replace the outside contractor's employees with the trained plant employees. Since there was an absence of any mention of retro-active monetary liability for affected plant employees by the umpire, this request, when raised by the union, received a neg-ative response from plant management and, in addition, the management referred the union representatives to the umpire's decision. Plant management was, of course, of the opinion that back pay was not required by the umpire's decision because it had not been specifically directed to take such remedial action. This conclusion found further support in the dicta of previous arbitration cases which had indicated that back pay would not necessarily follow in adverse contracting-out decisions. As a con-sequence of the diametrically opposed positions taken by local management and the union on back pay, the matter was again placed before the umpire almost a year later—in September 1970. On this occasion the umpire's lack of specificity in the award with respect to remedy was partially clarified when he orally advised the parties that a back-pay remedy had been in-tended with respect to those plant employees who, except for the contracting out, would have worked the jobs in question. Unfortunately, this belated clarification of the riddle created by the initial award has now been followed by additional conflict over the amount of liability due each affected employee. As a result, the remedy, after more than a year and a half, remains in contention.

A third problem which we at Bethlehem on more than one occasion have jointly faced with the union is the less-than-timely implementation of an adverse award even when the remedy called for is clear and unambiguous. To illustrate this implementation difficulty, I might note that our collective bar-gaining agreement with the Steelworkers has a number of rather complex and, in certain respects, amorphous incentive provisions which specify, among other things, that the management, when establishing a new incentive for work which has not previously been incentive rated or when replacing an existing incentive, must create a plan that provides equitable compensation. The answer to the question of whether any given new or revised incentive plan provides equitable compensation is, on occasion, a very nebulous one and, as a consequence, grievances **are** frequently filed alleging that a specific incentive plan does not meet the contractual standard. Upon the issuance of arbitration awards in this area, we, unfortunately, find from time to time that the disputed incentive plan has not met the standard of equitable compensation. In such a situation, the company normally is directed to adjust the plan in accordance with the decision and to compute and pay retroactively the monies due under the revised plan to the employees who have been covered by the plan during the period since the filing of a grievance. Because the passage of time in some of these incentive cases amounts to years instead of months and because some of these incentive plans cover large numbers of employees (several hundred in a few instances) and because considerable employee movement occurs into and out of jobs covered by the disputed plan, it has taken months and even years after the award has been issued before a precise retroactive pay calculation can be made. This, of course, is a most unsatisfactory end result because both parties are frustrated in their desire to dispose of the problem as finally decided at arbitration. The employees, on the one hand, cannot enjoy the fruits of their victory in terms of obtaining monies due, and the management continues to be saddled with a problem that in all likelihood affects employee morale and hence productivity, not to mention the burden of horrendous accounting costs.

Still another award-implementation problem of a recurring nature is probably best depicted by an arbitration decision at our Johnstown plant dealing with a crew-size question. Several years ago the management at this plant eliminated the job of powerhouse assistant engineer. The eliminated job was, for pay purposes and for upward and downward movement into other positions, located at about the midpoint in an established seniority unit. As a result of the abolition of the assistant engineer job, a general downward job reassignment occurred. Disgruntled over the job elimination and their resultant downgrading, the displaced assistant engineers filed a grievance claiming a violation of the past-practice provisions of the contract by the management. In his decision, the arbitrator sustained the claim and directed that the assistant engineers be restored to their former jobs and be made whole for any difference in earnings. After the issuance of the decision, the union, on behalf of a number of other employees in the seniority unit—nongrievants who had been displaced by the incumbents of the eliminated assistant engineer's job when they had been bumped back—also requested to be made whole. Being made whole, they say, includes not only the payment of wages lost because of being in the lower-rated jobs but also compensation for lost opportunities to have filled temporary vacancies in higher-rated jobs which would have been open to them had they not been bumped out of their jobs, lost overtime opportunities, and so on ad infinitum. In response, local management took the tack that only the original grievants were to be reimbursed. A dispute delaying implementation of the award ensued. Of course this problem also arises in a simpler way when only some of an affected class file a grievance. The issue arises where the grievance is sustained: Should the company, in the interest of equity, apply the relief granted by the arbitrator to all in the class regardless of whether they had filed a grievance and even though the arbitrator did not have authority to make such an application?

As another implementation problem, I cite a case which arose in 1966 at one of our large eastern plants when a number of employees objected to the scheduling of their 1966 vacations during various weeks other than those weeks which they had designated as their choice when canvassed during the scheduling period. Unfortunately, the preferred vacation periods designated by the grievants were unavailable because employees with greater lengths of service (a contractual criterion in assigning vacation weeks) had filled the established quotas for the weeks in question. When the vacation scheduling complaints of certain junior service employees could not be resolved, a rash of grievances was filed, claiming that the company had not complied with the contractual requirements that called for the notification of employees as to their vacation schedules for the year by January 1, 1966. The arbitrator, in deciding the grievances, concluded that the management's failure to notify employees of their vacation schedules by January 1 violated the agreement. As a consequence of this conclusion, the arbitrator directed that the grieving employees be granted their original vacation preference requests or paid in lieu of vacation time off. Unhappily, the first directive conflicted with the contractual right of more senior length-of-service employees to be given superior preference for certain of the weeks in question, while the second directive—which provided the grievants with the option of taking pay in lieu of vacation time off—was specifically precluded by the contract.

A final example of an arbitration-implementation problem is one in which the implementation thereof results in the parties' breaking virgin territory. This arose at a Bethlehem operation where the agreement establishing the seniority units provided that nonscheduling for up to a period of two weeks would not be considered a seniority event. The union, several years after the agreement was consummated, challenged the company's right to nonschedule employees for up to two weeks rather than to re-shuffle the employees to give the oldest employees the work available. The umpire reviewed the history of the agreement and found that the *quid pro quo* for the company's agreement to the seniority units was the local union's agreement to permit nonscheduling for a period of two weeks. He found that this latter provision violated the basic terms of the labor agreement and, therefore, the entire seniority agreement had to fall. This left the parties without any seniority agreement or, at best, one forged through the practices that had been followed prior to the creation of the invalid seniority unit agreement. The parties found that their ill adventure to arbitration resulted not in a resolution of one problem but the creation of hundreds of problems.

There are, of course, other award-implementation examples which have arisen at Bethlehem. These six situations, however, are sufficient to indicate that difficulties can and do occur when applying vague, impractical, or contractually ill-conceived awards. Invariably, when this happens, it results in delay as to the final disposition of the problem. Fortunately, this is an infrequent occurrence for Bethlehem.

Nonetheless, I think that all of you would agree that even on an infrequent basis delay in award implementation and the resultant animosity which it inevitably generates result in an unsatisfactory conclusion to arbitration. Admittedly, part of the blame in several of our specific illustrations could be laid at the feet of the advocates themselves for possibly not bending every effort to arrive at a satisfactory solution either before arbitration or in implementing the arbitrator's decision. I believe, however, that the greater responsibility must rest with the arbitrator who, for example, fails to specify any remedy as in the contracting-out case referred to earlier, apparently adopting an approach which is espoused by many in this profession; that is, that the arbitrator's chief and possibly sole function is to determine whether or not the collective bargaining agreement has been violated—the remedy aspect of the grievance being of no concern or, at best, only of secondary importance.

In contrast, many of us who are in an advocate's role are of the opinion that it would be most helpful initially to have more thorough consideration given to the question of an appropriate remedy in a given award. This is true even when the parties have a mature collective bargaining and grievance handling relationship. Frankly, an award which provides only the vaguest of guidelines to the parties for resolving what has been held to be a contract violation ignores the practical reality of arbitration, namely, that at least with respect to the particular problem presented to the arbitrator, the parties were unwilling bedmates. Consequently, it would appear that lack of specificity in the award frequently continues the strife which existed prior to arbitration—a very unsatisfactory result.

In contrast, a salutary side effect occurs, we have discovered, when an arbitrator has given more than cursory consideration to the remedy in that the decision is more tightly written because of a greater awareness which he acquires of the problems which can result during implementation from loosely worded decisions—a fact that tempers the tone of the decision in a significant way so that arbitral justice and equity are more delicately honed.

There are, of course, a number of specific corrective measures which might also be introduced by the advocates or the arbitrator to reduce implementation controversies and insure a greater clarity in awards. Illustrative of specific corrective measures that might be introduced are the following: First, pre-arbitration stipulations might be developed setting forth each party's position with respect to the appropriate remedy with differences in position, if any, being argued before the arbitrator. Second, absent a prehearing stipulation on the appropriate remedy, the arbitrator might well want to establish a practice of seeking the respective position of each party at the hearing on possible award approaches. Third, the arbitrator might arrange, in the absence of prehearing stipulations or in the absence of sufficient evidence on remedy being presented at the hearing, to discuss approaches to an award prior to issuing a decision. Fourth, as a broader and less practical alternative, the parties might, in certain instances, consider the negotiation of specific contract provisions dealing with award-implementation problem areas. Which of these courses of action, if any, are appropriate will vary and depend primarily upon the established collective bargaining relationship of the parties and the arbitrator's past experience. For example, under a permanent umpire system it is less likely that the arbitrator will feel compelled to go into the remedy aspect of recurring but similar disciplinary cases if the parties have a proven past record for successful dealings on questions of this type. In contrast, the opposite tack clearly might be appropriate when the arbitrator is presiding over an ad hoc hearing.

From a negative standpoint, one might also argue that the adoption of contract provisions specifying the boundaries for awards in a given situation is at best of limited value because of the impossibility of covering more than a narrow range of circumstances. It might also be urged that the extension of all hearings to allow for sufficient development of information going to the remedy is impractical in terms of cost and/or time. Likewise, post-hearing conferences could also be criticized. This is not to say, however, that each approach may not be useful in certain circumstances. In the vacation case referred to earlier, for example, the parties subsequently negotiated language which provided that not only must the vacation schedule be firmed up prior to the beginning of the vacation year, but also grievances dealing with vacation preferences must be arbitrated and a decision rendered prior to the commencement of the vacation period.

In closing, I would like to take the liberty of broadly paraphasing a comment made by Irving Bernstein nearly a decade ago when he noted before this body that arbitration decisions, like Caesar's Gaul and its three parts, may be divided into three groups: First, there are those decisions involving only conclusions of contract. Second, there are those decisions involving conclusions of contract and equity. Third, there are those decisions which I don't understand. It could well be that some of the Bethlehem implementation problems have arisen from this latter group.

CHAPTER VI

FEDERAL LABOR RELATIONS: PROBLEMS AND PROSPECTS

ARNOLD R. WEBER*

As I was traveling to Los Angeles, I experienced a minor identity crisis. First, I am honored to be a member of this organization. Second, when I was invited to speak I was Assistant Secretary of Labor for Manpower. Third, I am now with the Office of Management and Budget in the Executive Office of the President.

It's not clear whether I'm appearing before you as an aging arbitrator, a tired bureaucrat, or a passé professor. All of those identifications give me a certain invulnerability, and I would only say that if I have anything clear or concise to say, it reflects my training as an arbitrator; if I obfuscate, it reflects the disabilities that have been put on me in the past two years.

I spent most of my time in government as Assistant Secretary of Labor for Manpower—with responsibility for the administration of various training programs. However, I decided that this was an inappropriate topic for my remarks today since arbitrators can't be classed as disadvantaged, and certainly not in these surroundings—which I would classify as Cecil B. De-Mille's middle period.

Thus, I decided to fix upon my present responsibilities. In my present position I'm most concerned with the federal budget, which is presently being presented to the public and the Congress with much fanfare and hyperbole. I must confess that I had a shock when I came over to OMB. It is the only place in the world where, when you say ".1," you mean $100 million. The standard unit of currency is a billion dollars. When we go into the Director's reviews, where decisions are made with re-

---

* Member, National Academy of Arbitrators; Associate Director, Office of Management and Budget, Executive Office of the President, Washington, D. C.

spect to budget recommendations to the President, we have to transact business at a rate of $20 million a minute or we fall behind.

Technically, I'm the "M" in OMB and am concerned with developing effective management in government. Part of my responsibility, within the broad category of management, is for federal labor relations, working in concert with the Civil Service Commission and other agencies that impact upon this area.

The specific institutional responsibility goes from the Office of Management and Budget to one of these arcane groups called Federal Labor Relations Council. The Federal Labor Relations Council is charged with the broad administration and supervision of Executive Order 11491, which establishes the framework for federal labor relations.

The Federal Labor Relations Council is comprised of the Secretary of Labor, the Chairman of the Civil Service Commission, and the Director of the Office of Management and Budget, who is George Shultz. I am Mr. Shultz's representative on the Council. It is instructive that the broad administration of the critical area of labor relations in the Federal Government is a responsibility imposed upon three men who are very busy and have a wide range of responsibility. It is important that labor relations policy in the Federal Government be determined by top-level officials, but this arrangement poses some difficulty in assuming that this area receives the continued attention that it warrants.

As my text, then, I would like to talk about the development of federal labor relations: where it came from, where it is now, and the problems it will have to deal with in the immediate future. The lessons here are important ones, both in their own right and for what they can contribute to the understanding of the broader phenomenon of collective bargaining outside the private sector.

The federal labor relations system impacts on three million workers. Those three million workers represent a microcosm of the work force, from blue-collar workers in the naval shipyards and on soil conservation projects to the host of white-collar employees all over the country.

The federal labor relations system is also an important part of what will be the most exciting development in the industrial relations area in the 1970s—the emergence of bona fide labor relations in the public sector. The most visible and dramatic developments in this area have come at the state and local levels, with the Federal Government lagging behind in terms of the application of what we would view as professional industrial relations concepts. However, future developments at the federal level will undoubtedly have a major impact on the overall development of public sector labor relations.

Finally, the federal labor relations system provides a new basis for testing the transferability of the wisdom and genius that has accumulated in the labor relations field in the private sector over the past 35 years. This is one of the persistent issues in public sector labor relations, as I am sure you are aware from your involvement in cases in the public sector. Just as persistent are the two schools of thought in this area: those who believe that the idiosyncrasies of the public sector overwhelm private sector precedents, and those who argue that NLRB decisions and private sector contract provisions can be adopted, *in corpus,* in the public sector including the federal sector.

In order to understand the development of federal labor relations, it is important to understand the federal personnel administration system. Collective bargaining—or what passes for collective bargaining—is superimposed on a well-developed, elaborate, and explicit system of personnel administration that is calculated to deal with the wide range of substantive and procedural matters that are of concern to any group of employees. There are several specific elements of this system which are of particular significance.

First, the basic conditions of employment are essentially established by statute which reduces the opportunity to negotiate or to bargain over policy issues that would be the normal fare for collective bargaining. The statute goes back to 1884 and to the passage of the Pendleton Act which established the civil service system. It sets the basic rules of hiring, dismissal, promotion, and other rules governing the allocation of the labor force as codified over an 80-year period.

Second, basic levels of compensation have not been subject to managerial discretion or the exercise of economic sanctions by employee organizations. Rather, the wages of nearly two million classified employees in grades GS-1 through GS-18 who dominate federal employment have been set by Congress within a political framework, as opposed to the framework of an economic system subject to a continuous market test.

There is a Comparability Act, providing for wage surveys covering classified employees, which has been on the books since 1962. However, wage and salary increases over the past eight years have been a result of congressional action which has not been directly linked to principles of comparability. Congress does not always act in economic wisdom, and cannot reasonably be expected to, because it is not minimizing costs or maximizing profit. Congressmen must be concerned primarily with their relations with constituents and the probability of reelection. Thus, it is not surprising that over the past eight years the wage increases initiated by the Congress have exceeded the wage increases that would be justified by strict application of the comparability principle.

Third, elements of wage structure, as well as levels of compensation, are determined by statute and by Congress: in the first instance, by the Ramspeck Act of 1927, which sets up the various grades, and in the second instance, by various aspects of the wage board system which covers blue-collar employees. In this latter respect, the recent Wage Board bill which was vetoed by the President provides a classic example of legislative efforts to determine wage structure. Specifically, it represented an example of congressional action to define the number of steps in each grade of a job classification system.

Presently, all Wage Board employees—the blue-collar workers —have three in-grade steps with 4-percent differentials which are specified by law. The Wage Board bill would have added a fourth step. The cost of that little extra step would have been $130 million, which is big money even if we do identify it as ".13."

The extra step for blue-collar workers is, at best, difficult to justify in terms of established principles of job evaluation, independent of its cost. However, if you asked, "Why do you need the fourth step?" the unanimous reply was, "Because it's fair." It was "fairness" that ruled the day in Congress because standards of equity were more persuasive in the political process than arguments based on technical principles of wage and salary administration or standards of economic logic. This is perhaps a difficult reality to accept, but it is, in fact, a reality which anyone dealing with labor relations or personnel administration in the federal sector must accept.

Fourth, it is important to recognize the size and complexity of the federal personnel or labor relations system as a force and factor in its own right. There are three million employees in the system, and these employees are covered by seven different wage and personnel systems, all of which are linked by statute, regulation, or administrative practice. Overall, it is instructive to note that every time wages of federal employees are increased by 1 percent, the budget increases by $365 million. Thus, the recent 6-percent comparability increase cost $2,137,000,000.

It is possible to cope with and overcome the cultural shock of dealing with nine- and 10-digit numbers, but the magnitude of the issues involved, and the problems of applying them with some consistency across the board, continually pose a special technical requirement which is often difficult to meet. The structure of decision-making in the system tends to complicate this difficulty.

The departments generally can be viewed as line divisions, but in the area of personnel administration this is not the case. In fact, the departments have very little discretion. They deal with what you might call second-order administrative aspects: seeing that the rules are followed, but generally not being concerned with the development of the rules themselves or the character of the rules. Those are the preserve of a central agency of government—the Civil Service Commission.

Within the departments we generally find that personnel and industrial relations are left to the Assistant Secretary for Administration. The Assistant Secretary for Administration is the king of the hill, as far as the career civil service is concerned, but normally he is not on the main line of substantive developments and policy formulations in the department. It is a rare Cabinet member, as the operating head of his "division," who can find the time and the attention to give consideration to matters of industrial relations, personnel management in its own right.

Even the Secretary of Labor, who has a professional bias, or institutional bias, in this area, will find very little time and attention and capacity to deal with these in a constructive way between congressional committee hearings and making speeches to constituent groups and keeping Assistant Secretaries happy. If this is the case for the Secretary of Labor, who has a positive professional bias and who presides over one of the smallest departments, with only 10,400 employees, woe betide the poor Secretary of the Interior who has to worry about the Bureau of Indian Affairs and a host of other issues and who presides over 74,000 employees.

In fact, the only place where you will find that the divisional managers are really concerned with personnel or labor relations is in the Department of Defense. The Defense Department has had to give institutional energy and commitment to personnel and labor relations primarily because it has such a sizable blue-collar work force and because there has been strong spillover from private sector labor relations due to the activity of private sector unions, most notably the metal trades unions, in the blue-collar work force.

The basic responsibility for personnel administration and labor relations lies with the Civil Service Commission. The Commission's role is an interesting one because it has two somewhat inconsistent operational imperatives—bipartisanship and impartiality. The bipartisan imperative of the Commission is built into its structure. There are three commissioners and only two can be of one political party. At the same time, the Chairman of the Civil Service Commission is appointed by the President. He's an instrument of the President. He's there to serve the President and to be responsive to the President's and the Administration's desire and policy directives, but the nature of his job also requires him to be impartial.

Overall, the federal personnel system may be characterized as unstable and structurally amorphous. Most of the major decision-making in primary substantive areas is done by Congress. As a result, there is an element of indifference, if you will, associated with efforts to implement industrial relations in the department. The Civil Service Commission really assumes the lead, struggling to be bipartisan and impartial while also being responsive to the President and the needs of the executive branch, that is, management.

Against this background the unions historically played a rather interesting, if not peculiar, role. They were never visible and until recently had little direct impact. In fact, few of them functioned like unions; most were primarily lobbying organizations. The reason they were lobbying organizations is clear. The primary power is held by Congress, and one does not negotiate with Congress in the classical way; one lobbies for its attention and favor. Indeed, the unions, as lobbyists, generally have been extremely effective because they know how the game should be played.

Under this system, the unions reacted to their environment rather than actively shaping it. Over the past 10 years, however, we have seen something of a revolution in union behavior and tactics. That revolution has brought the first steps toward power to the shop stewards, not to the people—albeit in an ungainly and unpredictable way.

Clearly, the first step was taken in the early years of the Kennedy Administration, with the promulgation by the President of Executive Order 10988. Notice—this was an executive order, which is an instrument of art in government. It does not involve Congress, but is an expression of the President's power as Chief Executive or top manager, if you will, of the federal establishment. Thus, Executive Order 10988 was much like Section 7A in the NIRA of 1934.

Executive Order 10988 provided for collective bargaining; it provided for recognition of unions. In effect, it provided for the protected right to organize. However, its primary significance was not that it engendered a system of collective bargaining, because that system of collective bargaining still isn't in place in government, but that it removed the legal impediments that had limited such activities in the past. Specifically, it broke the nexus with the sovereignty issue, and with the notion that somehow unions didn't belong in government service.

Although that executive order was a very courageous and innovative act on the part of President Kennedy, it did have major deficiencies which reflected a persistent ambivalence. Clearly, one of the deficiencies was that the executive order never really made up its mind on the concept of exclusivity as one of the keystone concepts in the development of the American system of industrial relations, as contrasted to systems that have developed elsewhere.

As most of you know, the order provided for three levels of representation: exclusive, formal, and informal. In part, this was an effort to accommodate the unions, which dealt less by collective bargaining than by what might be called institutional dealing—the capacity to make extra-legal or informal arrangements with government officials in key administration positions. In this respect, it is interesting to note that the reaction of government unions to the concept of exclusivity in the new executive order has not been one of unanimous enthusiasm. For some unions, exclusivity means that they cannot make the best of two worlds, but they must choose formal collective bargaining while being denied the advantages of informal dealing.

A second deficiency in Executive Order 10988 was the fact that primary responsibility for the enforcement of the executive order was lodged with the agencies, the departments, and the Civil Service Commission. Thus, if there was an allegation that the executive order was violated, it was the department, in the first instance, that judged itself. Now it is true that all public officials are wise, compassionate, and aloof from their own concerns, but it is also true that they do make mistakes because of their particular interests and angle of vision.

Third, the executive order permitted only a narrow scope of collective bargaining. This had an impairing effect on the development of normal collective bargaining. Wages were still enacted by Congress; most of the other elements that are meat for collective bargaining were covered by the Civil Service Commission. The order ruled out negotiating over the mission of the agency; all that was left were a few interstices in this wall of exclusion.

Finally, Executive Order 10988 made no provision for the constructive development of impasse resolution techniques. The order did not address itself to this problem because it was gratuitous in the structure of that executive order. It did not provide for the shift in power and discretion that was necessary to make true bargaining work. And the notion of an impasse, as we understand it, was alien to the concept of discussions or negotiation that was engendered by the order.

Toward the end of the last Administration, the executive order was subjected to reevaluation and reanalysis. In the early part of this Administration, in 1969, an amended executive order was issued—11491. The major chore then became to forget 10988 and remember 11491 as the appropriate executive order.

The new order provides for exclusive recognition and for the phasing out of the other vestigial forms of recognition which are really inconsistent with bona fide collective bargaining. This step may be noncontroversial to those schooled in the private sector, but it has proven to be a painful step to take in the federal sector. The loss of formal recognition based on 10-percent membership excludes large numbers of organizations from dues check-off privileges. The outgrowth of this has been a clamor for dues check-off independent of representative status.

Executive Order 11491 also provided for an impartial mechanism for administration of that order. The old executive order was administered primarily by the Civil Service Commission and the agency heads. The new executive order is administered, in the first instance, by the Assistant Secretary of Labor for Labor-Management Affairs. He makes unit determinations and initial hearings on unfair labor practices. Much of what the NLRB does with respect to Taft-Hartley, the Assistant Secretary of Labor does with respect to this executive order.

This is an important step. The Assistant Secretary of Labor is still a management official who is put in the position of acting as an impartial party in cases involving other management officials and presidential appointees. By conventional private sector standards, one is still left with a feeling of unease. The administration of the order has been taken out of the hands of all Cabinet officers and placed in the hands of a single official in a department which has a professional bias in favor of good industrial relations, but that official is a manager himself.

A parallel change was made in the structure of the central administrative authority under the order with the establishment of the Federal Labor Relations Council. In effect, the creation of the Council modified the authority of the Civil Service Commission in the interest of managerial balance by substituting a troika—the Director of OMB, the Secretary of Labor, and the Chairman of the Civil Service Commission—for the Civil Service Commission as the final authority.

Walter Reuther used to talk about what he called the clean-shirt theory of government. While you are recovering from the shock of a Republican Administration official's quoting Walter Reuther, I'll present his theory: People reflect particular interests, but when they come down to Washington to serve on a board, they put on a clean shirt and suddenly become disinterested public servants. This analogy highlights the problem rather than indicating the solution.

The experience in this regard has not been as bad as a priori projection would imply. As a matter of fact, it has been good. But let me say as one of the delegated trinity, "it ain't easy." One always has to self-consciously address oneself to the questions: How am I to behave? And, what should my role be in this situation?

The third major change in Executive Order 11491 involves explicit attention to the problem of impasse resolution. The order did not change the status of strikes, but it did create a Federal Impasse Panel and injects the FMCS into impasses. Overall, it provides a range of impasse resolution methods which encompasses the arsenal of techniques which have been used so widely in the public sector.

The order, however, did very little about the problem of the narrow scope of collective bargaining. The scope of collective bargaining is now as constrained as it was under the previous executive order.

Coincidental with the movement from one executive order to another were other developments which also conditioned the character of evolution of this federal labor relations system.

One was the postal strike that took place in March of last year—clearly a watershed in the history of federal labor relations. It was a traumatic event; it was the Homestead strike and the Boston police strike and the sitdown strikes of the thirties all rolled into one. When those postmen went out in New York and Boston and parts of Chicago, what was a matter of labor relations—accumulated grievances, wage structure, and wage compression—became politics, and big politics at the highest level.

For the first time we had a massive withdrawal of the supply of labor—an exercise of a traditional sanction by government employees. It was interesting to see the wrench this action caused all the way down the line on the part of the old-line union leadership, who are deeply committed to the notion that a strike is not an acceptable weapon in collective bargaining. In a sense, although 11491 was controversial, it now seemed to be almost de minimis in view of the magnitude of the problems which were emerging in the federal sector.

The second major development involved a major piece of legislation, the Pay Comparability Act, which passed in the last days of the last session. It was an Administration bill which provided for a shift of authority away from the Congress to the President in the setting of wages for classified employees. Now the President receives the comparability survey and, if he accepts comparability, it goes into effect automatically. If he chooses to recommend that the pay increase be either more or less than comparability indicates, he must submit his decision to Congress where it requires a so-called reorganization-plan-type approval. That is, it becomes effective within 60 days unless Congress votes it down. In a way, this is a bureaucratic subtlety, but the shift of power is critical. For the first time since this republic has been hiring and paying people, the President now has a considerable element of discretion in determining what the rate of increase in compensation should be.

Overall, what do we have? Where are we?

At this point in time we are in the early stages of the development of a framework for collective bargaining which involves a shift in decision-making power away from the traditional sources of decision-making power in this area—from the Congress in the compensation area and from the Civil Service Commission in the administration of labor relations. We are witnessing weakening of the established institutions and the development of a framework of new institutions, but those new institutions have not developed at this point.

I would like to end, as is the wont of every government official, with a list of problems and prospects in this area that have to be addressed in some conscious way as we go forward.

First, we have to consciously try to depoliticize the process of collective bargaining in labor relations in the federal sector. The burden here, particularly, seems lodged with the unions. Many of the unions, as I have indicated, grew up when unions were really mutual aid societies for the purchase of legal representation before the Congress. Now they are in a situation where they have to bargain collectively, but at the same time they all want that second bite through the Congress. This dual approach is clearly inconsistent with meaningful collective bargaining, but it is difficult to eliminate because it is responsive to both the needs of unions and the understandable desire of Congress to maintain control over those elements of industrial relations which are important in terms of economics and politics.

The head of the new postal corporation tried to deal with this problem in a forthright way by saying that union officers should not be able to consult with congressmen on matters associated with collective bargaining. This immediately became "a gag rule." There was an invocation of the LaFollette-Jones Act of 1911, which was passed after President Theodore Roosevelt tried to do the same thing, and Mr. Blount prudently indicated that the order had been misunderstood and withdrew it.

The second point involves the viability of existing administrative arrangements. After one year of operation under Executive Order 11491, we conducted a review in which unions and management indicated what they thought was wrong with us and wrong with the executive order. We will shortly be recommending amendments to the order based on that review. The reaction to these recommendations will be an important short-run factor in the stability of the existing structure in any event. The structural deficiencies or problems associated with the existing administrative arrangement, as contrasted with a public board or an independent agency, will have to be self-consciously addressed as we proceed.

Third, we have to give attention to the question of the structure of collective bargaining and the scope of collective bargaining. For example, there's still great pressure on the notion of exclusivity. One of the requests of the unions during the review was to postpone the phasing out of formal consultation. The whole set of issues associated with craft and industrial unions still has to be addressed. Indeed, people have to learn to think in those terms. I must say in this regard that the greatest need for upgrading lies with management, because management is not accustomed to thinking of these things and doesn't realize that the character of the bargaining unit, in fact, will set the whole structure of power through the federal establishment into the next 20 years.

The scope-of-bargaining issue centers on wages. Here the experience at the state and local levels is helpful. Initially, wages were not bargainable; now they are the subject of negotiations. It is difficult to maintain collective bargaining where the main element of tradeoff, the principal element that affects the welfare of the employees and members that the union represents, is excluded.

It may be fateful that the movement of authority concerning wages from the Congress to the President as the Chief Executive is taking place at the same time that collective bargaining is coming into play. That shift of authority may provide the basis for collective bargaining to affect the President's discretion in terms of what he recommends to Congress, or it may stand on its own, separated from the process of collective bargaining. The system provides for union representation on the Comparability Council, which makes recommendations to the President's agents—the OMB and the Civil Service Commission—concerning wage increases. I am not sure that the unions are aware, yet, of the possibility of using this structure for collective bargaining.

Last, parties on both sides have to cultivate an understanding of, and a respect for, the integrity of collective bargaining. This means they should not go to the Congress to attempt to remedy every grievance; they should not politicize all bargaining issues. Instead, they should accept the bargaining process as the primary channel through which the problems of employee-employer relations are worked out. At this point that is the missing ingredient. One way or another, through some amalgam of procedures, experience, and drawing on the wisdom of the private sector, this is a job which will have to be done.

CHAPTER VII

CRITERIA IN PUBLIC SECTOR INTEREST DISPUTES

HOWARD S. BLOCK *

Introduction

The difficulties of addressing oneself to a subject as paramount and as broad as the title of this paper can hardly be overstated. Although many of the basic interest criteria developed in the private sector are often applicable in public employment, dispute settlement criteria for the public sector are, on the whole, still in the trial-and-error stage. Considering the relative inexperience of the parties in collective negotiations (or collective bargaining, if you will), the problem of formulating interest criteria for the newly transformed public sector is two-fold in nature. Not only must the criteria be *realistic,* but, however unpalatable to those adversely affected, they must be ultimately *acceptable* to the protagonists.

That interest criteria, meaning realistic standards for resolving disputes over new terms and conditions of employment, will often be denounced and resisted in the public sector is not surprising. Three decades of sophisticated bargaining in the private sector have not resulted in a ready acceptance of interest criteria, not when contrasted with private industry consensus of basic standards for resolving disputes during the term of a written collective agreement.

The private sector can, of course, afford the luxury of disagreement on interest criteria. After all, the weapon of a threatened or an actual strike contest is readily at hand for determined, committed negotiators to strive for a settlement on their own minimum terms. But public management and those who legislate still lean heavily toward a stringent prohibition of public employee strikes. Even if recent legislation by Pennsyl-

---

* Member, National Academy of Arbitrators; Attorney, Santa Ana, Calif.

vania and Hawaii legalizing strikes for most state employees augurs a reverse trend, and I think it does, the basic situation will, for the foreseeable future, remain unchanged. Public sector strikes, legal or not, bear within themselves a potential for political crisis—an unsettling tendency to rend the social fabric —even for European democracies, accustomed as they are to highly politicized labor strife. Perhaps the United States will be an exception in this regard, as it has been in other basic aspects of labor relations.

At the present time, we live in a halfway house, as is evidenced by the insistence of so much of public management that dealings with employee organizations be designated as collective negotiations, a designation widely believed to be a euphemism for collective bargaining. I do not share this belief; I do think that management's refusal to call a rose a rose is motivated, at least partially, by a concern that the adoption of the word "bargaining" might lead to an undesirable linkage of the public sector with labor laws, administrative rulings, and precedents of the private sector. However, a close analysis of the semantic differences between the two terms suggests a much more basic reason for public management's overwhelming preference for the term "collective negotiations." The term "bargaining" inescapably implies an exchange of consideration between negotiating parties. The bargain in the private sector has for its consideration the union's giving up its *legal* right to strike for a defined period of time in return for acceptable conditions of employment and rates of pay. But, what can a public employee organization offer as meaningful consideration in bargaining when it has no *legal* strike weapon to relinquish? Any other consideration offered by unions, public or private, such as improved employee morale and more efficient work performance, can be obtained through other methods, such as enlightened personnel policies, outside the bargaining relationship. There is a precise difference in meaning between the term "negotiations" and the term "bargaining." Collective negotiations, the argument goes, is merely a quantitative pooling of individual interests of separate employees—a collective lobbying as it were—without producing the element of coercion that would be present if the employee group were bargaining in the accepted sense of the word.

Whatever the future trends, the fact remains that if the parties in the public sector are unable, with the help of mediation, to resolve their differences over new terms and conditions of employment, they must turn to the alternatives of interest arbitration or fact-finding as a substitute for a strike contest. Let me stress immediately, however, that interest arbitration in the public sector cannot be the exceptional expedient it is in our private economy. Within a milieu where the right to strike is generally proscribed, arbitration or fact-finding will unavoidably become the rule for the settlement of troublesome interest disputes, and not a seldom-used emergency measure. It seems to me that the expertise which has fashioned workable rights criteria for stabilizing the contractual relationship in the private sector is still present to a sufficient degree and extent for the development of interest criteria that will be ultimately acceptable to the parties in the public sector.

I share the point of view described by Professor Russell Smith, in his analysis of the New York ("Taylor Committee") Report of March 1966: ". . . that since novel approaches may be required to deal with the unique problems in the public sector, the necessary expertise should be permitted to develop unhampered by any preconceptions associated with the administration of private sector legislation." [1]

Currently, innovative applications of interest criteria are undergoing severe trials in a number of public jurisdictions, most notably perhaps in Detroit where cumulative dissatisfactions by the city administration with a number of arbitral findings on cost items have become acute. But more on this later. Suffice it to say that those of us, beset by timidity, who are called upon to impart their wisdom to the parties embroiled in public sector conflict will find the area of decision-making brilliantly delineated for them in the following extract from Mr. Justice Cardozo's classic inquiry into *The Nature of the Judicial Process:*

". . . What is it that I do when I decide a case? To what sources of information do I appeal for guidance? In what proportions do I permit them to contribute to the result? In what proportions ought they to contribute? If a precedent is applicable, when do I refuse to follow it? If no precedent is applicable, how do I reach the rule

---

[1] "State and Local Advisory Reports on Public Employment Labor Legislation: A Comparative Analysis," 67 *Mich. L. Rev.* 891, 899 (1969).

that will make a precedent for the future? If I am seeking logical consistency, the symmetry of the legal structure, how far shall I seek it? At what point shall the quest be halted by some discrepant custom, by some consideration of the social welfare, by my own or the common standards of justice and morals? Into that strange compound which is brewed daily in the caldron of the courts, all these ingredients enter in varying proportions. . . . The elements have not come together by chance. *Some* principle, however unavowed and inarticulate and subconscious, has regulated the infusion. It may not have been the same principle for all judges at any time, nor the same principle for any judge at all times. But a choice there has been, not a submission to the decree of Fate; and the considerations and motives determining the choice, even if often obscure, do not utterly resist analysis." [2]

One of the most compelling reasons which makes it necessary for neutrals in public interest disputes to strike out on their own is the dearth of public bargaining history. The main citadels of unionism in private industry have a continuity of bargaining history going back at least to the 1930s. Public sector collective negotiations, on the other hand, is still a fledgling growth. In many instances its existence is the result of an unspectacular transition of unaffiliated career organizations responding to competition from AFL-CIO affiliates. As we know, a principal guideline for resolving interest disputes in the private sector is prevailing industry practice—a guideline expressed with exceptional clarity by one arbitrator as follows:

"The role of interest arbitration in such a situation must be clearly understood. Arbitration in essence, is a quasi-judicial, not a legislative process. This implies the essentiality of objectivity—the reliance on a set of tested and established guides.

"In this contract making process, the arbitrator must resist any temptation to innovate, to plow new ground of his own choosing. He is committed to producing a contract which the parties themselves might have reached in the absence of the extraordinary pressures which led to the exhaustion or rejection of their traditional remedies.

"The arbitrator attempts to accomplish this objective by first understanding the nature and character of past agreements reached in a comparable area of the industry and in the firm. He must then carry forward the spirit and framework of past accommodations into the dispute before him. It is not necessary or even desirable that he approve what has taken place in the past but only that he understand the character of established practices and

---

[2] New Haven: Yale University Press, 1921, at 10.

rigorously avoid giving to *either party* that which they could not have secured at the bargaining table." [3]

Viewed in the light of the foregoing principles, the public sector neutral, I submit, does not wander in an uncharted field even though he must at times adopt an approach diametrically opposite to that used in the private sector. More often than in the private sector, he must be innovative; he must plow new ground. He cannot function as a lifeless mirror reflecting pre-collective negotiation practices which management may yearn to perpetuate but which are the target of multitudes of public employees in revolt.

Comparisons—The Fundamental Criterion

These observations are not meant to suggest that the whole slate of pre-collective negotiation standards in the public sector for setting salaries and other conditions is wiped clean. Far from it. The prevailing wage concept of comparison of similar occupational classifications in appropriate enterprises and areas, though honored today more in the breach than in the observance, will always remain, at the very least, as a useful frame of reference. Prevailing wage, of course, is one aspect of the general operating concept of comparisons. Let me stress, at this point, that comparisons are still, and in all likelihood will remain, the predominant criterion for setting salaries.

Comparisons, as UCLA Professor Irving Bernstein expounded in his authoritative book on wage arbitration:

". . . are preeminent in wage determination because all parties at interest derive benefit from them. To the worker they permit a decision on the adequacy of his income. He feels no discrimination if he stays abreast of other workers in his industry, his locality, his neighborhood. They are vital to the union because they provide guidance to its officials upon what must be insisted upon and a yardstick for measuring their bargaining skill. In the presence of internal factionalism or rival unionism, the power of comparisons is enhanced. The employer is drawn to them because they assure him that competitors will not gain a wage-cost advantage and that he will be able to recruit in the local labor market. Small firms (and unions) profit administratively by accepting a ready-made solution; they avoid the expenditure of time and money needed for working one out themselves. Arbitrators benefit no less from comparisons. They have 'the appeal of precedent and . . . awards

[3] *Des Moines Transit Co.*, 38 LA 666, 671 (1962) , John J. Flagler et al.

based thereon are apt to satisfy the normal expectations of the parties and to appear just to the public.' " [4]

I should add on this subject that comparisons provide a much wider range of choice for the interest neutral than might appear at first blush. For example, at a particular stage of a Los Angeles transit strike some time ago, the parties cast about for an arbitrator to decide the rate of pay for auto mechanics. Had the issue gone to arbitration, and had the arbitrator been held to the single criterion of comparison, the following interesting choices would have presented themselves: (a) the mechanics' rates for transit systems in comparable cities such as Chicago, Detroit, and Philadelphia; (b) the transit rates for high-wage Pacific Coast areas as far north as Seattle; (c) the San Francisco Bay Area transit rates; and (d) the general rate paid in the Los Angeles community labor market for truck repair mechanics.

As it turned out, the parties negotiated their own figure with the aid of mediators, fixing the mechanics' rate at the average level paid in large garages throughout Los Angeles County and its environs, which resulted in a substantial increase for the transit mechanics.

Wage comparisons, it must be added, are not to be taken as an assortment of mirrors in a closed circle endlessly reflecting one another without a primary image. In each of the basic categories of our economy—manufacturing, service trades, building and construction, etc.—primary settlements are reached which provide guidelines or reference figures for other negotiations that take place in these respective categories. The term "guideline" or "reference figure" is just that: an approximation, not an inflexible figure. It might be useful to take an overview of our experience with wage patterns, guidelines, and reference figures in the private sector during the past three decades because it seems quite likely that administrative guidelines and reference figures will play an even larger role in the public sector than they have in the past.

During World War II, wages were generally held to the Little Steel Formula limiting increases to 15 percent above the January 1941 level. Increases over and above that formula depended

---

[4] *Arbitration of Wages,* Publications of the Institute of Industrial Relations (Berkeley: University of California Press, 1954), 54.

for the most part on a showing of increased productivity on a plant-wide basis. Wages in the immediate aftermath of that war centered on an 18½-cent "reconversion figure" won in steel and auto industry strikes in early 1946. For five years following World War II, steel and auto settlements provided pace-setting guidelines for most industries. From 1951 to 1953, wage controls were instituted by the Federal Government to combat the inflationary spiral generated by the Korean War. From 1953 to 1961, very loose wage guidelines were adopted by private industry, most of them inspired by steel or auto settlements.

In 1961, a 3.2-percent Administration guideline formulated by Labor Secretary Arthur Goldberg became an established annual national average for wage settlements in manufacturing which prevailed until 1966. Since 1966, a stepped-up rise in the consumer price index has blurred the overall picture. Nevertheless, some kind of comparison is still the governing criterion even when there is no recognized guideline. Many, if not most, negotiators in manufacturing rely heavily on average wage settlement figures published monthly by the Bureau of Labor Statistics, or those published by The Bureau of National Affairs, Inc. Public management, however, can take no solace from the fact that the burden of pace-setting is not thrust upon them. They have all they can do to cope with increasing employee pressures, as wage settlements in the public sector lag further and further behind those in the private economy. This lag has been accentuated in recent years by the steep rise in the cost of living, a factor that has given substantial impetus to the organizational efforts of public employee organizations.

Although one cannot overstress comparisons as the primary criterion for resolving interest disputes over economic issues, other criteria of major importance should not be ignored. Several states that have enacted dispute settlement procedures in the public sector have equipped interest neutrals with a broader range of criteria for their use. The criteria listed in Michigan's Public Act 312 (1969), providing for compulsory arbitration of police and fire disputes, are a good representative selection. Section 9 of the Act sets forth the following criteria:

"(a) The lawful authority of the employer.

"(b) Stipulation of the parties.

"(c) The interests and welfare of the public and the financial ability of the unit of government to meet those costs.

"(d) Comparison of the wages, hours and conditions of employment of the employees involved in the arbitration proceeding with the wages, hours and conditions of employment of other employees performing similar services and with other employees generally:

"(i) In public employment in comparable communities.

"(ii) In private employment in comparable communities.

"(e) The average consumer prices for goods and services, commonly known as the cost of living.

"(f) The overall compensation presently received by the employees, including direct wage compensation, vacations, holidays and other excused time, insurance and pensions, medical and hospitalization benefits, the continuity and stability of employment, and all other benefits received.

"(g) Changes in any of the foregoing circumstances during the pendancy of the arbitration proceedings.

"(h) Such other factors, not confined to the foregoing, which are normally or traditionally taken into consideration in the determination of wages, hours and conditions of employment through voluntary collective bargaining, mediation, fact-finding, arbitration or otherwise between the parties, in the public service or in private employment."

Arvid Anderson's summary analysis of the foregoing criteria is worth repeating here:

"The enumeration of the criteria seems designated not to limit the arbitrators, but to allow them the broadest scope in considering whatever factors they deem important in the particular case so long as they pay attention to the other factors. The long list of criteria would also seem to offer insurance that the award of arbitration boards could not be easily upset upon judicial review. While judicial review is provided by the Michigan statute, the grounds for reviewing or modifying the award are narrow. Awards of arbitration boards will be difficult to upset in litigation in Michigan. The aggrieved party must prove that the award 'is unsupported by competent, material and substantial evidence on the whole record,' a difficult task. Additional grounds for reversal of the award of arbitrators are that the panel exceeded its jurisdiction or that the order was procured by fraud, collusion or unlawful means. Such problems of proof are most difficult as the record in private grievance arbitration attests." [5]

---

[5] "Compulsory Arbitration Under State Statutes," New York University Twenty-Second Annual Conference on Labor (New York: Matthew Bender, 1969).

Ability to Pay: The Problem of Priorities

Nowhere in the public sector is the problem of interest criteria more critical than in the major urban areas of the nation. Municipal governments are highly dependent, vulnerable public agencies. Their options for making concessions in collective negotiations are at best limited, and are often nullified by social and economic forces which command markets, resources, and political power extending far beyond the city limits. City and county administrations are buffeted by winds of controversy over conflicting claims upon the tax dollar. On the federal level, the ultimate source of tax revenues, the order of priorities between military expenditures and the needs of the cities are a persistent focus of debate. On the state level, the counterclaims over priorities in most states seem to be education over all others.

The source of most local government revenue, as any homeowner will irately confirm, is the property tax. In urban areas, the political thrust of municipal government is to ease somewhat the utterly disproportionate tax levied on homeowners and to turn more insistently to state and federal sources for funds. On a personal note, I live in Orange County, Calif., and it has been some years since I have seen the once-prevalent bumper sticker, "Please Uncle Sam, I want to do it myself." I doubt if the problem can be better summarized than in the choice comment of Detroit Mayor Gribbs: "The money is in Washington, the power is in Lansing, and the human problems are at the local level of government." [6]

Thus, the unique aspect of applying interest criteria to local government negotiations becomes clear. When an employer in private industry argues inability to pay, he implies that if his labor costs are forced above a tolerable level, he will liquidate his holdings and reinvest his capital in another enterprise affording him a more acceptable rate of return. In short, he will go out of business. We have witnessed the same economic forces at work in the past—when federal and state minimum wages were enacted and subsequently raised, large numbers of marginal enterprises closed their doors.

One other example will illustrate why ability to pay is seldom

[6] BNA, *Government Employees Relations Report* No. 361, B-12 (Aug. 10, 1970).

controlling in the private sector. Some 20 years ago there were 175 retail hand bakeries in Long Beach, Calif., and its environs. Gradually, their number dwindled as these bakeries were forced to the wall by competition from frozen pastries and ready-mixed type of powders sold in the supermarkets. Each year or two the survivors met with the Bakers' Union to renegotiate wages and other cost items. The union's demands were modest, but firm. They remained impervious to the depressed conditions of the industry. As the local union president put it, "What would be the point of forgoing a wage increase? Next year they won't be any better off, or the year after. We can't keep them in business. They've got to solve that themselves. In the meantime, for as long as the jobs last, we're going to maintain a decent wage." It is only necessary to add that arbitral findings in the private sector disclose a substantial concurrence with the reasoning expounded by this representative. In the relatively few instances in which inability to pay has been given significant weight, it has usually been relied upon to justify some postponement of wage adjustments called for by the labor market but not to deny them permanently.

Unlike private management, an assertion by government of inability to pay will rarely be a prelude to closing its doors. For government to go out of business is not a very realistic alternative. Even curtailment or elimination of government services because of a budgetary squeeze is often more than offset by the necessity of providing additional benefits to meet growing social problems, or by the assumption of new government services such as interurban transit systems that private enterprise can no longer operate at a profit. The point is, operating decisions of the private sector are economic in nature, rooted in the profit motive. Identical decisions in a public enterprise are political; that is, economic factors are often dominated by political considerations. Harvard Professors Dunlop and Bok have perceptively contrasted the impact of economic constraints in the public and private sector in their recent book from which the following extract is highly pertinent to this discussion:

"In the private sector, union demands are usually checked by the forces of competition and other market pressures. Negotiators are typically limited by such restraints as the entry of nonunion competitors, the impact of foreign goods, the substitution of capital for higher-priced labor, the shift of operations to lower-cost areas, the contracting out of high-cost operations to other enterprises, the shut down of unprofitable plants and operations, the redesign of products to meet higher costs, and finally the managerial option to go out of business entirely. Similar limitations are either nonexistent or very much weaker in the public sector. While budgets and corresponding tax levies operate in a general way to check increases in compensation, the connection is remote and scarcely applicable to particular units or groups of strategically located public employees. Unhampered by such market restraints, a union that can exert heavy pressure through a strike may be able to obtain excessive wages and benefits."[7]

At any rate, whatever the complexities presented by the ability-to-pay argument on state and federal levels, it is on the local level that the problem is most resistant to a solution. The current experience of the City of Detroit with compulsory arbitration of police and fire wage disputes exemplifies the difficulties for the entire nation in all their awesome proportions. How does an arbitration panel respond to a municipal government that says, "We just don't have the money"?

Pioneering decisions of interest neutrals have assigned no greater weight to such an assertion than they have to an inability-to-pay position by private management. An arbitration panel constituted under Michigan's Public Act 312 rejected an argument by the City of Detroit which would have precluded the panel from awarding money because of an asserted inability to pay. What would be the point of an arbitration, the panel asks in effect, if its function were simply to rubber-stamp the city's position that it had no money for salary increases? What employer could resist a claim of inability to pay if such claim would become, as a matter of course, the basis of a binding arbitration award that would relieve it of the grinding pressures of arduous negotiations? While the panel considered the city's argument on this point, it was not a controlling consideration.

Inability to pay may often be the result of an unwillingness to bell the cat by raising local taxes or reassessing property to make more funds available. Arnold Zack gives a realistic depiction of the inherent elasticity of management's position in the following comment:

"It is generally true that the funds can be made available to pay

---

[7] Derek C. Bok and John T. Dunlop, "Collective Bargaining and the Public Sector," in *Labor and the American Community* (New York: Simon & Schuster, 1970), 334-335.

for settlement of an imminent negotiation, although the consequences may well be depletion of needed reserves for unanticipated contingencies, the failure to undertake new planned services such as hiring more teachers, or even the curtailment of existing services, such as elimination of subsidized student activities, to finance the settlement." [8]

The very fact of this elasticity places an additional burden on public management to hold the line against treasury raids by strong aggressive employee groups, who are able to gain a disproportionate share of available funds at the expense of the weak and the docile. Understandably, management will be prone to assert an inability to pay rather than to antagonize an employee group needlessly by declaring it has the money but will not make one-sided disbursements to accommodate partisan interests.

Also, an inability-to-pay declaration, or at least a restricted ability-to-pay stance, has another useful purpose: that of enabling public management to maintain a bargaining position. The very concept of bargaining carries with it as a logical corollary the necessity for the bargaining teams to limit the extent of information furnished to each other and to justify withholding possible concessions until they can be made at strategic times in order to exact reciprocity from each other. With budgetary information a matter of public record, management often has to overcome this inherent disadvantage by stubbornly refusing to revise allocations or redistributing reserve funds until an acceptable economic package can be agreed upon at the bargaining talks.

The dilemma of the interest neutral became nowhere more conspicuous than in the fallout from an arbitral award in the early summer of 1970 which granted fifth-year Detroit patrolmen an 11.1-percent salary increase.[9] The city announced a major austerity plan necessitated by the cost of the increase. Hundreds of layoffs in other departments followed, while the workweek for all city employees was increased from 35 to 40 hours a week. Because of the layoff, the city teetered on the brink of a sanitation strike, which might have triggered an all-city-employee strike. Eight employee organizations immediately

---

[8] "Ability to Pay in Public Sector Bargaining," New York University Twenty-Third Annual Conference on Labor (New York: Matthew Bender, 1970).

[9] BNA, *Government Employee Relations Report* No. 361, B-9 (Aug. 10, 1970).

filed unfair labor practice charges before the Michigan Employment Relations Commission, not to speak of a group lawsuit filed
in the Wayne County Circuit Court by other aroused employees.

Uniform Wage Policy v. Inequities

The near upheaval following the Detroit award is not atypical.
In many, if not most, inability-to-pay situations, the impasse is
not due to the economic cost of reaching an agreement with
the employee group directly involved in the negotiations.
With some notable exceptions (for example, teachers), such a
cost is often easily absorbed in the budget. The underlying problem for management is to avoid a settlement figure with one
group which arouses unrealistic expectancies among large numbers of other employees who are being pressed to go along with
a uniform wage policy pegged at a lower figure. In estimating
the cost of an award higher than the uniform figure, interest
neutrals must evaluate the validity of an argument by management that an award which overturns the uniform figure for one
group will irresistably become a new pattern for everyone else.
Public management has in the past been accustomed to making judicious inequity adjustments in response to employee organizations who pursue their objective by patient and persistent
lobbying. But employee relations of that day are a far cry from
the aggressive, militant campaigns of strong employee organizations today, campaigns which culminate, in an increasing number
of localities, in binding impasse procedures.

In current salary disputes, the apprehension that an inequity
adjustment for one group may have a disastrous impact upon a
uniform wage policy is often well founded. I do not think that
a rigid application of the prevailing wage principle which results
in a disproportionate increase for a favored group, an attitude of
let-the-chips-fall-where-they-may, is the answer. I have no sweeping alternative approach to offer, other than the thought that
a uniform wage policy merits a high degree of support from interest neutrals. I do not mean that I would rule out inequity
increases in every instance in which a uniform wage policy is en-
dangered. I would try to steer a highly flexible course. Much
would depend upon how big a tail was trying to wag how big a
dog. Most important would be an assessment of whether the re-
percussions of an inequity award to one group could be contained,

while all others are being held to a uniform wage increase. In recent years, for example, there has been a broad national consensus on the need for substantial increases to policemen and firemen and, in some jurisdictions, for teachers. Many times, an arbitral award is the only way an inequity can be remedied without arousing other employee groups to challenge a uniform wage policy. Arvid Anderson makes the point: "The employer may want arbitration as a means of settlement in order to persuade other employee organizations that he had no choice but to accept the terms ordered by the Arbitrator."[10]

Funding the Findings

The interest neutral finds himself in an unenviable position. If he simply accepts, uncritically, the claim of inability to pay as presented to him by management, he abandons all pretense of carrying out his quasi-judicial function. On the other hand, if he makes findings which compel a significant redistribution of funds in the budget, or a search for new sources of revenue, his position can become analogous to that of Will Rogers when he advanced a plan for combating the German submarine menace during World War I. The thing to do, said Rogers, was to heat the Atlantic Ocean to the boiling point, which would force the U-boats to surface where they could be picked off by Allied naval vessels.

"Very good," his listeners replied, "very ingenious. But just how do we go about heating the whole ocean?"

"That's your problem," said Will. "I've given you the solution. You work out the details."

My own experience in the past year as an interest neutral trying to cope with inability-to-pay impasses has not suggested any single basic criterion I can offer with self-assurance. Obviously, interest arbitration or fact-finding would be a mere ritual, unacceptable to employee organizations, if neutrals were to permit a management financial statement to become a privileged sanctuary—a document to be reviewed only as to its internal consistency. I am inclined to agree with those who insist that when a neutral rules out inability to pay as a valid defense, he should also assume some responsibility for suggest-

---

[10] Anderson, "Compulsory Arbitration Under State Statutes," at 12.

ing where to find the funds to implement his award, provided the parties have authorized him to do so. The preferable way to make clear his authority on this issue is in the submission agreement.

In suggesting that the parties impose this responsibility upon the neutral, I am fully aware that the expertise which he brings to these economic matters will rarely equal that of the persons entrusted with making up the budget. Nonetheless, the interest neutral must venture upon this uncertain terrain. His function does not permit him to shirk the responsibility of suggesting the possible sources of funds to implement his award. His insight into the fiscal aspects of the problem may be inferior to those of the negotiators, but they are objective insights. Because the neutral provides an *impartial* expertise, it becomes the only viewpoint acceptable to both parties.

Los Angeles Teachers' Dispute

In the public sector any controversy over ability to pay invariably focuses on priorities in public spending. Major disputes on the local level often become staging grounds for assaults on priorities of spending on state and federal levels of government. Nowhere was this phenomenon more featured than in the Los Angeles teachers' strike in the spring of 1970. The point should be made at once that the principal issues of the strike were meaningful recognition of the teachers union (United Teachers of Los Angeles) and the teachers' insistence on a substantive participation in decision-making on salaries, class size, and other matters vital to their profession. These issues, however, were not the focus of public concern until the final phase of the strike, when the resistance of school administrators brought them to the fore. Until then, the problem of the school board's inability to pay and the legality of the strike dominated the stage.

Prior to the strike, a tax override for education was voted down overwhelmingly by the electorate. Even persons who had previously regarded tax appropriations for education as sacrosanct voted "No," in order to keep the pressure on the state legislature to provide needed funds. When the strike began, if there was one fact unquestioned by both parties, it was that the Los Angeles city school board had no money to make any basic economic concessions. When Don Baer, the executive director of the Teachers Union (UTLA), was asked on television: "Why are you striking?" he replied with unexpected candor: "To create a crisis."

He meant, of course, exactly what he said. Since both sides agreed that there were no funds, the issue on this point was totally political. The target of the strike was avowedly the state's contribution to Los Angeles schools, which was 28 percent of the budget, as against a state contribution for other school districts averaging 35 percent. A succession of governors, including the incumbent, had at one time or another endorsed the principle of a 50-percent state contribution for all school districts as a millennial objective, but none of them had ever come close.

On the June primary ballot, to be voted on more than a month later, was an initiative measure making a 50-percent contribution by the state a constitutional requirement. The crisis the teachers' leaders had in mind was no softening-up process to reintroduce the rejected tax override. They were going for the jackpot—a majority vote of the electorate for the initiative measure requiring a 50-percent state contribution. A four-week strike produced a crisis, but not one which would overcome widespread opposition to the initiative measure. There was opposition even from the labor movement which supported the other goals of the strike.

UCLA Law Professor Benjamin Aaron was asked by the parties to mediate the bargaining issues of the strike. After a period of extensive exploration with the parties, Aaron made written recommendations, which doubtless he had good reason to believe would encompass the expectations of the teachers' leaders and a majority of the school board. The school board majority was less cohesive than had been foreseen. It very nearly collapsed under the impact of opposition from school administrators who declared that the recommendations would result in an unacceptable diminution of their authority and function.

To comprehend fully the inner nature of the marathon discussions which ensued between the parties, one will be greatly helped by Ida Klaus's account in the *Michigan Law Review* of March 1969 describing the New York City experience with teacher unionism. Curiously, the Los Angeles discussions telescoped in a matter of days the essential problems that had been encountered in New York City's then-seven-year history of teacher bargaining. Of particular interest is Miss Klaus's account of the evolution of the New York situation from the pioneering first stage of the bargaining relationship when ". . . the parties negotiated from knowledge of the amount of money available, and the Board was not committed to promoting improvements beyond its budgetary capacity . . ." [11] to the next stage where the teacher organization asked for definite commitments on salaries and working conditions:

". . . without conditioning their extent on the availability of funds. In other words, the teachers now wished to negotiate directly for improvements in their welfare. They wanted the substance of change and were leaving the financial means and budgetary consequences to the Board's ingenuity." [12]

The transition to the second stage of their evolving relationship was marked by the Board's acceptance of the teachers' approach. Miss Klaus summed up the turning point:

"In order to obtain a two-year contract and to absorb most of the increased salary costs in the second year, the Board was prepared to take its chances that its estimates of future financial ability were accurate. If necessary, it would have to divert to salaries and other negotiated items funds that would otherwise be utilized for educational needs and services. *The result was a shift in the order of priorities.*" [13] (Emphasis added.)

She added in a footnote:

"The Board in fact negotiated with the Union the order of priorities for the disbursements of the moneys that would be made available to the Board in its budget for the second year of the agreement." [14]

Returning now to the Los Angeles teachers' strike, the settlement proposed by Professor Aaron very nearly foundered on a similar problem of priorities. At issue was the positioning of a single word, "if," which had been moved up to the beginning of a key sentence at the insistence of the school board. Aaron proposed that the board restore $41 million in budget cuts for 1970-1971, reduce class sizes, and establish special reading courses,

---

[11] "The Evolution of a Collective Bargaining Relationship in Public Education; New York City's Changing Seven Year History," 67 *Mich. L. Rev.* 1033, 1040 (1969).

[12] *Id.* at 1041.

[13] *Id.* at 1042.

[14] *Id.* at 1042.

along with some other measures advanced by the teachers to make up a quality education program.

As reported by Harry Bernstein, the labor editor of the *Los Angeles Times* (May 17, 1970):

> "But Aaron had a big 'if' in his recommendation—all of his proposed expenditures would be cancelled if money was not available from the State or some other source.
>
> "Unlike Aaron's recommendation, the final agreement simply put the 'if' first, saying that if money became available, the 'quality education' program would be adopted.
>
> "For many teachers, and for the School Board majority, the placement of the word 'if' was crucial, apparently on the theory that the Board would be more firmly committed to spend money under Aaron's plan than under the final settlement plan."

The importance attached by the parties to the positioning of the word "if" may have been due to an overemphasis on the psychological factors in the dispute, because as Aaron himself pointed out, under either his own proposal or the final agreement, the Board could not spend money it did not have. At any rate, the entire episode graphically illustrates how inability to pay and a struggle over priorities are opposite sides of the same coin.

A parting comment on the matter of priorities. Although I have tended to dwell on inability to pay as a form of conflict over priorities in spending, I would not want to leave the impression that a local or state government cannot, in a very real and practical sense, be dead broke. To cite a highly pertinent analogy, even an enterprise that goes bankrupt—especially one that goes bankrupt—produces a conflict among creditors over priorities in the disbursement of the remaining assets.

The Combination Mediator/Fact-Finder

Early in my remarks, the point was made that where the right to strike is legally proscribed or effectively inhibited, arbitration and fact-finding will inevitably become more frequently resorted to by the parties to resolve impasses rather than seldom-used emergency measures. A close observation of Professor Aaron's role in the Los Angeles teachers' strike suggests another type of impasse procedure that merits serious consideration as a standard technique.

Descriptively, the role calls for a person to begin as a mediator, to function entirely as an intermediary, a go-between, exploring the issues in depth as a confidant of both parties. It should be reiterated: He is at this stage a mediator, no more and no less. If the parties are responsive to his efforts, as they often are to those of any competent mediator, all well and good. He will have enabled them to bridge the gap and effect a settlement.

If the deadlock cannot be resolved by his role as an intermediary, he is still in a position to make another effective move with the consent of the parties. Possessing an insider's knowledge obtained as an intermediary, he is in a peculiarly advantageous position to make fact-finding recommendations which should encompass both the equities and the realistic expectancies of the parties.

The objection will probably be raised that the parties will be less than cooperative with a mediator who has the reserved powers to make a finding of fact. The parties will not level with a mediator, they will argue, because to make premature disclosures of areas of compromise may prejudice the outcome of his fact-finding if mediation fails. Even if that assumption were valid (which I do not concede), the reticence of the parties to cooperate with a mediator often results from the fact that his role and function are terminated if the talks are unproductive. Not so with a mediator/fact-finder. It has been demonstrated on many occasions that the parties are highly motivated to cooperate with him precisely because he combines both functions in one person. They tend to respond positively to his mediation efforts if for no other reason than because of a desire to influence his findings should he assume his ultimate role as a fact-finder. I do not advocate the use of a mediator/fact-finder as a solution for any and all disputes in the public sector. I would stress only that there are situations where it is workable, and that alternatives to strikes in the public sector are not in such abundance that we can afford to ignore any technique which offers promise.

Conclusion

Some closing thoughts of a more general nature concerning public sector developments are in order. There was a time, and it seems only recently, that labor relations in public and private employment were sealed off from each other by disparate benefits and challenges. Ideally, the public sector offered civil service, a term synonymous with job security, substantial vacations, holidays, sick-leave plans, and other generous fringe benefits. Salaries, of course, always lagged behind the private sector.

In less than 30 years, "Big Labor" has set a pace for all of private industry which has outstripped the public sector in overall fringe benefits and widened the salary gap. The one area in which the public sector still offers a substantial advantage is that of job tenure. The incidence of layoffs, although on the increase in public employment, is still negligible when compared to the conditions prevalent in private industry.

Another major contributing factor to developments in the public sector is that the proportion of white-collar and professional employees in public employment has shifted from the offspring of middle-class parents with status hangups about joining unions to the offspring of higher paid blue-collar parents who accept unions as much a part of their lives as the church, the PTA, or the local Legion post.

The one constant factor in the linkage between the public and private sectors is the long-range pull of the applicable prevailing wage in private industry. It is a primary fact of life for both sectors that they compete in the same labor market for competent personnel. The public sector tends to lag behind the private sector, even far behind, in salaries and other benefits when unemployment is more than 4 percent. But let the labor market become tight, as it has been during periods of great industrial activity, and then the public sector is compelled to make accelerated adjustments to bring their salaries and benefits much closer to the average prevailing conditions in private industry. This long-term regulative aspect of the labor market, I suggest, will never become obsolete.

Comment—

Russell A. Smith *

Mr. Block's observations concerning the subject of his paper, "Criteria in Public Sector Interest Disputes," are interesting and provocative, and I have a few reactions to some of his com-

* Member and Past President, National Academy of Arbitrators; Professor of Law, University of Michigan, Ann Arbor, Mich.

ments. But I note that, acting under a nonreviewable but prov-idential excess of jurisdiction, he has actually gone somewhat beyond the labelled subject of his remarks, so I assume it is within the prerogative of a discussant to range at least as broadly.

In his introductory comments our speaker referred to the at-tempted distinction, currently in vogue in some jurisdictions in this country and abroad, between collective negotiations and collective bargaining—or, as sometimes expressed, between a meet-and-confer concept of collective discussions and the col-lective bargaining concept as we know it in the private sector. I did not understand that Howard is to be taken necessarily as approving the attempted distinction as a basis for public sec-tor labor relations legislation, but I did understand that he con-siders the distinction a valid one—that is, one that is theoretically sound and, I gather, one that is perhaps even theoretically re-quired, as a matter of analysis, in public sector labor relations in any jurisdiction or context in which strike action is pro-hibited by law. "Bargaining," he says, connotes that a legal "consideration" is exchanged, and, on the union side, this is the giving up, for the term of the agreement, of the legal right to strike.

Howard's legal analysis may be sound enough. But if he is im-plying that because of this the meet-and-confer model has to prevail in the public sector, I guess I have to register some doubt. It seems to me the evidence, up to this point, is that public sector unions will use the strike weapon either in its outright form or some variant, whatever the state of the law, in support of bargaining demands unless they are provided with an acceptable alternative. If this is so, what we have is a de facto recognition, or at least public tolerance, of strike action, within limits. This means that unions are in a position, as a practical matter, to offer public employers a de facto, if not Willistonian, consideration to support the agreement reached in bargaining. This is *their own* promise not to strike during the term of the agreement, and I suggest that while this may not be a legal consideration, it is nevertheless a valuable one in that it consists of a pledge willingly assumed by the contract-ing party, not imposed from without, and hence is a commit-ment more likely to be observed. In other words, I suggest that the public as well as the private sector employer, through gen-uine collective bargaining, can and does buy labor peace.

The final question I would raise about this attempted "ne-gotiations"—"bargaining" distinction is whether, as a practical matter, it can prevail. Will American unions accept an approach that makes the union's role simply that of lobbyist, even though it is through a process called conferring or negotiating, under circumstances where binding agreements do not result and where employees are expected to abstain from the use of any form of pressure other than the force of reason or the ballot box? I doubt it, although it may be that they will accept and even approve as a plus this more limited role as to some of the subjects of potential bargaining that, in some jurisdictions, are now expressly excluded entirely from the area of discussions or bargaining.

After delineating the "negotiations"—"bargaining" distinc-tion, Howard proceeded to say that in the public sector if dif-ferences cannot be resolved with the help of mediation, the parties "must turn to the alternatives of interest arbitration or fact-finding as a substitute for a strike contest." Of course, if the meet-and-confer analysis were accepted fully, this would not, presumably, be true, since strike action would be foresworn in any event. But, whatever the approach, and even if we were to move increasingly toward a legal acceptance of public em-ployee strike action, at least within limits, I think, as Howard does, that there will be steadily increasing resort to the use of neutrals in a role that goes beyond that of mediation and in-cludes arbitration. And it may even turn out, contrary to orthodox view, that neutrals will increasingly be given the dual roles of mediator-arbitrator or mediator/fact-finder. Preferably, this would come about through agreement of the parties, as in the case of Sam Kagel's current involvement with the San Fran-cisco nurses. I don't profess to be an expert on the mysteries, techniques, and art of the mediation process, but I have a hunch that a neutral who starts in a given dispute as mediator, but who has been given authority, finally, to decide unresolved is-sues, is likely to be pretty productive in his initial role as mediator.

Criteria for the resolution of public sector interest disputes obviously are important, as Howard says, whether in relation to the processes of negotiation, bargaining, mediation, fact-find-ing, or arbitration. Howard recognizes the unique problems of the public sector in this regard, but has confidence, at least as to neutrals who may participate, that their expertise will result in the development of "criteria that will be ultimately acceptable to the parties in the public sector." Moreover, he believes "the public sector neutral . . . does not wander in an uncharted field even though he must at times adopt an approach diametrically opposite to that used in the private sector," although "he must be innovative" and "must plow new ground." He turns to a consideration of comparisons as the fundamental criterion, then to the matter of ability to pay and the related problem of priorities, and finally, as regards criteria, to what he terms "uniform wage policy v. inequities."

Public sector negotiations can involve difficult noneconomic problems, some of which are not easily handled in terms of readily available or easily developed criteria. Among the more complex in this category are the issues arising out of union demands that, allegedly, cannot or should not be granted because of legal limitations on the authority of the public body doing the negotiating by virtue, for example, of civil service laws, teacher tenure legislation, home rule city charters, and a wide variety of specific legislation which arguably is prescriptive concerning the right of the public body to foreclose, through bargaining, the authority of the body to retain discretion. Some very sticky legal problems exist in these areas, and the threshold question facing the neutral is whether he should duck them altogether. If he gets to the merits of a specific proposal, either bypassing or deciding the legal question, he faces the question of suitable criteria. Comparisons—that is, what has been done about such issues elsewhere—may be useful. But in many instances this will indeed be a "plow new ground" area. Union security, including agency shop, is another and related kind of issue. Absent enabling legislation, legal questions may be raised. But if resolved, a neutral may have trouble developing the basis for an answer on the merits. He may believe that private sector trends ought *not* to be controlling, and public sector practice in his state may be varied and hence of little help. Does he then eschew pioneering, wait for a bargaining pattern to develop, in effect thereby removing the issue from the case, or does he proceed, as did his predecessors in the private sector before him (including the War Labor

Board and the railroad emergency boards functioning after the enabling amendment of the Railway Labor Act) to deal with the pros and cons? In so doing, are there considerations peculiar to public sector employment which should be considered relevant?

The economic issues arising in the public sector negotiations are much like those of the private sector—that is, they are wages and fringes. As to these, my own view is that the development and application of suitable criteria for their resolution pose either no insuperable or especially unique problems, or, on the other hand, some extremely difficult and unique ones, depending almost entirely on the relevance of the question of ability to pay. If inability to pay is not pleaded, or if pleaded is deemed irrelevant, the analysis on the merits in most respects can proceed on the basis of criteria (comparisons, cost-of-living increases, inequities, and so forth) characteristic of the private sector. Some might say certain public sector issues are unique, such as the question of parity between police and firefighters, but they really aren't. Tandem relationships are common in the private sector.

But if the fiscal position of the public authority (city or school board, for example) is brought into the case and deemed relevant, the neutral's task is frequently difficult to the point of utter inability to cope with the problem, and, I might add, exhaustion, unless the finding is that the employer is utterly without the financial resources to fund *any* increase in labor costs. In that case, if the neutral regards (or is required by law to regard) ability to pay as a supervening criterion, his task is simple. He denies the union's demands. And there are some municipalities and school boards which, to use Howard Block's term, are just "dead broke," at least in terms of revenues balanced against liabilities already assumed (including those attending a retention of the existing work force). Moreover, under principles of municipal law presumably in force in many jurisdiction, deficit budgets are not supposed to exist.

But these simplistic remarks dodge a whole series of problems for the neutral ranging from the factual to the basic questions of principle. I suggest that among the very serious questions are several that are not within the realm of expertise of labor dispute arbitrators on the basis solely of their private sector experience. The initial question is in a sense factual only. It is: What is the public body's actual fiscal position in terms of its ability to absorb *any* increased operating costs? Any sound analysis of this matter often requires an exhaustive and knowledgeable inquiry into budget allocations, revenue sources, transferability of appropriations, borrowing capability, and the like. The second question is whether, if the public body's ability to absorb increased operating costs is limited (which is probably the typical situation), the neutral should attempt to determine the gross amount of increased labor costs, if any, which the public body can finance. This in itself may turn out to be a fairly complicated problem. But, assuming this gross amount can be determined, the next and crucial question is whether the neutral should assume that this fund is all that can be provided, by way of increases, for any and all groups of employees—given the repercussionary effects of an increase awarded to the group before him—or should act on the basis that this fund can be enlarged by the public body by reductions in force or rearrangements of priorities. Obviously related is the question whether the neutral should attempt to determine the impact his award will have in terms of affecting the economic demands of other groups of employees and their ultimate settlement. Bear in mind, of course, that it is assumed that these other groups of employees, and their bargaining representatives, if any, are not parties to his proceeding or represented in it.

Now I submit that inquiries of these kinds pose problems which are so serious and difficult as to make the criterion ability to pay or, more realistically, alleged inability to pay, one which, if deemed to be relevant or required by law to be taken into consideration, is likely to be taken less seriously than others, such as comparison data. One of Howard Block's observations is that he "is inclined to agree with those who insist that when a neutral rules out inability to pay as a valid defense, he should also assume some responsibility for finding the funds to implement his award," although he also adds, apparently as a proviso, "if the parties have authorized him to do so." I interpret this remark as implying that Howard not only regards ability to pay as a proper criterion for consideration, where advanced by a party, but further as stating that the neutral does, indeed, have the full responsibility, somehow, of dealing with the series of problems which, I have suggested, then must be addressed. But I doubt very much that he can or should attempt any assignment of that magnitude except perhaps in a situation where all parties concerned, including other unions, have deliberately vested in him what would be tantamount to the full authority of the public body with respect to its budget, allocations, and priorities.

What, then, is the likely result where ability to pay is accepted by the neutral, or by law forced upon him, as a factor to be taken into account? Only a searching analysis of arbitral decisions would provide anything like an accurate answer. I have knowledge of some, however, including several in which I have participated. My impression is that a number of arbitrators, absent any statutory compulsion to take fiscal matters into account, tend to regard them as substantially irrelevant. But my impression, further, is that where, as under the Michigan police and firefighter compulsory arbitration law, this is one of the several factors specified for consideration as applicable, there has been a more or less valiant effort to analyze the public body's fiscal position, and, upon finding a very tight situation, to make an award on economic issues which would be somewhat less, or stated as being somewhat less, than otherwise would have been considered justified, but yet not to let the fiscal factor predominate.

A good example of this is Harry Platt's recent award, achieved unanimously—and miraculously—in the Detroit firefighters' case. Earlier, but with respect to the same fiscal year, an award had been handed down by Bill Haber (with a rather stinging dissent by the city's nominee) granting police (patrolmen) a base (*i.e.,* top) rate of $12,000, effective July 1, 1970, as against a prior rate of $10,800 and a city offer of 6 percent. For 63 years a parity relationship on base salaries had obtained between police and firefighters. In the firefighter case the city sought to break parity, primarily, I judge, because of its assertedly desperate financial straits. Harry held for maintenance of the parity principle, but, in light of the city's financial plea, made the $12,000 salary effective as of January 1, 1971, rather than July 1, 1970, and made effective as of July 1, 1970, the city's substantially lower offer of 6 percent. Other examples in Michigan awards may be cited in which the city's fiscal position was given some, although not predominant, effect.

This review suggests that parties and legislators face sub-stantial uncertainties concerning how arbitrators will deal with the ability-to-pay factor, if argued or imposed for considera-tion. For policymakers considering compulsory arbitration legis-lation, and whether to specify criteria, it seems to me to be clear that they cannot reasonably expect the ability-to-pay factor to be regarded as controlling if listed among several factors, some inconsistent with it in particular fact situations, unless they specify that it shall be. Then, if they do, they ought to rea-lize the extreme difficulties of applying the criterion. The up-shot, of course, is that they might decide to omit it as a cri-terion, or, as has been done in some jurisdictions, to make awards on economic issues advisory only. But the difficulties in doing this are obvious and considerable.

Comment—

ARNOLD M. ZACK *

Howard's paper has dealt effectively with the several criteria that are usually invoked by the parties in their effort to win the neutral to their point of view, and the critical view he raises of each of these criteria brings into focus the dangers of the neutral's embracing any one to the exclusion of the others. They are not separable, and no one should be embraced with-out recognition of the consequence to the other.

What fascinates me in this criterion or "crutch shopping" exer-cise we find ourselves enmeshed in as neutrals, is the prospect of the collision course on which it tends to lead us. The compara-bility criterion, and I would include internal comparability herein, which Howard refers to in his discussion of uniform wage policy v. inequities, has always been particularly appealing on an equity basis, satisfying our egos that our proposed solutions to disputes help to erase the unfair treatment of one group of work-ers compared to another.

When neutrals initially began to be involved in public sector disputes, a scant three or four or five years ago for most of us, the conventional regarding of the public sector employees was that they lagged behind their private sector counter-parts by virtue of long deprivation of effective bargaining

---

* Member, National Academy of Arbitrators, Boston, Mass.

rights or procedures. This made it convenient to rely on comparability as a means of rectifying what we believed to be basic
inequities in treatment in comparison to the private sector.
Inequities in comparison to similar jobs and wage increases in
the private sector, inequities in comparison to neighboring
and/or competing communities, and the internal inequities
within the bargaining unit or the larger government unit itself
provided a satisfying rationale for proposing higher settlements. In many instances the employers themselves acquiesced
to this criterion—anxious to compete with the private sector and
other government units in recruitment and retention of personnel, hopeful of using the mediator's proposal or the fact-
finder's recommendations as leverage for increasing their budgets, and to the extent that many administrators' salaries are pegged
to their employee's salary schedules, increasing their own personal income in the process.

In those early days it was often equally convenient, and legitimate, to chastise employers who invoked an already-com-
pleted, fixed budget to bar even minimal discussion of raising
salaries above the figures unilaterally determined by the fiscal
authorities as the point beyond which they would not move.
Neutrals often recognized the illegitimacy of this negotiation
ploy by uncooperative management by proposing settlements
in excess of budgetary allocations when they believed equity
so required. As a result the employers, whose negotiating season
followed budget submission dates, began to bury extra fall-back
funds somewhere in their budgets. An increasing number of
parties moved to negotiate prior to budget drafting, arguing,
when appropriate, the more pertinent unwillingness to pay and,
in the event that the resources, tax base, or taxing authority
limitations warranted it, true inability to pay.

Thus, in the early days of public sector collective bargaining, the two disparate criteria could be fairly easily reconciled
if neutrals undertook to prove the legitimacy of claimed inequities, on the one hand, and to delve into the true financial
status of the employer, on the other, to distinguish unwillingness from inability to pay. The times have changed in many
areas of the country where public sector bargaining has become
more firmly established, whether or not legislatively authorized. The economic crunch is closing ever tighter on the public

employer faced with an inflated economy, constitutionally fixed tax basis, escalating costs, and many of the revenue-raising problems Howard outlined.

Comparability, when raised now, is less likely to refer to the private sector. Competitive collective bargaining among the myriad of public school districts and local government units has escalated salaries and reduced or eliminated the lag behind the private sector or out-stripped private sector raises. Rather, it is more often likely to refer to inter/intra government comparisons. The police-fire parity situation in New York City and the other internal inequity issues Howard raised exacerbate the situation. Yet the comparability criteria, now more often phrased in terms of inequity, continue to confront the neutral. Pick the criterion you want to show that you're worse off compared to your neighbor: rates in "X" community, rates in the average of neighboring communities, closing the gap between you and the competitor, the cost-of-living increases, rates of increase in past years compared to this year, keeping at a fixed position in the scale of salaries, starting or top, of "X" communities within "Y" miles. And the list goes on.

This charade of comparability and its appeal to precedent-oriented arbitrators serving as neutrals masks what unfortunately is becoming the real criterion for salary adjustment, and that is muscle—the service, or group of employees who can exert the greatest pressure. The more essential the service, the higher the ante, the more likely the disproportionate share of funds. The paramount criterion is not even economics; it is politics.

Clearly the reality of the strike threat is what provides the muscle. To this extent I would dispute Howard's differentiation of the role of the illegal strike in the public sector as contrasted to the legal strike in the private sector. The strike may be illegal, as it is in 48 states, and indeed in a particular district employee sentiment may be opposed to it, but only if the price is right. The occurrence of the illegal strike anywhere is the testament to the effectiveness of the threat of the strike everywhere. In virtually every public sector dispute in which I have been involved, at some early point the issue of the strike is raised. "Will they strike?" or "Can they afford a strike?" or "Won't the public kill them if they strike?" or

"But they struck next door." The answer to these questions is bound to affect the money or benefits put into the pot.

It does appear that there is a rising pressure for the strike by those who have traditionally foreclosed that avenue, claiming at least that they have lost out by peaceful means and recognizing the value of the threat. And it is this pressure, in light of the pitiful financial posture of an increasingly large number of local government units, that brings us to the collision point. Employers' arguments increasingly have a much more cogent and realistic sound in terms of true inability to pay, particularly as increasing unionization among employees in a community escalates the cost impact of settlement with any particular group.

Certainly nonessential programs can be cut, eliminated, or deferred, and certainly the threatening employee organizations can have their bluff called. But it can't be denied that some day soon, unless radical change takes place, frequent interruption in essential services and increasing hostility will more likely become the order of the day.

One radical change that I personally would deplore would be strict final and binding adjudication of wage disputes— that is, final and binding arbitration carried out in the context of aloofness from the parties which has been the hallmark of success in grievance arbitration. The stakes are much higher in new contract disputes. Howard's emphasis on acceptability of the neutral, as well as the product of his involvement, whether as mediator, fact-finder, or arbitrator, is eminently well founded. To expect conformity to an arbitrator's award on a whole range of wages, hours, and working conditions when he is deprived of the opportunity of exploring the parties' true anticipations, and range of acceptability, is to expect an obedience to authority that ignores the movements of the times. It also anticipates strong enforcement authority which contradicts the very nature of all our dispute settlement procedures to date. The cost of hostility to the parties during the life of such an ordered contract just can't be measured. The Montreal police strike, which was called in protest to a final and binding arbitration award and succeeded in reopening it for a higher settlement, is a realistic example of the problem. So too are instances of Michigan communities' refusing to accept arbitration awards.

Arbitration as we now know it in grievance processing is much less likely to succeed than the combined mediation/fact-finding or mediation-arbitration, of which Block speaks. If the parties embrace such innovations and they prove their effectiveness, then perhaps their time has come, to the detriment of our present procedural prejudice.

Although troublesome and foreign to many neutrals geared to language interpretation, such inquiry into financial data is an essential responsibility when a claim of inability to pay is challenged. Maybe it requires a new breed of neutrals with public finance or economics experience. It may become incumbent on the neutral to investigate to determine to his satisfaction whether a community's fiscal position precludes granting certain demands.

Joint acceptability of the "solution" must inevitably remain the key to dispute settlement. It becomes increasingly difficult when the neutral recognizes that he may be barred from being seduced into a settlement acceptable to the two immediate parties by a political situation where a multiplier or parity impact might cause a crisis on a much larger scale, and even face statutory bars, as noted by Russ.

With this standard in mind, several ways in which public sector interest disputes may be more readily resolved are discussed below.

Increase the Size of the Bargaining Unit

Most states handle their disputes on a community basis. In education in New York State that means a possibility of 714 disputes, with each settlement attempting to whipsaw its neighbors'. There are also problems arising from the anachronisms in structure, duplication in costs, and so forth. Impoverished urban areas, with low tax bases and depleted treasuries, are expected to pay the same salaries as wealthy suburbs; yet the surpluses of the latter are barred from use in the adjacent big cities.

Civic pride, chauvinism, school board egos, and our tradition of grassroots democracy deter any dramatic change, but continuation of the present political structures promises to out-price education and further divide the middle class from the poor.

Countywide teacher negotiations, as in Maryland, is one step toward solving this problem. Statewide negotiations, particularly where state subsidy of local education is, or ought to be, heavy, appears to be the only sensible alternative to providing equal education for all communities, rich and poor, and to keep costs better under control.

On the city level, or indeed within any community, internal whipsawing is even more of a problem than it is among or between communities. New York City is one extreme, with 300 competing units. Philadelphia, with its all-embracing citywide unit and one negotiating season, is another, far more appealing and presumably less costly.

Bring All Competing Internal Organizations Into One Coordinated Bargaining Effort

Even if there are multiple units, coordinated bargaining as in the private sector would tend to curb escalation. The difficulty of achieving this is seen in what is occurring in New York City on the current police-fire parity issue, where the city finds itself negotiating with a half dozen police-type units and their employee organizations in various departments of city government.

Attempt to Remove Wage Determination From Collective Bargaining

The alternatives to the strike are so rare that we cannot afford to ignore any possibility for resolving public employee disputes. One possibility is to develop a procedure between the parties which will voluntarily remove wage determination from annual collective bargaining.

Most public sector classifications are unique and difficult to match in counterpart form in the private sector—police, firemen, and teachers, for example. If the parties could agree to a job evaluation system setting values for the various elements, as in the private sector, and tie these evaluations of bench-mark positions to comparable private sector positions, it might be possible to tie government employee wages and increases to variations in the private sector for comparable positions. This would assure that the impact of private sector bargaining would be peacefully reflected in the public sector.

Although this approach may seem a repetition of the Davis-Bacon concepts or federal wage boards, as well as the prevailing rate concepts used in many jurisdictions, it differs in its negotiated auspices. The development of job evaluation criteria, the identification of the bench-mark jobs, and the percentage of salary differential vis-à-vis the private sector would be matters of mutual or tripartite discussion—true collective bargaining.

Once that comparability is established, the prime function of the parties' relationship becomes one of enforcement, as well as resolution of disputes over job changes, new jobs, and other applications of the guidelines. These latter could be readily arbitrated, as they are now in the private sector.

This comparability concept has long been in effect in the Federal Government, but solely by virtue of the employer's unilateral or legislated edict, and it is this which in part is inspiring ever more vocal rumblings of federal employees for a voice in wage determination. As proposed here, the guidelines of comparability, the job evaluation procedures, and rankings would be subject to negotiation between the parties—the key to acceptability; hopefully they would do it alone, but if needed, perhaps with the aid of a mutually selected neutral party.

Needless to say this sketchy proposal does considerably curtail the bread-and-butter responsibilities of the employees' staff organizations, and that political fact alone might kill it; but it provides an approach that should be explored in local communities and one which may be necessary for both parties if our cities and towns are to continue to have equitably paid staffs and are to provide services to which the public is entitled. Indeed, it may be the last remaining means of preserving any semblance of peaceful resolution of public employee disputes.

CHAPTER VIII

ETHICAL RESPONSIBILITIES OF THE ARBITRATOR

I. The Case for a Code of Professional Responsibility for Labor Arbitrators

Alex Elson *

Our session today on the ethical responsibilities of the arbitrator is somewhat unusual. We have had a standing Committee on Ethics in existence since the Academy was founded. In 1950, this committee drafted our present Code of Ethics in conjunction with representatives of the American Arbitration Association and the Federal Mediation and Conciliation Service. From the reports of the Committee on Ethics over the years, it would appear that there is little grist for its mill. Should we therefore assume that the members of the Academy are living up to the Academy's purposes, as set forth in our Constitution, "to establish and foster the highest standards of integrity, competence, honor and character among those engaged in the arbitration of industrial disputes on a professional basis," and "to adopt and encourage the acceptance of and adherence to canons of ethics that govern the conduct of arbitrators"? Having received no complaints, should we not further assume that there are none of any substantial character? Why then do we continue our intensive soul-searching? Perhaps if we could put the Academy on the couch long enough, some skillful psychoanalyst could help dredge up from our collective unconscious the conflicts that lead us to this afternoon and this particular session. Please be assured that I will not attempt any Freudian or neo-Freudian interpretation. I am abysmally ignorant of my own unconscious, and it would be presumptuous of me even to think about the deep recesses of my fellow arbitrators' unconscious. But such probing, if it were possible, is indeed unnecessary. There are reasons for our concern we can identify. I begin by reviewing these reasons.

First, we are in a period of change characterized by great pres-

---

* Member, National Academy of Arbitrators, Chicago, Ill.

sure to reorder our priorities to place foremost the task of strengthening our societal systems to help realize our most deeply cherished values and goals. These goals include the dignity and worth of each individual, a just and fair society, peace and order in a troubled nation and world, growth and stability in our economy, and emphasis on those elements of life our founding fathers may have envisaged as appropriate to the pursuit of happiness.

As a result of the winds of change violently circulating in this country for the past few years, attention has focused on the professions. The gap between our preachments and our practices has been mercilessly exposed. Fortas, Haynsworth, and cases involving conduct of state court judges have produced concern and anxiety on the part of the judiciary and have led to the adoption of codes of conduct by various federal and state judicial bodies. The American Bar Association has approved a set of rules having to do with conflict of interest of judges. It is now in the process of reconsidering the canons of judicial conduct adopted many years ago. It has recently approved a far-reaching and comprehensive Code of Professional Responsibility to take the place of its former Canons of Ethics. Many state bar associations have adopted this Code. Even the American Medical Association and constituent local medical societies have taken a fresh look at the problem of delivery of medical services, particularly to the low- and middle-income groups, and have relaxed their traditional opposition to group- and government-sponsored programs providing medical services. The teaching profession, particularly the faculties of universities, has for several years been engaged in intensive evaluation of its obligations, not only in the area of university governance, but in relation to its responsibilities to the consumers of its efforts. Many of the clergy have left their cloisters and are putting their religion to work where "the action is."

The second reason, directly related to the first, is that in the two decades since our Code of Ethics was adopted, the profession of labor arbitration has come of age. The growth has been tremendous. Labor arbitration has become an important system in industrial conflict resolution. Nevertheless, we are still troubled by whether we can claim for ourselves the status of a profession. William Loucks described a key distinguishing characteristic of a profession in his most insightful paper, "Arbitration—

A Profession," given at the Thirteenth Annual Meeting of the Academy:

> "It consists of a membership composed solely of those who are willing and anxious to follow an enlightened consensus on what activities and acts are permissible, demanded, or precluded to the practitioner—basically without fear of organized sanction against the individual. . . . The concern of the classic professions is to see that established emphases upon function, service, and codes of behavior are not chiseled away—our concern is to see that more and more emphasis is put upon performance of function, that more and more we build, through our individual behavior as arbitrators, those codes of right and wrong which keep our efforts focused on performance of function."

Human nature being what it is, it follows that an individual arbitrator will give more weight and attention to his professional obligation when there is an organized and persistent reminder and stimulus coming from the Academy.

Third, a substantial number of arbitrators are not members of this Academy. Over the years, but less so in recent years, rumors of serious misconduct have circulated. These have included charging very high fees which have no relationship to the amount of time spent, rigged awards, and, I believe, an isolated case or two of an arbitrator who indicated he would throw the case one way or the other for a side payment. Almost without exception these rumors involved nonmembers of the Academy. Our concern indeed was and is not about our members, most of whom, except for the founders, have been carefully screened in advance and were admitted only after careful investigation, but for all arbitrators outside of the Academy. I should add, parenthetically, that we may suffer here from a parochial bias. Indeed, at this point there is little hard evidence that demonstrates that the ethical conduct of arbitrators outside of the Academy falls below the standard of conduct of members of the Academy. The concern, nevertheless, remains and provides some of the impetus for our inquiry.

Fourth, there have been constant and recurring complaints having to do with both the expense and the delay involved in the arbitration process. I am informed that the FMCS receives an average of three letters a week from parties complaining about delay—both in setting hearing dates and in the issuance of awards. Complaints on fees are somewhat fewer, averaging two or three a month. But these statistics are but the tip of an ice-berg. We must remember that most parties, for a variety of rea-sons, are reluctant to make complaints. Inherent in the problems of delay and expense are standards of conduct, to some extent touched on in our present Code of Ethics, which need further inquiry and elaboration.

Within the limitations of time, I do not believe I can make a fruitful contribution by discussing isolated problems involv-ing specific questions of ethical conduct. Instead, I should like to focus on what I believe should be the immediate role of the Academy in this area. The Code was superbly drafted. It was an exceptional document considering the difficulty then con-fronting the draftsmen in formulating rules of conduct for the widely varied collection of individuals engaged in labor arbitra-tion; there was also proper concern about moving too fast in a field where flexibility is a prime consideration. The developments of the past 20 years make clear that we need to take a fresh look at the Code. The time has come for a complete restatement of the Code of Ethics. We should commence immediately to draft a Code of Professional Responsibility for Labor Arbitrators. I will not pre-sume to do more than to indicate the bare outline of such a code and some of the subjects which I believe need special attention and consideration in any revision.

You will note that I use the term "Code of Professional Re-sponsibility." This is a title borrowed from the American Bar Association's recent revision of its Canons of Ethics. Canons are like commandments. They are basically negative in tone and commitment. The time is past for simply a string of "thou shalt nots." We should accentuate the affirmative obligations growing out of membership in a profession. In particular, we should artic-ulate the positive obligations of arbitrators to achieve the high objectives of the arbitration process—that of an impartial, com-petent, expeditious, and relatively inexpensive method of dis-pute resolution.

Much of the content of the present Code of Ethics belongs in a new Code. I would hope that what is retained will be restated in affirmative form. It should be made clear to all arbitrators that it is not enough to avoid engaging in improper conduct but that it is the responsibility of each individual arbitrator to do everything in his power to achieve the objectives of the arbitration process. Beyond the tone of the Code, there is need, as I see it, for more content indicating in more specific terms what arbitrators should do to fulfill their responsibility as professionals. I intend to do so only in summary fashion and to relate this content to the four objectives I have previously mentioned: impartiality, competency, expedition, and reasonableness of cost. I shall take these up in turn.

I. Impartiality

In general we assume that impartiality is achieved when the arbitrator has been accepted by the parties. But acceptability is no guarantee of impartiality. In the case of the permanent arbitrator, or one who has regularly served the parties over a period of years, impartiality may be assumed by his acceptability. But in the case of ad hoc arbitration, in many cases one or both parties may have had no prior experience with the arbitrator selected. As is true in the judicial field, appearance of impartiality may be just as important as impartiality itself, and this brings us to the conflict-of-interest area which is the subject of Herbert Sherman's paper. I will not trespass on his topic except to say that there is an affirmative duty on the part of an arbitrator to remove himself from any case in which he believes his impartiality is compromised or when there are circumstances which may lead to doubt as to his impartiality. There is need for amplification of conflict-of-interest situations. I should note in passing that the report of the Special Committee on Standards of Judicial Conduct appointed by the American Bar Association took about eight pages, double-spaced, to set forth the standards that should apply. While part of the report is not directly relevant to the labor arbitrator, the bulk of it will provide a frame of reference for the draftsmen of a new Code of Professional Responsibility.

II. Competency

We come next to the matter of competency. Here the emphasis should be put upon performance of function. There are obligations related to competency, of course, which may be regarded as institutional or as belonging to the Academy, and obligations and responsibilities which can be identified as individual. The Academy has been aware of the keen need for training of arbitrators and also for the encouragement of all efforts to mark out an educational route which can be preparatory to entering the profession of arbitration. As an Academy we have not accomplished a great deal in either of these respects, but there has been some progress. Far more economics departments, departments of industrial relations, and law schools are including courses in arbitration, and the literature in the field has grown substantially, the best part of it being the annual proceedings of the Academy.

There are a number of areas in which the individual arbitrator has primary responsibility. The first I mention is more negative than positive. Clearly, no arbitrator should undertake an arbitration beyond his competence. One illustration should suffice and that is the review of a wage incentive. I need not tell this group that an arbitration involving a wage incentive cannot be properly handled by a novice or one who has never previously been involved in the establishment of incentive rates. The least that an arbitrator who first encounters a case of this character should do is to make clear to the parties his lack of experience. If, notwithstanding this disclosure, the parties wish him to proceed, he should raise with the parties the advisability of providing consultation with an industrial engineer, certainly in his early ventures in the field. Other problems of this character likewise require an arbitrator without adequate experience to proceed with care and caution. Clearly, an arbitration involving a determination of contract terms, particularly of wages, should not be undertaken by an arbitrator devoid of requisite economic background and of knowledge of established criteria for wage determination.

On the positive side, the Code should make clear that individual arbitrators should do everything in their power to help train beginners in the field by taking on assistants where their caseload warrants it, and by advising and counseling them. In addition, arbitrators should be available for instruction and training of the representatives of the parties. It is axiomatic to say that the success of the arbitration process depends not only on the arbitrator but on the labor and management representatives that appear before him. The AAA has been active for many years in arranging training sessions for the parties, and it should be accepted as an obligation of the individual arbitrator that he be generous with his time when he is asked to participate in this type of training.

Finally, the individual arbitrator has an obligation to keep himself abreast of developments in the field. Among lawyers the continuing education of the bar has received tremendous impetus in recent years, and arbitrators should not assume that they can simply get by with the experience of arbitrating cases. They should expand their horizons to include the benefit of research and education wherever that is made available to them.

The American Bar Association Code of Professional Responsibility, Ethical Considerations, Rules 6-1, 6-2, and 6-5, relate to competency and are relevant to this discussion. They read:

> "EC 6-1. Because of his vital role in the legal process, a lawyer should act with competence and proper care in representing clients. He should strive to become and remain proficient in his practice and should accept employment only in matters which he is or intends to become competent to handle.

> "EC 6-2. A lawyer is aided in attaining and maintaining competence by keeping abreast of current legal literature and developments, participating in continuing legal education programs, concentrating in particular areas of the law, and by utilizing other available means. He has the additional ethical obligation to assist in improving the legal profession, and he may do so by participating in bar activities intended to advance the quality and standards of members of the profession. Of particular importance is the careful training of his younger associates and the giving of sound guidance to all lawyers who consult him. In short, a lawyer should strive at all levels to aid the legal profession in advancing the highest possible standards of integrity and competence and to meet those standards himself.

> "EC 6-5. A lawyer should have pride in his professional endeavors. His obligation to act competently calls for higher motivation than that arising from fear of civil liability or disciplinary penalty."

III. Expedition

We come next to the matter of expedition. I need not tell this group that delay presents one of the most serious problems in the arbitration process. Delay is behind a good deal of the discontent that exists with the process and forms the basis for the bulk of complaints. It is a truism that delay in the process is the responsibility not only of the arbitrator but of the parties. Arbitrators can do little or nothing about delays which occur prior to the time they are approached. But there are two types of delay which follow the appointment of the arbitrator. First, delay in scheduling, and second, delay in issuing the award after the case has been submitted by the parties. As to the first type of delay, the parties who agree to a long delay are at least put on notice by the arbitrator. Parties may be reluctant to change once their choice is made. Accordingly, there may be an affirmative duty on the part of the arbitrator, in the interest of expedition, to make clear to the parties that they are free to name another arbitrator to hear the case. When it comes to delays following the submission of the case, the responsibility is entirely on the arbitrator. Most complaints about arbitrators relate to the long time taken to issue awards. More than any other factor, a delayed award discredits the arbitration process and the arbitration profession. It defeats one of the most cherished objectives of arbitration—an expeditious resolution of the dispute. The new Code should place an affirmative obligation on the part of the arbitrator to decline appointment when he has a backlog of aged cases that have not been reduced to awards.

IV. Expense

Finally, we come to the matter of expense. This subject has also been extensively considered in the past. We all agree that excessive fees should be avoided. But when are fees excessive? While we cannot say very much specifically about what fees should be without running the risk of being charged with price-fixing, we can say more than our present Code states. The present Code simply states that fees "should be reasonable and consistent with the nature of the case and the circumstances of the parties." We should be able to relate the factors to be taken into consideration in the fixing of fees with greater particularity. Time taken by itself cannot and should not be the sole criterion. The parties should not be expected to pay for the education of the arbitrator. If a young and inexperienced arbitrator takes a week or 10 days to write an award on a relatively simple case, he should charge not on the basis of the time spent, but what would be a fair fee considering the nature of the issue involved. On the other hand, the undertaking of an arbitration involving the determination of contract terms, fixing rates of pay, rules, and working conditions for a substantial number of employees carries with it responsibility warranting compensating at a higher level than that of the ordinary grievance arbitration.

Then there is the problem of parties with limited financial resources—the small company or small union. An important characteristic of a profession is its willingness to place service first and to provide that service to all who need it on a basis on which they can afford to pay. Some years ago, our president, Jean McKelvey, suggested a device which would serve two purposes, providing entry into the field of young arbitrators and a low-cost arbitration service. That device was the sponsoring of arbitration clinics in some of our larger cities, perhaps with the help of the appointing agencies, to provide arbitration at modest fees for clients unable to afford customary fees and to enable young arbitrators to gain experience. I am not suggesting that any specific proposal of this character be incorporated in the Code, but I do think the Code should make clear the obligation of the profession to provide services on a low-cost basis for parties whose financial circumstances warrant this treatment.

Miscellaneous Comments

There are a number of miscellaneous matters that should be considered.

Part III of the present Code relates to the conduct and behavior of the parties. I am not certain in my own mind that a Code of Professional Responsibility should include material of this character. If a decision is made to cover the parties as well as the arbitrators, then it would seem to me that the parties should be drawn into the drafting process. If we expect the parties to be guided by our Code, I am sure it would be generally agreed that they should have a voice in its formation.

Some additional developments during the past two decades should be reflected in the new Code of Professional Responsibility. They arise out of one of the central considerations of the Landrum-Griffin Act—the recognition of the need to protect individual employee's rights. What is the responsibility of the arbitrator to protect the rights of an affected individual employee caught between the claims of the company and the union or possibly victimized by collusion of the parties? What should be said about the informed or rigged award? Along with these problems are the due process problems set forth with deep insight by Willard Wirtz in his paper at the Eleventh Annual Meeting of the Academy in 1958.

Finally, should the Code of Professional Responsibility extend to the other roles played by neutrals? One of the significant changes that has taken place in recent years, primarily because of the growth of public employee bargaining, is the increasing involvement of arbitrators in mediation and fact-finding. I would suppose that most members of the Academy have served in a neutral role other than arbitrator. Consideration should be given to including provisions in the Code relating to these special neutral roles after weighing the differences in practices and procedures of such neutrals and arbitrators.

Conclusion

Each period through which we live seems troubled and beset with difficulties. Today we are overwhelmed with problems that seem insoluble. I will not recite the litany all too familiar to you. The ethics of our profession seem inconsequential by comparison with the major crises that confront the nation, the states, and the cities, but the fact remains that we are the mainspring of an important system of dispute resolution and that the improvement of this system and the functioning of those who profess to arbitrate is one of the primary goals of this Academy. To this end I have attempted to suggest in bare-bone fashion some of the principal factors that should be taken into consideration in the drafting of the new Code. But I am fully aware that the generalities of my remarks mask a morass of difficult and delicate problems which will confront the draftsmen. We have not heretofore avoided challenge, and I trust you will agree that the time has come for a Code of Professional Responsibility for Labor Arbitrators.

II. Arbitrator's Duty of Disclosure—A Sequel

Herbert L. Sherman, Jr. *

The choice of the title for this paper is explained by the fact that it is a sequel to my prior article on the labor arbitrator's duty of disclosure, which was published last year in the

* Member, National Academy of Arbitrators; Professor of Law, University of Pittsburgh, Pittsburgh, Pa.

University of Pittsburgh Law Review[1] and in the *Arbitration Journal*.[2] At the outset of this paper I shall summarize the contents of that article, which will serve as an introduction to a discussion of some developments not covered in the prior article.

Summary of Prior Article

Part I of the prior article covers the basis and general nature of the duty of disclosure. Compliance with this obligation is important because an arbitrator's award may be invalidated by a court if the arbitrator has not properly fulfilled his duty. Part I discusses relevant provisions of the Code of Ethics of the National Academy of Arbitrators, the Rules of the American Arbitration Association, the Regulations of the Federal Mediation and Conciliation Service, the United States Arbitration Act, the three-way split of the Supreme Court of the United States in a commercial arbitration case involving the duty of disclosure, and the Canons of Judicial Ethics. These sources are in general accord with that part of Rule 3 of the Code of Ethics of the National Academy of Arbitrators which requires an arbitrator ". . . to disclose to the parties any circumstances, associations or relationships that might reasonably raise any doubt as to his impartiality . . . for the particular case." However, unlike some of the other sources cited, the Code of Ethics does not require an arbitrator to disqualify himself for any given case. The Code simply requires an arbitrator to comply with his duty of disclosure, and the parties are then free to regard him as qualified or not qualified.

Part II of the prior article notes that there are varying philosophies concerning the function of arbitration. Some see arbitration as primarily a substitute for litigation, while others view labor arbitration as primarily a substitute for the strike. Some consider an arbitrator to be like a judge, but others stress the differences between a judge and a labor arbitrator. These differing views concerning the functions of arbitration and the role of the labor arbitrator frequently affect the position that one takes on the question of what a labor arbitrator must disclose to the parties.

---

[1] 31 *U. Pitt. L. Rev.* 377 (1970).
[2] 25 *Arb. J.* 73 (1970).

Part III of the prior article describes a survey, which I made, of the views of arbitrators and of labor and management representatives on what an arbitrator must disclose to the parties. A questionnaire, with 30 questions based on actual situations, was prepared. Each question could be answered by "Yes" or "No" or "It Depends." The purpose of the questionnaire was to give some concrete meaning to the legal, ethical, and moral abstractions that are used to characterize the arbitrator's duty of disclosure. The prior article described the general conditions, assumptions, and limitations involved in the survey, and it reports the comments of many of the respondents.

The results of the survey were tabulated for arbitrators as a category, for union representatives as a category, and for company representatives as a category. An Appendix attached to the prior article also breaks down the returns from arbitrators into four categories: (1) lawyer and teacher, (2) neither, (3) lawyer, non-teacher, and (4) non-lawyer, teacher. For the most part there was no significant variation in the answers of these four categories.

Part IV of the prior article reports the tabulated results of the answers of arbitrators and of union and company representatives to the 30 questions in the questionnaire and analyzes the returns. The 30 questions cover the following 12 topics: prior consulting work of an arbitrator, lectures and conference participation, the professor-arbitrator's role at a university, stock ownership, travel and hotel problems, prior social and civic contacts with representatives of the parties, membership in a "conflict of interest" organization, prior contacts in arbitration, prior memberhip in a union, hortatory expressions to arbitrator, fellow arbitrator as representative of a party, and the role of the arbitrator in political maneuvers.

Subsequent Developments

Several relevant developments have taken place since my prior article was published. During the past year a New York court has invalidated a labor arbitrator's award because of the arbitrator's failure to comply with his duty of disclosure. The Special Committee of the American Bar Association on Standards of Judicial Conduct has issued a preliminary statement and interim report on matters which are relevant to the arbitrator's duty of disclosure. I have reviewed a series of cases involving disqualification of a justice or judge and a series of commercial arbitration cases. Moreover, I have made further analyses of the answers of arbitrators and of company and union representatives to my 30-question questionnaire.[3] For example, I have compared the answers of arbitrators from the Northeast, the Midwest, the South, and the Far West to determine whether there is any significant difference in the answers to the questions on the basis of geographical regions. I have also compared the answers of company and union representatives from the Northeast and the Midwest to determine whether there is any significant difference in the answers to the questions from these representatives. This paper will relate these subsequent developments to the specific topics analyzed in the prior article.

As a general observation, however, it should be noted that my recent studies show that there are only a few significant variations in the answers of arbitrators from the various parts of the country to the 30 questions in the questionnaire. And the prevailing views of company representatives from the Northeast are the same as the prevailing views of company representatives from the Midwest (except for answers to two questions concerning ownership of shares of stock). Likewise, the prevailing views of union representatives from the Northeast are essentially the same as the prevailing views of union representatives from the Midwest.

Appendix A to this paper shows the number and percentage of arbitrators in the Northeast, the Midwest, the South, and the Far West who answered each of the 30 questions with a "Yes," a "No," or "It Depends."[4] Appendix B shows the number and percentage of union representatives and company representatives in the Northeast and the Midwest who answered each of the 30 questions with a "Yes," a "No," or "It Depends."[5]

---

[3] The author gratefully acknowledges the assistance rendered by Miss Geraldine Sabol, a law student at the University of Pittsburgh School of Law, in connection with these studies.

[4] Responses of Canadian arbitrators were included in the tabulations published in the prior article. However, the number of such responses was insufficient to tabulate them as a separate group, and such responses were excluded from the tabulations contained in Appendix A to this article.

[5] Included in the tabulations for the original article were responses from a few union and company representatives not located in the Northeast or Midwest. These responses have been excluded from the tabulations in Appendix B to this article.

I turn now to the specific topics covered in the prior survey.

Prior Consulting Work of Arbitrator

A majority of the arbitrators and union representatives (but not company representatives) who responded to my questionnaire indicated that a labor arbitrator has a duty to disclose to the parties that 10 years ago he received a consulting fee of $500 from one of the parties for a matter not related to labor relations, but the vast majority of all respondents took the position that an arbitrator has no duty to disclose that 10 years ago he received a consulting fee of $500 from *another* company in the same industry for a matter not related to labor relations.

Such views are consistent with the recent holding of the Appellate Division of the New York Supreme Court in *Colony Liquor Distributors* v. *Teamsters Local 699.*[6] In that case the arbitrator, who was a staff member of the New York State Board of Mediation, was not a member of the National Academy of Arbitrators. The court vacated his award in favor of a local union because he failed to disclose to the employer that he had been employed as an attorney by other locals of the same international union, apparently within six months of the arbitration hearing, that during the calendar year preceding the arbitration hearing he received $10,000 from these other local unions for his services, and that he had a close relative still employed by the international union as an accountant at the time of the hearing.

The court pointed out, "The mere fact that there has been a prior association of an arbitrator with one of the parties, in and of itself, does not necessarily require disqualification." But even though the employer did not claim that the arbitrator was guilty of actual bias, the court notes that the nondisclosure of the arbitrator's prior association with the other locals of the international union deprived the employer of pertinent information which he was entitled to have to make an independent decision as to whether he would accept the arbitrator in spite of his previous associations. The court correctly finds that the relationship of the arbitrator to one of the parties was more than insignificant. This conclusion is amply supported by the cumulative effect of the *recency* of the association of the arbitrator

---

[6] 312 N.Y.S.2d 403, 74 LRRM 2945 (1970), *revs'g* the decision below, 74 LRRM 2942 (1970).

with another branch of a party to the arbitration, the *professional* nature of the relationship, and the fact that the *amount of money* which he received for his services indicated that the relationship was significant.

The holding in this case is consistent with the holding in *Commonwealth Coatings Corp.* v. *Continental Casualty Co.*,[7] a commercial arbitration case in which a majority of the Supreme Court of the United States vacated an arbitration award because the neutral member of an arbitration panel for a dispute between a prime contractor and a subcontractor failed to disclose to the subcontractor that he had received $12,000 in consultant's fees from the prime contractor over a period of four to five years and that he in fact had rendered service as a consultant on the very projects which became involved in arbitration. The prior business relation of the neutral arbitrator with one of the parties was clearly significant in that case and should have been disclosed.

In other commercial arbitration cases, state courts have set aside arbitration awards where an arbitrator failed to disclose that business transactions between him and one of the parties increased substantially during the pendency of the arbitration proceedings,[8] where an arbitrator failed to disclose that in a regular course of dealing with one of the parties he had made purchases running into millions of dollars,[9] and where an arbitrator failed to disclose that he had been on the staff of the law firm representing one of the parties within three years of the arbitration hearing.[10] On the other hand, it has been held that a relationship which is "peripheral, superficial or insignificant" need not be disclosed.[11]

It is interesting to note that in an AAA case, disclosure by

---

[7] 393 U.S. 145 (1968).

[8] *Dukraft Mfg. Co.* v. *Bear Mill Mfg. Co.*, 22 Misc.2d 1057, 151 N.Y.S.2d 318 (1956). Cf. *Dulien Steel Products* v. *The Ogeka*, 147 F.Supp. 167 (D.C. Wash. 1956) (arbitrator not deemed to be partial merely because prior to his retirement his company had been represented by the law firm representing one of the parties in arbitration) and *Texas Eastern Transmission Corp.* v. *Barnard*, 177 F.Supp. 123 (D.C. E.D. Ky. 1959) (mere fact that counsel for one of the parties was also counsel for bank for which arbitrator was an officer did not establish "evident partiality" of arbitrator).

[9] *Milliken Woolens, Inc.* v. *Weber Knit Sportswear, Inc.*, 202 N.Y.S.2d 431 (1960).
[10] *Id.*

[11] *In the Matter of Cross Properties, Inc. and Gimbel Bros., Inc.*, 225 N.Y.S.2d 1014 (1962).

the arbitrator to the AAA of a prior business relationship may not prevent his award from being set aside. In a commerical case in which the arbitrator advised the tribunal clerk of the AAA of the arbitrator's $2,200 business transaction with one of the parties a little over a year prior to the arbitrator's appointment, a federal court in New Jersey set the award aside because the tribunal clerk had not transmitted the disclosure to the parties.[12]

Lectures and Conference Participation

Over 90 percent of the respondents to the questionnaire agree that an arbitrator has no duty to disclose to the parties that last year he received a free lunch when he gave a general talk to a personnel association meeting which included some representatives of the company now seeking his services, or that last year he participated in a conference, sponsored by the AAA for representatives of various unions, on how to be more effective in labor arbitration, and the conference included a representative of the union now seeking his services. The prevailing view seems to be that service as a lecturer or a conference participant, even on labor arbitration, need not be disclosed and that something with as trifling monetary value as a free lunch need not be disclosed.

The Interim Report of the Special Committee on Standards of Judicial Conduct of the American Bar Association proposes that a judge "should not accept gifts or loans from lawyers or litigants, or any gift of a value in excess of $100 unless it is from a member of his family or is reported by him in the same manner as receipt of outside compensation." [13] Theoretically a gift of a free lunch from a lawyer to a judge would fall within this provision, but it seems probable that such a gift, whether or not the recipient gave a lecture, would be deemed to be de minimis.

One interesting aspect of this interim report is that it applies only to full-time, and not part-time, judges. But most arbitrators serve as such only on a part-time basis. Thus, the provisions of this report are not applicable to the typical arbitrator even if the role of an arbitrator is analogized to that of a judge, since the typical arbitrator is only a part-time judge. This report sim-

---

[12] *Rogers* v. *Schering Corp.*, 165 F.Supp. 295 (D.C. N.J. 1958).
[13] Interim Report, Section 6 (c).

ply suggests some possible standards which might be considered by the National Academy of Arbitrators.

The Professor-Arbitrator's Role at a University

Although the interim report of the ABA committee provides that a judge should not serve as an arbitrator except under extraordinary circumstances, the report does recognize that a judge "may speak, write, lecture, teach, or participate in seminars on matters pertaining to the law and the legal system" provided that he does not take a position that would affect his impartiality.[14] Likewise, it is clear that an arbitrator may properly perform these normal functions of a professor on matters pertaining to arbitration and that a professor who performs these functions is not doing something that is incompatible with the role of an arbitrator.

But to what extent must a professor-arbitrator disclose his academic contacts to the parties? The vast majority of the respondents to my questionnaire agree that an arbitrator has no duty to disclose to the parties that a company now seeking his services has sent representatives to a university to attend a management training program for various companies, and that the arbitrator teaches a course in industrial relations in that program. And most respondents agree that the arbitrator has no duty to disclose that a representative of one of the parties is a former degree-seeking student of the arbitrator, at least where there was no close relationship between the student and the arbitrator. In fact, many a professor-arbitrator who has taught for many years would not recognize, or be sure, that a representative is a former student. Although the arbitrators from the Far West are closely divided on the proper answer to this question, the prevailing view among arbitrators from other regions, in accord with the view of most company and union representatives, is that there is no duty to disclose that a representative of one of the parties is a former degree-seeking student of the arbitrator. But most respondents believe that an arbitrator does have a duty to disclose that a representative of one of the parties is a former student-research assistant for the arbitrator. The same would probably be true of a representative whose graduate thesis was supervised by the professor-arbitrator.

---

[14] Interim Report, Sections 2 and 9 (a) .

In addition to faculty-student contacts, a professor, of course, has contacts with other faculty members and speakers at the university. Most respondents to my questionnaire take the position that an arbitrator has no duty to disclose that the union or company representative has given a talk to the arbitrator's class at the request of the arbitrator. This position is consistent with the holding in *MacNeil* v. *Cohen*,[15] in which the First Circuit Court of Appeals held that the chief judge of that court was not disqualified to sit on a case against a defendant simply because the chief judge had been a lecturer at Harvard Law School when one of the defendant's partners, James Landis, was dean of that law school. The court found that the relationship of the chief judge and former Dean Landis did not fall within the federal disqualification statute, which states, "Any justice or judge of the United States shall disqualify himself in any case in which he has a substantial interest, has been of counsel, is or has been a material witness, or is related to or connected with any party or his attorney as to render it improper, in his opinion, for him to sit on the trial, appeal, or other proceeding therein." [16]

Stock Ownership and Other Financial Interests

Most respondents to my questionnaire believe that an arbitrator has a duty to disclose to the parties that he or his wife owns 500 shares of the stock of the company now seeking his services, or that he or his wife owns only five shares, or that he owns 50 shares in an affiliate or subsidiary corporation. Although it has been held that ownership by a judge of 20 shares of common stock of RCA, which had issued over 13 million shares, was not a substantial interest,[17] the prevailing view seems to be that any amount of stock ownership must be disclosed by an arbitrator, whether it is significant or insignificant.

The interim report of the special committee of the ABA states that a full-time judge should *disqualify* himself in any case in which he knows that he has an interest, which "includes any legal or equitable interest, no matter how small," in the party

---

15 264 F.2d 186 (1st Cir. 1959).

16 28 U.S.C. § 455 (1948).

17 *Lampert* v. *Hollis*, 105 F.Supp. 3 (D.C. N.Y. 1952).

or issue in litigation.[18] Apparently ownership of one share of stock requires disqualification under this proposal. Another provision of the report says that a judge "should not hold any investment or other financial interest in an enterprise that is likely to be involved in proceedings in his court." [19] Although the report states that "Ownership of shares in a mutual fund or other entity is also an 'interest' if the mutual fund or other entity holds a substantial interest in a party to the litigation," my correspondence with the reporter for the committee indicates that this provision may be modified. How many judges or arbitrators would know whether a mutual fund in which they hold shares has a substantial interest in a party appearing before the adjudicator?

My correspondence with the reporter for the committee also indicates that special rules may be developed to cover the ownership of government bonds and the ownership of shares in a corporation affiliated with a party to the proceeding.

But again a full-time judge can be distinguished from a part-time arbitrator, not only because the interim report of the ABA committee recognizes a distinction between the role of a full-time judge and that of a part-time judge but also because of the difference in the job security of a judge and the job security of an arbitrator. Senator Birch Bayh of Indiana, a strong advocate of more rigid controls over federal judges to compel them to disqualify themselves on certain grounds, recognizes a distinction between a full-time judge who has lifetime tenure and a member of Congress who has little job security because he is elected for a limited term and his conduct is subject to review by his constituents. He advocates *disqualification* of a federal judge in certain situations, but only a *duty of disclosure* for a member of Congress because of the difference in job security.[20] On the basis of this line of reasoning an arbitrator could be deemed to be more like a member of Congress than a judge.

One point that should be raised is whether a judge should be disqualified to sit on a case simply because he has *some* financial interest in the outcome. If he is disqualified by *any* financial interest, then no judge of the United States could be qualified

---

[18] Interim Report, Section 8. But a judge who was a depositor in a bank was held not to have a disqualifying pecuniary interest in a suit against trustees of stock of the bank in *Long* v. *Stites,* 63 F.2d 855 (6th Cir. 1933).
[19] Interim Report, Section 6 (b).
[20] *Trial,* April-May 1970, p. 48.

to pass on the constitutionality of a broad-based tax such as the federal income tax. The ABA special committee report says that a judge is disqualified if he has any interest in the proceeding, but that when disclosure of the nature of the interest shows that the judge's interest is insubstantial in the opinion of *all* parties, they may waive the judge's disqualification.[21] A literal reading of this section of the report would mean that a party who objected to a suit challenging the constitutionality of a broad-based tax could prevent any court test by refusing to waive the disqualification of all judges.[22] In any event, it has been held that a judge is not disqualified to pass on the validity of bonds of a county of which he is a taxpayer simply because he is a taxpayer.[23]

Compare the status of an arbitrator who is asked to arbitrate a public employee dispute between a state government and a union of its employees. Is every arbitrator who is a *resident* of that state disqualified to serve as a neutral arbitrator because the result of the case could affect his taxes? Is every arbitrator who is a *nonresident* of that state disqualified from arbitrating in that state if there is a business privilege tax applicable to performance of services by nonresidents in that state and the result of the case may affect the amount of the business privilege tax in the future?

Rule 11 of the 1970 Voluntary Labor Arbitration Rules of the AAA states that "no person shall serve as a neutral Arbitrator in any arbitration in which he has any financial . . . interest in the result of the arbitration, unless the parties, in writing, waive such disqualification." But suppose that one party refuses to waive the disqualification. If all judges and all arbitrators are disqualified by any financial interest in the outcome of the case, no matter how small the interest, the judicial process and the arbitration process can be frustrated by the refusal of

---

[21] Interim Report, Section 8.

[22] In *Tumey* v. *State of Ohio*, 273 U.S. 510, 523 (1927), the Supreme Court held that there is a violation of due process where the judge has "a direct, personal, substantial pecuniary interest" in the result of the case. But this statement was made in the context of a case involving a criminal trial before a mayor of a village who would receive no fee unless he found the defendant guilty. The mayor received about $100 a month from the procedures in question. Bribery, discussed *infra* in connection with playing poker or golf (under "Prior Social and Civic Contacts With Representatives of the Parties"), is another example of an improper financial interest in the outcome of a case.

[23] *Wade* v. *Travis*, 75 F. 985 (W.D. Texas, 1896).

one party to waive the disqualification. Perhaps the arbitrator may interpret AAA Rule 11 in such a way that it does not cover a remote and very slight financial interest. Under Rule 46 it is provided that "[t]he Arbitrator shall interpret and apply these Rules insofar as they relate to his powers and duties."

Does an arbitrator have a duty to disclose his status as a tax-payer in all public employee disputes, such as disputes involving policemen and firefighters? In a case involving a public utility for gas, electricity, or water, does an arbitrator have a duty to disclose that he is a customer of the utility and that the result of the case could affect his utility bill? Even if he is not a customer of that utility, an award affecting the rates of that utility could have an indirect effect on other similar utilities in the area, including the utilities of which the arbitrator is a customer. From my experience I believe that the parties are already aware of the taxpayer status of the arbitrator and his status as a customer of a public utility when they select him as an arbitrator for these types of cases. It is doubtful whether these matters involve disqualification. If they do, parties who know the location of the residence and office of the arbitrator should be deemed to have waived any disqualification on these grounds when they selected the arbitrator.[24]

Perhaps it is wise for the arbitrator to disclose these matters out of an excess of caution, but undue disclosure can have undesirable consequences. A party has been known to seize upon disclosure of relatively insignificant matters as an excuse for causing delay in the arbitration proceedings, or as an excuse for seeking another list of arbitrators from an appointing agency in the hope that another arbitrator more sympathetic to that party may be selected. Undue disclosure by an arbitrator may cause these undesirable tactical maneuvers, thus promoting injustice under the legal disguise of preserving due process.

Travel and Hotel Problems

Most respondents to my questionnaire believe that an arbitrator has no duty to disclose that he found himself sitting beside the union representative for the next day's hearing on the plane

---

[24] Cf. *Newburger v. Rose*, 228 App.Div. 526, 240 N.Y.S. 436, *aff'd* 254 N.Y. 546, 173 N.E. 859 (1930) (court noted that parties could have discovered by reference to a telephone directory that the arbitrator was a broker).

trip to the hearing. But the arbitrators from the Midwest are closely divided on whether the arbitrator has a duty to disclose that he has discovered during the hearing that the union representative has a reservation on the same flight to return to their home city after the hearing and that the union representative plans to sit with the arbitrator. Most arbitrators from other regions, however, and the vast majority of company and union representatives, take the position that there is no duty to disclose this information. And although the arbitrators from the South are closely divided on whether an arbitrator must disclose that the union has arranged for its representative to drive him from the airport to the plant after the arbitrator has asked the parties in a joint letter how to reach the plant, the prevailing view of arbitrators from other regions, in accord with the views of the vast majority of company and union representatives, is that there is no duty to disclose this information.

Most respondents in all categories also believe that an arbitrator has no duty to disclose that the union representative, seeing the arbitrator in the hotel lobby the night before the hearing, offered him a drink, or that one of the parties reserved for the arbitrator a hotel room customarily reserved on a continuing basis for that party.

Prior Social and Civic Contacts With Representatives of the Parties

Most respondents in all categories believe that an arbitrator has no duty to disclose that he and the company representative belong to the same neighborhood civic association, or that a neighbor-friend of the arbitrator is a production superintendent of the company now seeking the arbitrator's services—as long as the superintendent's department is not involved in the case.[25] These relationships are more remote than the relationship in the New York case which invalidated an arbitrator's award because the arbitrator failed to disclose that he recently had been employed as an attorney by other locals of the same international union and had received $10,000 from these other locals dur-

---

[25] In a commercial arbitration case it was even held that an arbitrator had no duty to disclose that he occasionally bought raw silk from one of the parties. *E. Richard Meining Co.* v. *Katakura & Co.*, 241 App. Div. 406, 272 N.Y.S. 735, *aff'd* 266 N.Y. 418, 195 N.E. 134 (1934).

ing the preceding calendar year. See discussion of this case under "Prior Consulting Work of Arbitrator," *supra.*

Most respondents in all categories believe that an arbitrator has no duty to disclose that the company representative took him out to dinner at the last annual meeting of the National Academy of Arbitrators. The clearly prevailing view is that an arbitrator cannot be "bought" with a drink or a meal. But there is no majority view among arbitrators in any of the regions of the country on whether an arbitrator has a duty to disclose that he has played poker or golf with the union representative on prior occasions. Nevertheless, most company and union representatives believe that there is no duty to disclose this information despite the possible risk of bribery through betting at poker or golf.

If a permanent umpire has not simply won money from a union representative on prior occasions while playing poker or golf but the umpire has been bribed by one of the parties to decide some of his cases in favor of that party, should all of the decisions of that umpire in that bargaining relationship be invalidated? If the holding of a recent Oklahoma case were to be followed, the answer would seem to be no. In *Johnson* v. *Johnson,*[26] Oklahoma Supreme Court Justice N. S. Corn had received bribes over a period of many years to vote as directed by the attorney who was the briber. A specially constituted court in that case stated the issue and answer as follows (at p. 417):

> "Where a judge secretly agrees to take bribes from an individual and does take them consistently, but such fact is unknown except to him and the bribe-giver, does he thereby automatically forfeit his office or automatically become disqualified to participate in any future decision of the Court, so that his every vote thereafter is a nullity, even in cases where no wrongdoing occurred? Our answer is in the negative."

The court noted that over a period of 20 years there were more than 1,000 cases where the bribed judge had cast the deciding vote. The court was concerned about the consequences if all of these decisions were set aside. Thus it held that those cases in which no corruption can be found must be allowed to stand.[27]

---

[26] 424 P.2d 414 (1967).

[27] Cf. *Restatement of Judgments* § 124, Corruption of or Duress upon the Court.

Membership in a "Conflict of Interest" Organization

Most respondents to my questionnaire agree that an arbitrator has a duty to disclose that he is a member of an organization which is working against the interest of one of the parties. Examples would be an economist who is working against an increase in milk prices when he is asked to arbitrate for a dairy which wants the increase, or an arbitrator who is a member of a black coalition which is trying to force construction unions to admit more blacks to their membership when he is asked to arbitrate for one of these construction unions.

Tumey v. *State of Ohio* [28] presents a good example of a conflict of interest. In that case the Supreme Court of the United States held that to subject a defendant to a trial in a criminal case before a judge having a direct and substantial interest in convicting him was a denial of due process of law. The judge in that case was the mayor of a village which was in poor financial condition. The greater the fines assessed by the judge, the more he helped the coffers of the village.

Prior Contacts in Arbitration

The vast majority of all respondents to my questionnaire agree that an arbitrator has no duty to disclose that the union representative has presented prior arbitration cases to the arbitrator even though the company representative has not had the benefit of this experience. Apparently this advantage is simply accepted as one of the realities of the arbitration process, and there is no duty to put the other party on notice of it.[29]

However, a commercial arbitration award has been set aside where an arbitrator failed to disclose that his company had received an award for $31,000 in a prior arbitration proceeding, and the president of one of the present parties was the arbitrator.[30]

---

[28] 273 U.S. 510 (1927).

[29] But an arbitrator has a duty to disclose that the attorney for one of the parties also represented the arbitrator and a company in which the arbitrator has a substantial interest. *Matter of Atlantic Rayon Corp.*, 277 App. Div. 554, 100 N.Y.S.2d 849 (1950).

[30] *Shirley Silk Co., Inc.* v. *American Silk Mills, Inc.*, 260 App. Div. 572 (1940). Accord: *Knickerbocker Textile Corp.* v. *Sheila-Lynn, Inc.*, 172 Misc. 1015, 16 N.Y.S.2d 435, aff'd 259 App. Div. 992, 20 N.Y.S.2d 985 (1939).

Prior Membership in a Union

A majority of the arbitrators in the Far West believe that an arbitrator should disclose that, for a *short period* of time, as a college student *many years ago,* he was an *inactive* member of a local union affiliated with the international union now seeking his services. But most arbitrators in the Northeast, the Midwest, and the South disagree. And the vast majority of company and union representatives also take the position that an arbitrator has no duty to disclose this information. It has aptly been stated that undue disclosure tends to raise unnecessary doubts in the minds of the parties as to the arbitrator's ability to deal with the case objectively and honestly.

Of course, if the arbitrator were an officer of the local union now seeking his services, a different situation would be presented. An arbitrator should disclose to the employer this close and responsible relationship which would be more like the relationship of an attorney for the union—a relationship which the Appellate Division of the Supreme Court of New York has indicated the arbitrator must disclose.[31]

Hortatory Expressions to Arbitrator

Most arbitrators take the position that an arbitrator has no duty to disclose that after the hearing a representative of a party has stated to him that "this is a very important case which we cannot afford to lose." Such oral expressions are viewed as general propaganda. Most company representatives agree that there is no duty of disclosure of such a remark. Although union representatives from the Midwest are fairly evenly divided on the answer to this question, the prevailing view of union representatives from the Northeast is that there is no duty of disclosure.

Fellow Arbitrator as Representative of a Party

A clear majority of the respondents to my questionnaire believe that an arbitrator has no duty to disclose that he recognizes one of the representatives of the parties as a fellow mem-

---

[31] See discussion of this case, *supra,* under Prior Consulting Work of Arbitrator. But cf. *Darlington* v. *Studebaker,* 261 F.2d 903 (7th Cir. 1959) (Judge Grant not disqualified merely because several years ago he had served as an attorney for defendant) and *Voltmann* v. *United Fruit Co.,* 147 F.2d 514 (2nd Cir. 1945) (judge not disqualified because his son-in-law, who had nothing personally to do with the case, was a member of the law firm representing defendant).

ber of the National Academy of Arbitrators. Although some arbitrators believe that a member of the Academy should never represent a party in labor arbitration, the Canons of Ethics of the Academy do not contain any such bar. And the membership requirements of the Academy simply state that an applicant must not be "primarily identified" as an advocate or consultant for labor or management in labor-management relations.

By way of comparison it is interesting to note that the Second Circuit Court of Appeals has held that a judge is not disqualified because of the professional relationship of the judge and a defendant in certain international legal associations and common attendance at meetings of such associations.[32]

Role of the Arbitrator in Political Maneuvers

Most arbitrators tend to believe that an arbitrator has a duty to disclose that the union representative has advised the arbitrator that a hearing must be held for "political" reasons, but that he has asked the arbitrator to agree, in advance of the hearing, to adopt the company position because the union representative agrees with the company position. But a substantial number have reservations. Company representatives tend to say that there is no duty of disclosure, and union representatives tend to say that there is a duty of disclosure. Under the Academy's Code of Ethics the arbitrator could not properly agree in advance of the hearing to hold in favor of the company.

Where the union representative does not ask the arbitrator to make a prior commitment on the decision that he will render but simply tells the arbitrator that a hearing must be held for "political" reasons even though the union representative agrees with the company's position, the prevailing view among arbitrators (except in the South) is that there is no duty of disclosure. Most union and company representatives also believe that there is no duty of disclosure in this situation in which the arbitrator has not been asked to make a commitment on how he will decide the case and in fact he has made no such commitment.

In a third situation involving a political maneuver the union representative may hint, after the hearing, that he expects to

---

[32] *Weiss* v. *Hunna*, 312 F.2d 711 (2nd Cir. 1963) .

lose the case. Most respondents to my questionnaire believe that an arbitrator has no duty to disclose that on a plant visit, after the hearing, the union representative who presented the union's case indicates that he has done his best in presenting the case but that he will understand if the arbitrator rules in favor of the company under the contract.

Many arbitrators are concerned about the impact of these political maneuvers on individual rights. In considering the duty of disclosure or withdrawal from the case, some would make a distinction between a discharge case involving a particular individual and a general case of wage determination affecting all employees. Others would make a distinction between an ad hoc arbitrator and a permanent umpire. Still others make distinctions in terms of whether they adopt the philosophy that an arbitrator is "like a judge" or the philosophy that arbitration is an extension of the collective bargaining process. As pointed out by Bob Fleming in 1961 in his article on due process in arbitration, some arbitrators view their handling of an agreed case (also known in some circles as an "informed award" or "rigged award") as an act of statesmanship.[33] Judge Paul Hays clearly disagrees with this view. In his lectures on "Labor Arbitration —A Dissenting View," he maintains that a rigged award clearly should be vacated by a court on public policy grounds.[34]

As yet, however, there are no clearly correct answers to these questions arising out of the agreed case because no clearly defined theory of the nature of the arbitration process has been adopted.

Conclusion

Various canons of ethics, rules, regulations, and court decisions make it clear that an arbitrator has a duty of disclosure. But the nature of the duty is expressed in very general terms. It is my hope that this paper, considered in conjunction with

---

[33] Fleming, "Some Problems of Due Process and Fair Procedure in Labor Arbitration," 13 *Stan. L. Rev.* 235, 248-251 (1961), also published in *Arbitration and Public Policy*, Proceedings of the 14th Annual Meeting, National Academy of Arbitrators, ed. Spencer D. Pollard (Washington: BNA Books, 1961), at 87-90. For an earlier study see Wirtz, "Due Process of Arbitration," in *The Arbitrators and the Parties*, Proceedings of the 11th Annual Meeting, National Academy of Arbitrators, ed. Jean T. McKelvey (Washington: BNA Books, 1958), at 26-32.

[34] See 74 *Yale L.J.* 1019, 1033 (1965).

my prior article on this subject, has provided some concrete guidance for the arbitration profession, and for those who use its services, on precisely what the parties can reasonably expect an arbitrator to disclose with respect to many specific situations which arbitrators have encountered in their practice.

APPENDIX A

Arbitrators' Answers by Regions

Does a Labor Arbitrator Have a Duty to Disclose to the Parties at any Stage of the Arbitration Process—

1. That 10 years ago he received a consulting fee of $500 from one of the parties for a matter not related to labor relations?

	Yes	No	It Depends
Northeast	58 (64%)	30 (33%)	3 (3%)
Midwest	59 (64%)	29 (32%)	4 (4%)
South	17 (49%)	14 (40%)	4 (11%)
Far West	27 (77%)	5 (14%)	3 (9%)

2. That 10 years ago he received a consulting fee of $500 from another company in the same industry for a matter not related to labor relations?

	Yes	No	It Depends
Northeast	5 (5%)	83 (91%)	3 (3%)
Midwest	2 (2%)	87 (95%)	3 (3%)
South	4 (11%)	29 (83%)	2 (6%)
Far West	2 (6%)	29 (83%)	4 (11%)

3. That last year he received a free lunch when he gave a general talk to a personnel association meeting which included some representatives of the company now seeking his services?

	Yes	No	It Depends
Northeast	2 (2%)	86 (95%)	3 (3%)
Midwest	1 (1%)	89 (97%)	2 (2%)
South	2 (6%)	32 (91%)	1 (3%)
Far West	0 (0%)	34 (97%)	1 (3%)

4. That last year he participated in a conference, sponsored by the American Arbitration Association for representatives of various unions, on how to be more effective in labor arbitration, and the conference included a representative of the union now seeking the arbitrator's services?

	Yes	No	It Depends
Northeast	0 (0%)	87 (96%)	4 (4%)
Midwest	2 (2%)	90 (98%)	0 (0%)
South	1 (3%)	31 (89%)	3 (9%)
Far West	2 (6%)	32 (91%)	1 (3%)

5. That a company now seeking his services has sent representatives to a university to attend a management training program for various companies, and the arbitrator teaches a course in industrial relations in that program?

	Yes	No	It Depends
Northeast	5 (5%)	76 (84%)	10 (11%)
Midwest	10 (11%)	78 (85%)	4 (4%)
South	5 (14%)	27 (77%)	3 (9%)
Far West	3 (9%)	29 (83%)	3 (9%)

6. That a representative of one of the parties is a former degree-seeking student of the arbitrator?

	Yes	No	It Depends
Northeast	31 (34%)	47 (52%)	12 (13%)
Midwest	34 (37%)	45 (49%)	13 (14%)
South	15 (43%)	17 (49%)	3 (9%)
Far West	15 (43%)	14 (40%)	6 (17%)

7. That a representative of one of the parties is a former student-research assistant for the arbitrator?

	Yes	No	It Depends
Northeast	59 (65%)	21 (23%)	11 (12%)
Midwest	60 (65%)	18 (20%)	14 (15%)
South	21 (60%)	12 (34%)	2 (6%)
Far West	26 (74%)	7 (20%)	2 (6%)

8. That the union or company representative has, at the arbitrator's request, given a talk to the arbitrator's class at a university?

	Yes	No	It Depends
Northeast	19 (21%)	63 (70%)	8 (9%)
Midwest	20 (22%)	61 (67%)	10 (11%)
South	8 (23%)	23 (66%)	4 (11%)
Far West	9 (26%)	20 (57%)	6 (17%)

9. That the arbitrator owns 500 shares of stock of the company now seeking his services?

	Yes	No	It Depends
Northeast	78 (86%)	5 (5%)	8 (9%)
Midwest	88 (96%)	3 (3%)	1 (1%)
South	31 (89%)	0 (0%)	4 (11%)
Far West	31 (89%)	1 (3%)	3 (9%)

10. Five shares?

	Yes	No	It Depends
Northeast	61 (67%)	25 (27%)	5 (5%)
Midwest	70 (76%)	17 (18%)	5 (5%)
South	23 (66%)	10 (29%)	2 (6%)
Far West	24 (69%)	5 (14%)	6 (17%)

11. That his wife owns 500 shares?

	Yes	No	It Depends
Northeast	71 (78%)	12 (13%)	8 (9%)
Midwest	82 (89%)	6 (7%)	4 (4%)
South	29 (83%)	2 (6%)	4 (11%)
Far West	30 (86%)	4 (11%)	1 (3%)

12. That his wife owns five shares?

	Yes	No	It Depends
Northeast	55 (60%)	32 (35%)	4 (4%)
Midwest	63 (68%)	23 (25%)	6 (7%)
South	20 (57%)	12 (34%)	3 (9%)
Far West	23 (66%)	8 (23%)	4 (11%)

13. That the arbitrator owns 50 shares in an affiliate or subsidiary corporation?

	Yes	No	It Depends
Northeast	58 (64%)	19 (21%)	13 (14%)
Midwest	66 (72%)	16 (17%)	10 (11%)
South	21 (60%)	11 (31%)	3 (9%)
Far West	25 (71%)	6 (17%)	4 (11%)

14. That the arbitrator found himself sitting beside the union representative for the next day's hearing on the plane trip to the hearing?

	Yes	No	It Depends
Northeast	24 (26%)	57 (63%)	10 (11%)
Midwest	27 (29%)	51 (55%)	14 (15%)
South	8 (23%)	23 (66%)	4 (11%)
Far West	8 (23%)	18 (51%)	9 (26%)

15. That the arbitrator has discovered during the hearing that the union representative has a reservation on the same flight to return to their home city after the hearing and that the union representative plans to sit with the arbitrator?

	Yes	No	It Depends
Northeast	28 (31%)	48 (53%)	15 (16%)
Midwest	41 (45%)	38 (41%)	13 (14%)
South	11 (31%)	20 (57%)	4 (11%)
Far West	11 (31%)	18 (51%)	6 (17%)

16. That the company representative took the arbitrator out to dinner at the last annual meeting of the National Academy of Arbitrators?

	Yes	No	It Depends
Northeast	13 (14%)	60 (66%)	17 (19%)
Midwest	22 (24%)	63 (68%)	7 (8%)
South	6 (17%)	23 (66%)	6 (17%)
Far West	7 (20%)	21 (60%)	7 (20%)

17. That the union representative happened to see the arbitrator in the hotel lobby the night before the hearing and offered him a drink?

	Yes	No	It Depends
Northeast	8 (9%)	79 (87%)	4 (4%)
Midwest	11 (12%)	75 (82%)	6 (7%)
South	3 (4%)	30 (86%)	2 (6%)
Far West	1 (3%)	31 (89%)	3 (9%)

18. That upon the arbitrator's asking the parties in a joint letter how to reach the plant, the union has arranged for its representative to drive the arbitrator from the airport to the plant?

	Yes	No	It Depends
Northeast	35 (39%)	41 (46%)	14 (16%)
Midwest	38 (41%)	44 (48%)	10 (11%)
South	15 (43%)	14 (40%)	6 (17%)
Far West	14 (40%)	18 (51%)	3 (9%)

19. That one of the parties reserved a hotel room for the arbitrator and he later learned, after using the room, that this room customarily is reserved on a continuing basis for that party? (But assume that the arbitrator pays for the room.)

	Yes	No	It Depends
Northeast	14 (16%)	68 (76%)	8 (9%)
Midwest	15 (16%)	72 (78%)	5 (5%)
South	8 (23%)	24 (69%)	3 (9%)
Far West	7 (20%)	26 (74%)	2 (6%)

20. That the arbitrator has played poker or golf with the union representative on prior occasions?

	Yes	No	It Depends
Northeast	28 (31%)	38 (42%)	25 (27%)
Midwest	37 (40%)	35 (38%)	20 (22%)
South	16 (46%)	13 (37%)	6 (17%)
Far West	15 (43%)	13 (37%)	7 (20%)

21. That the company representative and arbitrator belong to the same neighborhood civic association?

	Yes	No	It Depends
Northeast	21 (23%)	66 (73%)	4 (4%)
Midwest	17 (18%)	54 (59%)	21 (23%)
South	8 (37%)	20 (57%)	7 (20%)
Far West	8 (23%)	23 (66%)	4 (11%)

22. That the arbitrator is a member of an organization which is working against the interest of one of the parties (*e.g.*, opposition to milk price increase, black coalition, etc.) ?

	Yes	No	It Depends
Northeast	56 (62%)	16 (17%)	18 (20%)
Midwest	63 (68%)	13 (14%)	16 (17%)
South	20 (57%)	8 (23%)	7 (20%)
Far West	26 (74%)	5 (14%)	4 (11%)

23. That a neighbor-friend of the arbitrator is a production superintendent of the company now seeking the arbitrator's services (but the superintendent's department is not involved in the case) ?

	Yes	No	It Depends
Northeast	24 (26%)	57 (63%)	10 (11%)
Midwest	34 (37%)	51 (55%)	7 (8%)
South	8 (23%)	18 (51%)	9 (26%)
Far West	8 (23%)	20 (57%)	7 (20%)

24. That the union representative has presented prior arbitration cases to the arbitrator (but the company representative has not) ?

	Yes	No	It Depends
Northeast	8 (9%)	81 (89%)	2 (2%)
Midwest	6 (7%)	85 (92%)	1 (1%)
South	0 (0%)	34 (97%)	1 (3%)
Far West	1 (3%)	34 (97%)	0 (0%)

25. That, for a short period of time, as a college student many years ago, the arbitrator was an inactive member of a local union affiliated with the international union now seeking his services?

	Yes	No	It Depends
Northeast	32 (36%)	52 (58%)	6 (7%)
Midwest	39 (42%)	51 (55%)	2 (2%)
South	12 (34%)	19 (54%)	4 (11%)
Far West	19 (54%)	12 (34%)	4 (11%)

26. That a representative of a party, after the hearing but before issuance of the decision, has advised the arbitrator that "this is a very important case which we cannot afford to lose"?

	Yes	No	It Depends
Northeast	20 (22%)	56 (62%)	14 (16%)
Midwest	24 (26%)	50 (54%)	18 (20%)
South	13 (37%)	18 (51%)	4 (11%)
Far West	7 (21%)	18 (53%)	9 (26%)

27. That the arbitrator recognizes one of the representatives of the parties as a fellow member of the National Academy of Arbitrators?

	Yes	No	It Depends
Northeast	30 (33%)	51 (57%)	9 (10%)
Midwest	28 (31%)	56 (62%)	6 (7%)
South	7 (20%)	27 (77%)	1 (3%)
Far West	8 (23%)	21 (60%)	6 (17%)

28. That a union representative has advised the arbitrator that he agrees with the company's position (but that a hearing must be held for "political" reasons), and that the union representative has asked the arbitrator to agree in advance of the hearing to adopt the company position?

	Yes	No	It Depends
Northeast	40 (45%)	32 (37%)	15 (17%)
Midwest	46 (52%)	24 (27%)	18 (22%)
South	21 (60%)	10 (29%)	4 (11%)
Far West	19 (54%)	6 (17%)	10 (29%)

29. Same question as #28 except that the arbitrator is not asked to make a commitment on the decision that he will render.

	Yes	No	It Depends
Northeast	25 (29%)	48 (55%)	14 (16%)
Midwest	35 (38%)	39 (42%)	18 (20%)
South	18 (51%)	13 (37%)	4 (11%)
Far West	11 (31%)	15 (43%)	9 (26%)

30. That on a plant visit, after the hearing, the union representative, who presented the union's case, indicates that he has done his best in presenting the case but that he will understand if the arbitrator rules in favor of the company under the contract?

	Yes	No	It Depends
Northeast	4 (4%)	79 (87%)	8 (9%)
Midwest	9 (10%)	68 (74%)	15 (16%)
South	6 (17%)	23 (66%)	6 (17%)
Far West	3 (9%)	28 (80%)	4 (11%)

APPENDIX B

Company and Union Answers (Northeast and Midwest)

Does a Labor Arbitrator Have a Duty to Disclose to the Parties at any Stage of the Arbitration Process—

1. That 10 years ago he received a consulting fee of $500 from one of the parties for a matter not related to labor relations?

	Yes	No	It Depends
Company (Northeast)	48 (39%)	66 (54%)	8 (7%)
Company (Midwest)	8 (22%)	27 (75%)	2 (5%)
Union (Northeast)	51 (58%)	36 (41%)	1 (1%)
Union (Midwest)	15 (48%)	11 (35%)	5 (16%)

2. That 10 years ago he received a consulting fee of $500 from another company in the same industry for a matter not related to labor relations?

	Yes	No	It Depends
Company (Northeast)	10 (8%)	108 (89%)	4 (3%)
Company (Midwest)	2 (5%)	35 (95%)	0 (0%)
Union (Northeast)	11 (13%)	75 (85%)	2 (2%)
Union (Midwest)	4 (13%)	26 (84%)	1 (3%)

3. That last year he received a free lunch when he gave a general talk to a personnel association meeting which included some representatives of the company now seeking his services?

	Yes	No	It Depends
Company (Northeast)	1 (1%)	120 (98%)	1 (1%)
Company (Midwest)	0 (0%)	37 (100%)	0 (0%)
Union (Northeast)	5 (6%)	81 (92%)	2 (2%)
Union (Midwest)	1 (3%)	29 (94%)	1 (3%)

4. That last year he participated in a conference, sponsored by the American Arbitration Association for representatives of various unions on how to be more effective in labor arbitration, and the conference included a representative of the union now seeking the arbitrator's services?

	Yes	No	It Depends
Company (Northeast)	3 (2%)	118 (97%)	1 (1%)
Company (Midwest)	2 (5%)	35 (95%)	0 (0%)
Union (Northeast)	9 (10%)	77 (88%)	2 (2%)
Union (Midwest)	2 (6%)	29 (94%)	0 (0%)

5. That a company now seeking his services has sent representatives to a university to attend a management training program for various companies, and the arbitrator teaches a course in industrial relations in that program?

	Yes	No	It Depends
Company (Northeast)	1 (1%)	120 (98%)	1 (1%)
Company (Midwest)	2 (5%)	34 (92%)	1 (3%)
Union (Northeast)	10 (11%)	70 (80%)	8 (9%)
Union (Midwest)	4 (13%)	26 (84%)	1 (3%)

6. That a representative of one of the parties is a former degree-seeking student of the arbitrator?

	Yes	No	It Depends
Company (Northeast)	30 (25%)	76 (62%)	16 (13%)
Company (Midwest)	7 (19%)	27 (75%)	3 (8%)
Union (Northeast)	30 (34%)	49 (56%)	9 (10%)
Union (Midwest)	9 (29%)	21 (68%)	1 (3%)

7. That a representative of one of the parties is a former student-research assistant for the arbitrator?

	Yes	No	It Depends
Company (Northeast)	76 (62%)	36 (30%)	10 (8%)
Company (Midwest)	18 (49%)	17 (46%)	2 (5%)
Union (Northeast)	59 (67%)	25 (28%)	4 (5%)
Union (Midwest)	18 (58%)	11 (35%)	2 (6%)

8. That the union or company representative has, at the arbitrator's request, given a talk to the arbitrator's class at a university?

	Yes	No	It Depends
Company (Northeast)	30 (25%)	86 (70%)	6 (5%)
Company (Midwest)	2 (6%)	32 (89%)	2 (6%)
Union (Northeast)	23 (26%)	62 (70%)	3 (3%)
Union (Midwest)	3 (10%)	25 (81%)	3 (10%)

9. That the arbitrator owns 500 shares of stock of the company now seeking his services?

	Yes	No	It Depends
Company (Northeast)	90 (74%)	16 (13%)	16 (13%)
Company (Midwest)	25 (68%)	8 (22%)	4 (11%)
Union (Northeast)	74 (84%)	9 (10%)	5 (6%)
Union (Midwest)	30 (97%)	1 (3%)	0 (0%)

10. Five shares?

	Yes	No	It Depends
Company (Northeast)	64 (53%)	41 (34%)	15 (13%)
Company (Midwest)	20 (54%)	12 (32%)	5 (14%)
Union (Northeast)	62 (70%)	21 (24%)	5 (6%)
Union (Midwest)	26 (84%)	4 (13%)	1 (3%)

11. That his wife owns 500 shares?

	Yes	No	It Depends
Company (Northeast)	86 (70%)	20 (16%)	16 (13%)
Company (Midwest)	27 (73%)	7 (19%)	3 (8%)
Union (Northeast)	66 (75%)	13 (15%)	9 (10%)
Union (Midwest)	29 (94%)	2 (6%)	0 (0%)

12. That his wife owns five shares?

	Yes	No	It Depends
Company (Northeast)	62 (51%)	39 (32%)	21 (17%)
Company (Midwest)	18 (50%)	15 (41%)	3 (8%)
Union (Northeast)	56 (64%)	23 (26%)	9 (10%)
Union (Midwest)	23 (74%)	5 (16%)	3 (10%)

13. That the arbitrator owns 50 shares in an affiliate or subsidiary corporation?

	Yes	No	It Depends
Company (Northeast)	62 (51%)	35 (29%)	25 (20%)
Company (Midwest)	18 (49%)	13 (35%)	6 (16%)
Union (Northeast)	59 (67%)	22 (25%)	7 (8%)
Union (Midwest)	26 (84%)	4 (13%)	1 (3%)

14. That the arbitrator found himself sitting beside the union representative for the next day's hearing on the plane trip to the hearing?

	Yes	No	It Depends
Company (Northeast)	14 (11%)	104 (85%)	4 (3%)
Company (Midwest)	4 (11%)	27 (75%)	6 (16%)
Union (Northeast)	19 (22%)	59 (67%)	10 (11%)
Union (Midwest)	6 (19%)	23 (74%)	2 (6%)

15. That the arbitrator has discovered during the hearing that the union representative has a reservation on the same flight to return to their home city after the hearing and that the union representative plans to sit with the arbitrator?

	Yes	No	It Depends
Company (Northeast)	25 (21%)	95 (79%)	1 (1%)
Company (Midwest)	12 (32%)	22 (58%)	4 (11%)
Union (Northeast)	19 (22%)	64 (73%)	5 (6%)
Union (Midwest)	4 (13%)	24 (77%)	3 (10%)

16. That the company representative took the arbitrator out to dinner at the last annual meeting of the National Academy of Arbitrators?

	Yes	No	It Depends
Company (Northeast)	14 (11%)	106 (87%)	2 (2%)
Company (Midwest)	3 (8%)	34 (92%)	0 (0%)
Union (Northeast)	18 (20%)	61 (69%)	9 (10%)
Union (Midwest)	1 (3%)	28 (90%)	2 (6%)

17. That the union representative happened to see the arbitrator in the hotel lobby the night before the hearing and offered him a drink?

	Yes	No	It Depends
Company (Northeast)	2 (2%)	114 (93%)	6 (5%)
Company (Midwest)	1 (3%)	35 (95%)	1 (3%)
Union (Northeast)	14 (16%)	68 (77%)	6 (7%)
Union (Midwest)	0 (0%)	28 (90%)	3 (10%)

18. That upon the arbitrator's asking the parties in a joint letter how to reach the plant, the union has arranged for its representative to drive the arbitrator from the airport to the plant?

	Yes	No	It Depends
Company (Northeast)	24 (20%)	95 (78%)	3 (2%)
Company (Midwest)	8 (22%)	28 (76%)	1 (3%)
Union (Northeast)	28 (32%)	55 (63%)	5 (6%)
Union (Midwest)	9 (29%)	21 (68%)	1 (3%)

19. That one of the parties reserved a hotel room for the arbitrator and he later learned, after using the room, that this room customarily is reserved on a continuing basis for that party? (But assume that the arbitrator pays for the room.)

	Yes	No	It Depends
Company (Northeast)	12 (10%)	107 (88%)	3 (2%)
Company (Midwest)	5 (14%)	30 (81%)	2 (5%)
Union (Northeast)	15 (17%)	68 (77%)	5 (6%)
Union (Midwest)	4 (13%)	26 (84%)	1 (3%)

20. That the arbitrator has played poker or golf with the union representative on prior occasions?

	Yes	No	It Depends
Company (Northeast)	42 (34%)	66 (54%)	14 (11%)
Company (Midwest)	6 (16%)	27 (75%)	4 (11%)
Union (Northeast)	31 (35%)	50 (57%)	7 (7%)
Union (Midwest)	11 (35%)	15 (48%)	5 (16%)

21. That the company representative and arbitrator belong to the same neighborhood civic association?

	Yes	No	It Depends
Company (Northeast)	34 (28%)	81 (66%)	7 (6%)
Company (Midwest)	4 (11%)	32 (86%)	1 (3%)
Union (Northeast)	16 (18%)	69 (78%)	3 (3%)
Union (Midwest)	1 (3%)	29 (94%)	1 (3%)

22. That the arbitrator is a member of an organization which is working against the interest of one of the parties (e.g., opposition to milk price increase, black coalition, etc.)?

	Yes	No	It Depends
Company (Northeast)	94 (77%)	15 (12%)	13 (11%)
Company (Midwest)	24 (65%)	10 (27%)	3 (8%)
Union (Northeast)	70 (80%)	10 (11%)	8 (9%)
Union (Midwest)	24 (77%)	3 (10%)	4 (13%)

23. That a neighbor-friend of the arbitrator is a production superintendent of the company now seeking the arbitrator's services (but the superintendent's department is not involved in the case)?

	Yes	No	It Depends
Company (Northeast)	26 (21%)	88 (72%)	8 (7%)
Company (Midwest)	6 (16%)	28 (76%)	3 (8%)
Union (Northeast)	31 (35%)	54 (61%)	3 (3%)
Union (Midwest)	8 (26%)	19 (61%)	4 (13%)

24. That the union representative has presented prior arbitration cases to the arbitrator (but the company representative has not) ?

	Yes		No		It Depends	
Company (Northeast)	4	(3%)	115	(94%)	3	(2%)
Company (Midwest)	1	(3%)	34	(94%)	1	(3%)
Union (Northeast)	16	(18%)	69	(78%)	3	(3%)
Union (Midwest)	1	(3%)	29	(94%)	1	(3%)

25. That, for a short period of time, as a college student many years ago, the arbitrator was an inactive member of a local union affiliated with the international union now seeking his services?

	Yes		No		It Depends	
Company (Northeast)	24	(20%)	93	(76%)	5	(4%)
Company (Midwest)	7	(19%)	30	(81%)	0	(0%)
Union (Northeast)	34	(39%)	52	(59%)	2	(2%)
Union (Midwest)	10	(32%)	21	(68%)	0	(0%)

26. That a representative of a party, after the hearing but before issuance of the decision, has advised the arbitrator that "this is a very important case which we cannot afford to lose"?

	Yes		No		It Depends	
Company (Northeast)	44	(36%)	70	(57%)	5	(4%)
Company (Midwest)	9	(24%)	25	(68%)	3	(8%)
Union (Northeast)	40	(46%)	38	(44%)	9	(10%)
Union (Midwest)	11	(35%)	15	(48%)	5	(16%)

27. That the arbitrator recognizes one of the representatives of the parties as a fellow member of the National Academy of Arbitrators?

	Yes		No		It Depends	
Company (Northeast)	28	(23%)	91	(75%)	3	(2%)
Company (Midwest)	8	(22%)	28	(76%)	1	(3%)
Union (Northeast)	29	(34%)	53	(62%)	4	(5%)
Union (Midwest)	9	(29%)	22	(71%)	0	(0%)

28. That a union representative has advised the arbitrator that he agrees with the company's position (but that a hearing must be held for "political" reasons), and that the union representative has asked the arbitrator to agree in advance of the hearing to adopt the company position?

	Yes		No		It Depends	
Company (Northeast)	50	(41%)	58	(48%)	14	(11%)
Company (Midwest)	10	(27%)	23	(62%)	4	(11%)
Union (Northeast)	44	(50%)	30	(34%)	14	(16%)
Union (Midwest)	16	(52%)	12	(39%)	3	(10%)

29. Same question as #28 except that the arbitrator is not asked to make a commitment on the decision that he will render.

	Yes	*No*	*It Depends*
Company (Northeast)	30 (25%)	82 (67%)	10 (9%)
Company (Midwest)	8 (22%)	25 (69%)	3 (8%)
Union (Northeast)	37 (42%)	43 (49%)	8 (9%)
Union (Midwest)	9 (29%)	18 (58%)	4 (13%)

30. That on a plant visit, after the hearing, the union representative, who presented the union's case, indicates that he has done his best in presenting the case but that he will understand if the arbitrator rules in favor of the company under the contract?

	Yes	*No*	*It Depends*
Company (Northeast)	14 (11%)	106 (87%)	2 (2%)
Company (Midwest)	3 (8%)	33 (89%)	1 (3%)
Union (Northeast)	23 (26%)	61 (69%)	4 (5%)
Union (Midwest)	6 (19%)	23 (74%)	2 (6%)

NATIONAL ACADEMY OF ARBITRATORS OFFICERS AND COMMITTEES, 1971-1972

I. *Officers*

Lewis M. Gill, President

Clair V. Duff, Vice President

Edgar Jones, Jr., Vice President

Peter Seitz, Vice President

Rolf Valtin, Vice President

Eva Robins, Treasurer

Alfred C. Dybeck, Secretary

Gerald A. Barrett, President-Elect

II. *Board of Governors*

Howard S. Block

William J. Fallon

Howard G. Gamser

Robert G. Howlett

David L. Kabaker

John Phillip Linn

Clare B. McDermott

Thomas J. McDermott

John F. Sembower

Ralph Roger Williams

Benjamin H. Wolf

Harry D. Woods

235

III. *Appointments and Committee Rosters*

(a) *1972 Annual Meeting*

Arrangements Committee

William J. Fallon, Chairman

Mortimer H. Gavin, S.J.	John W. Teele
George Savage King	Donald White

Leslie E. Woods

Program Committee

Milton Friedman, Chairman

Thomas G. S. Christensen	Eva Robins
William J. Fallon	Arthur Stark
Patrick J. Fisher	Arnold M. Zack

(b) *Editors*

Proceedings of Annual Meeting	Gerald G. Somers
Newsletter	Seymour Strongin

(c) *The Standing Committees*

Executive Committee

Lewis M. Gill, President

Gerald A. Barrett	Jean T. McKelvey
Alfred C. Dybeck	Eva Robins

Membership

Alexander B. Porter, Chairman

Arvid Anderson	George S. Ives
Raymond L. Britton	Mark L. Kahn
John E. Dunsford	Morris L. Myers
John A. Hogan	Earl E. Palmer

Ethics and Grievance

Richard Mittenthal, Chairman

Benjamin Aaron	Eli Rock
Leo C. Brown, S.J.	Ralph T. Seward
Alex Elson	Russell A. Smith
Patrick J. Fisher	Abram H. Stockman
Sylvester Garrett	Seymour Strongin

Law and Legislation

William B. Gould, Chairman

Harry W. Arthurs	Peter Seitz
Merton C. Bernstein	Clyde W. Summers
David M. Helfeld	Ted T. Tsukiyama
Adolph M. Koven	Bertram F. Willcox
Lennart V. Larson	Jerre S. Williams

(d) *The Special Committees*

Liaison

Martin Wagner, Chairman

Milton Friedman	Robert G. Howlett
Howard G. Gamser	Edwin R. Teple

Legal Affairs

John E. Gorsuch, Chairman

Hillard Kreimer	Herbert L. Sherman, Jr.

Overseas Correspondents

William H. McPherson, Chairman

Benjamin Aaron	Morrison Handsaker

Public Employment Disputes Settlement

Jean T. McKelvey, Chairman

Howard S. Block	Zel S. Rice II
Jacob Finkelman	Eva Robins
Milton Friedman	Eli Rock
Howard G. Gamser	William E. Simkin
James C. Hill	Russell A. Smith
Robert G. Howlett	Robert L. Stutz
Earl E. Palmer	James C. Vadakin

Arnold M. Zack

Development of New Arbitrators

Thomas J. McDermott, Chairman

Harold W. Davey	Milton Friedman
John E. Dunsford	John C. Shearer

Seymour Strongin

Regional Chairmen

Clair V. Duff
Coordinator of Regional Activities

Region 1	Mark Santer
Region 2	Thomas G. S. Christensen
Region 3	Walter J. Gershenfeld
Region 4	George S. Ives
Region 5	Paul H. Sanders
Region 6	David R. Kochery
Region 7	John F. W. Weatherill
Region 8	Charles L. Mullin, Jr.
Region 9	Paul W. Walter
Region 10	David P. Miller
Region 11	Arthur A. Malinowski
Region 12	John E. Dunsford
Region 13	Leonard Oppenheim
Region 14	Harry Seligson
Region 15	Morris L. Myers
Region 16	William Levin

ARBITRATION AND FEDERAL RIGHTS UNDER COLLECTIVE AGREEMENTS IN 1970 *

William B. Gould ** and James P. Kurtz ***

During 1970 the single most significant development affecting arbitration was the Supreme Court decision in *Boys Markets, Inc.* v. *Retail Clerks Union* [1] permitting federal courts to issue injunctions against strikes in violation of collective bargaining agreements in which the employer is willing to arbitrate the dispute under the agreement and is suffering irreparable injury by reason of the strike. The *Boys Markets* decision and similar cases are discussed separately below. The greatest amount of litigation was centered on employee actions under Section 301 (a) of the Labor Management Relations Act (LMRA) [2] against an employer and/or labor organization, alleging a breach of a collective bargaining agreement on the part of the employer and a breach of the duty of fair representation on the part of the labor organization. Also, on the state level, at least in the lower courts, there is a rise in the number of decisions involving collective bargaining, arbitration, and public employees, including a few compulsory arbitration decisions, especially in police and fire departments. Discussed and cited below are the most sig-

---

* Report of the Committee on Law and Legislation for 1970, National Academy of Arbitrators. Although all reported federal and state cases touching upon arbitration were read and studied, the focus of this report is on Sec. 301 actions under the Labor Management Relations Act (LMRA) reported in 1970. By the second week in January 1971, approximately 150 federal court cases had been reported, including those involving the civil rights-arbitration area, not counting cases where both the lower court and an appellate opinion were handed down during the year. In addition, there were approximately 60 Railway Labor Act cases reported and about 60 state court actions reported, most of which involved the State of New York. Also there are a large number of NLRB opinions touching upon arbitration, and federal court decisions dealing with recognition of awards of the National Joint Board for the Settlement of Jurisdictional Disputes; some of those cases are referred to herein. No representation is made that this report is necessarily exhaustive.

** Member, National Academy of Arbitrators; Professor of Law, Wayne State University, Detroit, Mich.; Member of the Michigan Bar.

*** Trial Examiner, Michigan Employment Relations Commission; Member of the Michigan Bar.

[1] 398 U.S. 235, 74 LRRM 2257 (1970).
[2] 29 U.S.C. 185.

nificant decisions, and cases with the clearest statement of principles impinging upon the arbitral process.

I. Strikes, Injunctions, and Arbitration

Under the Supreme Court's 1962 decision in *Sinclair Refining Co.* v. *Atkinson*,[3] federal courts were forbidden to issue injunctions against strikes in violation of a collective bargaining agreement, since such strikes constituted "labor disputes" within the meaning of the Norris-LaGuardia Act.[4] In view of the *Steelworkers* trilogy [5] and the Court's subsequent decision approving removal of state court injunctive proceedings involving violations of collective bargaining agreements to federal courts in *Avco Corp.* v. *Aero Lodge No. 735*,[6] the Supreme Court held in *Boys Markets* that *Sinclair* was "a significant departure from our otherwise consistent efforts upon the congressional policy to promote the peaceful settlement of labor disputes through arbitration." [7] Therefore, the Court held, in substance, that an employer may obtain injunctive relief against a strike by a union in breach of a no-strike clause in a collective bargaining agreement in which the grievance was subject to arbitration under the contract, the employer was ready to proceed with arbitration, and the employer suffered irreparable injury by reason of the union's breach of its no-strike obligation. Thus, the *Boys Markets* decision restates the overriding importance of arbitration in the labor-management relations of this country, while at the same time providing another entree for the action of courts in our industrial relations.[8]

Of course, *Boys Markets* did not change the fact that employers could collect damages under 301 caused by the union's

---

[3] 370 U.S. 195, 50 **LRRM** 2420 (1962).

[4] 29 U.S.C. 104.

[5] *United Steelworkers* v. *American Mfg. Co.*, 363 U.S. 564, 46 **LRRM** 2414 (1960); *United Steelworkers* v. *Warrior & Gulf Navigation Co.*, 363 U.S. 574, 46 **LRRM** 2416 (1960); *United Steelworkers* v. *Enterprise Wheel & Car Corp.*, 363 U.S. 593, 46 **LRRM** 2423 (1960).

[6] 390 U.S. 557, 67 **LRRM** 2881 (1968).

[7] 398 U.S. at 241, 74 **LRRM** at 2259.

[8] See generally, Gould, "On Labor Injunctions, Unions, and the Judges: The Boys Markets Case," 1970 *Sup Ct. Rev.* 215. See also, Isaacson, "A Fresh Look at the Labor Injunction," *Labor Law Developments*, Proceedings of the 17th Annual Institute on Labor Law, The Southwestern Legal Foundation (New York: Matthew Bender, 1971).

breach of contract,[9] even after the contract expired,[10] or where the no-strike clause was implied because the contract contained a broad arbitration provision.[11] An arbitrator's award ordering a labor organization to cease and desist from continuing a work stoppage in violation of contract is also enforceable under Section 301.[12] In view of the presumption of arbitrability,[13] the courts have often stayed employer's suits for damages for breach of contract and ordered the parties to proceed to arbitration,[14] and may even dismiss an employer's suit where arbitrable issues are presented.[15]

Even after *Boys Markets* one court has denied injunctive relief where the contract does not bind the parties to arbitration on the no-strike clause in addition to the underlying issue[16] or where there is no dispute subject to arbitration under the contract, as in the *Simplex Wire* case.[17] In *U.S. Steel Corp.* v. *Mine Workers*,[18] the Third Circuit reversed a district court's grant of an injunction, holding that the court must still determine the appropriateness of injunctive relief in a given case, the strike being over hazardous conditions in the coal mines.

A New York district court granted an employer a temporary restraining order against a strike, but made stringent requirements for the arbitration of the dispute, even to the point of setting an early deadline (six days) for the submission of the

---

[9] *Blue Diamond Coal Co.* v. *Mine Workers,* 436 F.2d 551, 76 LRRM 2003 (6th Cir. 1970) (judgment for almost $250,000).

[10] *Union Tank Car Co.* v. *Truck Drivers, Local 5,* 309 F.Supp. 1162, 73 LRRM 2425 (E.D. La. 1970).

[11] *Colts, Inc.* v. *Local 376, UAW,* 314 F.Supp. 578 LRRM 2252 (D. Conn. 1970). See the leading case of *Teamsters* v. *Lucas Flour Co.,* 369 U.S. 95, 49 LRRM 2717 (1962).

[12] *New Orleans Steamship Ass'n* v. *Local 1418, ILA,* 423 F.2d 38, 73 LRRM 2613 (5th Cir. 1970).

[13] *ITT World Communications, Inc.* v. *Communications Workers, Local 1174,* 422 F.2d 77, 73 LRRM 2244 (2d Cir. 1970).

[14] *Fluor Corp.* v. *Carpenters District Council,* 424 F.2d 283, 74 LRRM 2004 (5th Cir. 1970); *Howard Electric Co.* v. *IBEW, Local 570,* 423 F.2d 164, 73 LRRM 2785 (9th Cir. 1970).

[15] *Johnson Builders, Inc.* v. *Carpenters Local 1095,* 422 F.2d 137, 73 LRRM 2664 (10th Cir. 1970); but see *Rounds Co.* v. *Joint Council of Teamsters,* 8 Cal. App. 3d 830, 75 LRRM 2198 (1970), where the court held that an order to compel arbitration and not a complete dismissal was the proper remedy.

[16] *Stroehmann Bros. Co.* v. *Local 424, Bakery Workers,* 315 F.Supp. 647, 74 LRRM 2957 (M.D. Pa. 1970).

[17] *Simplex Wire & Cable Co.* v. *Local 2208, IBEW,* 314 F.Supp. 88, 75 LRRM 2475 (D. N.H. 1970).

[18] —— F.2d ——, 74 LRRM 2611 (3rd Cir. 1970), *rev'g* 74 LRRM 2607 (W.D. Pa. 1970).

arbitrator's award.[19] However, in a plant-closing situation in which the union was seeking to compel arbitration of the dispute, the court held that the union did not waive its right to arbitration where it had engaged in a strike in violation of the contract and despite the employer's offer of expedited arbitration.[20] In sum, courts seemed disposed to grant injunctions to prevent a strike,[21] or a slowdown,[22] where the dispute is subject to arbitration.

II. Rights of Individual Employees Under Section 301

The progeny of *Vaca* v. *Sipes* [23] continue to proliferate, but the formidable obstacles to a successful result on the part of individual employees remain. Illustrative of the pitfalls of such litigation is the recent decision of the Sixth Circuit Court of Appeals in *Dill* v. *Greyhound Corp.,* [24] reversing and dismissing an employee's suit for breach of contract and unfair representation over seniority placement in which a judgment for substantial damages had been awarded by the lower court. The Sixth Circuit held that the employer's construction of the contract was reasonable. Further, the court held that there was no violation on the part of the union of its duty to represent fairly its members since there was no proof of hostility, malice, or bad faith on its part in settling the grievance at a lower step than arbitration in the grievance procedure,[25] despite the lower court's finding that the union acted arbitrarily and in reckless disregard of the employee's rights. The Sixth Circuit noted that

---

[19] *American Tel. & Tel. Co.* v. *Communications Workers,* 75 LRRM 2178 (S.D. N.Y. 1970).

[20] *Teamsters Local 757* v. *Borden, Inc.,* 433 F.2d 41, 75 LRRM 2481 (2d Cir. 1970), *aff'g* 312 F.Supp. 549, 74 LRRM 3020 (S.D. N.Y. 1970).

[21] *W. R. Grace & Co.* v. *Local 759, Rubber Workers,* 76 LRRM 2113 (N.D. Miss. 1970); *Holland Constr. Co.* v. *Operating Engineers, Local 101,* 315 F.Supp. 791, 74 LRRM 3087 (D. Ky. 1970); but see *California Council of Carpenters* v. *Orange County Super. Ct.,* 11 Cal. App. 3d 144, 75 LRRM 2364 (1970); *cf. Tri-Cities Newspapers, Inc.* v. *Local 349, Printing Pressmen,* 427 F.2d 325, 74 LRRM 2285 (5th Cir. 1970), concerning the procedural issue as to whether the international union was an indispensable party in the employer's action.

[22] *Pittsburgh Press Co.* v. *Printing Pressmen,* 75 LRRM 2800 (W.D. Pa. 1970).

[23] 386 U.S. 171, 64 LRRM 2369 (1967).

[24] 435 F.2d 231, 76 LRRM 2070 (6th Cir. 1970), *rev'g* 76 LRRM 2060 (W.D. Tenn. 1969).

[25] In regard to the refusal of the union to proceed to arbitration, see also *Lomax* v. *Armstrong Cork Co.,* 433 F.2d 1277, 75 LRRM 2585 (5th Cir. 1970), *aff'g* 75 LRRM 2580 (S.D. Miss. 1969). In this regard the courts usually refuse to distinguish between the step of arbitration and earlier steps in the grievance procedure.

an employee does not have an absolute right to require his bargaining representative to press his complaint to the end of the grievance procedure, and that proof that the union acted negligently or exercised poor judgment is not enough to support a claim of unfair representation.[26]

The only individual employee 301 action, also based upon a seniority dispute, that was noticeably successful was a breach-of-contract judgment against an employer, but the Court of Appeals for the First Circuit at the same time dismissed the unfair representation action against the union as barred by the one-year statute of limitations applicable to tort actions in Puerto Rico.[27] The First Circuit also held that reinstatement was a perfectly acceptable form of relief for 301 suits against an employer and remanded the action to the lower court to enter such an order, or to submit the question of the amount of future lost earnings to a jury.

Perhaps the most important fair-representation decision of the past year is the Supreme Court's decision in *Czosek* v. *O'Mara*,[28] applying *Vaca* rationale to employees covered by the Railway Labor Act. In *Czosek* the Court upheld the complaint of discharged railroad employees against the union for the alleged breach of its duty of fair representation. The Court held that breach of the duty of fair representation is not within the jurisdiction of the National Railroad Adjustment Board (NRAB) nor subject to the ordinary rule that administrative remedies should be exhausted before resort to the courts. The Court further denied the union's claim that it was error for the lower courts to dismiss the suit against the employer in the absence of any allegation that the employer was in any way implicated in the union's alleged discriminatory conduct, noting that the union is responsible only for the damages flowing from its own conduct, and citing the *Vaca* decision. The Court said that the union would not be materially prejudiced by the possible absence of the railroad as a codefendant. Thus, it is clear that

---

[26] The Court quoted from *Bazarte* v. *United Transportation Union*, 429 F.2d 868, 75 LRRM 2017 (3d Cir. 1970), *rev'g* 305 F.Supp. 442, 73 LRRM 2379 (E.D. Pa. 1969).

[27] *Figueroa* v. *Trabajadores Packinghouse*, 425 F.2d 281, 74 LRRM 2028 (1st Cir. 1970), *aff'g in part and reman'g*, 302 F.Supp. 224, 72 LRRM 2585 (D.P.R. 1969).

[28] 397 U.S. 25, 73 LRRM 2481 (1970).

in employee 301 actions neither the employer [29] nor the union [30] are indispensable parties in actions brought against one of the parties individually. The *Czosek* case was cited by the Ninth Circuit Court of Appeals in a 301 suit by nonunion employees attacking the use of agency shop fees for political purposes as precedent for rejecting the union's contention that the matter was within the exclusive jurisdiction of the National Labor Relations Board (NLRB) .[31] Despite *Czosek,* employee suits against employers and unions subject to the Railway Labor Act encounter the same difficulties as other *Vaca*-type suits.[32] But what remains unresolved and unclear is the extent to which the court's assumptions about the irrelevance of NRAB to fair representation suits apply to *Vaca* cases arising under the NLRA. In both *Czosek,* and to a lesser extent in the *Glover* [33] case which was decided in the previous term, the Court seemed to emphasize the fact that union and employer together controlled Railway Labor Act machinery. Query: May the same be said about the impartial arbitration *selected* by the two parties and not the complaining individual or group?

Where the employer has broad power under the collective bargaining agreement to perform the action complained of in the 301 breach-of-contract action, the courts are powerless to rewrite the agreement for the parties.[34] In regard to the finality to be accorded to the grievance procedure, one court refused to determine whether the settlement of the grievance breached the contract where it found no breach of the duty of fair representation on the union's part.[35] Further, the courts have required the dissenting employee to exhaust available remedies, even in-

---

[29] *Young* v. *United Steelworkers,* 49 F.R.D. 74, 74 LRRM 2165 (E.D. Pa. 1969).

[30] *Sandobal* v. *Armour & Co.,* 429 F.2d 249, 74 LRRM 2781 (8th Cir. 1970), but reversing the lower court on its application of the Nebraska four-year statute of limitations for oral contracts rather than the five-year limitation applicable to written contracts, 74 LRRM 2778 and 2780 (D. Neb. 1968 and 1969). See also, *LaSalle* v. *Associated Press,* 2 FEP Cases 818 (W.D. Mo. 1970) involving the Civil Rights Act of 1964.

[31] *Seay* v. *McDonnell Douglas Corp.,* 427 F.2d 996. 74 LRRM 2600 (9th Cir. 1970).

[32] See, for example, *Jackson* v. *Trans World Airlines, Inc.,* 75 LRRM 2251 (S.D. N.Y. 1970) wherein the court found no "hostile discrimination" by the employer or the union regarding a change in the contract, within the meaning of *Steele* v. *L. & N. RR,* 323 U.S. 192, 15 LRRM 708 (1944).

[33] *Glover* v. *St. Louis-San Francisco Ry,* 393 U.S. 324, 70 LRRM 2097 (1969).

[34] *Shields* v. *General Electric Co.,* 73 LRRM 2144 (N.D. Ky. 1970).

[35] *Bowen* v. *Lockheed Georgia Co.,* 309 F.Supp. 1210, 74 LRRM 2367 (N.D. Ga. 1970). See also *Hunter* v. *Locher,* 74 LRRM 2761 (E.D. Mich. 1970).

tra-union remedies,[36] unless facts are shown that such appeal would be futile.

A court has also directed arbitration, "with appropriate participation by plaintiff," in an individual employee action under 301 and stay court proceedings pending such arbitration.[37] However, the Fourth Circuit pointed out in its affirmance of the dismissal of an employee 301 action that it was error for the lower court to ground its dismissal on the theory that plaintiffs were required to submit their claim to arbitration and the arbitrator's holdings were binding on the court, where the plaintiffs based their case upon an illegal conspiracy between the union and the employer to deprive them of their rights.[38] The court pointed out that in such cases the complaining employees would be entrusted to parties charged with combining to defraud them. Therefore, the court dismissed the suit on its merits for failure to state a claim of improper representation.

In another case involving bumping rights, a Colorado district court refused a defendant union's offer to arbitrate and to permit plaintiffs to be represented by counsel at such arbitration, because the union had previously taken a position adverse to that of the plaintiffs and thereby, in effect, had already wrongfully refused to take their grievance to arbitration.[39] The court also objected to the fact that the plaintiff employees, as the true adverse parties, had no choice in the selection of the arbitrator chosen and paid by the employer and the union under the contract, finding that this placed the arbitrator in a difficult position, "open to the charge that he is interested in the outcome." Further, an appellate court in Indiana was faced with a breach-of-contract action by a discharged employee against the employer and overruled the trial court's denial of a new trial based upon findings of no breach of contract and failure to exhaust contractual remedies.[40] The appellate court held, apparently on the basis of the fact that the plaintiff was discharged after a meeting of employer and union representatives, that the evi-

---

[36] *Anderson* v. *Ford Motor Co.*, 75 LRRM 2687 (E.D. Mich. 1970).

[37] *Nuest* v. *Westinghouse Air Brake Co.*, 313 F.Supp. 1228, 74 LRRM 2564 (S.D. Ill. 1970).

[38] *Lusk* v. *Eastern Products Corp.*, 427 F.2d 705, 74 LRRM 2594 (4th Cir. 1970), *aff'g on different grounds* 74 LRRM 2592 (D. Md. 1969).

[39] *Watson* v. *Cudahy Co.*, 315 F.Supp. 1286, 75 LRRM 2632 (D. Colo. 1970).

[40] *Landaw* v. *Tucker Freight Lines, Inc.*, 263 N.E.2d 756, 76 LRRM 2029 (Ind. App. 1970).

dence "clearly demonstrates that the actions and words of the Union officials . . . would have made any appeal [by plaintiff] fruitless and, at most, a hollow gesture . . . ," and that "any attempt by [plaintiff] to prosecute a written appeal through his Union would have been for naught." Thus the court held that plaintiff's "only logical recourse" was to the courts since the alternative of arbitration would be an exercise in futility under the circumstances. In contrast, however, a Michigan appellate court held that an employee was entitled to proceed with his wrongful discharge and unfair representation suit where the allegations were that the union failed to follow *mandatory* steps of the grievance procedure and intra-union remedies would be so time-consuming as to be futile.[41] In one other case where an employee was contesting his discharge for violation of the no-strike clause of the collective bargaining agreement and the local union membership voted not to proceed further with the employee's grievance, the court dismissed the action holding that the plaintiff had no standing to substitute himself for the local union as the enforcement agency of the agreement, which explicitly gave the union final authority to decline to process a grievance.[42] However, the Ninth Circuit, reversing the district court, held that employees who had been reinstated to their jobs as a result of an arbitration award were entitled to arbitration over the interpretation of the back-pay provision of the collective bargaining agreement where the employees disagreed with the disposition proposed by the employer and the union.[43] The court disposed of the allegation that the plaintiffs had no standing to order the employer to proceed to arbitration by holding that this was a question of procedure to be decided by the arbitrator, citing *Wiley* v. *Livingston*.[44]

As might be expected, most employee suits involve alleged

---

[41] *Harrison* v. *Arrow Metal Products Corp.*, 20 Mich. App. 590, 174 N.E. 2d 875, 73 LRRM 2712 (1969). (This case also involved extensive discussion of plaintiff's allegations of libel, slander, and blacklisting flowing from his discharge for theft.)

[42] *Encina* v. *Tony Lama Co.*, 316 F.Supp. 239, 75 LRRM 2012 (W.D. Tex. 1970).

[43] *Bealmer* v. *Texaco, Inc.*, 427 F.2d 885, 74 LRRM 2635 (9th Cir. 1970), *cert. den.* 400 U.S. 926, 75 LRRM 2612 (1970).

[44] 376 U.S. 543, 55 LRRM 2769 (1964). But see *Hackett* v. *McGuire Bros., Inc.*, 2 FEP Cases 1076 (E.D. Pa. 1970), holding that a retired employee had no standing to contest the hiring practices of the employer under Title VII of the Civil Rights Act of 1964.

wrongful discharges,[45] and most result in adverse results for the plaintiffs. Resolutions of seniority placement are also a fruitful source of employee 301 litigation,[46] especially pursuant to agreements involving merger of facilities and dovetailing of seniority in the transportation industry.[47] Also, during the past year employee suits have frequently been aimed at disputes concerning overtime compensation [48] or other wage losses.[49] Courts have also become involved with employee suits involving libel or slander connected with grievances or the proceedings thereon.[50] In summary, employee suits under Section 301 and the *Vaca* case appear to be increasing, but their chances of success appear slight except in the unusual circumstances where both the breach of contract is clear and hostility, bad faith, or malice on the part of the union is shown.

Whether there had been exhaustion of remedies under the

---

[45] See, for example, *Abrams* v. *Carrier Corp.*, 434 F.2d 1234, 75 LRRM 2736 (2d Cir. 1970), *reman'g* 75 LRRM 2724 (N.D. N.Y. 1968) ; *Young* v. *Southwestern Bell Tel. Co.*, 424 F.2d 256, 74 LRRM 2256 (8th Cir. 1970), *aff'g* 309 F.Supp. 475, 74 LRRM 2154 (E.D. Ark. 1969); *Barefoot* v. *Teamsters, Local 886*, 424 F.2d 1001, 73 LRRM 2885 (10th Cir. 1970); *Alessandrini* v. *Fed. of Musicians*, 75 LRRM 2338 (S.D. N.Y. 1970) ; *Patrick* v. *I. D. Packing Co.*, 308 F.Supp. 821, 74 LRRM 2060 (D. Iowa 1969) (possibility of exemplary damages also discussed) ; *Bartels* v. *Lithographers No. 1-P*, 306 F.Supp. 1266, 73 LRRM 2154 (S.D. N.Y. 1969); *Boutte* v. *Beaumont City Lines, Inc.*, 450 S.W.2d 383, 73 LRRM 2791 (Tex. Civ. App. 1970); *Jakubus* v. *Associated Truck Lines, Inc.*, 76 LRRM 2013 (Mich. Cir. Ct. 1970) ; *DeLosa* v. *Transport Workers Union*, 73 LRRM 2620 (N.Y. Sup. Ct. 1970) .

[46] See *Walters* v. *Teamsters, Local 612*, 425 F.2d 115, 74 LRRM 2379 (5th Cir. 1970); and *Bruen* v. *Local 492, IUE*, 425 F.2d 190, 74 LRRM 2169 (3d Cir. 1970), *aff'g* 75 LRRM 2212 (D. N.J. 1969); see also cases involving both fair representation and the Civil Rights Act of 1964, *Tippett* v. *Liggett & Myers Tobacco Co.*, 316 F.Supp. 292, 2 FEP Cases 904 (M.D. N.C. 1970) ; *Austin* v. *Reynolds Metals Co.*, 2 FEP Cases 451 (E.D. Va. 1970) ; *Sciaraffa* v. *Oxford Paper Co.*, 310 F.Supp. 891, 2 FEP Cases 398 (D. Me. 1970).

[47] See *Fuller* v. *Truck Drivers, Local 107*, 428 F.2d 503, 74 LRRM 2497 (3rd Cir. 1970); *Safely* v. *T.I.M.E. Freight, Inc.*, 307 F.Supp. 319, 74 LRRM 2075 (W.D. Va. 1969) , *aff'd* 424 F.2d 1367, 75 LRRM 2047 (4th Cir. 1970) ; *Taylor* v. *Dealers Transport Co.*, 73 LRRM 2106 (W.D. Ky. 1968), *aff'd* 73 LRRM 2110 (6th Cir. 1969) *cert. denied* 396 U.S. 1008, 73 LRRM 2120 (1970); *Farkas* v. *Printing Pressmen's Union No. 2*, 312 F.Supp. 161, 74 LRRM 2362 (S.D. N.Y. 1970) ; *Humphrey* v. *Dealers Transport Co.*, 304 F.Supp. 104, 73 LRRM 2103 (W.D. Ky. 1967) ; *Crowley* v. *Locomotive Engineers, Div. 28*, 472 P.2d 106, 75 LRRM 2036 (Ariz. App. 1970). See also the leading case of *Humphrey* v. *Moore*, 375 U.S. 335, 55 LRRM 2031 (1964).

[48] See *Centeno* v. *Puerto Rico Aggregates Co.*, 312 F.Supp. 907, 74 LRRM 2276 (D. P.R. 1970); and *Adams* v. *Knox Glass, Inc.*, 73 LRRM 2390 (N.D. Ga. 1969) .

[49] See *Amaya* v. *Hilton Hotel Corp.*, 74 LRRM 2486 (Cal. App. 1970) ; and *Livingston* v. *Kaplan*, 73 LRRM 2272 (N.Y. Sup. Ct. 1969).

[50] *Harris* v. *Hall's Motor Transit Co.*, 73 LRRM 2274 (D.C. Gen. Sess. 1969); and *Bird* v. *Meadow Gold Products Corp.*, 302 N.Y.S. 2d 701, 73 LRRM 2100 (1969).

grievance procedure is a question of fact to be determined by the court at a trial, where the plaintiff employee alleges his efforts to comply with the grievance machinery were blocked by the wrongful acts of the company and the union.[51] Failure to make such allegations and to pursue contract remedies can lead to summary dismissal of a 301 action by an employee.[52]

III. General Judicial Problems Under 301

A. *Actions Cognizable Under 301*

During the past year there were a number of unusual court actions brought under Section 301 which deserve comment. Section 301 actions usually involve suits by unions and employers on a collective bargaining agreement, but in one case involving a union representing entertainers, the union filed suit for past-due wages for individual employees based upon breach of both a collective bargaining agreement and the employees' individual contracts with the employer.[53] The collective bargaining agreement provided for minimum compensation with the specific provision that the employees could make their own individual contracts for greater compensation. The court held that the suit on both the individual and collective agreements was cognizable under Section 301, especially since the individual rights sought to be enforced by the union have their basis in the collective bargaining agreement. The case also involved the rather novel question of whether the union could bind an individual defendant who signed the contract as well as the corporate defendant, and held that under the form contract used in this case it was a question of fact to be answered at trial as to whether the individual defendant signed as an agent or whether he bound himself personally on the contract.

Following the leading case of *Parks* v. *IBEW*,[54] a number of 301 suits between local unions and their internationals arose during the past year, based on the holding that the union constitution is a contract between labor organizations within the

[51] *Sandobal* v. *Armour & Co., supra* note 30.

[52] See *Anderson* v. *Ford Motor Co., supra* note 36; *Lindsey* v. *General Dynamics Corp.,* 450 S.W. 2d 895, 73 LRRM 2671 (Tex. Civ. App. 1970) ; but see *Landau* v. *Tucker Freight Lines, Inc., supra* note 40.

[53] *Musical Artists* v. *Atlanta Municipal Theater, Inc.,* 310 F. Supp. 944, 74 LRRM 2459 (N.D. Ga. 1970) .

[54] 314 F.2d 886, 52 LRRM 2577 (4th Cir.), *cert. denied,* 372 U.S. 976, 52 LRRM 2943 (1963).

meaning of 301 (a). In one case a millwrights local of the Carpenters Union sued its international for injunctive relief and
damages for failure to recognize its statewide claim to jurisdiction under its charter over all millwrights, who prior to the issuance of the charter to the plaintiff had been represented by
regular carpenter locals.[55] The suit was dismissed on the
ground that there was no exhaustion of intra-union remedies
or excuse for its failure to do so, since the matter had not been
appealed by the complaining local to the general executive
board of the union or to its convention, as provided in the union
constitution.

In another unusual case, in which the union constitution was
not mentioned as such, a local of the Steelworkers Union sued
its international, the employer, and a second Steelworkers local
union.[56] The company whose employees were represented by
the plaintiff local was sold to the employer whose employees were
represented by the defendant local. The suit alleged a breach
of the collective bargaining agreement between the plaintiff and
the predecessor company and an award of an arbitrator interpreting that agreement after the sale of the company. A second
cause of the action was predicated on a breach of the duty of
fair representation. The court denied the motions of the defendants to dismiss the complaint, except for the fair representation cause of action against the employer.

Two local unions which were formerly affiliated with the defendant international union brought state court actions to recover local assets after disaffiliation.[57] The federal court permitted removal because the international constitution would be
involved in determining the rights of the parties. In a Ninth
Circuit case, a local union brought suit under Section 301 against
a member in order to collect a fine for crossing a picket line.[58]
Even though the fine was based upon a violation of the union

[55] *Local 1219 Carpenters* v. *United Bro. of Carpenters,* 314 F.Supp. 148, 74
LRRM 2527 (D. Me. 1970).
[56] *Local 4076, Steelworkers* v. *United Steelworkers,* 75 LRRM 2457 (W.D. Pa.
1970).
[57] *Locals 10 and 20, Paper Workers* v. *Int'l Bro. of Pulp, Sulphite, and Paper
Mill Workers,* 75 LRRM 2399 (W.D. Wash. 1970).
[58] *Hotel and Restaurant Employees, Local 400* v. *Svacek,* 431 F.2d 705, 75
LRRM 2427 (9th Cir. 1970); but see *Ballas* v. *McKiernan,* 312 N.Y.S. 2d 204, 74
LRRM 2647 (1970). See generally, Gould, "Some Limitations Upon Union Discipline Under the National Labor Relations Act: The Radiations of Allis Chalm-
ers," 6 *Duke L. J.* 1067 (1970).

constitution, the court dismissed the suit on the ground that it was an intra-union dispute unrelated to a collective bargaining agreement and that 301 does not give a basis for a suit by a union against its members. Thus, where members of a union brought an action under Section 301 to compel their officers to comply with the alleged requirements of the union constitution in regard to the conduct of elections, the suit was dismissed on the ground that the grant of jurisdiction under 301 does not extend to internal union affairs.[59]

In a rather complicated case, 225 former employees of Carrier Corp. brought a 301 action for breach of contract and unfair representation against Carrier and the two unions, Steelworkers and Sheet Metal Workers, that replaced in succession the original independent union representing the employees of Carrier.[60] In response to the allegation that there was no contract at the time of the discharges of the plaintiffs, the court held that where the Steelworkers merely replaced the former independent, which had not reopened its contract at the time of the election petition, that contract provided the basis for the suit against Carrier and the Steelworkers. However, the court expressed some doubt, but permitted amendment of the complaint, as to whether suit under 301 against the Steelworkers could be based on the charter and bylaws granted by the international to the local on the theory that plaintiffs were third-party beneficiaries. As for the Sheet Metal Workers, which replaced the Steelworkers as bargaining representative of the employees, the court held that the plaintiffs had no standing under Section 301 to maintain a suit for a breach of a special no-raiding agreement applying to the Carrier situation and entered into by the Sheet Metal Workers and other international unions, since such agreement was for the benefit of the particular union winning the certification election, and not for the benefit of the plaintiffs.

Section 301 suits involving pension fund disputes become intertwined with the provisions of Section 302 of the LMRA.[61]

---

[59] *Antal* v. *Budzanoski,* 75 LRRM 2828 (W.D. Pa. 1970). But compare trusteeship cases under Section 302 of the Labor Management Reporting and Disclosure Act (LMRDA), 29 U.S.C. 462, where the courts take an activist role; and see *Local 167 Luggage Workers* v. *International Leather Goods Workers,* 316 F.Supp. 500, 75 LRRM 2056 (D. Del. 1970); *Smith* v. *Distillery Workers,* 75 LRRM 2049 (E.D. Ky. 1970).

[60] *Abrams* v. *Carrier Corp., supra* note 45.

[61] See *Doyle* v. *Shortman,* 311 F.Supp. 187, 73 LRRM 2657 (1970).

Whether a dispute under a pension plan is arbitrable or not depends upon the provisions of the collective bargaining agreement and the pension agreement.[62] A 301 action by a committee of pensioned miners has been maintained against the union and the pension fund trustees in order to force the defendants to recover delinquent royalty payments against mine operators.[63] In another case by retired employees, the District of Columbia circuit court of appeals held that the eligibility requirement of a pension fund was invalid as being arbitrary and without rational basis, and ordered the retirees to be granted pensions if they met the other lawful requirements of the pension plan.[64]

B. *Existence of a Contract*

A necessary prerequisite to a suit to determine rights under a contract is the existence of the contract itself. Thus, the Eighth Circuit recently held that declaratory judgment procedure could be used under Section 301 to determine that a valid and enforceable contract, which had neither been modified nor terminated by mutual consent, existed between the parties.[65] The parties modified a previous agreement by signing a "letter of understanding," which the district court found to be a valid collective bargaining agreement, contrary to the contention of the union that it was only a temporary or preliminary agreement. The district court held that the agreement was unconditional, and parol evidence was not permitted to alter or contradict its terms. Although the parties later discussed altering the agreement, they never mutually agreed to reopen it and then be bound by subsequent negotiations. Similarly, the Sixth Circuit enforced a settlement memorandum and a supplemental agreement pursuant thereto with respect to certain pay rates, even though the time limits for reaching the agreement had elapsed.[66]

Under 301 a party may obtain reformation of a contract that does not accurately reflect the agreement reached during nego-

---

[62] *Sigismondi* v. *Queens Transit Corp.,* 73 LRRM 2479 (N.Y. Sup. Ct. 1969).

[63] *Thomas* v. *Honeybrook Mines, Inc.,* 428 F.2d 981, 74 LRRM 2337 (3rd Cir. 1970). (This particular decision involved the payment of attorney fees for the plaintiffs by the pension fund.)

[64] *Roark* v. *Boyle,* 439 F.2d 497, 74 LRRM 3025 (D.C. Cir. 1970).

[65] *Heavy Contractors Ass'n* v. *Laborers, Local 1140,* 430 F.2d 1350, 75 LRRM 2117 (8th Cir. 1970), *aff'g* 312 F.Supp. 1345, 75 LRRM 2113 (D. Neb. 1969).

[66] *Kentucky Skilled Craft Guild* v. *General Electric Co.,* 431 F.2d 62, 75 LRRM 2122 (6th Cir. 1970), *aff'g* 75 LRRM 2117 (N.D. Ky. 1969).

tiations, since a party cannot be required to submit to arbitration any dispute he has not agreed to submit. Thus, the Ninth Circuit, in a 301 suit by an employer, reformed the contract to accurately reflect the agreement of the parties by making certain changes in disputed wage schedules.[67] The court rejected the union's motion that the dispute should be sent to arbitration, noting that where the employer seeks a change in the terms of a written agreement, "it can be said with positive assurance that such an issue is not arbitrable under the agreement." The court also denied that it was usurping the function of an arbitrator in examining the bargaining history to resolve the issue on the merits, since it was reviewing the negotiations not to aid it in *interpreting* the wage scales as written in the contract, but to determine if the scales, as written, reflected the actual agreement of the parties. The court rejected the union's contention that the dispute related to a mere ambiguity, but held, rather, that it involved the failure of the written contract to record the actual agreement reached. Under *Smith* v. *Evening News Ass'n*,[68] the Supreme Court held that relief under 301 was available, even though the employer could have redrafted the contract and presented it to the union, and if the union refused to sign the tendered contract a charge of refusal to bargain could have been filed with the NLRB under Section 8 (b) (3) of the NLRA.

The existence of the contract is closely tied with the problem of the repudiation, cancellation, or termination of a collective bargaining agreement.[69] Thus, it is very clear that a union's violation of a no-strike clause does not automatically entitle the employer to repudiate the contract and its arbitration clause.[70] Further, the withdrawal of employees from the union does not serve to nullify the contract.[71]

The Sixth Circuit recently had occasion to discuss the effect of union ratification on the existence of a contract upon which a suit under Sections 301 and 303 of the LMRA could be

---

[67] *West Coast Tel. Co.* v. *Local 77*, IBEW, 431 F.2d 1219, 75 LRRM 2469 (9th Cir. 1970), *aff'g* 75 LRRM 2464 (W.D. Wash., 1968).

[68] 371 U.S. 195, 51 LRRM 2646 (1962).

[69] See the discussion in *Teamsters, Local 745*, v. *Braswell Motor Freight Lines, Inc.*, 428 F.2d 1371, 74 LRRM 2717 (5th Cir. 1970).

[70] *Cast Optics Corp.* v. *Textile Workers*, 75 LRRM 2169 (S.D. N.Y. 1970).

[71] *Livingston* v. *Electro Film Offset Printing Co.*, 73 LRRM 2267 (N.Y. Sup Ct. 1970).

based.[72] The case arose when the union which represented all the production and maintenance employees demanded, in order to achieve employee ratification of the tentative agreement between the parties, that the employer bargain separately with the skilled employees. Under a relatively new provision of the union constitution, production employees and skilled employees were permitted to vote separately on ratification. The production workers, who comprised about 90 percent of the bargaining unit, voted to ratify, but the skilled workers rejected the tentative agreement. The Sixth Circuit approved the lower court dismissal of the employer's 301 action for damages, rejecting the employer's claim that on the basis of past bargaining history a contract came into existence when a majority of the total bargaining unit voted for ratification of the tentative agreement. The court held that the method of ratification, unless otherwise stipulated by the parties, is an internal concern of the union, and until it ratifies the formal instrument the contract does not become operative. However, as to the novel claim for damages under Section 303 [73] by reason of the alleged inducement by the union of the employees to strike to force the employer to bargain with a labor organization (i.e., "skilled employees") other than the one which was the certified representative of the employees, the court held that a factual issue was presented as to whether the "skilled employees" constituted a "labor organization" under Section 2 (5) of the NLRA.[74]

The question of the existence of an arbitration provision in a contract arose in several state cases involving the Musicians Union, whose arbitration clause was contained in its bylaws and incorporated by reference in its standard form contracts. A California appellate court confirmed an arbitration award under such a contract, despite the employer's contentions that he was not aware of the arbitration provision or the proceedings thereon, he had not read the contract prior to signing it, and the procedure before the union trial board was not an impartial one since the board was composed of union members rather than a neutral arbitrator.[75] The court rejected all of the employer's claims under the California Arbitration Act. A New York court,

---

[72] Lear Siegler, Inc. v. UAW, 419 F.2d 534, 73 LRRM 2097 (6th Cir. 1969).
[73] 29 U.S.C. 187.
[74] 29 U.S.C. 152 (5).
[75] Federico v. Frick, 3 Cal. App. 3d 872, 73 LRRM 2810 (1970).

on the other hand, granted a stay of arbitration under such a contract, finding no clear and unequivocal agreement to arbitrate and noting, *inter alia,* that the employer was not aware of the bylaw and had not been given a copy thereof.[76] An earlier decision of the same court, however, did compel arbitration under what would appear to be the same contract.[77]

Public employment offers special problems as to the existence of a collective agreement since statutory authority underlines the ability of the public employer to enter into an enforceable contract or contractual provisions.[78] Thus, the Washington Supreme Court denied specific performance of an alleged agreement in regard to a wage increase which was not in writing as provided in the authorizing legislation, the court noting that anyone contracting with a municipal corporation is bound to take notice of the limitations in its power to contract.[79] In the case of *West Allis Policemen's Ass'n* v. *City of West Allis,* the court found no agreement on a wage increase where the city council did not ratify the agreement as required by state law, the court noting: [80]

> "Public employee labor negotiations and wage determinations must be conducted within the framework of existing political structures and related legislative restraints upon the municipality relative to budget and spending matters."

C. *Application of Contract Outside Its Term*

Few cases were decided during the past year in regard to application of contracts to matters preceding their execution or following their expiration, and most of the problems in this area pertain to successorships or plant closures treated below. In a Puerto Rico case the court set aside an arbitrator's award of back wages for work done during rest periods in violation of a three-year contract, where he ordered back pay for a 12-year period pursuant to a Puerto Rico statute permitting employees to claim back wages not received from their employer for a maximum period of 10 retroactive years.[81] The court held

---

[76] *Iona College* v. *William Morris Agency,* 73 LRRM 2592 (N.Y. Sup. Ct. 1970).
[77] *Fenton* v. *Lipsius,* 73 LRRM 2271 (N.Y. Sup. Ct. 1969).
[78] *Zderick* v. *Silver Bow County,* 460 P.2d 749, 73 LRRM 2076 (Mont. 1969).
[79] *State of Washington* v. *Callam County Comm'rs,* 77 Wash. 2d 549, 73 LRRM 2493 (1970).
[80] 73 LRRM 2339, at 2342 (Wis. Cir. Ct. 1970).
[81] *Dorado Beach Hotel Corp.* v. *Local 610, Hotel Employees,* 317 F.Supp. 217, 75 LRRM 2383 (D. P.R. 1970).

that under the explicit terms of the contract the arbitrator had no jurisdiction to go back further than the five-day period prior to the submission of the grievance, and that the statute applied only to legal actions and not to the processing of grievances under a collective bargaining agreement.

In another case the Ninth Circuit confirmed an arbitration award of a joint area committee established under a 1964 Teamster contract covering grievances unresolved when the prior 1961 collective bargaining agreement expired, at which time the focus of the grievance machinery shifted from a regional to a national basis under the 1964 contract.[82] The court held that the 1964 area committee that considered the grievances was substantially the same institution as the prior committee and was the proper forum to consider unresolved disputes arising from the 1961 agreement, and that the question of jurisdiction to decide the grievances was for the committees involved to decide.

Reaffirming the principle that rights created and arising under a collective bargaining agreement are not expunged by the expiration of that agreement, a court has compelled a union to arbitrate an employer's claim for strike damages where the permanent arbitrator had held the matter of damages open pursuant to the request of the parties.[83] Further, it has been held that an employer may not avoid arbitration of a dispute arising during the term of a new contract on the ground that the matter is governed by a strike settlement understanding reached prior to the execution of the contract in which it was allegedly agreed that the dispute was not subject to arbitration.[84]

D. *Plant Closure and Removal, Accretion, and Successorship*

A complete cessation of business by an employer with a single operation presents the clearest situation as to contract rights, since, unlike a merger of facilities or companies, the identity of the contracting parties is not usually a matter in dispute. For example, in the past year a Pennsylvania district court was called

---

[82] *Freight Drivers Local 208* v. *Braswell Motor Freight Lines, Inc.,* 422 F.2d 109, 73 LRRM 2543 (9th Cir. 1970).

[83] *Honeywell, Inc.* v. *Instrument Workers Local 116, IUE,* 307 F.Supp. 1126, 73 LRRM 2210 (E.D. Pa. 1970). (The court also held that the permanent arbitrator was not an indispensable party in the action.)

[84] *Associated Press* v. *Local 222, Newspaper Guild,* 73 LRRM 2908 (S.D. N.Y. 1970).

upon to rule on a 301 suit by a union claiming vacation pay under a collective bargaining agreement, where the employer had sold its physical assets and dissolved the corporation.[85] The court granted the union's motion for summary judgment and awarded the vacation pay on a pro rata basis as deferred compensation without any reference to the grievance procedure of the contract. The problem, however, often becomes more difficult to resolve when the employer closing its plant has more than one place of business.[86]

Even where there is a successor employer, the union may decide to proceed against the selling employer with which it has a contract. Thus, the Seventh Circuit has compelled an employer that sold its business to arbitrate a union's claims for separation allowances and vacation pay, denying the employer's request for a judicial construction of the contract.[87] Citing the *Wiley* case, the defendant employer also claimed that the purchaser of the business, who had hired the former unit members as new employees, was bound by operation of law to observe the provisions of the contract. The court held that the possible legal rights of the union against the purchaser, as a successor, carry no implication of a release of the seller from obligations arising under the bargaining agreement prior to the transfer of ownership. The court specifically refused to consider what rights the union has against the purchaser for the seller's obligations, or what continuing liabilities the seller might have for damages incurred by the employees at the hands of the purchaser.

Under the *Wiley* doctrine, an arbitration clause of a collective bargaining agreement remains in effect when a successor employer replaces its predecessor by way of merger, purchase, lease, or otherwise, the principal test being whether there is a "substantial continuity of identity in the business enterprise."[88] If the employing industry remains essentially the same despite the change of ownership, then the new company is a successor employer and is obligated to arbitrate under the terms of its predecessor's contract. A number of federal court decisions finding successorship and ordering arbitration or confirming awards

---

[85] *United Automobile Workers* v. *Aluminum Alloys Corp.*, 310 F.Supp. 213, 73 LRRM 2796 (E.D. Mich. 1970).
[86] See *Teamsters Local 757* v. *Borden, Inc., supra* note 20.
[87] *Packinghouse Workers* v. *Cold Storage Corp.*, 430 F.2d 70, 74 LRRM 3055 (7th Cir. 1970), *aff'g* 74 LRRM 3051 (N.D. Ill. 1969).
[88] 376 U.S. at 551, 55 LRRM 2773.

were handed down during the past year.[89] However, courts are frequently confronted with a demand by a labor organization to declare an entire collective bargaining agreement binding upon a successor employer, but they refrain from doing so on the ground that this would be passing on the merits of the union's claims and would usurp the function of the arbitrator.[90]

Nevertheless, the courts must still determine whether there is a successor employer who has a duty to arbitrate under its transferor's contract. Thus, a court dismissed a union's action for specific performance of its contract with the seller against the purchaser, where the latter continued its operations at its former place of business with its own employees, who were represented for purposes of collective bargaining by another labor organization, and where it did not hire any of the seller's employees.[91] While not specifically requested by the union, the court assumed that it also demanded enforcement of the arbitration clause of its contract, and held that the duty to arbitrate did not survive this transaction. The court also noted that forcing the purchaser to bargain with the plaintiff union when its employees were already represented by another labor organization would expose the purchaser to a charge of unfair labor practices under the NLRA.

In another breach of contract action, the Oregon district court ruled that the defendant partnership was a new business entity which was not bound by the contract entered into with the inactive corporation.[92] The partnership took over the corporation's commercial rock-crushing plant and its employees, but the heavy construction business of the corporation was discontinued entirely. The same person was the principal owner-manager of both the partnership and the corporation. The partnership refused the union's demand to abide by the construc-

[89] *Retail Clerks Local 1552* v. *Lynn Drug Co.*, 421 F.2d 1361, 73 LRRM 2814 (6th Cir. 1970), *aff'g as modified* 299 F.Supp. 1036, 72 LRRM 2009 (S.D. Ohio 1969); *Garment Workers* v. *Senco, Inc.*, 310 F.Supp. 539, 74 LRRM 2501 (D. Mass. 1970); *DeLaurentis* v. *Towne Nursing Center, Inc.*, 74 LRRM 2396 (S.D. N.Y. 1970).

[90] For a discussion of the courts being limited to compelling arbitration in successorship cases and not granting what amounts to specific performance of the contract, see the District Court opinion in *Retail Clerks* v. *Lynn Drug Co.*, supra note 89.

[91] *Printing Pressmen No. 447* v. *Pride Papers—Aaronson Bros. Paper Corp.*, 75 LRRM 2185 (S.D. N.Y. 1970).

[92] *Operating Engineers, Local 701* v. *Pioneer Constr. Co.*, 313 F.Supp. 753, 73 LRRM 2839 (D. Ore. 1970).

tion contract covering the employees of the corporation, but did offer to accept the contract that the plaintiff union had with other commercial gravel producers in the area which provided for lower wages. In denying the union's claims of successorship, the court noted that the end product of the old business and range of skills of the work force was far more complex, that the work force of the new operation was much smaller, and that the nature of the new gravel operation did not require the higher rate of pay enjoyed by construction workers.

The Third Circuit recently held that a union had no right to compel arbitration concerning the applicability of its contract to the employees of the employer's wholly owned subsidiary.[93] The subsidiary had been acquired before execution of the agreement and nothing was stated therein as to the application of the contract to the subsidiary. Also, the employees of the subsidiary had twice voted against representation by the union in elections conducted by the NLRB. Therefore, it was held that the dispute fell outside the collective bargaining agreement and there was no duty on the part of the employer to arbitrate.

A California appellate court also was faced with the application of a contract covering retail stores to a new location and the question of joinder of the new corporate entity in the proceedings.[94] The employer sought an order to restrain arbitration proceedings ordered by a lower court at the request of the union. The court set aside the order to arbitrate, holding that it was a question of "substantive arbitrability" to be determined by the court, not an arbitrator, as to whether or not the "additional locations" clause of the union contract could be applied to the new store, in which the employer claimed it had no interest, financial or otherwise. The court also held that it was an error to determine whether the new corporate entity was owned, operated, or controlled by the employer without joinder of the new corporation. Under the California arbitration statute it was held that neither the arbitrator nor a party to the arbitration has the power to compel a stranger to become a party to the arbitration proceedings.

[93] *Local 464, Bakery Workers* v. *Hershey Chocolate Corp.*, 433 F.2d 926, 75 LRRM 2845 (3d Cir. 1970), *aff'g* 310 F.Supp. 1182, 73 LRRM 2538, amended 75 LRRM 2239 (M.D. Pa. 1970).

[94] *Food Giant Markets, Inc.* v. *California Superior Court*, 73 LRRM 2122 (Cal. App. 1969).

E. *Multiparty Arbitration*

Other than the few factual situations treated in the text above which involved questions as to tripartite arbitration, there were few court decisions in the past year dealing directly with the problem of multiparty arbitration. A classic work-assignment dispute in a procedural posture was presented to the Third Circuit, and the court affirmed the dismissal of the plaintiff union's 301 action to compel arbitration because of its refusal to join the second union, whose members were then performing the work, as an additional party defendant under the Federal Rules of Civil Procedure.[95] The court noted that without the joinder the employer would be exposed to the risk that the second union would in turn institute a separate grievance leading potentially to conflicting awards. In view of the dismissal on procedural grounds, the court noted that it did not need to consider the propriety of an order for tripartite arbitration under the important *CBS* decision of the Second Circuit in 1969.[96]

A rather complex case was presented to the Seventh Circuit in which a trade association of milk dealers received from the district court a summary judgment compelling the union to arbitrate a dispute over the union's alleged violation of a clause in the contract regarding the granting of more advantageous terms and conditions to other dealers in the area (most-favored-nation clause).[97] The court rejected the union's argument for dismissal on the ground that since the contract was signed by the individual milk dealers after its negotiation by the association, the association was not a proper party to demand arbitration and then enforce the standard area contract. The court held that to require each of the individual dealers to make perfunctory demands before joining as plaintiffs would be an excessively technical and meaningless gesture, and that the presence of various individual dealers in the suit cured any defect as to whether there was a proper plaintiff, there being at most a harmless misjoinder of parties. The suit, however, was remanded to the district court because of its summary rejection of the union's defense against arbitration on the ground that the clause

[95] *Window Glass Cutters League* v. *American St. Gobain Corp.*, 428 F.2d 353, 74 LRRM 2749 (3d Cir. 1970).

[96] *CBS, Inc.* v. *American Recording & Broadcasting Ass'n*, 414 F.2d 1326, 72 LRRM 2140 (2d Cir. 1969).

[97] *Associated Milk Dealers, Inc.* v. *Local 753, Teamsters*, 422 F.2d 546, 73 LRRM 2435 (7th Cir. 1970).

in question violated the antitrust laws, holding that the district court, rather than an arbitrator, must interpret the antitrust laws and possible violations thereof. The court further held that the district court failed to fully consider the union's claim that the matter was not arbitrable under the contract and a memorandum of understanding between the parties, and indicated that it should have considered parol evidence of the bargaining history to determine whether the parties intended to submit the particular dispute to arbitration, noting that its ruling on arbitrability will not affect an arbitrator's interpretation of the most-favored-nation clause.

F. *Exhaustion and Court Decisions on Merits*

As noted in many of the cases cited above, before a court will entertain a 301 suit for violation of a collective bargaining agreement, available grievance machinery must be exhausted even though it does not lead to arbitration in the usual sense, and once a final decision on the merits is reached the courts will not permit relitigation of the decision. A district court recently discussed three exceptions to the usual refusal of courts to consider the merits of final awards under the grievance procedure: namely, cases involving breach of duty of fair representation by the union in handling the employee's grievance; unavailability or inadequacy of the grievance procedure; and refusal of the decision-maker under the contract to consider the merits of the grievance.[98] The court then concluded that the latter exception applied to the case at hand in which a state joint grievance committee under a Teamster contract decided that it did not have authority to make a decision on the matter in dispute and dismissed the grievance without rendering a decision on the merits. Since the decision of the committee was "final and binding" under the contract, the court decided it must inquire into the merits of the grievance. The court found no violation of the contract by the company and the union and dismissed the employee suit.

The fact that a union continues to bargain with an employer over employment conditions does not mean that it waives its rights under the argeement or is estopped from asserting such rights. Thus, a court found that bargaining was contemplated

---

[98] *Safely* v. *T.I.M.E. Freight, Inc., supra* note 47.

by the agreement, and that it would denigrate the arbitration process to penalize the union because it tried to settle the dispute by bargaining while at the same time seeking to have the arbitration award enforced.[99] However, where an employee accepts an informal settlement of his discharge grievance and fails to pursue his remedies under the contract further, he cannot later bring suit for wrongful discharge in the absence of factual allegations that he was coerced by the employer and the union into abandoning his grievance and accepting a settlement.[100]

IV. Compelling Arbitration or Reviewing Awards

Almost all 301 litigation involves the issue of either compelling arbitration or review of an award, as is apparent from the cases discussed or cited above. The following subheadings will introduce some of the other cases reported in the past year that are of particular interest. The courts have continued, with minor exceptions, to exercise their responsibility in seeing that contractual means of disposition of disputes are followed and carried out without unnecessary interference or usurpation from the courts or other outside sources.

A. *Suits to Compel Arbitration and Arbitrability*

Unless a dispute is clearly precluded from arbitration, it must be resolved by the agreed-upon method of resolution, but it is for a court to decide whether or not an employer is required to arbitrate and the issues it must arbitrate. Once a court finds that there are contractual provisions that govern a dispute or that it cannot be said with positive assurance that the contract excludes the dispute from arbitration, that is, finds that the dispute is arbitrable, then it will compel the parties to submit the interpretation of the contractual provisions to an arbitrator. So strong is the presumption of arbitrability that a court will compel arbitration, even though it is "crystal-clear" that the arbitrator could decide the merits only one way.[101] Even frivolous or weak claims may be arbitrable, and doubts by the court should

---

[99] *Teamsters, Local 745* v. *Braswell Motor Freight Lines, Inc., supra* note 69.

[100] *Gutierrez* v. *Gaffers & Sattler Corp.*, 74 LRRM 2022 (Cal. App. 1970).

[101]*Local 286, IUE* v. *General Electric Co.*, 429 F.2d 412, 74 LRRM 2645 (1st Cir. 1970); *Operating Engineers, Local 103* v. *Crown Constr. Co.*, 75 LRRM 2184 (N.D. Ind. 1970). (Judgment on pleadings in union suit granted.)

be resolved in favor of contract coverage.[102] Where there is a broad arbitration provision, the courts will not speculate in advance as to what the arbitrator will award or whether any such award can be enforced.[103]

Suits for breach of contract may result instead in the court's compelling arbitration, and the commencement of such action does not constitute a waiver of the arbitration provisions of the contract.[104] In one such recent case based upon breach of a settlement agreement, the Fifth Circuit affirmed the lower court's order that the settlement agreement became an integral part of the then-existing collective bargaining agreement and that the dispute be submitted to the arbitration proceedings under the contract.[105] The court also approved of the order for discovery by the parties under the Federal Rules of Civil Procedure in aid of the arbitration proceedings and the retention of jurisdiction by the court pending the determination by the arbitrator.

It has been clearly established under the Supreme Court's *Wiley* decision that where the substantive issues of a dispute are a proper subject for arbitration, procedural matters arising out of that dispute, such as whether preliminary steps of the grievance procedure may be disregarded, are for the arbitrator, not the court, to determine because procedural matters are often intertwined with the merits of the dispute.[106] Thus, even in a situation where the contract explicitly requires strict adherence to the grievance procedure and specifically requires that "no step shall be used until all previous steps have been ex-

---

[102] *F & M Schaefer Brewing Co.* v. *Local 49, Brewery Workers*, 420 F.2d 854, 73 LRRM 2298 (2d Cir. 1970).

[103] *United Ins. Co.* v. *Insurance Workers*, 315 F.Supp. 1133, 75 LRRM 2053 (E.D. Pa. 1970).

[104] *Local 66, Pointers Pension Fund* v. *Horn Waterproofing Corp.*, 74 LRRM 2397 (S.D. N.Y. 1970); see also *Teledyne Wisconsin Motor* v. *Local 283, UAW*, 75 LRRM 2472 (E.D. Wis. 1970).

[105] *Asbestos Workers Local 66* v. *Leona Lee Corp.*, 434 F.2d 192, 76 LRRM 2026 (5th Cir. 1970), *aff'g* 76 LRRM 2024 (W.D. Tex. 1969).

[106] *Meat Cutters, Local 405* v. *Tennessee Dressed Beef Co.*, 428 F.2d 797, 74 LRRM 2722 (6th Cir. 1970), *rev'g* 74 LRRM 2720 (M.D. Tenn. 1969). See also *Bealmer* v. *Texaco, Inc.*, *supra* note 43 (standing of individual employees, binding effect of agreement, and timeliness as procedural in nature); *Air Engineering Metal Trades* v. *ARO, Inc.*, 307 F.Supp. 934, 74 LRRM 2167 (E.D. Tenn. 1969) (lapse of 15-day period for submitting to arbitration).

hausted," a South Dakota district court ordered arbitration,[107] noting in strong language:

> "Technical or strict construction will be disregarded . . . even as it is agreed on, will not be permitted as a method to nullify the policy back of the Labor Management Relations Act and moreover may not be used as a defense against arbitration."

Further, the court will not require a party to submit to the expense and inconvenience of separate arbitration hearings for procedural and substantive issues.[108]

Cases refusing to compel arbitration are, relatively speaking, few in number and often involve special circumstances which dictate the result. Thus, in an employer's damage action under Section 303 of the LMRA, the Fifth Circuit refused the union's motion to stay the action pending arbitration under the broad arbitration clause in the contract between the parties.[109] The court restated the established principle that courts must hear and determine the validity of tort damage claims "absent a clear, explicit statement in the collective bargaining contract directing an arbitrator to hear and determine" such claims. Also, where the contract clearly does not require the matter to be submitted to arbitration, such as "jurisdictional disputes" subject to the National Joint Board for the Settlement of Jurisdictional Disputes, or the grievance has been adjusted satisfactorily and the matter is now moot, the courts will not compel arbitration.[110] However, where the employer requested and was denied a stay of arbitration pending an appeal as to arbitrability, the Tenth Circuit held that the case was not moot because "implementation of the arbitration award depends on the validity of the court order requiring arbitration." [111] In the somewhat unusual case of a suit to compel arbitration under the provisions of a terminated contract regarding the terms of a new collec-

[107] *Local Lodge 862, IAM* v. *Schweigers, Inc.*, 314 F.Supp. 585, 74 LRRM 2682 (D. S.D. 1970).
[108] *Steelworkers* v. *Jones & Armstrong Steel Co.*, 74 LRRM 2374 (N.D. Ala. 1970) (timeliness issue).
[109] *Vulcan Materials Co.* v. *Steelworkers, Local 2176*, 430 F.2d 446, 74 LRRM 2818 (5th Cir. 1970).
[110] *Tobacco Workers Local 317* v. *P. Lorillard Corp.*, 314 F.Supp. 513, 75 LRRM 2437 (M.D. N.C. 1970); see also *Communications Workers* v. *Southern Bell Tel. & Tel. Co.*, 419 F.2d 1210, 73 LRRM 2206 (5th Cir. 1970); *Vincent J. Smith, Inc.* v. *Brennan*, 33 App. Div.2d 1099, 74 LRRM 2254 (N.Y. Sup. Ct. 1970); *Central Steel Erecting Co.* v. *Carpenters, Local 125*, 33 App. Div.2d 876, 73 LRRM 2622 (N.Y. Sup. Ct. 1970).
[111] *Automobile Workers, UAW* v. *Folding Carrier Corp.*, 422 F.2d 47, 73 LRRM 2632 (10th Cir. 1970).

tive bargaining agreement which would supersede the terminated contract, the court stayed proceedings and held that the matter was not ripe for determination at that time where the parties had resumed negotiation and, therefore, were not at an impasse.[112]

B. *Reviewing, Enforcing, or Vacating Awards*

In view of the national policy to encourage arbitration as a device to settle industrial disputes and the fact that the parties have bargained for a determination of their disputes by an arbitrator or other means of final determination, rather than by a court, the courts must not substitute their judgment for that of the arbitrator by reviewing the merits of an award.[113] As long as the award "draws its essence" from the collective bargaining agreement and is not in manifest disregard of the agreement, of the submission to the arbitrator, or of the law of the shop, the award must be enforced, and any ambiguity is to be resolved in favor of the award.[114] An arbitrator may decide that certain issues are beyond his authority to decide under the contract, and the courts will respect such awards.[115]

To be enforceable an award must be "final and binding" or a "definitive settlement" under the collective bargaining agreement.[116] Thus, an otherwise final award was enforced against an employer, even though the union could have elected under the terms of the agreement to strike but did not do so, rather than seeking court enforcement of the award.[117] Where there has been more than one award in connection with a particular dispute, the court will have to determine which award is final,

---

[112] *South Pittsburgh Water Co.* v. *Utility Workers, Local 174,* 315 F.Supp. 305, 75 LRRM 2477 (W.D. Pa. 1970).

[113] *New Orleans Steamship Ass'n* v. *Local 1418, ILA, supra* note 12; *Teamsters Local 249* v. *Motor Freight Express, Inc.,* 48 F.R.D. 294, 73 LRRM 2799 (W.D. Pa. 1966); but see *Communications Equipment Workers* v. *Western Electric Co.,* 75 LRRM 2776 (D. Md. 1970) where the court correctly cited the law but engaged in "a careful review of all the evidence presented before the Board of Arbitrators" and found no error in their decision.

[114] *District 50, UMW* v. *Bowman Transp., Inc.,* 421 F.2d 934, 73 LRRM 2317 (5th Cir. 1970); *Steelworkers* v. *Reynolds Aluminum Supply Co.,* 75 LRRM 2180 (N.D. Ala. 1970); *IUE, Local 103* v. *Radio Corp. of America,* 74 LRRM 2883 (S.D. N.Y. 1970).

[115] *Federal Labor Union No. 18887* v. *Midvale-Heppenstall Co.,* 421 F.2d 1289, 73 LRRM 2384 (3d Cir. 1970).

[116] See *General Drivers Local 89* v. *Riss & Co.,* 372 U.S. 517, 52 LRRM 2623 (1963). See also the case discussed at note 118.

[117] *Freight Drivers Local 208* v. *Braswell Motor Freight Lines, Inc., supra* note 80.

and a procedural dismissal does not preclude a second award unless the agreement specifically bars reinstituting the complaint.[118] In one case a district court enforced, in an employee's suit, the second of four arbitration awards as the final and binding award, noting that in order to do so the court had to examine the merits of the various decisions and holding that once an award is made, the rights of the parties thereto are vested and cannot be destroyed by a later attempted modification.[119] Attempts by a party to vacate an award or enjoin its enforcement without evidence of fraud or other substantial ground meet with little success in the courts.[120]

Occasionally the courts are faced with a challenge to an award on the ground that it violates another statute or some public policy, and the courts must dispose of such contentions on the merits.[121] Other defenses to the enforcement of an award are that the employer is not bound by the agreement in question,[122] that the arbitrator exceeded his contractual authority or the scope of the issue submitted to him,[123] or that the award as rendered is indefinite or vague.[124] In the latter case, where the findings that support an award are not intelligible or complete, the court may remand the case for more definite findings.[125] The fact that a union has engaged in an illegal strike against a hospital in violation of state law is not necessarily a defense to an arbitration award.[126] As in other areas of public em-

[118] *Local 616, IUE* v. *Byrd Plastics, Inc.,* 428 F.2d 23, 74 LRRM 2550 (3rd Cir. 1970).

[119] *Parker* v. *Mercury Freight Lines, Inc.,* 73 LRRM 2189 (N.D. Ala. 1969) (Attorney fees were denied to the plaintiffs, however, even though they prevailed; *cf. District 50, UMW* v. *Bowman Transp., Inc., supra* note 114); *cf. Hunter* v. *Locher, supra* note 35.

[120] *Iron City Indus. Cleaning Corp.* v. *Local 141, Laundry & Dry Cleaners Union,* 316 F.Supp. 1373, 75 LRRM 2797 (W.D.Pa. 1970); *Teamsters Local 807* v. *West Farms Express, Inc.,* 73 LRRM 2414 (N.Y. Sup. Ct. 1970).

[121] *Employees' Ind. Union* v. *Wyman Gordon Co.,* 314 F.Supp. 458, 75 LRRM 2425 (N.D. Ill. 1970); *Doyle* v. *Shortman, supra* note 61; *Consolidated Edison Co.* v. *Rigley,* 73 LRRM 2220 (N.Y. Sup. Ct. 1970).

[122] *Local 11, IBEW* v. *Jandon Elec. Co.,* 429 F.2d 584, 74 LRRM 2892 (9th Cir. 1970) *aff'g* 74 LRRM 2888 (C.D. Cal. 1968).

[123] *Pulp & Paper Mill Workers, Locals 359 & 361* v. *Allied Paper, Inc.,* 76 LRRM 2031 (S.D. Ala. 1970); *Pontiac Osteopathic Hospital* v. *Service Employees, Local 79,* 24 Mich. App. 585, 180 N.W.2d 510, 75 LRRM 2702 (1970).

[124] *Bowman* v. *Ruchti Bros.,* 74 LRRM 2064 (Cal. App. 1970).

[125] *New England Tel. & Tel. Co.* v. *Telephone Workers,* 74 LRRM 2685 (D. Mass. 1970); *Railroad Trainmen* v. *Ill. Cent. R.R.,* 75 LRRM 2556 (E.D. Ill. 1969), *aff'd sub nom. United Transp. Union* v. *Ill. Cent. R.R.,* 433 F.2d 566, 75 LRRM 2557 (7th Cir. 1970) (remand to National Railroad Adjustment Board because of its failure to consider alleged hearsay evidence).

[126] *In re David (Adelphi Hospital),* 35 App. Div. 2d 737, 75 LRRM 2605 (N.Y. 1970).

ployment arbitration, the confirmation of an award depends upon the enabling legislation involved.[127]

V. Relationship of 301 to Other Legislation

A. *National Labor Relations Act*

As noted above in a number of cited cases, potential conflicts with the NLRA and other statutes are frequently raised as defenses to arbitration. However, as pointed out in *Federal-Mogul Corp.* v. *Local 985, UAW*,[128] since arbitrators are familiar with the principles of labor law, there is no basis for assuming that they would fashion a remedy that would require the losing party to violate the law. The case involved a union's suit to compel arbitration concerning the employer's failure to recognize the union at a newly acquired plant. The employer's contention that such recognition, where it had already recognized another union, would cause it to commit an unfair labor practice was held to be premature, until the award has issued.

Arbitration does not control the Board in its determination of bargaining unit issues. Thus, a unit clarification by the NLRB deprived the union of any right to recognition as the representative of the employees, and the union cannot thereafter compel arbitration of the same question.[129] However, the Ninth Circuit dismissed a 301 action by a union seeking a declaratory judgment in regard to the inclusion of certain employees in the bargaining unit after the NLRB had declared that they were excluded by reason of their supervisory status, holding that arbitration was, by agreement, the exclusive method of resolution.[130] In jurisdictional dispute cases the NLRB has always deferred to the National Joint Board for the Settlement of Jurisdictional Disputes where both unions and the employer have agreed to be bound by its decision, but some courts are not in

---

[127] *Rockland Firefighters Ass'n* v. *City of Rockland*, 261 A.2d 418, 73 LRRM 2463 (Me. 1970); cf. *Mellon* v. *Fitzgerald Public Schools*, 22 Mich. App. 218, 177 N.W.2d 187, 74 LRRM 2516 (1970) (testing the right of individual presentation of grievances under the Michigan act permitting collective bargaining among public employees).

[128] 74 LRRM 2961 (E.D. Mich. 1970). See also *Heavy Contractors Ass'n* v. *Laborers. Local 1140, supra* note 65.

[129] *Smith Steel Workers* v. *A. O. Smith Corp.*, 420 F.2d 1, 73 LRRM 2028 (7th Cir. 1969).

[130] *Local 89, IBEW* v. *General Tel. Co. of the Northwest*, 431 F.2d 957, 75 LRRM 2112 (9th Cir. 1970), rev'g 75 LRRM 2109 (E.D. Wash. 1968).

agreement as to the necessity for the employer to be a party to such agreement.[131]

In a recent case involving the suspension of a union steward for violation of a no-solicitation rule, the employer brought a 301 action to compel arbitration, and the union filed an unfair labor practice charge with the NLRB.[132] The court held that there are areas of overlapping jurisdiction between the NLRB and the arbitrator, and where there is an arbitration clause there is concurrent contract and Board jurisdiction, with neither preempting the other. Therefore, the court compelled the union to arbitrate the employer's grievance despite the fact that the NLRB had issued a complaint and held a hearing in regard to the same matter. The court specifically refused to consider to what extent the Board should defer to an arbitrator's decision, or whether the Board should postpone its own proceeding until arbitration was concluded. It is clear that the two procedures can complement one another in some instances, as in those situations where the employer is refusing to furnish information in order to permit the union to evaluate the merits of grievances before proceeding to arbitration,[133] or in those involving a union's breach of its duty of fair representation.[134]

As for the NLRB itself deferring to arbitration in other areas of its activity, the courts continue to uphold its refusal to defer, [135] except under the rather restricted circumstances set forth in its *Spielberg Mfg. Co.* decision.[136] However, within the Board itself there has been a split in opinion as to its policy of deferral, with Member Brown consistently dissenting in favor of a more liberal policy of deferral and withholding of NLRB action and review until the existing contractual remedies have

---

[131] *Plasterers Local 79* v. *NLRB,* 440 F.2d 174, 74 LRRM 2575 (D.C. Cir. 1970) ; *Vincent* v. *Local 532, Carpenters,* 75 LRRM 2819 (W.D. N.Y. 1970). Compare, for example, *Laborers, Local 42 (R. B. Cleveland Co.),* 184 NLRB No. 77, 74 LRRM 1562 (1970); *Millwrights Local 1862 (Jelco, Inc.),* 184 NLRB No. 58, 74 LRRM 1485 (1970).

[132] *United Aircraft Corp.* v. *Canel Lodge 700, Machinists,* 436 F.2d 1, 76 LRRM 2111, aff'g 314 F.Supp. 371, 74 LRRM 2518 (D. Conn. 1970) ; see also *Cast Optics Corp.* v. *Textile Workers, supra* note 70, citing *Carey* v. *Westinghouse Elec. Corp.,* 375 U.S. 261, 55 LRRM 2042 (1964).

[133] *NLRB* v. *Twin City Lines, Inc.,* 425 F.2d 164, 74 LRRM 2024 (8th Cir. 1970).

[134] *Local 485, IUE (Automatic Plating Corp.),* 183 NLRB No. 131, 74 LRRM 1396 (1970) ; *Port Drum Co.,* 180 NLRB No. 90, 73 LRRM 1068 (1970) .

[135] *Steve's Sash & Door, Inc.* v. *NLRB,* 430 F.2d 1364, 74 LRRM 2765 (5th Cir. 1970).

[136] 112 NLRB 1080, 36 LRRM 1152 (1955).

been exhausted.[137] However, the recent decision of *Terminal Transport Co.*,[138] by a majority of a three-member panel, composed of the newly appointed Chairman of the Board Miller and Member Brown, presages a possible shift in policy on the Board's deferral policy. The majority opinion held that the NLRB would honor the arbitration award of a joint arbitration panel, where the employee refused to submit to a test in regard to his qualifications, the lack of which was the asserted reason for the employer's discharge action. Member Jenkins issued a strong dissent and would proceed to consider the grievant's case on the merits, finding that, contrary to *Spielberg*, there was not a "voluntary settlement" by the employee involved, that the committee did not directly consider and decide the issue of discrimination under Section 7 of the NLRA, and that the procedure of the joint committee was not "fair and regular" since it had no outside neutral member to provide impartial consideration of the alleged discrimination. A second new appointee, Ralph E. Kennedy, was sworn in December 14, 1970, succeeding Frank McCulloch, so it is still too early to know whether there may be a shift in Board policy in regard to deferral to arbitration, but the national policy as reaffirmed in such 1970 Supreme Court decisions as *Boys Markets* and *Czosek* would indicate that such change is likely.

B. *Arbitration and Civil Rights Legislation*

This past year there were a number of important decisions involving the relationship between arbitration and civil rights legislation, most particularly Title VII.[139] The most important of these involved the question of whether the grievant, pursuing contractual remedies available to him as the result of a collec-

---

[137] See, for example, *Englehardt, Inc.*, 186 NLRB No. 81, 75 LRRM 1401 (1970) (Chairman Miller not on panel); *Sunbeam Corp.*, 184 NLRB No. 117, 74 LRRM 1712 (1970) (three-way split in disposition of case involving question as to whether employee was engaged in protected activity); *International Paper Co.*, 184 NLRB No. 38, 74 LRRM 1438 (1970) ; *Iron Workers, Local 229 (Bethlehem Steel Corp.)*, 183 NLRB No. 35, 74 LRRM 1317 (1970).

[138] 185 NLRB No. 96, 75 LRRM 1130 (1970).

[139] See in addition to the cases discussed below, *Waters* v. *Wisconsin Steel Works, Int'l Harvester Co.*, 427 F.2d 476, 2 FEP Cases 574 (7th Cir. 1970) *rev'g* 301 F.Supp. 663, 1 FEP Cases 858 (N.D. Ill. 1969), *cert. denied* 2 FEP Cases 1059 (1970): *Fakete* v. *U.S. Steel Corp.*, 424 F.2d 331, 2 FEP Cases 540 (3d Cir. 1970), *rev'g* 300 F.Supp. 22, 2 FEP Cases 104 (W.D. Pa. 1969); *Oubichon* v. *North American Rockwell Corp.*, 3 FEP Cases 12 (C.D. Cal. 1970); *Evans Local 2127, IBEW*, 313 F.Supp. 1354, 2 FEP Cases 483 (N.D. Ga. 1970) ; *Newman* v. *Avco Corp.*, 313 F.Supp. 1069, 2 FEP Cases 517 (M.D. Tenn. 1970); *Bremer* v. *St. Louis Southwestern R.R.*, 310 F.Supp. 1333, 2 FEP Cases 509 (E.D. Mo. 1969) .

tive bargaining agreement, could be said to have made an effective election of remedies which would preclude further litigation in the courts under Title VII. Last year the Seventh Circuit had refused to apply this doctrine to the Title VII area.[140] As the result of decisions this year by the Fifth and Sixth Circuits, the courts are now split on this issue.

In *Hutchings* v. *U.S. Industries, Inc.*,[141] the Fifth Circuit held that a black worker's prior use of contractual grievance-arbitration machinery to protest alleged promotion discrimination did not result in an election of remedies. The court held that an arbitration award, whether adverse or favorable to the employee involved, was not per se conclusive of a determination of his rights under Title VII. Moreover, the court stated that in a case like *Hutchings,* where there was an intermediate grievance determination through which the matter was deemed settled, there was no conclusive effect flowing from such a resolution of the issue. In ascertaining the legislative intent of Congress when it passed Title VII, the court, referring specifically to the national labor policy in favor of arbitration of labor disputes and the Court's holding in *Boys Markets,* stated the following: [142]

> "Congress . . . has made the federal judiciary, not the EEOC or the private arbitrator, the *final* arbiter of an individual's Title VII grievance. . . . The EEOC serves to encourage and effect voluntary compliance with Title VII. So also may the private arbitrator serve consistent with the scope of his authority. Neither, however, has the power to make the ultimate determination of Title VII rights."

The Fifth Circuit in *Hutchings* then noted its agreement with the Seventh Circuit's statement to the effect that its holding was not to be used to obtain a duplicate relief in both public and private forums ". . . which would result in an unjust enrichment or windfall to him [the plaintiff or grievant]." Moreover, the court specifically noted that arbitration awards and determinations might be properly considered as evidence, even though they are not to be regarded as conclusive upon the judiciary.

The Sixth Circuit has reached a contrary result in *Dewey* v.

---

[140] *Bowe* v. *Colgate-Palmolive Co.,* 416 F.2d 711, 2 FEP Cases 121 (7th Cir. 1969).

[141] 428 F.2d 303, 2 FEP Cases 725 (5th Cir. 1970), *rev'g and reman'g* 309 F.Supp. 691, 2 FEP Cases 599 (E.D. Tex. 1969).

[142] *Id.* at 313-314, 2 FEP Cases at 732-733.

Reynolds Metals Co.[143] In *Dewey,* a case involving alleged religious discrimination, the court held that where grievances are based upon alleged civil rights violations and the parties to a collective bargaining agreement consent to a mutually accept- able arbitrator, the arbitrator's decision concerning such griev- ances is "final." The court cited both the *Steelworkers* trilogy as well as *Boys Markets* for the proposition that the arbitration process was to be encouraged as a matter of national labor law. If, said the Sixth Circuit, the arbitrator's award was not re- garded as final,[144]

> "This result could sound the death knell to arbitration of labor disputes, which has been so usefully employed in their settlement. Employers would not be inclined to agree to arbitration clauses in collective bargaining agreements if they provide only a one- way street, i.e., that the awards are binding on them but not on their employees.
>
> "The tremendous increase in civil rights litigation leads one to the belief that the Act will be used more frequently in labor disputes. Such use ought not to destroy the efficacy of arbitration."

The Sixth Circuit did not make reference to the fact that the arbitrator in *Dewey* did not deal with the legal and consti- tutional issues involved. Moreover, there are a substantial num- ber of arbitrators who believe that such matters are beyond their scope of jurisdiction or competence. And, finally, the Sixth Circuit opinion in *Dewey* ignores the fact that the plaintiff or grievant is alleging discrimination on the part of one or both parties who are involved in the selection of the impartial ar- bitrator—and the very serious need for reform of discrimination arbitration cases.[145] Suffice it to say, this split in the circuits makes it clear that the Supreme Court may be called upon before long to resolve the matter and determine whether the public character of Title VII overrides the thrust of decisions like the *Steelworkers* trilogy and *Boys Markets* which were used by the Sixth Circuit to argue for adherence to a "business as usual" policy in the very important civil rights arena.

---

[143] 429 F.2d 324, 2 FEP Cases 687 (6th Cir. 1970), *rev'g* 300 F.Supp. 709, 71 LRRM 2406, 1 FEP Cases 759 (W.D. Mich. 1969), *rehearing den.* 429 F.2d 324, 2 FEP Cases 869 (1970), *aff'd by equally divided Court,* 402 U.S. 689, 3 FEP Cases 508 (1971). Accord *Oubichon* v. *North American Rockwell Corp., supra* note 139, discussing *Dewey, Newman,* and *Hutchings; Pompey* v. *General Motors Corp.,* 24 Mich. App. 60, 179 N.W.2d 697, 2 FEP Cases 1027 (1970).

[144] *Id.* at 332, 2 FEP Cases at 691.

[145] See Gould, "Labor Arbitration of Grievances Involving Racial Discrimina- tion." 118 *U. Pa. L. Rev.* 40 (1969) and McKelvey, "Sex and the Single Arbitrator," 24 *Ind. & Lab. Rel. Rev.* 355 (1971).

C. *Other Statutes*

There are a few additional noteworthy cases dealing with the relationship of Section 301 to other legislation. In one case the Second Circuit affirmed the lower court's permanent injunction against a union from conducting grievance proceedings regarding unpaid benefits against the alleged successor of a motor carrier in reorganization under Chapter XI of the Bankruptcy Act.[146] The referee in bankruptcy had confirmed a plan or arrangement whereby the carrier would pay 10 percent of its claims, and the union is seeking the remaining 90 percent from the alleged successor. The court affirmed the finding that there was no successorship, and even if there had been, attempting to arbitrate the claim would be in violation of the bankruptcy order.

In another case, the court refused to set aside an arbitration award reinstating a discharged truck driver on the ground that it would violate safety regulations and Interstate Commerce Commission requirements.[147] The court noted that the employer's defense had been fully litigated in the arbitration proceedings and had been found to be a subterfuge to get rid of the employee, and that the employer had an obligation to make a bona fide effort to secure a waiver of ICC requirements in view of the employee's past history of a physical defect.

The district court in New York was required to rule on whether an arbitrator's opinion construing a contract clause forbidding the employer from selling ice cream from its Philadelphia area plant in the New York City area violated antitrust laws.[148] The court held that the construed provision is not a territorial restriction of the type prohibited by the antitrust laws, but is an attempt to preserve minimum standards for wages, hours, and working conditions and is within the labor exemption under said laws.

In the *U.S. Steel* case,[149] the Third Circuit remanded the case to the district court to determine whether the work stop-

---

[146] *Eastern Freight Ways Inc.* v. *Local 707 Teamsters*, 422 F.2d 351, 73 LRRM 2270 (2d Cir. 1970), *aff'g* 300 F.Supp. 1289, 71 LRRM 2641 (S.D. N.Y. 1969).

[147] *Int'l Auto Sales & Serv., Inc.*, v. *Teamsters, Local 270*, 311 F.Supp. 313, 73 LRRM 2829 (E.D. La. 1970).

[148] *National Dairy Products Corp.* v. *Teamsters, Local 680*, 308 F.Supp. 982, 73 LRRM 2444 (S.D. N.Y. 1970).

[149] *Supra* note 18.

pages, which were the subject of the employers' action for injunctive relief, were labor disputes at all, or whether they were a mass protest against the Federal Government for its failure to enforce provisions of the new Federal Coal Mine Health and Safety Act of 1969. The appeals court also questioned that if an "abnormally dangerous condition" were found to exist, this would be a proper subject of arbitration under the contract, and if so, how.

VI. Conclusion

It is fair to conclude that the *Boys Markets* decision will have an immediate impact on arbitration, although perhaps limited in relation to the overall number of arbitration cases. As of this time, *Boys Markets* simply provides for the granting of an injunction in a *Boys Markets* strike in violation of a no-strike clause which must be conditioned upon both the availability and the willingness of the employer to avail itself of the arbitral process immediately. In view of the fact that injunctive orders are extraordinary relief, it can be anticipated that the courts will require immediate and expedited arbitration which will place demands upon both the time and expertise of arbitrators. It can also be expected that the courts will be much more willing to scrutinize the arbitral process in a *Boys Markets* situation where the arbitration is being conducted in conjunction with a pending court proceeding. Therefore, a great deal of accommodation between courts and arbitrators will be required so that each process does not intrude upon the other.

Employee suits can be expected to cause problems for employers and unions, in view of the increased militancy of minority positions or groups as well as the greater emphasis on individual freedoms and procedural due process. Accordingly, arbitrators will have to be increasingly aware of the problems and positions of dissenting minority employees in grievance arbitration disputes and take pains to see that their rights are protected as far as possible. While increasing awareness among arbitrators of the problems of individual suits will not necessarily reduce the number of such suits substantially, it may help to alleviate any conflict or tension that those suits might cause between the courts and the arbitral process.

Finally, the field of public employment arbitration would

appear to be a new arena which may require some inventive thinking for many arbitrators. The increasing use of compulsory arbitration in interest disputes in public employment, especially in the protected services, will require much more attention to the surrounding problems of other bargaining units of employees of the public employer involved and to the public itself because of the impact that the award will have on such third parties. It is possible that the viability of compulsory arbitration statutes will be in large measure determined by how successful the arbitration awards are in resolving public employment disputes, not only as to the employees immediately involved, but also in regard to the other employees of the public employer.[150]

The developments of 1970 clearly indicate an increased use of arbitration in all sectors of our economy and a broader responsibility for arbitrators than ever before. The arbitrators must be equal to the task of new problems in such controversial areas as public employee and racial discrimination disputes.

---

[150] See *Mount St. Mary's Hospital* v. *Catherwood*, 26 N.Y.2d 493, 74 LRRM 2897 (1970) *aff'g* 305 N.Y.S.2d 143, 73 LRRM 2127 (1969). See also, Michigan act to provide for compulsory arbitration of labor disputes in municipal police and fire departments, which the legislature made effective for a trial period until June 30, 1972, M.C.L.A. 423.231ff, M.S.A. 17.455 (31) ff. The initial experience with the act is that it has caused dissatisfaction among other employees of the public employer involved, who do not have the same right and thus are left to negotiate with an employer who has an empty purse, or one who refuses to negotiate until the compulsory arbitration is completed.

BIBLIOGRAPHY

Block, "Race Discrimination in Industry and the Grievance Process," 21 *Lab. L.J.* 627 (1970).

Comment, "Federal Arbitration Act in State Courts: Converse Erie Problems," 55 *Cornell L. Rev.* 623 (1970).

Comment, "Impact of John Wiley Revisited: From the Vindication of Policy to the Verge of Inequity," 21 *Syracuse L. Rev.* 875 (1970).

Gould, "On Labor Injunctions, Unions, and the Judges: The Boys Markets Case," 1970 *Sup. Ct. Rev.* 215.

Isaacson, "A Fresh Look at the Labor Injunction," *Labor Law Developments,* Proceedings of the 17th Annual Institute on Labor Law, The Southwestern Legal Foundation (New York: Matthew Bender, 1971).

Krislov and Peters, "Grievance Arbitration in State and Local Government: A Survey," 25 *Arb. J.* 196 (1970).

Mack, "Improving Mediation and Fact Finding in the Public Sector," 21 *Lab. L.J.* 259 (1970).

Markson, M., "The End of an Experiment in Arbitral Supremacy: The Death of Sinclair," 21 *Lab. L.J.* 645 (1970).

McDermott, "Types of Seniority Provisions and the Measurement of Ability," 25 *Arb. J.* 101 (1970).

Petersen, "Consequences of the Arbitration Award for Unions," 21 *Lab. L.J.* 613; "Union Prediction in Arbitration," 21 *Lab. L.J.* 787 (1970).

Rains, "Dispute Settlement in the Public Sector," 19 *Buffalo L. Rev.* 279 (1970).

Sherman, "The Duty of Disclosure in Labor Arbitration," 25 *Arb. J.* 73 (1970).

Staudohar, "Compulsory Arbitration of Interests Disputes in the Protective Services," 21 *Lab. L.J.* 708 (1970).

Symposium: "Arbitration and Antitrust," 44 *N.Y.U. L. Rev.* 1069 (1969).

Symposium: "Collective Bargaining, Contract Enforcement and Arbitration—1969," 22 *N.Y.U. Conf. Lab.* 81 (1969).

Unkovic, "Enforcing the No-Strike Clause," 21 *Lab. L.J.* 387 (1970).

SURVEY OF THE ARBITRATION PROFESSION
IN 1969 *

The Executive Committee of the Board of Governors of the National Academy of Arbitrators authorized this survey of the arbitration profession in 1969.

The questionnaire was reviewed and copies were mailed to members of the Academy in June 1970. By mid-October 1970, 222 responses had been received. This represents 60.5 percent of the Academy's membership at that time. This is the fourth statistical survey conducted by the Academy, others having been made for the years 1952, 1957, and 1962.[1]

In the following narrative summary, comparisons with the 1962 data have been drawn, wherever possible.

I. The Arbitrator

The average age of the respondents as of December 31, 1969, was 57 years. This compares with 52.7 years in 1962. Only four respondents (1.8 percent) were under 40; in 1962, eight (4.6 percent) were under 40; in 1957, 10 (11.2 percent) were under 41. In 1962, 36 (20.7 percent) were 60 years of age or older; at the end of 1969, 93 (41.9 percent) were in this category. While the 1962 data showed that the majority of arbitrators were in their

---

* This survey was made by Jean T. McKelvey and Derek L. Rogers, Graduate Assistant, New York State School of Industrial and Labor Relations, Cornell University, Ithaca, N.Y.

[1] See "Survey of the Arbitration Profession in 1952," Appendix E, in *The Profession of Labor Arbitration*, Cumulative Selection of Addresses at First Seven Annual Meetings, National Academy of Arbitrators, 1948 through 1954, ed. Jean T. McKelvey (Washington: BNA Books, 1954), 176-182; "Research and Education Committee Report and Recommendations," Appendix D, and "Statistical Tables Based on the Survey of Arbitration Work of Members of the Academy in 1957," Appendix E, in *Arbitration and the Law*, Proceedings of the 12th Annual Meeting, National Academy of Arbitrators, ed. Jean T. McKelvey (Washington: BNA Books, 1959), 179-190; and "Survey of Arbitration in 1962," Appendix C, in *Labor Arbitration—Perspectives and Problems*, Proceedings of the 17th Annual Meeting, National Academy of Arbitrators, ed. Mark L. Kahn (Washington: BNA Books, 1964), 292-316.

forties and fifties, the latest study finds almost three quarters of the arbitrators (72.5 percent) to be in their fifties and sixties.

The average number of years of schooling reported by the respondents has remained constant with the exception of years in high school. Arbitrators spent an average of 4.0 years in high school (3.9 in 1962), 3.9 years at college, and 3.6 years in graduate or professional schools.

As was evident in previous surveys, the typical arbitrator is well educated. Only three of 222 do not hold any college degree. The others, among them, have 546 degrees. At the collegiate level there are 129 B.A. degrees and 60 B.S. degrees. The most widely held advanced degrees are LL.B., 81; M.A., 75; and Ph.D., 65. Among the leading fields of concentration in college are economics (70), political science (46), history (21), and law and prelaw (14). While most arbitrators received their basic college training in the social sciences, it is noteworthy that 11 arbitrators majored in English, 10 in engineering, four in accounting, two in agronomy, one in library science, and one in zoology. Arbitrators did their professional or graduate study in two primary fields: law (122) and economics (75).

Only 19 (8.6 percent) of the arbitrators have worked full time with unions or the labor movement. A larger number, 37 (16.8 percent), have worked full time with companies or employers' associations. In the former group the average amount of time spent in such work was 5.0 years; in the latter, 8.3 years. On the other hand, the arbitrators have performed a large amount of service for the Federal Government in labor relations. A total of 139 (64.6 percent) have done such work full time or part time. This service was primarily with three agencies—NWLB, WSB (1950-52), and NLRB—in that order. Experience in working with state or municipal agencies was reported by 33 (15.2 percent), with the New York State Board of Mediation as the leading agency.

The great majority entered arbitration work between 1940 and 1950. There were 42 (19.4 percent) who received their first case in the period 1940-44; 52 (24.0 percent) in 1945-49; and 45 (20.7 percent) in 1950-54. Thirty-one (14.3 percent) got their first case in 1960-64, and five (2.3 percent) got theirs during the following year. No respondent reported a more recent initial case. The typical arbitrator received his first case at the age of 37.4 years.

Sixty-six (30.3 percent) of the arbitrators first arbitrated between the ages of 30 and 34; 59 (27.1 percent) between 35 and 39; and 36 (16.5 percent) between 40 and 44 years. The principal sources of the first case in descending order were the parties (30.4 percent), the AAA (19.1 percent, as compared with 24.2 percent in 1962), a state mediation board (13.2 percent as against 11.6 percent in 1962), and the NWLB (11.4 percent compared to 16.8 percent in 1962).

Seventy-seven arbitrators waited an average of 8.4 months from the time of acceptance on an AAA, FMCS, or state agency panel to receipt of the first case. During the first five years of the arbitrators' membership in the profession, they heard an average of 14.8 cases in the first year, 19.7 in the second, 22.8 in the third, 28.4 in the fourth, and 33.6 in the fifth. A majority of 173 (79.7 percent) have been continuously available for arbitration since entering the field.

At the outset of their arbitration careers, most of the respondents derived their income primarily as teachers (115 or 52.2 percent) or as lawyers (55 or 25.1 percent). Among the other principal sources of income were consulting (8), government employment (7), and membership in state mediation agencies (7). Arbitrators ascribed their achievement of initial acceptability chiefly to their NWLB experience (63), other governmental board experience (61), and reputation as a teacher (59).

Thirty-one respondents (14 percent) served an arbitration apprenticeship. In the 1962 study, 19 arbitrators (10.9 percent) reported that they had served as apprentices. One arbitrator began his apprenticeship in 1939, five during the 1940s, 12 during the 1950s, and nine began during the last decade. The average duration of these apprenticeships was approximately 3.1 years as compared with 2.6 years reported after the 1962 survey. The principal activities performed during the apprenticeship in descending order of incidence were sitting in at hearings, writing entire decisions subject to review, drafting decisions, and performing background research. In all but four cases the parties were aware of the apprenticeship. The average amount of time spent in the apprenticeship during the period was 49.6 percent compared with 55 percent noted in the previous survey. Again, the method of compensation was varied: six apprentices received annual salaries averaging $7,133; seven received no remuneration; five received a per diem averaging $90. Other apprentices received a board salary, a weekly salary, hourly pay, and remuneration on a per case basis. Four apprentices received their first cases concurrently with their apprenticeships; 18 others waited an average of 17 months; six others had received their first cases before the commencement of their apprenticeships. Twenty-nine respondents (15.8 percent) have trained apprentices, the average number trained per trainer being 3.3. In 1962, 24 (14.5 percent) had trained an average of 3.1 apprentices.

Almost three quarters of the respondents (74.8 percent) arbitrate on a part-time basis. On the average, these arbitrators devote 30.9 percent of their time to arbitration as compared with 33.4 percent in 1962. Ninety-seven of the 160 part-time arbitrators cited teaching as their regular occupation; 36 are lawyers; 10 are consultants; six are educational administrators; and six are members of governmental labor relations agencies.

II. Opinions on Shortage of Arbitrators

Of 214 respondents to the first question in this section of the survey, 131 (61.2 percent) had recourse to a waiting list of cases yet to be heard during 1969. Ten arbitrators, an additional 4.7 percent, either scheduled cases from two to six months in advance or declined appointments when they were not available. Eighty-three arbitrators specified how frequently they had a waiting list: 62 (74.7 percent) reported that they had a continual backlog; 10 (12.0 percent) that they had a list on two to five occasions; and three (3.6 percent) that they had a list monthly. Thiry-five (34.3 percent) of 102 respondents had waiting lists which averaged from one to five cases; 28 (27.4 percent) averaged six to 10 cases; and 19 (18.6 percent) averaged more than 20 cases.

Eighty-seven percent of the 186 respondents to the second question asserted that certain educational backgrounds are particularly suited for gaining entry into the arbitration profession. Law, industrial and labor relations, and economics, the most frequently cited fields of study, were suggested by 130, 65, and 51 arbitrators, respectively. Numerous proponents of legal training reasoned that through it the potential arbitrator could obtain knowledge of the rules of evidence, procedures, and contract interpretation, and practice in analysis and the exercise of judgment. Others argued that the value of a legal background has grown due to the increasing use of lawyers by the parties. Advocates of the study of industrial and labor relations and economics proposed education in these fields as the means by which the novice could gain familiarity with the techniques of collective bargaining, knowledge relevant to substantive issues, and insight into industrial problems. Generally these arbitrators believed that education in these three disciplines would impart superior understanding of labor relations issues and would encourage the parties to place more confidence in, and thus be more likely to select, the aspiring arbitrator. The 24 respondents who denied the importance of any specific educational background emphasized the desirability of a broad educational experience and the significance of personal traits and abilities in the achievement of acceptance.

Suggestions as to the most important criteria for gaining acceptance as an arbitrator, in descending order of incidence, were (1) impartiality and fairness; (2) technical competence, especially with respect to knowledge of industrial relations principles and practices; (3) analytical ability and intelligence; (4) suitable temperament and personality; (5) integrity; (6) ability to write lucid and reasonable discussions; (7) related experience; (8) recommendations of established arbitrators and prior personal relations; (9) exposure to the parties; (10) objectivity; (11) ability to conduct an orderly hearing; and (12) education. Similarly, respondents proposed the following means of acquiring acceptance as an arbitrator: (1) apprenticeship and association with, and sponsorship by, senior arbitrators; (2) experience with government agencies such as the FMCS, NLRB, and state mediation and labor boards; (3) teaching, especially in the fields of labor law, labor economics, or industrial and labor relations; (4) educational background in the aforementioned areas; (5) contacts with management and union representatives; (6) making availability known by listing with AAA, FMCS, and appointing agencies; (7) exposure to the parties; and (8) writing on subjects of collective bargaining.

In all, 176 respondents offered their opinions on the possibility of a shortage of qualified arbitrators upon the retirement of the "war-labor-board" arbitrators. Ninety-three (52.8 percent) asserted that there would be a shortage because they felt that: (1) generally, the parties are reluctant to select new and unknown neutrals; (2) new arbitrators are not being trained in sufficient numbers; (3) arbitrators establish themselves slowly, and failure to provide for the effective entry of aspirants limits the number of new arbitrators who gain wide acceptability; and (4) the growth of demand for arbitrators in the public sector threatens the supply available to the private sector. The 83 respondents (47.2 percent) who took the opposite view argued that: (1) young people are available and can be trained as replacements through apprenticeship and training programs under the auspices of the AAA and the FMCS; (2) younger arbitrators are gaining acceptance, especially as a result of their work in the public sector; (3) other qualified but underutilized neutrals will be drawn upon when the "war-labor-board" arbitrators are no longer available; and (4) demand has its way of causing supply to appear.

Eighty-five percent of the 200 arbitrators who expressed a definite opinion in response to Question 6 opposed the institution of standardized entrance requirements for facilitating the acceptance of new arbitrators. The major arguments advanced by this group were that the field is too varied to yield itself to standardization and that inasmuch as it is the parties' right to select arbitrators on the basis of their qualifications, the profession should offer flexibility and diversity of training and experience. Others asserted that standards would not facilitate acceptance or change the attitudes of the parties and appointing agencies, but rather would tend to restrict entry to the field. Finally, it was argued that rather than risk the exclusion of desirable candidates by the institution of standardized requirements, the doors should be left open and the selection process would serve to eliminate the unfit. The remaining 30 arbitrators suggested that the employment of standardized entrance requirements would be useful: (1) in that rigid criteria would be in keeping with the responsibility of the profession; (2) so that aspirants will know what is necessary in order to become an arbitrator; and (3) in placing a visible imprint on the potential arbitrator which may contribute to his acceptability. Some of these arbitrators noted, however, that the requirements would facilitate acceptance only insofar as the standards met with the approval of companies and unions.

III. Arbitration, Mediation, and Fact-Finding

The 174 arbitrators who responded to the first question in the final section of the 1969 survey had a total of 8,875 cases; of these,

65.5 percent were received on an ad hoc basis, 24.4 percent were heard by permanent umpires, and 10.1 percent were decided by a permanent panel of arbitrators. The percentage of ad hoc to all cases has declined since 1962; on the other hand, the percentage of permanent umpire cases showed a marked increase, reversing somewhat the trend discovered in the previous survey. Of a total of 201 respondents, 151 arbitrators served as umpires under 489 collective agreements and/or as panel members under 425 agreements. By way of contrast, in 1962 arbitrators served as umpires and panel members under 235 and 308 agreements, respectively. In descending order of incidence, umpireships are most common in steel, garment, rubber, electrical and electronics, airlines, and metal fabrication. Similarly, panels are most common in airlines, electrical and electronics, steel, trucking, rubber, and metal fabrication. Arbitrators have become active as panel members and/or umpires in several areas of employment not included in the 1962 survey statistics; most notable among these fields are public education, government service, shipping, aluminum, aerospace, communications, and broadcasting.

Among the major sources of ad hoc cases the parties themselves led with 40.7 percent of the total, a moderate decline from 44.0 percent in 1962. In this respect, however, it is interesting to note that appointment by the parties characterized 64.7 percent of the ad hoc cases reported in 1952. The parties were followed in order by AAA (23.7 percent), FMCS (21.5 percent), NMB-NRAB (8.0 percent), and state agencies (5.5 percent). The AAA and FMCS raised their shares since 1962, as they had over the previous decade; however, the state agencies have fallen off noticeably, while the percentage of NMB-NRAB appointments increased slightly.

During the calendar year 1969, 83 respondents served in a neutral third-party capacity in a labor dispute in which they were not acting as arbitrators. The total number of cases in which arbitrators performed such service was 806; in 1962, 37 arbitrators were similarly engaged in 499 cases. A majority of arbitrators, 72.2 percent, have participated in dispute settlement in the public sector at some time. During the past three years, 86 served as fact-finders (490 cases), 77 mediated (604 cases), 37 arbitrated (163 cases), and 27 were involved in elections (125 cases). In 1969, 73 (35.1 percent) of the arbitrators served as fact-finders in 214 cases and

58 (28.7 percent) served as a neutral in 225 mediation and conciliation cases in the public sector.

SURVEY STATISTICS

I. The Arbitrator

1. *Age as of December 31, 1969* (222 responses) :

	1969	1962
Average age	57	52.7

Age by decade intervals:

	1969		1962	
	Number	*Percent*	*Number*	*Percent*
30-39	4	1.8	8	4.6
40-49	43	19.4	59	33.9
50-59	82	36.9	71	40.8
60-69	79	35.6	28	16.1
70-79	14	6.3	8	4.6
	222	100.0	174	100.0

2. *Average number of years of schooling:*

	Years	
	1969	*1962*
High school (205 responses)	4.0	3.9
College (208 responses)	3.9	3.9
Graduate or professional (207 responses)	3.6	3.6

3. *Degrees held* (responses exceed 222 due to the fact that many persons hold more than one degree) :

Degree	*1969*	*1962*
None	3	3
B.A.	129	113
B.S.	60	40
M.A.	75	65
M.S.	9	8
M.E.	4	2
LL.B.	81	79
LL.M.	19	8
J.D.	49	8
S.J.D.	12	6
Ph.D.	65	66
D.D.	0	0
LL.D.	10	6
M.B.A.	5	5
M.P.A.	2	2
Ph.B.	2	1
L.H.D.	1	1
D.Litt.	1	1

M.L.	1	—
A.M.P.	1	—
B.B.A.	2	—
B.S.P.	1	—
B.C.S.	1	—
B.L.S.	1	1
B.S.A.E.	1	—
B.S.S.	1	—
B.S.M.E.	1	—
B.Ed.	1	1
B.Sc.	—	1
L.S.T.	1	—
S.T.L.	—	1
M.C.L.	—	1
J.S.D.	—	1
LL.D. hon.	4	3
D.C.S. hon.	1	—
D.H.L. hon.	1	—
L. H. D. hon.	—	1
D.Sc. hon.	1	—
	546	424

4. *Major field of concentration in college* (215 responses; 18 double majors, 1 triple major) :

	1969	1962
Economics	70	63
Political Science	46	28
History	21	25
Law & Pre-Law	14	15
English	11	4
Engineering	10	6
Industrial Relations	8	6
Business & Business Administration	6	8
Philosophy	5	4
Accounting	4	3
Social Science	4	5
Sociology	4	3
Agronomy	2	—
Chemistry	2	3
Finance	2	—
Liberal Arts	2	1
Literature	2	5
Physics	2	—
Psychology	2	2
Statistics	2	1
None or General	2	2
Biology	1	—
Education	1	—

Economic History	1	—
Industrial Management	1	—
Insurance	1	—
Journalism	1	—
Library Science	1	1
Marketing	1	—
Meteorology	1	—
Political Economy	1	—
Science	1	2
Social Service Administration	1	—
Theology	1	—
Zoology	1	—
Mathematics	—	4
Oriental Languages	—	1
Social Institutions	—	1
	235	193

Minor field of concentration in college (177 responses; 15 double minors, 3 triple minors) :

	1969	1962
Economics	36	30
English	23	14
History	23	16
Political Science	23	29
Philosophy	15	9
Psychology	11	5
Mathematics	10	6
None	8	3
Engineering	6	—
Sociology	6	4
Business Administration	4	4
Speech	3	—
Statistics	3	2
Accounting	2	2
Biology	2	1
Chemistry	2	—
Education	2	2
French	2	—
Social Sciences	2	1
Aviation	1	—
Comparative Literature	1	—
Farm Management	1	—
Humanities	1	2
Finance	1	—
Industrial Management	1	—
Industrial Relations	1	—
Foreign Languages	1	7
Journalism	1	3

Latin	1	—
Pre-Medical Science	1	—
Romance Languages	1	—
Public Speaking	1	—
Social Studies	1	—
Industry	—	3
Geology	—	2
Science	—	2
Literature	—	1
Anthropology	—	1
Advertising	—	1
Mechanical Engineering	—	1
Labor Law	—	1
Music	—	1
Chemistry-Physics	—	1
Personnel	—	1
	198	155

5. *Fields of graduate and professional study* (213 responses; many double and triple fields) :

	1969	1962
Law	122	80
Economics	75	68
Industrial and Labor Relations	22	19
Political Science	16	18
Unspecified	11	18
Business Administration	5	—
Industrial Engineering	5	—
Sociology	5	4
History	3	4
Personnel Administration	3	—
Public Administration	3	—
Education	3	—
International Relations	2	—
Labor History	2	—
Psychology	2	3
Statistics	2	2
Adult Education	1	—
Accounting	1	—
Economic History	1	—
Finance	1	1
Industrial Engineering & Administration	1	—
Insurance	1	—
Marketing	1	—
Political Economy	1	—
Social Insurance	1	—

Speech	1	—
Theology	1	—
Administration	—	10
Mathematics	—	1
Cost Analysis & Control	—	1
Comparative Literature	—	1
Library Science	—	1
	292	231

6. *Full-time work with union or labor movement* (222 responses):

	1969		1962	
	Number	*Percent*	*Number*	*Percent*
Had none	203	91.4	163	93.7
Had some	19	8.6	11	6.3

(Of the 19 who specified the years of this work, the average was 5.0 years; in 1962, 10 arbitrators averaged 2.9 years in this work.)

7. *Full-time work with companies or employers' associations in labor relations* (220 responses):

	1969		1962	
	Number	*Percent*	*Number*	*Percent*
Had none	183	83.2	145	83.3
Had some	37	16.8	29	16.7

(Of the 37 who specified the years of this work, the average was 8.3 years; in 1962, 26 arbitrators averaged 5.5 years in this work.)

8. *Full-time or part-time work with Federal Government in labor relations* (215 responses):

	1969		1962	
	Number	*Percent*	*Number*	*Percent*
Had none	76	35.4	44	25.1
Had some	139	64.6	131	74.9

Federal Agency and Number of Years of Service:

	1969			1962		
	Full-Time	*Part-Time*	*Average Number of Years*	*Full-Time*	*Part-Time*	*Average Number of Years*
NWLB	53	30	2.4	51	35	2.5
WSB (1950-52)	28	20	1.4	27	20	1.6
NLRB	26	5	5.1	15	5	5.5
NWSB (1945-47)	8	9	1.5	9	12	1.1
FMCS	8	5	6.2	4	10	1.3
Conciliation Service	6	7	2.5	6	7	3.9
NRA	6	2	1.8	6	3	1.3
NMB	3	7	10.3*	2	10	7.1
Other	30	11	—	20	10	—

* Based on three responses only.

9. *Full-time work in state or municipal labor relations* (217 responses):

	1969		1962	
	Number	*Percent*	*Number*	*Percent*
Had none	184	84.8	144	83.7
Had some	33	15.2	28	16.3

(Of those with such service, the average number of years served was 8.2 in 1969 and 9.1 in 1962.)

	Number	
Agency	*1969*	*1962*
N.Y.S. Board of Mediation	16	8
State board of mediation (unspecified)	—	5
State labor relations board (unspecified)	—	4
City agency (unspecified)	1	2
N.Y.S. Labor Relations Board	5	2
Wisconsin Employment Relations Board	3	1
N.Y.C. Office of Collective Bargaining	2	—
Massachusetts Board of Conciliation	2	1
Pennsylvania Bureau of Mediation	1	—
Pennsylvania Labor Relations Board	1	1
Pennsylvania Department of Labor	—	1
Pennsylvania Workmen's Compensation Board	1	—
Missouri Employment Service	1	1
Michigan Employment Security Appeal Board	1	—
N.Y.S. Public Employment Relations Board	1	—
Division of Labor Relations, N.Y.C.	1	—
Louisville Labor-Management Commission	1	1
Alabama Department of Industrial Relations	1	1
Iowa Department of Labor	—	1
California Conciliation Service	—	1
	38	30

(Several persons worked for more than one agency.)

10. *Year of first arbitration case* (217 responses) :

	1969		1962	
Years	Number	Percent	Number	Percent
1915-19	0	0.0	1	0.6
1920-24	0	0.0	0	0.0
1925-29	1	0.5	1	0.6
1930-34	4	1.8	2	1.4
1935-39	12	5.5	17	9.7
1940-44	42	19.4	45	25.7
1945-49	52	24.0	57	32.6
1950-54	45	20.7	35	20.0
1955-59	25	11.5	17	9.7
1960-64	31	14.3	0	0.0
1965	5	2.3	0	0.0
	217	100.0	175	100.3

11. *Age at which first arbitration case heard* (218 responses) :
    Average age   37.4
    Age by five-year intervals:

Age	Number	Percentage
20-24	1	0.5
25-29	22	10.1
30-34	66	30.3
35-39	59	27.1
40-44	36	16.5
45-49	15	6.9
50-54	13	6.0
55-59	4	1.8
60-64	2	0.9
	218	100.1

12. *Source of first case* (220 responses) :

	1969		1962	
	Number	Percent	Number	Percent
Parties	67	30.4	52	30.0
AAA	42	19.1	42	24.2
State Mediation Board	29	13.2	20	11.6
NWLB	25	11.4	29	16.8
FMCS	19	8.6	8	4.6
Another Arbitrator	14	6.4	7	4.0
Conciliation Service	10	4.6	7	4.0
NMB	6	2.7	3	1.7
Other	8	3.6	5	2.9
	220	100.0	173	99.8

13. *Length of time from acceptance to AAA, FMCS, or state agency panel to receipt of first case* (77 responses) :

Average	8.4 months	
Months	Number	Percent
1	10	13.0
2	8	10.4
3	18	23.4
4	3	3.9
6	17	22.1
9	1	1.3
12	6	7.8
18	2	2.6
24	8	10.4
36	4	5.2
	77	100.1

14. *Average number of cases heard during first five years in arbitration profession* (188 responses) :

Year	Average Number of Cases
1st	14.8
2nd	19.7
3rd	22.8
4th	28.4
5th	33.6

Distribution:

Cases	1st	2nd	3rd	4th	5th
0- 20	159	152	135	120	107
21- 50	17	21	35	44	47
51-100	9	12	15	17	25
101-200	2	2	2	6	8
Over 200	1	1	1	1	1
	188	188	188	188	188

15. *Availability for arbitration* (217 responses) :

	1969		1962	
	Number	Percent	Number	Percent
Continuously available	173	79.7	132	75.4
Not continuously available	44	20.3	43	24.6

(Of those not continuously available, they were on the average unavailable for 4.9 years (1969) and 4.0 years (1962).)

16. *Principal source of income at outset of career in arbitration* (219 responses:

	Number	Percent
As a teacher	115	52.5
As a lawyer	55	25.1
As a consultant	8	3.6
From retirement income	3	1.4
Other	38	17.4
	219	100.0

17. *Grounds for achievement of initial acceptability as an arbitrator* (218 responses):

	Number
NWLB experience	63
Other governmental board experience	61
Reputation as a teacher	59
Experience as apprentice arbitrator	22
Affiliation with an institute of industrial relations or like institution	21
Publications in the field of labor	18
Other	41
Not known	16
	301

(Several persons cited more than one contributing factor.) The larger groups of "other" were: recommended by established arbitrators (10); labor law practice (5); prior labor relations experience (8); acquaintance with unions and employers (6); association with George Taylor (3).

18. *Arbitration apprenticeship* (222 responses):

	1969		1962	
	Number	Percent	Number	Percent
Did not serve	191	86.0	156	89.1
Served	31	14.0	19	10.9

19. *Starting year of apprenticeship* (31 responses):

	1969	1962
1926	—	1
1939	1	2
1940	2	2
1941	1	—
1942	1	2
1946	1	1
1947	—	2
1950	1	—
1952	2	1
1954	2	1
1955	1	1

1956	3	3
1957	2	1
1958	1	—
1960	2	—
1961	3	—
1962	2	—
1964	2	—
Unspecified	4	2
	31	19

Average duration of apprenticeship

	Years	
1969		*1962*
3.1		2.6

20. *Nature of the apprenticeship* (31 responses) :

	1969		*1962*	
	Number	Percent	Number	Percent
Sitting in at hearings	21	67.7	17	89.5
Office work	11	35.5	8	42.1
Background research	14	45.2	9	47.4
Drafting decisions	16	51.6	12	63.2
Writing entire decisions subject to review	17	54.8	12	63.2
Writing decisions without review	2	6.4	4	21.1
Hearing officer	10	32.3	8	42.1

21. *Awareness of parties of apprenticeship* (30 responses) :

	1969		*1962*	
	Number	Percent	Number	Percent
Were aware	26	86.7	17	89.5
Were not aware	4	13.3	2	10.5

22. *Percentage of time spent in apprenticeship* (30 responses) :

	Percent
1969	*1962*
49.6	55.0

23. *Rate of compensation during apprenticeship* (24 responses) :

	1969		*1962*	
Type of Compensation	Number	Average	Number	Average
None	7	—	5	—
Annual salary	6	$7,133.00	7	$5,709.00
Per Diem	5	90.00	4	39.50
Weekly salary	1	150.00	1	100.00
Board salary (unspecified)	1	—	1	—
Hourly pay	2	3.25	—	—
Pay per case	1	100.00	—	

One respondent began his apprenticeship with an annual salary of $7,500 and concluded with a *per diem* of $180.

24. *Length of time from inception of apprenticeship to receipt of first case* (28 responses) :

	1969	1962
	18 averaged 17 months	14 averaged 21 months
Received first case concurrently with apprenticeship	4	4
Received first case before inception of apprenticeship	6	—

25. *Those who trained apprentices* (183 responses) :

	1969		1962	
	Number	Percent	Number	Percent
Did not train	154	84.2	141	85.5
Did train	29	15.8	24	14.5

26. *Average number of apprentices trained by those who trained* (28 responses) :

1969	1962
3.3	3.1

27. *Time devoted to labor arbitration* (214 responses) :

	Number	Percent
Arbitrate on full-time basis	54	25.2
Arbitrate on part-time basis	160	74.8
	214	100.0

28. *Regular occupations of part-time arbitrators* (158 responses) :

	Number
Teacher	97
Lawyer	36
Consultant	10
Other	29
	172

(Several respondents indicated more than one regular occupation.)

29. *Percentage of time devoted to arbitration by part-time arbitrators* (152 responses) :

Average: 30.9 percent

Distribution:

Percentage of Time	Number	Percent
1-15	47	30.9
16-30	55	36.2
31-45	14	9.2
46-60	14	9.2
61-75	13	8.6
76-90	6	3.9
91-99	3	2.0
	152	100.0

II. Opinions on Shortage of Arbitrators

1. *Waiting list for cases to be heard in 1969* (214 responses) :

Did have a waiting list	131
Did not have a waiting list	73
Others *	10

* Eight respondents indicated that they scheduled cases from two to six months in advance and two more refused appointment when not available.

Frequency of overload (83 responses) :

Number of Responses	Percent of Year	Frequency Number of Times	Monthly
62	100		
3	75		
2	50		
1	25		
68			
1		1	
2		2	
2		2-3	
3		3	
2		3-4	
1		4-5	
1		10-12	
12			
3			x
83			

Number of cases waiting to be heard (102 responses) :

Number of Cases	Number of Responses
1-5	35
6-10	28
11-15	13
16-20	7
21-25	5
26-30	3
31-35	1
36-40	8
Over 40	2

2. *Special educational fields suited for facilitating entry to the field of arbitration* (186 responses) :

Yes	162
No	24

Educational Field	Number of Times Cited
Law	130*
Industrial and Labor Relations	65
Economics	51**
Business Administration	9
Social Sciences	6
Political Science	5
Engineering	3
Sociology	2
Mathematics	2
Physical Sciences	2
Labor History	2
Accounting	2
Industrial Management	2
Industrial Engineering	2
Psychology	2
Mechanical Engineering	1
Philosophy	1
Statistics	1
History	1
Social Psychology	1
Industrial Sociology	1
Behavioral Science	1
Banking and Finance	1

---

* Includes 21 suggestions of Labor Law.
** Includes 20 suggestions of Labor Economics.

3. *Important criteria for gaining acceptance as an arbitrator:*

Criteria	Number of Times Cited
Impartiality and fairness	100
Technical competence	63
Analytical ability and intelligence	53
Suitable temperament and personality	44
Integrity	41
Lucid, reasonable decisions, promptly rendered	39
Experience	31
Recommendations and prior personal relations	19
Exposure to the parties	15
Objectivity	12
Conduct orderly hearings	10
Education	6

4. *Possibility of a shortage of qualified arbitrators* (205 responses):

Yes	93
No	83
Do not know	29

5. *Means of acquiring acceptance as an arbitrator:*

Recommendations	Number of Times Cited
Apprenticeship and training	86
Related government experience	62
Related teaching experience	27
Related educational background	25
Contacts with parties	23
Availability and listing with AAA, FMCS, and appointing agencies	23
Exposure to parties	21
Related writing	14

6. *Desirability of standardized entrance requirements for facilitating acceptance* (207 responses):

Yes	30
No	170
Do not know	7

III. Arbitration, Mediation, and Fact-Finding

1. *Caseload by tenure of arbitrators* (174 responses):

	1969		1962	
	Number	Percent	Number	Percent
Ad hoc	5,814	65.5	4,684	72.7
Permanent umpire	2,161	24.4	1,160	18.0
Permanent panel of arbitrators	900	10.1	600	9.3
	8,875	100.0	6,444	100.0

2. *Service as umpire or member of panel of arbitrators* (201 responses) :

In 1969, 151 arbitrators served as umpires under 489 agreements and/or as panel members under 425 agreements. (115 arbitrators served as umpires under 489 agreements, and 112 served as panel members under 425 agreements.)

In 1962, 102 arbitrators served as umpires under 235 agreeements and/or as panel members under 308 agreements.

3. *Industry distribution of umpireships and panels* (179 responses) :

| | 1969 | | 1962 | |
	Umpireship	Panel	Umpireship	Panel
Plant	—	—	29	—
Steel	21	15	17	12
Garment	18	3	6	—
Rubber	15	10	6	3
Electrical & Electronics	13	16	7	6
Airlines	10	23	1	4
Metal Fabrication	9	10	8	5
Public Education	9	9	—	—
General Manufacturing	8	9	—	—
Construction	8	1	2	1
Textile	7	6	9	3
Food Products	7	6	—	2
Maritime	7	5	—	—
Machine Manufacturing	7	4	3	1
Railroad	7	4	3	—
Government Service	7	4	—	—
Auto Parts	7	3	6	—
Meat	—	—	7	1
Air & Motor Transportation	6	6	—	7
Aluminum	6	2	—	—
Plastics	6	1	2	2
Trucking	5	12	—	—
Newspapers	5	9	1	4
Aircraft	5	8	7	5
Shipbuilding	5	5	1	7
Auto	5	1	6	1
Chemical	4	9	8	7
Retailing	4	9	—	3
Aerospace	4	5	—	—
Printing	4	3	—	—
Utilities	4	2	1	3
Hotels & Restaurants	4	2	3	—
Paper	4	1	—	—
Mining	3	8	3	7
Copper	3	5	—	—
Shoes	3	3	1	2
Furniture	3	3	2	—
Cement	3	2	3	—

Hospitals & Nursing	3	2	2	—
Publishing	3	—	1	3
Munitions	3	—	—	—
Agricultural Equipment	3	—	2	1
Glass	2	8	3	8
Communications	2	5	—	—
Broadcasting	2	5	—	—
Warehousing	2	2	—	—
Appliances	2	2	—	—
Instruments	2	1	—	—
Optical	2	1	2	1
Office Equipment	2	1	1	2
Building Service	2	—	—	—
Laundry	2	—	—	—
Breweries	1	5	1	2
Refining	1	3	—	—
Wholesale Distribution	1	2	1	2
Oil	—	2	1	2
Auto Repairs	—	—	2	—
Truck Manufacturing	1	1	2	—
Bearing Manufacturing	—	—	2	—
Lumber	—	—	2	—
Hats	1	1	—	2
Woodworking	—	1	—	2
Nonferrous Metals	—	—	1	2

A substantial number of additional industries were represented by only one umpireship and/or panel.

4. *Participation as neutrals in labor dispute* (139 responses):

	1969	1962
Railway Labor Act Emergency Board	15	9
Taft-Hartley Title II Board	2	5
Presidential Board Other Than Railway or Taft-Hartley	—	24
Other:		
State Board of Mediation (unspecified)	—	116
N.Y.S. Board of Mediation	—	100
State Mediator & Hearing Officer	—	75
Private Mediator & Consultant	—	53
City	10	40
NRAB & NMB	1	35
Health, Welfare & Pensions	—	10
Atomic Energy Panel	—	9
FMCS & Labor Department	—	7
Railroad Public Law Boards	6	—
Executive Order 10988	6	—
Special Boards of Adjustment	—	6

N.Y.S. Public Employment Relations Board	3	—
AEC Labor-Management Relations Panel	2	—
State Minimum Wage Board	—	2
U.S. Minimum Wage Board	1	—
National Protection Agreement	1	—
Miscellaneous	4	8
	51	499

5. *Sources of ad hoc arbitrations* (184 responses) :

	1969		1962	
	Number	*Percent*	*Number*	*Percent*
Parties	2,466	40.7	2,337	44.0
AAA	1,440	23.7	1,096	20.6
FMCS	1,306	21.5	903	17.0
NMB–NRAB	485	8.0	418	7.9
State Agencies	334	5.5	518	9.8
Courts	6	0.1	12	0.2
Other	28	0.5	28	0.5
	6,065	100.0	5,312	100.0

6. *Cases in which arbitrators served as neutrals but not as arbitrators in labor disputes* (207 responses) :

1969		1962	
Arbitrators	*Cases*	*Arbitrators*	*Cases*
83	806	37	499

7. *Participation in dispute settlement in the public sector* (216 responses) :

	Number	*Percent*
Have participated at some time	156	72.2
Have never participated	60	27.8
	216	100.0

Area of participation in public sector dispute settlement during the past three years:

	Number of Arbitrators	*Number of Cases*
Fact-finding	86	490
Mediation	17	604
Election	27	125
Other:		
Arbitration	37	163
Hearing Officer	3	4
State Labor Relations Board	1	50
Unspecified	20	57

8. *1969 service as a neutral in fact-finding cases in the public sector* (208 responses):

	Number	Percent
Served	73	35.1
Did not serve	135	64.9
	208	100.0

73 arbitrators served in 214 cases (average: 2.9).

9. *1969 service as a neutral in mediation and conciliation cases in the public sector* (202 responses):

	Number	Percent
Served	58	28.7
Did not serve	144	71.3
	202	100.0

58 arbitrators served in 225 cases (average: 3.9).

SURVEY OF THE ARBITRATION PROFESSION IN 1969

I. The Arbitrator

1. How old were you on December 31, 1969? _____

2. How many years of schooling have you had?   Years
   High School _____
   College _____
   Graduate or professional _____

3. What degrees do you hold? (Check)
   None _____
   B.A. _____
   B.S. _____
   M.A. _____
   M.S. _____
   M.E. _____
   LL.B. _____
   LL.M. _____
   J.D. _____
   S.J.D. _____
   Ph.D. _____
   D.D. _____
   Other _____

4. What was your major field of concentration in college? _____
   Your minor field? _____

5. What type, if any, graduate or professional study did you do? _____

6. Have you ever worked for a union or the labor movement on a full-time basis? Yes _____ No _____
   If the answer is "yes," give the years of this experience: _____

7. Have you ever worked for a company or an employers' association in labor relations on a full-time basis? Yes _____ No _____
If the answer is "yes," give the years of this experience: _____

8. Have you ever worked for the federal government in labor relations work on a full-time or part-time basis? Yes _____ No _____

If the answer is "yes," give the agency and years:

Agency	Full-time	Part-time	Years
NRA	_____	_____	_____
NLRB	_____	_____	_____
Conciliation Service	_____	_____	_____
NWLB	_____	_____	_____
NWSB (1945-47)	_____	_____	_____
FMCS	_____	_____	_____
NMB	_____	_____	_____
WSB (1950-52)	_____	_____	_____
Other	_____	_____	_____

9. Have you ever worked for a state or municipal government in labor relations work on a full-time basis? Yes _____ No _____
If the answer is 'yes," give the agency and years:

Agency	Years
_____	_____
_____	_____

10. In what year did you hear your first arbitration case? _____

11. At what age did you hear your first arbitration case? _____

12. From whom did you receive your first case?

NWLB	_____
Conciliation Service	_____
FMCS	_____
NMB	_____
State Mediation Board	_____
AAA	_____
Parties	_____
Another arbitrator	_____
Other (name)	_____

13. If your availability was made through application to AAA, FMCS, or state agency, how long was it from the time of acceptance for the panel to first case received? _____

14. Approximately how many cases did you have during your first five years as an arbitrator?

1st year	_____
2nd year	_____
3rd year	_____
4th year	_____
5th year	_____

15. Excluding short periods, have you been available for arbitration continuously since that time? Yes _____ No _____
If the answer is "no," give the years during which you did no arbitration:
_____

16. When you started as an arbitrator what was your principal source of income?
    As a teacher _____
    As a lawyer _____
    From retirement income _____
    As a consultant _____
    Other (specify) _____

17. How do you believe you were able to achieve your first acceptability as an arbitrator?
    From your NWLB experience _____
    From your other governmental board experience _____
    From your publications in the field of labor _____
    From your experience as an apprentice arbitrator _____
    From your reputation as a teacher _____
    From your affiliation with an Institute of Industrial Relations or like institution
    Other (specify) _____
    Do not know _____

18. Did you serve arbitration apprenticeship with an established arbitrator? Yes _____ No _____

19. If the answer to No. 18 is "yes," give the years in which this apprenticeship took place: _____

20. What did the apprenticeship consist of? (check)
    Sitting in at hearings _____
    Office work _____
    Background research _____
    Drafting decisions _____
    Writing entire decisions subject to review _____
    Writing decisions without review _____
    Hearing officer _____

21. Were the parties aware of the apprenticeship? Yes _____ No _____

22. During the apprenticeship what proportion of your time was spent in the arbitration apprenticeship? _____ percent

23. What was the rate of compensation during the apprenticeship? (specify) _____

24. How long was it from the inception of the apprenticeship to the first case you received on your own? _____

25. Have you ever trained an apprentice arbitrator? (The means in an organized program and excludes occasional visitors to hearings.) Yes _____ No _____

26. If the answer to No. 25 is "yes," how many apprentices have you trained? _____

27. Do you do labor arbitration on
   Full-time basis _____
   Part-time basis _____

28. If part-time, what is your regular occupation?
   Teacher _____
   Lawyer _____
   Consultant _____
   Other (specify) _____

29. If part-time, what percent of your time is devoted to arbitration? _____

II. Opinions on Shortage of Arbitrators

1. During *1969* did you ever have a waiting list for cases yet to hear? Yes _____ No _____. If yes, how often did you have a list and what was the average number of cases: _____

2. Are there any special educational backgrounds particularly suited for facilitating entry into the field of arbitration? Yes _____ No _____ Why or why not _____

3. What is (are) the important criterion (criteria) for gaining acceptance as an arbitrator? _____

4. Will there be a shortage of qualified arbitrators when the "war-labor-board" arbitrators retire? Yes _____ No _____ Why or why not? _____

5. How would you recommend that a younger person interested in becoming an arbitrator should go about obtaining the necessary acceptance? _____

6. Should standardized entrance requirements be instituted for facilitating the acceptance of new arbitrators? Yes _____ No _____. Why or why not? _____

III. Arbitration, Mediation and Fact-Finding

1. Of your total *1969* caseload, how many were
   Ad hoc _____
   Permanent Umpire _____
   Permanent Panel of Arbitrators _____

2. Under how many collective bargaining agreements in *1969* were you serving as umpire (or with some other "permanent" title)? _____ Under how many were you designated as a member of a panel of arbitrators? _____

3. Indicate the industry or industries in which you held umpireships: _____

   In which you were designated on panels: _____

4. Have you participated in *1969* on any of the following: Number
   Railway Labor Act emergency board   _____
   Taft-Hartley Title II Board   _____
   Other Presidential boards   _____
   Other (specify)   _____

5. For your *ad hoc* arbitration in *1969* give the number obtained by each of
   the following means:
   Parties   _____
   FMCS   _____
   AAA   _____
   NMB and NRAB   _____
   State agencies   _____
   Courts   _____
   Other (specify) _____   _____
   _____   _____

6. During the calendar year *1969*, in how many cases did you serve in a
   neutral third-party capacity in a labor dispute on problems in which you
   were not acting as arbitrator? _____

7. Have you ever participated in dispute settlement in the public sec-
   tor? _____ How many cases have you had in the past *three* years of
   the following types:
   Mediation   _____
   Fact-finding   _____
   Election   _____
   Other   _____

8. During the calendar year *1969*, did you serve as a neutral in fact-finding
   cases in the public sector? _____
   If so, how many? _____

9. During the calendar year *1969*, did you serve as a neutral in mediation
   and conciliation cases in the public sector? _____
   If so, in how many cases? _____

THE DEVELOPMENT OF NEW ARBITRATORS: REPORT OF COMMITTEE, 1970-1971 *

Thomas J. McDermott, Chairman**

During May 1970, President Jean T. McKelvey appointed a special Committee for the Development of New Arbitrators. Its basic function was to determine if a type of continuing program for the entry of persons into the arbitration profession could be developed that would be both practical and within the capabilities of the Academy to carry out. In addition, attempts should be made to develop more specific factual data relating to those who seek to enter the arbitration profession. Throughout the year preliminary reports have been submitted to members of the committee, and meetings of the committee were held in October 1970 and January 1971. The following, therefore, constitutes the report for this committee for the year 1970-1971.

Prior Activities

The subject of entry into the arbitration profession is not a new one to the Academy. Almost from its very beginning as a professional organization, it has recognized the problem of a short supply of acceptable arbitrators and the need for some form of orderly process that would enable persons with appropriate talents to move into labor arbitration work. However, the organization has had great difficulty in coming up with much of a specific nature that would be directed at this objective. A summary of what consideration has been given to this problem in the past and what activities have taken place is therefore of importance to emphasize the need for action on the part of the Academy if it is to meet its responsibilities as a professional organization.

The need for the Academy to concern itself with entry into

---

* Members of the Committee on the Development of New Arbitrators are Harold Davey, John Dunsford, Milton Friedman, Seymour Strongin, and John C. Shearer.
** Professor of Economics, Duquesne University, Pittsburgh, Pa.

the profession was stressed by the late Edwin Witte in his address to the first annual meeting of the Academy in 1948. He stated that further progress in industrial arbitration depends upon a number of factors and among them is the development of "a larger group of qualified and experienced arbitrators." [1] In 1950, the Committee on Research and Education, Charles C. Killingsworth, chairman, issued a "Report on the Education and Training of New Arbitrators." [2] In that report the committee found no shortage of people able and willing to undertake arbitration work, but it did state that there was a shortage of *acceptable* arbitrators in several regions of the country. In pinpointing the basic problem, the report stated:

> "Since experience is unquestionably the best teacher in this field, as in so many others, and since there are many potentially able arbitrators whose services are not being used, the problem of maintaining an adequate supply of arbitrators now and in the future is to a large extent a problem of promoting the acceptability of newcomers." [3]

The committee called attention to the fact that practically nothing had been done with respect to the training of arbitrators; yet it did not feel that at that time it was ready to propose any program for the Academy to adopt. It did, however, point to the real basis why the Academy should concern itself with the training and development of new arbitrators when it stated:

> "If arbitration is to be recognized as a profession, we must give adequate attention to training for this new profession. In the opinion of this committee, it is most fitting that this Academy, the professional society of arbitrators, should make training for arbitration one of its major concerns." [4]

In 1954, a subcommittee on Education and Training, Lloyd Bailer, chairman, was established by the Committee on Research and Education. In an interim report dated October 1, 1955, the committee, in discussing the use of formal courses for training arbitrators, stated that while such courses were desirable for university students to study, ". . . the inherent factor of acceptability to the parties makes it unwise to represent the arbitrator's posi-

---

[1] Edwin E. Witte, "The Future of Labor Arbitration—A Challenge," in *The Profession of Labor Arbitration,* Cumulative Selection of Addresses at First Seven Annual Meetings, 1948 through 1954, National Academy of Arbitrators, ed. Jean T. McKelvey (Washington: BNA Books, 1954), 11.

[2] *Id.* at 170-175.

[3] *Id.* at 173.

[4] *Id.* at 175.

tion as one that can be achieved by pursuing a given curriculum —as one may become a civil engineer, for example." [5]

Insofar as to what the Academy should do about education and training of new arbitrators, the subcommittee made several recommendations, among them the following:

1. The Academy encourage the use of interns by such agencies as the Federal Mediation and Conciliation Service, American Arbitration Association, and state mediation boards.

2. The Academy encourage and sponsor conferences on arbitration at which students of arbitration be encouraged to participate.

3. The Academy establish a student advisory program to assist universities in advising students of the labor arbitration profession.

4. That arbitrators be encouraged to bring in apprentices for fixed terms of one or two years. [6]

No particular action was taken by the Academy on these recommendations, although the sponsorship of conferences and the use of apprentices were undertaken by individual members of the Academy.

In the Research and Education Committee report of 1959, it was noted that prior committees had given consideration to three activities. One was the preparation of a periodic casebook of arbitration by members of the Academy. A second was a survey of arbitration courses offered by American universities, and the third was a search for ways to implement the training of new arbitrators. Acting on the advice of the Board of Governors and from the comments of the members of the committee, it was determined that consideration that year would be given only to the first two activities. [7]

While this committee did not concern itself with the question

---

[5] "Interim Report of Subcommittee on Education and Training," in *Management Rights and the Arbitration Process*, Proceedings of the 9th Annual Meeting, National Academy of Arbitrators, ed. Jean T. McKelvey (Washington: BNA Books, 1956), 231.

[6] *Id.* at 232-234.

[7] "Research and Education Committee Reports and Recommendations," in *Arbitration and the Law*, Proceedings of the 12th Annual Meeting, National Academy of Arbitrators, ed. Jean T. McKelvey (Washington: BNA Books, 1959), 179.

of new arbitrators, the topic was very much alive. At the 1960 annual meeting, Member William C. Loucks presented a paper titled "Arbitration—A Profession." [8] In treating the criteria that mark a profession and applying them to labor arbitration, he stated:

> ". . . [T]here are no clearly marked educational routes generally recognized as preparatory for entering a profession of arbitration. Comparing our field with either the law, medicine, the ministry, or teaching we still have a long way to go in this regard and we probably should be devoting more attention to it over future years." [9]

Jean McKelvey, in her discussion of the above paper, called attention to the fact that the Academy was formed in part "to promote the study and understanding of the arbitration of industrial disputes" and that over the years had been interpreted to include "the education and training of new members of the profession." [10] She deplored the lack of specific progress by the Academy in implementing this function, despite prior concern with the problem.

In the same volume of proceedings appeared a paper by Arnold W. Zack, titled "An Evaluation of Arbitration Apprentices." [11] The paper concerned itself with a description of the nature of apprentice programs in effect at that time and an evaluation of their success. It included five recommendations as to what the Academy could do:

1. Institute a public relations program aimed at graduate and law schools to encourage individuals to enter the profession.

2. Formally endorse the concept of apprenticeship as the most effective means of training competent arbitrators.

3. Develop a clearing house where individuals interested in entering arbitration can obtain information as to the nature of and qualifications for apprenticeship, and availability of employment opportunities.

4. Establish a program of summertime or graduate clerkships with designating agencies.

---

[8] In *Challenges to Arbitration*, Proceedings of the 13th Annual Meeting, National Academy of Arbitrators, ed. Jean T. McKelvey (Washington: BNA Books, 1960), 20.

[9] *Id*. at 24.

[10] *Id*. at 32.

[11] *Id*. at 169-176.

5. Develop a pre-apprenticeship program with labor and industry to permit selected individuals to engage directly in work in labor relations.[12]

No specific actions resulted from these recommendations, and the question of what specific measures should be adopted continued to be a matter of discussion.

The American Bar Association also concerned itself with this problem of developing qualified, experienced, and acceptable arbitrators. In 1961, the Committee on Labor Arbitration to the Section of Labor Relations Law of the Association issued a report in which it found the problem to be a three-fold one.[13] First were the difficulties that talented and objective young men encountered in attempting to acquire the experience necessary both to qualify and to be accepted as arbitrators. In this regard the absence of any institution where training and acceptability might be acquired presents a formidable obstacle to any individual seeking to enter the field, no matter how great his qualifications.

The second was the absence of adequate machinery for passing judgment upon the qualifications of arbitrators and the communicating of that judgment to the parties. The report scored the appointing agencies as having failed to develop any standards of background or performance for arbitrators and of not imposing any meaningful restrictions on the admission of arbitrators to their panels. Because of this, the conclusion was drawn that there was no feasible means available to the parties to check the fitness of persons whose unknown names appear on panels of prospective arbitrators. As a result, selection tends to be confined to the familiar arbitrators who have acquired repute. The final facet of the problem was that many clients lack confidence in more youthful arbitrators, regardless of their exposure to industrial life, and many others are fearful of those whose experience was gained in working for the other side. Thus, in addition to the reluctance to entrust their case to the inexperienced, acceptability becomes difficult even for those experienced

---

[12] *Id.* at 175.

[13] "Report of Committee on Labor Arbitration to the Section of Labor Relations Law of the American Bar Association," in *Collective Bargaining and the Arbitrator's Role,* Proceedings of the 15th Annual Meeting, National Academy of Arbitrators, ed. Mark L. Kahn (Washington: BNA Books, 1962), 243-248.

in labor relations but whose experience was in the form of advocacy.[14]

In answer to these problems, the committee set forth three basic recommendations. The first was that the American Bar Association should take the initiative in organizing a tripartite structure made up of representatives of labor, management, and arbitrators for the establishment of a pilot program for the training of new arbitrators under the guidance and supervision of experienced and respected arbitrators. It was suggested that the model for this experiment be the program under the contract of Bethlehem Steel Corp. and the United Steelworkers of America, Ralph Seward, chairman. With respect to the problem of standards, the committee proposed that the Bar Association collaborate with the National Academy of Arbitrators, the Federal Mediation and Conciliation Service, and the American Arbitration Association in the formulation of certain minimal standards for labor arbitrators, and that these standards be used to condition admission to the panels of the appointing agencies. Finally, as a device for securing acceptability of those trained under the proposed training program and those admitted under the new set of minimal standards, it was recommended that an impartial group made up equally of labor and management representatives be established for the purpose of inducing client acceptance of the new arbitrators so approved.[15] To date, nothing concrete resulted from this report, although at the 1962 meeting of the Academy it engendered considerable discussion.

It was, however, in 1962 that the Academy, under the leadership of President Benjamin Aaron, moved from discussion to action. In conjunction with the AAA and the FMCS, a training program for potential arbitrators was initiated in Chicago. The program began with 14 trainees and ended with 10. It consisted of a one-day training institute and of arrangements for attendance at hearings conducted by Academy members. While the trainees were requested to prepare their own opinions and awards for analysis by the arbitrators, only a few chose to participate in this aspect of the training.[16]

---

[14] *Id.* at 244.

[15] *Id.* at 246.

[16] Committee on Training of New Arbitrators, "Report to the Membership, 1964," in *Labor Arbitration—Perspectives and Problems,* Proceedings of the 17th Annual Meeting, National Academy of Arbitrators, ed. Mark L. Kahn (Washington: BNA Books, 1964), 322.

Similar programs were initiated in Pittsburgh in 1963 and in Cleveland in 1965. Out of these there were approximately three persons who were successful in gaining a fair degree of acceptability as arbitrators. Thus the conclusion cannot be made that these programs were a total success, but neither were they a complete failure. Besides the few who were assisted in making the grade, some other benefit resulted. Former Director William Simkin of FMCS states:

> "If nothing else has been accomplished it has been worth something to get labor and industry people together to talk about the need to break in some new people. Even though few of the potential arbitrators have 'made it,' I suspect that there is a better awareness of the need, and it is possible that other new people—not in a training program—have benefitted." [17]

Current Programs

Currently several other comparable types of programs are in effect or are being initiated. During 1970, the Labor Law Committee of the Bar Association of Metropolitan St. Louis, in conjunction with the FMCS and the AAA initiated a program aimed at developing and training new arbitrators for that area. The central and immediate purpose of the program is to acquaint selected "trainees" with the arbitration process by arranging for their presence at hearings conducted in the St. Louis area.

Because the AAA does not have a regional office in St. Louis, the administration of this program is being conducted by John Canestraight, an FMCS commissioner in the St. Louis office. Initially Academy Member Father Leo Brown assisted in the determination and selection of the potential trainees. Currently Committeeman John Dunsford is serving as the Academy liaison to this program. His report on the nature of the program and its progress may be summed up as follows:

The names of approximately 20 potential arbitrators were solicited from various sources, and a committee from the Bar Association narrowed the list down to seven persons. That committee was made up of an attorney who represents unions in the St. Louis area, another who represents companies, and Commissioner Canestraight. The factors used for selecting the trainees included the availability of an individual to attend hearings,

---

[17] Letter to chairman, Committee for the Development of New Arbitrators, dated June 11, 1970.

current listing on the AAA or FMCS rosters, degree of interest in the project, lack of direct connection with either labor or management, and general acceptability of the individual.

The seven trainees included two practicing lawyers, two university professors (one in labor economics, the other in management), a retired NLRB staff member, a retired business executive, and a Presbyterian minister. Four of the trainees have law degrees, although two (the business executive and the minister) have apparently not practiced. Two of the seven are in their sixties, one is in his fifties, two are in their forties, and two are in their thirties.

No formal training program was scheduled, as the main thrust of the program was to attempt to gain exposure of trainees to the parties and the process by having them accompany arbitrators to actual hearings. Commissioner Canestraight has assumed the responsibility for the administrative details connected with arranging with arbitrators and the parties for attendance at the arbitration hearings. Also, the intention is to have the trainee draft a mock award which the arbitrator would then evaluate. After the trainee has had an opportunity to sit in on six hearings, the committee will review these awards and evaluations. Then, a majority approval of the trainee will automatically result in his being placed on the FMCS roster.[18] Actual appearances by trainees at hearings was to have begun during December 1970 and to continue through 1971. Evaluation of this program will, of course, have to be made at some future date. This program is likely to serve as a prototype for one that the FMCS hopes to initiate in Los Angeles.[19]

The AAA has a program under way in New York that was inspired by the International Association of Machinists through Steven Vladeck, Counsel for District 15.[20] Under this program, a special labor-management committee will select a group of arbitrators from those persons who have had only one or two arbitration cases, or who indicate good possibilities for gaining acceptability. These applicants will be in the age bracket of

---

[18] Letter to Committee Member Seymour Strongin from William J. Kilberg, General Counsel, FMCS, dated Jan. 4, 1971.

[19] Id.

[20] Letter to Committee Member Harold W. Davey from Joseph Murphy, Vice President, AAA, dated Mar. 15, 1971.

30 to 50, and the ones selected will be given a two-day orientation program followed by a period of internship. This internship will be mainly in the form of attendance at hearings with established arbitrators. Also, with the permission of the parties, the interns will write decisions which will be reviewed by the arbitrator conducting the hearing.

The AAA and the FMCS are also sponsoring a program in the Cleveland area, which is related to work being done by Academy Member Edwin R. Teple. Details on this program are not available at this time. Finally, the AAA is also seeking to initiate a program in the Philadelphia area, but as yet nothing concrete has been established for that program.

The Need for Arbitrators

The recent and rapid growth in the use of arbitrators in the public sector on top of a long-time-continuing increase in demand for arbitration in the private sector presents serious problems with respect to the future supply of arbitrators to meet this burgeoning demand. As this need for arbitrators continues to grow, the average age of the members of the arbitration profession continues to increase. As reported in the "Survey of the Arbitration Profession in 1969" (Appendix C), the average age of members of the Academy is more than four years greater than it was in 1962; the percentage of members over 60 years of age has doubled since 1962; and less than 2 percent of the members are under age 40, compared to 4.6 percent in 1962.[21]

In terms of age alone, the problem of developing and training new arbitrators appears to be growing more acute. Perhaps the last to recognize this potential shortage would be the profession itself. However, even here the realization is growing that a shortage may become a problem in the immediate future. In the 1969 survey, in answer to the question, "Will there be a shortage of qualified arbitrators when the 'war-labor-board' arbitrators retire?" slightly more than half of those responding thought that there would be and gave reasons for their opinions.[22] The 47.2 percent who did not foresee a shortage also backed their assertions with opinions.[23]

---

[21] See Appendix C for this volume, at 275-276.

[22] *Id.* at 279-280.

[23] *Id.* at 280.

Exclusive of the War Labor Board, which was a unique training ground for new arbitrators, one other important institutional source for the supply of new arbitrators has been through apprenticeship programs conducted by experienced arbitrators. These programs have long been the most successful method for insuring that persons with good potential backgrounds will gain the necessary degree of acceptability that insures their successful entry into the arbitration profession. Such programs are, however, limited by a number of serious restrictions. For the most part they are very costly and time-consuming for the experienced arbitrator who takes on an apprentice. As a result, such programs have been restricted mainly to umpireships with heavy case loads and with a willingness on the part of the parties both to finance the program and to agree to the use of the apprentice for hearing cases and writing decisions. In addition, there have been a few other full-time arbitrators who have been willing to sacrifice time and money in order to get particular individuals started in the field, but such persons have been the exception.

The 1969 survey indicates that some progress is being made in the movement of individuals into the profession via the apprenticeship route,[24] but despite these improvements, the small numbers involved prevent this avenue from being a primary source for the training and development of any substantial quantity of new arbitrators. The problem of a shortage of acceptable arbitrators will continue to be present, and the need for the adoption of a continuing program or programs aimed at alleviating this shortage will continue to be a matter of serious concern to the National Academy of Arbitrators.

Possible Programs for Consideration by the Academy

To date, the past activities of the Academy in the training and development of new arbitrators have been through participation with the appointing agencies in programs that primarily stressed training. While training is important, the route to acceptance as an arbitrator can come only through experience, for the problem has been in the past and will continue to be that the parties generally do not want to accept as an arbitrator anyone who has not had experience. Therefore, any program that is to be sponsored by the Academy must go beyond mere

[24] *Id.* at 277-278, for survey results on apprenticeship.

training and must seek to provide some channel for the gaining of experience.

Such a program should take into consideration those attributes which the parties believe distinguish an experienced arbitrator from an inexperienced one. Unfortunately, very little research has been carried out in this area. However, in a recent survey of attitudes of union and management representatives toward experienced versus inexperienced arbitrators by Brian L. King, several conclusions were drawn.[25] Not surprising, the first was that a significant preference prevailed in the attitudes of both labor and management representatives that was in favor of the experienced arbitrators. On the other hand, while union representatives favored the experienced arbitrator over the inexperienced, they had significantly more favorable attitudes toward the inexperienced arbitrator than those held by the management representatives. Finally, with respect to attributes upon which the respondents based their conclusions, it was believed by both sides that the inexperienced arbitrator would be less likely to base his decision on the specific facts of the particular case. Second, and related to the first, they were of the opinion that the experienced arbitrator would be more likely to develop pertinent information through his questions and his conduct of the hearing. Finally, both groups were convinced that inexperienced arbitrators were significantly less consistent in their rulings than were the experienced arbitrators.

While these three attributes were the only ones that the union respondents found to be significantly different as between experienced and inexperienced arbitrators, management representatives were convinced that, in addition, inexperienced arbitrators were more likely to accept a case despite an overloaded schedule, were more likely to attempt to improve the contract through arbitration, and were less likely to have as broad a viewpoint as the experienced arbitrator.[26]

This study emphasizes the point that any program aimed at developing new arbitrators must be directed at increasing the supply of persons who will become acceptable, rather than being solely concerned with training. To date, experience has shown

---

[25] Brian L. King, "Management and Union Attitudes Affecting the Employment of Inexperienced Labor Arbitrators," 22 *Lab. Law J.* 23-28 (1971).

[26] *Id.* at 25-27.

that the one proven method for accomplishing this objective has been through some form of apprenticeship relationship. Therefore, any continuing program adopted by the Academy should provide, in some degree, for such a relationship.

Several possible programs are currently under consideration by the Committee for the Development of New Arbitrators. One relates to the establishment of a program for arbitration fellowships. This would be done on a regional basis and in conjunction with university law schools and graduate schools of business and industrial relations. Under such a program, arrangements would be made with selected universities to provide for the appointment of one or two graduate or law students to serve as arbitration fellows in the last year or two of their graduate programs. Such students would be compensated under the fellowship program of the university. However, the individual would be relieved of most assistantship or fellowship duties at his university, and instead would be assigned to work as an assistant with one or two Academy members in the region. As an assistant, the fellow could work with the arbitrators in researching prior awards and cases. Under some circumstances, he might be used for preparing drafts of opinions and awards for the arbitrator's use, or even as a hearing officer.

It should be noted, however, that several limitations are present in the adoption of such a program. One is the problem of age. Most graduate school fellows would be in their late twenties at the oldest. In view of the fact that the parties tend to view anyone under 40 years of age as being inexperienced,[27] the chances of these assistants' gaining acceptability after their graduation would be minimal. Another would be the limited period of experience that any one individual would be able to achieve in such a program. Still another is that if the assistant is used only for research purposes, it is unlikely that such duties would contribute anything to his gaining any degree of acceptability, and the extent of experience obtained would be minimal. On the other hand, if he is used for preparing preliminary drafts of opinions and awards, his value to the arbitrator would be considerably enhanced. Also, the assistant would gain experience in writing decisions that would be invaluable. However, it is questionable if such experience could be trans-

---

[27] *Id.* at 25.

lated into acceptability, unless his name appeared on those decisions. Furthermore, there is a serious question of ethics involved in such use of assistants without the knowledge and consent of the parties. This question is presently under consideration by the Committee on Ethics and Grievances.[28]

Obviously the fullest use and best exposure for the assistant would be where he is used as a hearing officer and where, under the supervision of the arbitrator, he would prepare the opinion and award. Such use of assistants would actually make it an apprenticeship program, and it is doubtful that a system of using graduate fellows would permit time for the individual to develop to the stage of serving as a hearing officer.

In view of these limitations, it is improbable that a program for utilizing graduate fellows as arbitration assistants would be successful in increasing the supply of acceptable arbitrators. Perhaps the only contribution that the Academy could make with respect to the use of assistants would be to have the Committee for the Development of New Arbitrators serve as a clearing house for matching members who are seeking assistants with applicants who wish to serve in that capacity. In view of the growing demand for mediators, fact-finders, and arbitrators that is taking place in the public sector, such a program might render a genuine service to those persons working in that sector and at the same time serve as a training source for providing qualified personnel to serve in the public employment sector.

Another possible program is one that is under consideration by the AAA. That organization is interested in establishing a position of arbitrator in residence. The Association would seek money to finance a program wherein each year one of our senior and more respected arbitrators would be given the opportunity to serve a year in residence and to work with a selected group of new arbitrators carefully culled from the ranks of those persons recently added to the panel of the AAA. Such a program would be primarily an endeavor of the AAA, but it would require the cooperation of the Academy in the obtaining of members to assist the arbitrator in residence by advising and instructing those persons selected who live in their geographic areas.

---

[28] Letter from Russell A. Smith, chairman, Committee on Ethics and Grievances, dated Jan. 18, 1971.

Perhaps the most effective program that could be carried on by the Academy and which would be within its capabilities would be a continuing program of interns and mentors. The program would be conducted on a regional basis, and it would involve the selection of from five to eight persons to serve as interns.

The selection process for determining eligible candidates will require the working out of a number of details. It is likely that a joint labor and management committee should be appointed to pass on the applicants. This committee would have the further responsibility of seeking to gain acceptance of the graduates of the program as arbitrators by labor and management. Criteria for determining eligibility of persons for the internship program must be developed. Such things as age limits to be applied, the backgrounds to be sought, the manner in which the names of prospective applicants would be obtained, and the standards to be used for evaluation of the applications are all details that would have to be determined.

At any rate, once the list of interns was determined, the assistance of both the AAA and the FMCS would have to be secured. In addition, members of the Academy would have to volunteer to serve as mentors in those cases they would be hearing in their local areas. The lists of interns and mentors would be maintained in the regional AAA office. When an AAA case arose to be heard by one of the mentors in the regional office hearing room or in the city itself, the regional manager would obtain the necessary clearances, and he would send out a copy of the "Notice of Hearing" not only to the parties concerned but also to not more than three persons from the intern list. For FMCS cases, a system of interchange would have to be worked out between the FMCS, the AAA regional office, and the arbitrator.

The interns would attend the hearing as auditors. At its close, they would get together with the arbitrator for purposes of discussion that would, of course, avoid the merits of the case. During the hearing the interns should take copious notes, and each should prepare a draft of a decision. These drafts should be mailed to the regional manager of the AAA office, who would hold them until the arbitrator's decision was received.

A copy of his decision would then be sent to the interns, and their drafts would be released to the mentor-arbitrator. It is hoped that the mentor would then read these drafts and prepare a critical evaluation for the benefit of the intern.

Committee Member John Shearer proposes adding two additional phases to the program, which would take effect after each trainee had audited from two to four cases with each of three arbitrators in the region, thus making a total of from six to 12 auditing experiences. On the basis of their acquaintanceship with the particular intern, the arbitrators would recommend that he be advanced to the next phase, which would be to serve as an assistant to a particular arbitrator. The comments with respect to the use of assistants as given above would, of course, apply to this relationship, referred to as Phase 2. In addition, Mr. Shearer's proposal includes the requirement that the decision be signed by the arbitrator, followed by the notation "Assisted by" and the name of the assistant. This service as an assistant should be with two or three mentors for from two to four cases each.

Upon the recommendation of these mentors, the assistant would then be proposed for listing by the AAA and the FMCS which would be Phase 3. In this phase it is hoped that the intern would be selected by the parties for particular cases. A system of monitoring is then proposed whereby, for a period of two years, each of the three mentors would review from two to four ,cases with the intern, in the function of a monitor. At completion, the new arbitrator would be designated by the agencies as having completed the Academy training program.

With respect to remuneration for the intern, Mr. Shearer proposes that in the auditing phase the trainee would cover his own expenses. While serving as an assistant, one half of the arbitrator's fee would be paid to the assistant. During the monitoring stage, the trainee would receive his full fees and expenses.

Activities by Appointing Agencies

While emphasis in this report has been given to the need for establishing a continuing program that would provide for entry of qualified arbitrators into the profession, it is not intended that this will be the only avenue for entry. It is hoped that

entry via regular established apprenticeship programs will continue to grow. Also, entry as now provided for through the
American Arbitration Association and the Federal Mediation
and Conciliation Service is assumed to continue.

With respect to this latter form of entry, there are certain
things which could be done by the appointing agencies that
would do much to improve acceptance of new panel members
by the parties. One would be the collecting of more specific
data with respect to the numbers of persons added to the panels
of the appointing agency each year, the extent to which the
names are used by the regional offices in the case of the AAA
and the Washington office in the case of the FMCS, and the
extent to which the individuals are selected (1) by management, (2) by labor, and (3) by both. Also, there is a need for
establishing a system of follow-up for the purpose of determining
the reasons for acceptance or rejection of specific individuals. It
would appear that more success in the introduction of new
names to the profession might be achieved if criteria for acceptance were more specifically determined and applied. In the case
of admission to the AAA panels, a reduction in the number of
persons accepted and a more uniform program for insuring the
more frequent use of those accepted might result in more success
in the introduction of new arbitrators. In the case of the
FMCS, the basic criterion for admission to its roster is acceptability by labor and management representatives. For the most
part, actual arbitration experience has been viewed as absolute
proof of such acceptance. It may be that a review of its qualifications, with less emphasis on the need for actual experience,
might lead to an increase in the number of new names accepted
by the FMCS, and to an increase in the number of persons
with satisfactory acceptability ratios.[29]

Regardless of what program may be adopted by the Academy,
the ultimate question is, "Will he or will he not be jointly
picked for a case by the parties?" In this regard it may be
possible that some use could be made by both the AAA and
the FMCS of the power of direct appointment. In general, the
practice has been to give these appointments only to experi-

---

[29] A satisfactory acceptability ratio, according to Committee Member Davey, is an
acceptance by the parties in 10 percent or more of the times the person's name is
submitted to the parties.

enced arbitrators. On the other hand, if a small number of these appointments were given to graduates of an Academy-approved program, it would get them started with their first cases. However, the appointing agency would want some sort of control over the issuance of the decision, so that it could feel confident that no major mistakes would be made. Here, a committee of Academy members in each region could agree to serve as a board of review and go over with the intern the decision and award before it was released to the parties. This, however, may be too much to expect from individual Academy members and also might evoke considerable opposition from the parties.

It is evident, therefore, that through the years the Academy has been concerned with the problem of insuring a steady supply of qualified persons into the labor arbitration profession. To date, however, it has not been able to devise a continuing program that would achieve this objective. To some extent this has been due to the apathy of the membership with respect to this problem, but to a greater extent it has been because no practical program has been proposed that is within the capabilities of the Academy and its members to carry out. The matter of need for such a program is no longer in question. If the Academy is to fulfill its function as a professional organization, it must play some positive role in providing for the development of new arbitrators. The job for this committee for the year 1971-1972 will be one of determining what specific programs should be recommended to the Board of Governors for adoption.

ANNUAL REPORT OF SPECIAL COMMITTEE ON DISPUTES SETTLEMENT IN PUBLIC EMPLOYMENT, NATIONAL ACADEMY OF ARBITRATORS, 1970-1971 *

The committee was appointed by President McKelvey in April 1970, with a request that we continue the activities initiated by Chairman Rock and the 1969-1970 committee and, further, that we consider examining grievance arbitration practices in the public sector.

This report will review the 1970 Montreal Training Sessions which were planned by the 1969-1970 subcommittee, the activities of the past year, and our recommendations for future activities.

I. The Montreal Workshops

Because of membership interest in the subject, our workshop sessions in Montreal concentrated on the skills, special public sector problems, and techniques employed in mediation and fact-finding with recommendations. The workshops were scheduled for two days. On the first day, approximately 70 members attended small workshops under the leadership of members who had had considerable public sector mediation experience, for discussion and analysis of the mediation process. On the second day, the number increased to approximately 100 participants, who heard union and management representatives explain what they expect of the process of "fact-finding with recommendations." The participants then attended workshop sessions, led by members experienced in public sector impasse resolution.

The response of the participants and discussion leaders was enthusiastic, in part because some insights were gained into the

* Members of the Committee for 1970-1971 were: Howard Block, Milton Friedman, Howard Gamser, Ronald Haughton, Jean McKelvey (ex officio), Eli Rock, Ralph Seward, William Simkin, Russell Smith, Martin Wagner, Leo Walsh, Arnold Zack, and Chairman Eva Robins.

processes hitherto unknown to many members, and in part because the workshops for members only restored an opportunity for the free exchange of views, an opportunity not customarily available in the regular sessions.

II. Training Programs

The 1969-1970 report of the Rock committee explained in detail the growing need for training in the unaccustomed role of mediator and fact-finder in public sector disputes. It also included descriptions of the kind of training which had been initiated by public and private agencies, some with NAA members participating in the planning and taking an active role in the training sessions. In addition, the regions had been given the training material gathered by the committee, for their use as and when the regions recognized a need in their areas. Individual members of the committee have been consulted by members of the NAA for guidance in setting up training or workshop sessions on special problems, procedural and substantive, as they arose through the introduction of new legislation or new procedures.

As a result of the Montreal experience and the growing interest of some members in serving in a neutral capacity in public sector disputes, the committee decided to have one day of members-only workshops in public sector disputes at the California meeting in 1971.

In the second "teach-in," we wanted to describe the major substantive issues in public sector disputes and particularly to point up the differences between public and private sector substantive issues. We presented to the members, in short talks and in workshops, the kinds of issues and problems usually met in public sector disputes, particularly in police, fire, teacher, and other civil service employee contract negotiations. We also had one workshop continuing the discussion on skills of mediation and fact-finding with recommendations.

Eighty-eight people preregistered for the workshops. Of that number, 55 appeared and an additional 10 or 12, not preregistered, attended the sessions.

The workshop on techniques and skills of mediation and fact-finding with recommendations was well attended, and the participants were enthusiastic. Since the substantive issues workshops were intended to be descriptive of the issues rather than an evaluation of criteria, there was less discussion in those workshops. However, we believe they served a useful purpose, at least to familiarize neutrals with the kind and complexity of the issues in police, fire, teacher, and civil service negotiations.

The committee recommends the continuation of a day for members-only meetings, before the regular annual meeting, but not necessarily devoted to public sector subjects. The purpose would be to afford to the members, in small groups or large, the opportunity to discuss problems, become aware of new developments, and share opinions. The committee's recommendations were accepted by the Board of Governors, which authorized the additional day, for members only, prior to the 1972 Annual Meeting in Boston. The 1972 Program Committee will plan the day.

III. Public Sector Grievance and Interest Arbitration

The committee believes the experience, countrywide, in these areas is too spotty to warrant study at this time. However, grievance arbitration is a rapidly growing field in the public sector, and future committees may want to consider it. Interest arbitration appears to be very limited at this time, although it is growing as a result of statutory changes.

IV. Relationship of Public Sector
Training Programs to the Shortage of Arbitrators

The committee has discussed this subject only briefly. Committee members were present at the October 1970 meeting of Tom McDermott's Committee on the Development of New Arbitrators. We had hoped that the experience of new neutrals as mediators and fact-finders in the public sector might furnish a new source of grievance arbitrators, but, from what we have been told, grievance arbitration work in the public sector continues to be handled mainly by the arbitrators with many years of experience in the private sector. Probably the Committee on the Development of New Arbitrators should continue to consider the public sector as a source of new arbitrators. It is a subject which the Public Sector Disputes Settlement Committee should not handle, since it simply duplicates the work of the other committee.

V. Relationship to Membership Standards

The Stark committee considered and reported on the question of possible membership for persons whose experience was largely public sector mediation and fact-finding. In view of that committee's activities, the Public Sector Disputes Settlement Committee has not considered this subject.

VI. Liaison With Other Agencies

With the proliferation of public employment boards and committees, it may become necessary to establish liaison, on a regional or national basis, among the NAA and the local and national agencies. This committee was unable to take on this task, but recommends that it be considered by the Liaison Committee in the future.

VII. Additional Recommendations

A. We recommend that the regions attempt to meet the needs of the members by making known to them the training programs in public sector disputes settlement techniques which might be available in the regions. We also advocate the unstructured, informal, "one-to-one" type of training in which members who are experienced in mediation and fact-finding with recommendations are willing to give such guidance on techniques as may be requested by arbitrators new to the other processes. This could be handled regionally.

B. We recommend that the committee be continued, at least for another year. If the public sector workshops are to be discontinued for a time, it might be advisable to have the committee concentrate on such research as it may be able to undertake. It might also serve as a clearing house to the regions in reporting on research developments in the field, training sessions, and scheduled conferences. We recommend that the committee chairmanship be university based, where research assistance may be available. Eventually, valuable information to the regions and to individual members may come from studies of the public sector experience with matters such as: the satisfaction or dissatisfaction of public employers and public employee organizations with mediation, fact-finding with recommendations, and interest arbitration; the kind and quality of training available throughout the country; the cost, availability, and value of large conferences; and anticipated developments in the public sector.

The committee wishes to thank the officers and governors for their support during the past year and for the opportunity we have had, in our committee's work, to learn more about this field.

CUMULATIVE AUTHOR INDEX

NOTE: The Index Entry refers to the years of the various annual meetings. Titles of the volumes and the number of each annual meeting are listed below.

TOPICAL INDEX

343